DEMOCRATIC RHONDDA

DEMOCRATIC RHONDDA

Politics and Society, 1885–1951

CHRIS WILLIAMS

UNIVERSITY OF WALES PRESS
CARDIFF
1996

British Library Cataloguing-in-Publication Data

A catalogue record for this book is available from the British Library.

ISBN 0-7083-1334-5

PUBLISHED WITH THE FINANCIAL ASSISTANCE OF THE SCOULOUDI FOUNDATION AND THE HUMANITIES RESEARCH BOARD OF THE BRITISH ACADEMY

Typeset at the University of Wales Press
Printed in Wales by Dinefwr Press, Llandybïe

For my parents
Josephine Anne and Peter Hale Williams

Contents

List of tables		viii
List of maps		viii
Preface		ix
Abbreviations		xi
Maps		xiii
Introduction		1
Chapter 1	*Rhondda: 'The most active and thriving community in Great Britain or the World'*	12
Chapter 2	*The rise of Labour, 1885–1910*	29
Chapter 3	*Labour in command, 1910–1927*	83
Chapter 4	*Labour in crisis, 1910–1927*	119
Chapter 5	*The left divided, 1927–1951*	151
Conclusion:	*A Labour people*	206
Statistical Appendix		214
Notes		236
Bibliography		281
Index		297

Tables

Chapter 1

1.1   Distribution of birthplaces of Rhondda inhabitants,
      1901 and 1911   16

Chapter 2

2.1   Result of the 1885 Parliamentary Election   37
2.2   Result of the 1900 Parliamentary Election   39
2.3   Result of the January 1910 Parliamentary Election   41
2.4   Result of the December 1910 Parliamentary Election   43

Chapter 3

3.1   Result of the 1920 Parliamentary Election in Rhondda West   89
3.2   Result of the 1922 Parliamentary Elections   90
3.3   Result of the 1923 Parliamentary Elections   90

Chapter 5

5.1   Result of the 1929 Parliamentary Elections   158
5.2   Result of the 1931 Parliamentary Elections   159
5.3   Result of the 1933 Parliamentary Election in Rhondda East   160
5.4   Result of the 1935 Parliamentary Election in Rhondda East   161
5.5   Result of the 1945 Parliamentary Election in Rhondda East   161
5.6   Result of the 1950 Parliamentary Elections   164
5.7   Result of the 1951 Parliamentary Elections   165

(*See also* Statistical Appendix pp.213–35.)

Maps

1.   The south Wales coalfield   xiii
2.   Major settlements in the Rhondda Valleys, *c.* 1920   xiv
3.   Major collieries in the Rhondda Valleys, *c.* 1920   xv
4.   Parliamentary and Urban District Council boundaries,
      Rhondda Valleys, 1921   xvi

Preface

The origins of this work date from a March day in 1981 when, as a seventeen-year-old prospective university entrant, I journeyed to University College Cardiff to present myself at one of its regular open days. Eventually, having attended two meetings in the company of many other applicants, I found myself alone with Dr Dai Smith, of the Department of History of Wales. For the next thirty minutes the profession of the historian came alive as he brandished recent publications (*The Fed* and *Fields of Praise*), off-loaded spare copies of the magazine *Arcade* and enthused about the opportunities for communicating history through radio and television. His eagerness to attract me to Cardiff to study the multiple history of Wales did not take immediate effect, however: like him I studied first at Balliol College, Oxford, graduating with a BA in Modern History in 1985. Balliol provided the chance to study south-east Asian and Indian history, to learn about Marxism and post-structuralism, to dwell on historiography and, most of all, to debate with Jeremy Morris, Peter Wilding and Graham Wright the meaning of it all. Undoubtedly, Oxford opened doors that might otherwise have remained shut, but ultimately it could not compete with the magnetic pull of a history that I considered, in important ways, to be my own. Accordingly, in October 1985, I returned to Cardiff to take up a British Academy award and to read for a doctorate. Initially setting out to explore the history of the Labour Party in Wales between the wars, the project turned out to be something rather different, but my enthusiasm for this history and for the contemporary relevance of the historical profession has been strengthened, not deflected, by the decade of industry that has been committed to this enterprise. That this has been the case is due in large measure to Dai Smith, as to learn from his combination of intellectual power and passion for our history has been a rare privilege: I could not have wished for a better supervisor or a firmer friend.

In seeing the work through from idea to thesis to monograph I have incurred many other debts. First must be to my many interviewees, in Rhondda and beyond, who recalled their own lives or those of their loved ones and who gave me an invaluable 'feel' for the history and the spirit of that remarkable community. Librarians and archivists in many institutions have eased the path of enquiry, and I would like to pay particular tribute to those at the public libraries of Cardiff and Treorchy; the Glamorgan Record Office; the National Library of Wales; the South Wales Miners' Library; and the libraries of the University of Wales at Cardiff and Swansea. Comrades in Llafur, the Welsh Labour History Society, have provided both the wider context and an inspirational commitment to the subject, and to Dave Egan, Neil Evans, Hywel Francis, Rob Humphreys, Angela John, Keith Strange and Rob Turner I can offer only a single thanks for the multiple forms of their assistance. My thesis examiners David Howell and John Williams proffered helpful advice and repeated encouragement, Andy Croll and Angela Gaffney believed in my abilities when I did not, and Kevin Passmore set a standard which my competitive instincts then tried to reach. Deian Hopkin, Peter Stead and Duncan Tanner read the text in various forms, and suggested improvements and corrections. Even if I have not heeded all their advice, I am very grateful for their efforts. Ralph Griffiths kindly gave me the benefit of his experience in suggesting sources for additional funding, Ian Dennis drew the maps at very short notice, whilst at the University of Wales Press Ned Thomas and Liz Powell have handled me with expertise and patience. Finally, amongst my largely but never wholly intellectual debts I mention my colleague Bill Jones, who has also been a constant friend for a decade. He has given of his knowledge and wisdom with unstinting generosity, and I look forward to many more years working in his company.

The last three years would have been neither so productive nor so joyous had it not been for the love and companionship of Sara Spalding. Robespierre the cat and Newport RFC have made their own, unique contributions whilst brothers Jonathan and David and sister Kate were periodically on hand to refresh and to encourage. My sons Philip and Harri have been with this work from inception to completion and have seen it change first from so many piles of paper into a 'big book' and then change again into a much smaller one. My expression of thanks to them barely does justice to their immense commitment: I take heart from the fact that they both remain interested in history. Lastly, this work is dedicated to my parents, Josephine Anne and Peter Hale Williams, who have watched over my intellectual, political and personal journeys, and have constantly offered me a love that has given me the strength to carry on through both the worst and best of times.

Abbreviations

AL	Abergorky Lodge		MEA	Municipal Employees' Federation
ASRS	Amalgamated Society of Railway Servants		MFGB	Mineworkers' Federation of Great Britain
BUF	British Union of Fascists		ML	Mardy Lodge
CCC	Central Canteen Committee		*MP*	*Merthyr Pioneer*
CL	Cambrian Lodge		*MRG*	*Mid-Rhondda Gazette*
CLC	Central Labour College		*MRO*	*Mid-Rhondda Outlook*
CLP	Constituency Labour Party		MRTLC	Mid-Rhondda TLC
CMA	Cambrian Miners' Association		NAC	National Administrative Council
CP(GB)	Communist Party (of Great Britain)		NDL	National Democratic League
CT	*Cardiff Times*		NEC	National Executive Committee
CWM	*Colliery Workers' Magazine*		NLW	National Library of Wales
DLB	*Dictionary of Labour Biography*		NUM	National Union of Mineworkers
DLP	Divisional Labour Party		NUR	National Union of Railwaymen
DW	*Daily Worker*		NUT	National Union of Teachers
EC	Executive Committee		NUW(C)M	National Unemployed Workers' (Committee) Movement
EdC	Education Committee			
FC	Finance Committee		PAC	Public Assistance Committee
FL	Ferndale Lodge			
FPRL	*Free Press and Rhondda Leader*		PBG	Pontypridd Board of Guardians
GCC	Glamorgan County Council		*PC*	*Pontypridd Chronicle*
GCT	*Glamorgan County Times*		PD	Park and Dare Lodge
GFP	*Glamorgan Free Press*		*PG*	*Porth Gazette*
GFPRL	*Glamorgan Free Press and Rhondda Leader*		PLC	Porth Labour Committee
			PTCLP	Pontypridd Trades Council and Labour Party
ILP	Independent Labour Party			
LM	Lewis Merthyr Lodge		RAC	Relief Advisory Committee
LRC	Labour Representation Committee		RBLP	Rhondda Borough Labour Party
LRC9	LRC No.9 Ward			
MCW	Maternity and Child Welfare (Clinic/ Committee)		RBLP9	RBLP No.9 Ward
			RC	*Rhondda Clarion*

RCA	Rhondda Conservative Association	SWML	South Wales Miners' Library
RCTA	Rhondda Class Teachers' Association	SWN	South Wales News
RD	Rhondda No.1 District	SWRCL	South Wales Regional Council of Labour
RFG	*Rhondda Fach Gazette*	SWSS	South Wales Socialist Society
RFL	*Rhondda Fach Leader*		
RG	*Rhondda Gazette*	*SWW*	*South Wales Worker*
RHCMA	Rhondda House Coal Miners' Association	TL	Tylorstown Lodge
		TLC	Trades and Labour Council
RL	*Rhondda Leader*	TTLC	Treherbert TLC
RLA	Rhondda Liberal Association	TUC	Trades Union Congress
		UAB	Unemployment Assistance Board
RLLA	Rhondda Labour and Liberal Association	UCS	University College, Swansea
RoC	Roads Committee		
RS	*Rhondda Socialist*	UGC	Unemployment Grants Committee
RSCMA	Rhondda Steam Coal Miners' Association	URC	Unofficial Reform Committee
RSS	Rhondda Socialist Society	WCG	Women's Co-operative Guild
RUDC	Rhondda Urban District Council		
RV	*Rhondda Vanguard*	*WD*	*Workers' Dreadnought*
RWDLP	Rhondda West Divisional Labour Party	WEA	Workers' Educational Association
SAU	Shop Assistants' Union	*WHR*	*Welsh History Review*
SDF	Social Democratic Federation	*WL*	*Workers' Life*
		WM	*Western Mail*
SMC	School Management Committee	*WW*	*Workers' Weekly*
		YSB	Ystradyfodwg School Board
SSC	Special Staffing Committee		
SWDN	*South Wales Daily News*	YUDC	Ystradyfodwg Urban District Council
SWM	*South Wales Miner*		
SWMF	South Wales Miners' Federation	YUSA	Ystradyfodwg Urban Sanitary Authority

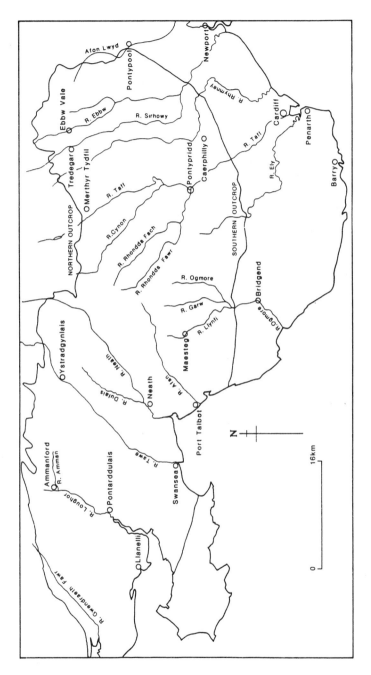

The south Wales coalfield

Afon Lwyd
Pontypool
Newport
R. Rhymney
R. Ebbw
Ebbw Vale
R. Sirhowy
Cardiff
Penarth
R. Taff
Tredegar
Merthyr Tydfil
Pontypridd
Caerphilly
R. Ely
Barry
R. Taff
R. Cynon
NORTHERN OUTCROP
R. Rhondda Fach
R. Rhondda Fawr
SOUTHERN OUTCROP
R. Ogmore
Bridgend
R. Garw
R. Ogmore
Ystradgynlais
R. Neath
R. Llynfi
Maesteg
R. Dulais
R. Afan
Neath
Port Talbot
Ammanford
R. Amman
R. Neath
R. Tawe
Pontardulais
R. Loughor
Swansea
Llanelli
R. Gwendraeth Fawr

N

0   16km

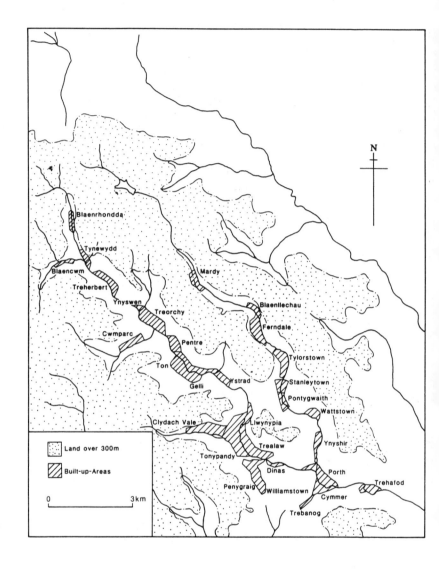

Major settlements in the Rhondda Valleys, *c.* 1920

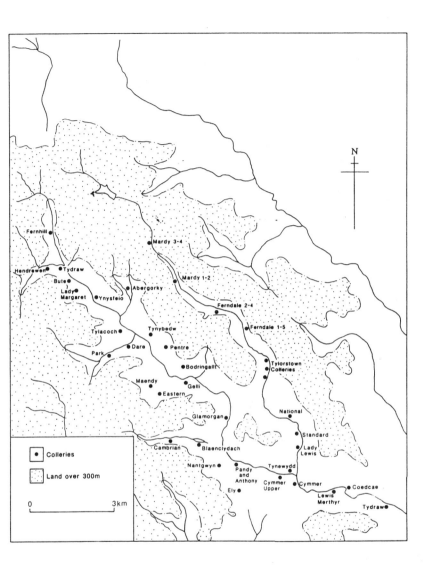

Major collieries in the Rhondda Valleys, *c.* 1920

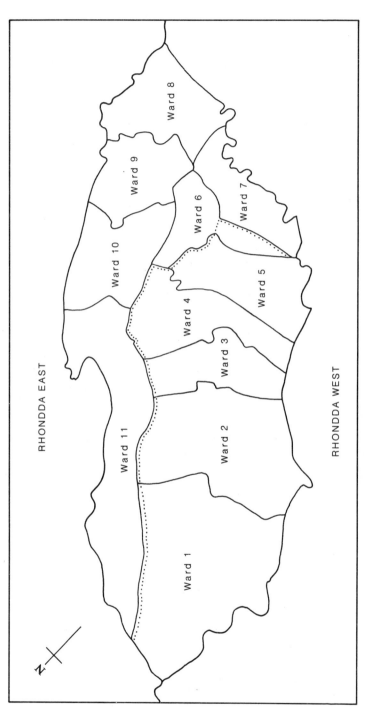

Parliamentary and Urban District Council boundaries, Rhondda Valleys, 1921

Introduction

Siting 'Democratic Rhondda'

I grew up among people who in the face of the most damnable and destructive adversity yet managed to sing their songs of resistant, rebellious belief in their own creative power and goodness. I keep singing with them until I drop . . . What I write about fundamentally is not the tragedy of a stricken and contracting community but about fulfilment and its opposite, arrogance and the servility it feeds on, death and the dreams it puts an end to . . .

Gwyn Thomas, 1952[1]

When speaking before his constituency party's executive committee in 1947, William John, Labour MP for Rhondda West since 1920, announced his intention of retiring from Parliament at the next general election. He also informed the meeting that there was an urgent need to collate a history of the growth of the Labour Party locally since the election of Rhondda's first MP, William Abraham or 'Mabon', in 1885: 'there were but a few records', said John, 'and it was necessary to do so while the men of this period were still alive.'[2] Unfortunately, Will John's call was not heeded, and studies of Rhondda politics, like those of local politics more generally in modern British history, have emerged only belatedly. Edward Thompson's 'call to arms' for scholars of local politics in his 'Homage to Tom Maguire' took some time to find a response, although in recent years an understanding of the regional mosaic of late nineteenth- and early twentieth-century politics has been enhanced by the works of, amongst others, David Howell, Michael Savage and Duncan Tanner.[3] Edward Thompson's influence has also been identified as partly responsible for the relative chronological and political imbalance of local studies: for Raphael Samuel and Gareth Stedman Jones, Thompson's magnificent *The Making of the English Working Class* inspired many historians to concentrate on 'alternative history', upon 'heroic periods of struggle', subjects that offered a contrast with the 'bureaucratic and social democratic' realities of the late twentieth century. This meant that where the Labour Party ('the main political tradition in twentieth-century working-class and left-wing politics') was studied at all, it was the period of the 'rise of Labour' that received attention, rather than the inter-war or post-war years.[4] If, as the Labour Party became more established and more institutionalized, it had also become more uniform, then the consequent fading of its local distinctiveness might have explained such neglect; but extant local studies of these decades show this to be a false impression.[5] The range of political choices for the working class may have narrowed by the 1920s, with the reorganization of the Labour Party around a new constitution and the consolidation of some left-wing currents in the Communist Party of Great Britain (CPGB or CP); but local formulations and traditions remained of crucial significance. Consequently, the local study is vital to the development of the history of working-class politics in that it asks new questions and sets new agendas.[6]

An awareness of the inescapable variety of local political histories has been complemented by a more sophisticated understanding of the relation between the 'local' and the 'national'. Whilst it is true that no strict division between the two domains is either feasible or desirable, and that the historian of the 'local' must guard against the possibility of over-estimating the significance of local experiences and initiatives, there may be a more significant place than hitherto believed for the 'local', even after the emergence of 'nationalizing' currents in British politics.[7] A measure of consensus has now been reached that the experience of 'class' (especially in the Victorian and Edwardian eras) was rooted in local occupational structures; but what has recently assumed a more significant role in twentieth-century political history has been the understanding of political parties as coalitions of regionally and locally based interests.[8] Principles and policies were determined at the local level, and projected upwards onto the national stage where they competed with each other in an unstable, flexible framework at various times dominated by regional or group priorities.[9] It can be argued that in the inter-war period a collection of industrial regions, including south Wales, came to constitute not only Labour's economic bedrock, but also its wider identity. In the longer term such strong, regionally-generated class consciousnesses have outlived both the erosion of their economic foundations and the passing of the historical 'moments' of their creation, and have continued to exercise a powerful influence upon the Labour movement.[10]

It is in the context of these trends in the writing of British labour history that this study of Rhondda politics from 1885 to 1951 has been conceived. The lengthy time-span of the work makes possible an understanding of local distinctiveness from the birth of an admittedly imperfect democratic polity in 1885 through to the operations of a mature political system, and thus breaks through any barrier between 'the rise of Labour' and its later stability.[11] As for the balance between the 'local' and the 'national', throughout this work emphasis has been placed on a 'microdynamic' explanation of political change: political change primarily explained by the internal dynamics of Rhondda and the wider south Wales coalfield rather than by the operation of exogenous forces. Only towards the end of the period covered do forces such as the rise of European Fascism, the Second World War, the reforms of the Attlee governments and the onset of the Cold War begin to take precedence over locally rooted stimuli. This is not to suggest that such stimuli were parochial in their concerns, as the rhythms of Rhondda society can be seen as national, if not international, from the expansion of the coal industry in the second half of the nineteenth century onwards. Rather, what began to diminish, particularly after 1945, was the consciousness that Rhondda was a creative rather than a reactive domain, with some control over its historical destiny rather than being largely dependent upon the intervention of external agents of change.[12]

As for the historical significance of this work, it is a study of a key segment of the south Wales coalfield, an area that became, in the inter-war years, a Labour 'heartland'. Although its parliamentary representation before the First World War was dominated by Liberal and 'Lib-Lab' MPs, by 1922 the sixteen constituencies of the coalfield, from Llanelli in the west to Pontypool in the east, were all returning Labour representatives to the Commons, and they and their successors have continued to do so for the last seventy years. Labour's monopoly of coalfield politics has outlived the coalfield itself. Labour has also exercised power at local level: in 1919 ten urban district councils in south Wales were returned with Labour majorities, and both the Glamorgan and the Monmouthshire County Councils soon followed suit. The importance of south Wales to the national fortunes of the Labour Party was never more evident than at the general election of 1931, when the party went into massive retreat across

Britain, its Commons representation falling from 288 seats to 52. It was saved from extinction by the staunch support still found in the coalfields of Yorkshire, Lancashire and south Wales.

Rhondda was at the core of this south-Walian political experience. The electoral reforms of 1884 and 1885 created it as a parliamentary constituency with a substantial working-class electorate, and it proceeded immediately to return Wales's first 'Labour' MP in the grand shape of the 'Lib-Lab' Mabon.[13] It saw, before the First World War, the development of an independent Labour movement, embracing working-class Liberals, Independent Labour Party (ILP) socialists and industrial unionists, and from 1910 this movement (whose energies were channelled through an organizational array of trade unions, trades councils and political bodies) replaced the Liberal hegemony with its own. An added dimension to the blanket coverage of the left, in the Rhondda valleys at least, was a political culture that not only nurtured and sustained a resilient Labour Party but also provided for a level of Communist Party support unparalleled in British terms, occasioning fierce political and ideological conflict on the left. How this Communist challenge was articulated, and then how it was contained and defeated by Labour, is a subject of great interest and importance. The scholar of British political and labour history will thus find in this work material that bears upon three conventional historical debates: the timing and dynamics of the replacement of the Liberals by Labour as the party of the left; the character of Labour domination in one of the party's most successful areas; and the fortunes of the spirited challenge made to that domination by the Communist Party.

Whilst the inspiration for this study and its methodological and historiographical precepts have come largely from British labour history, an understanding of Rhondda politics also makes a distinctive contribution to modern Welsh history. It would not be true to say that Rhondda's history has been neglected in the composite narratives that now surround and interpret the recent history of the south Wales coalfield and its people, for it has rightly been seen as central to that area's rise and fall. Rhondda is an internationally famous name that has, in its time, conjured up consecutive images of rapid economic and demographic growth (developments which in a very real sense made south Wales), followed by stagnation, slump and depression, when Rhondda's experience became a metaphor for that of the whole coalfield, and indeed for that of many of the depressed areas of Britain. Intertwined with this economic experience were industrial relations of an often volatile nature. Although in the late nineteenth century Rhondda and south Wales more generally were synonymous with the moderation of 'Mabonism', by the early twentieth century the coalfield was the site of momentous struggles between the trade union establishment and its radical challengers (some of whom embraced the exotic doctrines of industrial unionism and syndicalism). The riots in Tonypandy in 1910 not only threw these divisions into sharp relief but also highlighted the raising of the stakes concerning the future organization and control of the coal industry. Rhondda had already produced the first leader of the South Wales Miners' Federation (SWMF, 'Federation' or 'Fed') in Mabon: it went on, during successive decades of industrial struggle, to produce until well after the Second World War some of the most impressive, committed and articulate trade unionists seen in Britain this century, including Arthur Cook, Arthur Horner, and Will Paynter. South Wales was the storm-centre of the industrial relations battles of the 1920s, a crucial arena for the rebuilding of trade unionism in the 1930s, and in the vanguard of the successful struggles for the establishment of the National Union of Mineworkers (NUM) and the nationalization of the coal industry in the 1940s.

These economic and industrial relations histories are now available in multi-layered form, in works displaying not only great technical ability but often an admirable, even inspirational commitment to the human subjects of their studies.[14] The fascinating nature of south Wales is evident in the continuing flow of historical scholarship, enhancing our understanding as, slowly, a 'total' history of coalfield society begins to take shape.[15] A complementary route into the past lives of Rhondda people is available through literature, and no finer grasp of the spirit of the area is to be had than by immersion in the prose of writers such as Lewis Jones and Gwyn Thomas, the former himself an important figure in the history to be told here.[16] But if Rhondda has enjoyed a striking modern economic and industrial relations history, its necessarily intertwined political history has been no less vivid. Although 'the baton of class leadership' had been carried by the workers of Merthyr (and perhaps Monmouthshire) in the nineteenth century, by the early twentieth century it was firmly in the hands of Rhondda men and women.[17] Indeed, it was the fame of Rhondda's political radicalism that attracted this study, for that radical history, and its contemporary legacy, has all too often been the subject of prejudice, caricature and misunderstanding.

The Labour Party, the political expression of modern Rhondda and more generally that of south Wales, has not had a good press. Its detractors have identified it with chauvinism, corruption, and a narrow-minded philistinism that has precluded effective co-operation with sympathetic political parties and groupings. It has become commonplace at one end of the Welsh political spectrum to play up a craven image of Labour in order to celebrate less widespread manifestations of Welsh political allegiance in the hope of contemporary gain. Given its political strength in twentieth-century south Wales, Labour should occupy centre stage in any history. But in a distorted historical account what have captured the limelight are the milestones of the 'Welsh radical tradition': the 'Golden Age' of class-conciliatory Liberalism, the fierce burst of intellectual endeavour that was syndicalism, and the charismatic powers of Communism. By these important but in this context misunderstood phenomena, the Labour Party's historical contribution has been overshadowed and its relevance marginalized. And, with the disappearance of the pure strains of syndicalism and Communism from Welsh political life, in retrospect conveniently domesticated and rehabilitated, and with the Labour Party continuing to reproduce itself in a supposedly bastardized form, what remains of the Welsh radical tradition passes by sleight of hand to the anachronistic rootlessness of Welsh nationalism.[18]

A more academic distortion has occurred at the hands of those historians unwilling to embrace the more riotous and revolutionary dimensions of coalfield history, preferring to emphasize 'legal, constitutional, peaceful protest'.[19] Whilst it is true that '[e]ven in the worst horrors of the 1930s, with its mass unemployment and near-starvation in the valleys, the main thrust of radical endeavour went towards constructive, constitutional activity' it is a mistake to separate such activity from 'occasional violent upsurges or civil disorders'. For, as *The Miners' Next Step* cannot be understood in separation from its surrounding political history, so neither can the stay-down stoppages of 1935 be seen as anything but an essential part of the rebuilding of the SWMF. To divide these activities is to write a history unrecognizable to those who lived through it, and is to marginalize the admittedly irregular and atypical, but nevertheless revelatory instances of extra-parliamentary protest.

Such interpretations of modern Welsh political history may be found increasingly untenable as that history is written and rewritten but, as yet, local studies of modern Welsh politics remain few and scattered, and much of the most important work has either to be published or undertaken. The emphasis has remained upon the 'rise of Labour'.[20] A study of Rhondda complements extant local studies, but in its chronological range and in its refusal to accept the distorting simplicities of either nationalist or liberal historiography it restores the Labour Party to its rightful place in the history of modern Wales, whilst locating productive and fruitful ideological offshoots such as syndicalism and Communism within the common, socialist culture of mining communities.

Open Marxism: economy, society, politics

Historians are currently attending to the nuances of class behaviour, pondering its very existence and wondering if it ever translated itself from being to action by any discernibly connected route. They would do well to credit some practitioners at least with the doubts and sophistications they readily accrue to themselves.

Dai Smith, 1993[21]

This work rests upon a theoretical perspective that might best be labelled 'the relative autonomy of the political'. This perspective is, and remains in this work, essentially Marxist, although it acknowledges the common reference points it has with non-Marxist histories, and particularly with post-structuralist modes of historical enquiry. Accordingly it retains a heavy emphasis upon 'class' as a fundamental concept, both objectively identified and subjectively lived, but complements this with a sensitivity to the interactive realm of political discourse, and an attention to the complex refraction and construction of class identities through political organizations.

The 'relative autonomy of the political' should not be misunderstood as an attempt to cut politics free of its social and economic context in an over-reaction to crude, deterministic readings of Marxist historical materialism. Rather it is a way of coming to terms with a revised understanding of how that context operates, and how human agency and creativity exist within it. Edward Thompson, that champion of 'agency', redefined determinism not as the 'predetermined programming or the implantation of necessity, but . . . the "setting of limits" and the "exerting of pressures". It means retaining the notion of structure, but as structural actuation (limits and processes) within a social formation which remains protean in its forms.'[22] In this formulation the economic 'base' sets limits and creates circumstances within which 'superstructural' activity (politics, ideology – the 'making' of history) can be decisive, and in which this activity derives much of its momentum from its own history, language and conflicts.[23] This position allows the historian to re-evaluate the place of politics within social history, treating politics's own dynamics rather than importing politics as an illustration of a development with its essential dynamic elsewhere.[24]

The position of 'relative autonomy', whether historical materialist in origin or not, is one that is shared by many practitioners of modern British political history. As Duncan Tanner puts it, 'The logic of much recent analysis is to recognise the difficulties of making connections between "social" experience and "political" responses.'[25] But a rejection of 'reductionism' should not be seen as a dismissal of the 'social'. Rather it is a recognition of the complex interplay of historical forces.[26]

One important attempt at conceptualizing the interrelationship between the social and economic context and the political realm has been made by Michael Savage.[27] Savage's sophisticated categorization of various types of working-class politics (statist, mutualist, economist) and the capacities open to political organizations practising such politics should certainly be a starting-point for all future local political histories. However, Savage's ambition of providing a totalizing explanatory framework for working-class politics has resulted in his embracing certain propositions that seem inappropriate to an understanding of Rhondda politics and perhaps of the politics of the south Wales coalfield more generally. It is impossible, in such a context, to share his view that industrial conflict was largely irrelevant to the development of Labour politics, that 'the rise of the Labour Party owed little to intensified workplace conflict between capital and labour'.[28] More seriously, Savage also dismisses the importance of working-class cultures and consciousnesses in explaining political alignments: 'People have a variety of beliefs about different elements of their lives, and there is no reason to suppose that there is any coherence about these beliefs.'[29] The complexity of popular belief is not in itself an argument against its relevance: indeed, it may be argued that statist, mutualist and economist 'interests' can only be understood as constructed and given meaning by an admittedly variable and fractured working-class 'culture'. As John Marriott has argued in relation to Savage's work:

People do not negotiate in a direct and immediate way with material conditions; the negotiation is structured through consciousness. At an individual or party level discourses not only mediate between material conditions and their interpretation but can organise experience itself. It follows that in order to understand the efficacy of political parties or the ways in which political forms relate to everyday experience, account must be taken of the appropriate political discourses. This takes us into the realm of language.[30]

Indeed, the introduction of 'language' into the conceptual apparatus established by Savage provides a fruitful way in which future studies of local politics might be organized. For whilst the use made of the methods of discourse analysis is a subject of considerable controversy, not least for its own ambitious and sometimes misleading posturings, any emphasis upon 'the means and content of human communication' is welcome within the framework of the relative autonomy of the political.[31] As Neville Kirk has suggested, the project must be to 'incorporate study of language into a wider framework of analysis that embraces agency and structure, saying and doing, the conscious and unconscious, and the willed and unintended consequences of individual and social action and thought.'[32] Language is not free-floating, but as Gareth Stedman Jones admits, it is 'part of social being'.[33]

The importance of political languages is evident from recent debates on the modern history of the Labour movement.[34] As, increasingly, the economic and cultural differentiation of the British working class has been revealed, even in its 'classic' setting of the first half of the twentieth century, so gradually attention has been paid to the salience of the political unities and loyalties of the working class and of the Labour movement, however fragile the economic and social foundations of such unity in terms of workplace sectionalism, ethnic difference or cultural differentiation.[35] Often, the creation of shared visions and purposes based upon not necessarily self-evident assertions of a common identity took place in the political domain, and were manufactured with languages of class and justice that need to be taken seriously in their own terms, rather than seen as relating to a deeper socio-economic 'reality'. It is at this point that Savage's work is re-embraced, for his emphasis upon the important role played by local political institutions in the construction of working-class identities: ' . . . as Labour gained control of municipal authorities and so had greater ability to make the city in the image of the working class, so they could also facilitate working-class formation.'[36] The 'political' therefore, can be a creative as much as a reactive domain.

This work is influenced by the theoretical and methodological precepts outlined here in various ways. In keeping with the 'relative autonomy of the political', Chapter 1 sketches a portrait of Rhondda's social and economic history during the period, thus providing the basic framework within which its political history unfolded. The fact that Rhondda was a 'coal society', its economic fortunes and social institutions dominated by the rhythms of the mining industry, is manifestly vital to any understanding of its political trajectory, and yet cannot explain anything but the broad lineaments of political change. In contrast, Chapter 2 examines the 'rise of Labour' up to 1910 in the locality against the backdrop of the Liberal domination of local politics and the Lib-Lab parliamentary representation of the area through the personality of Mabon.[37] Inchoate but common conceptions of working-class identity permeated the 'rise of Labour', articulated through a language that stressed the human dignity and value of manual work.[38] Although, in Savage's phraseology, the 'formal' politics of the working class varied from Liberal to socialist, in 'practical' terms the agenda was shared, and was distinctive from that of the middle-class Liberals who at that time provided the nominal leadership of Rhondda society. Chapter 3 covers the establishment of a Labour political hegemony in the period 1910–27 and identifies its organizational and cultural underpinnings. The successful advocacy of the movement and of the party, welded together against rival political parties, employers and government in a common industrial and political struggle, was accompanied by a heightened vision of the movement's future as being linked to 'socialism'. At the same time this external unity barely concealed the tensions and conflicts that arose within the Labour movement over the meaning of socialism. Chapter 4 examines the most significant of these conflicts, over the uses (envisaged or real) to be made of local government power, and over the industrial and social trauma of 1926. The result of that crisis was, ultimately, the expulsion of the Communists and other left-wing elements from the Rhondda Labour Party against the backdrop of similar 'purges' across Britain. Chapter 5 traces the rise and fall of the consequent Communist challenge to the Labour Party's domination of the channels of representative government, and seeks to explain both the attractions of Communism and the limits set to its growth by Labour's response to this threat. This explanation operates from within a framework that refuses reductionist simplicities and pays attention instead to the competing (and complementary) approaches of these opposing wings of the Labour movement. Finally, the Conclusion draws together the major themes of this work within a re-evaluation of the popular meaning of the Labour Party's 'socialism'. Most importantly, it is hoped that, in the face of the detail of the newspaper reports and minute books, Rhondda people will still manage to 'sing their songs of resistant, rebellious belief in their own creative power and goodness'. If this historian owes only one thing to his subject of study, then it is to let its voice reverberate throughout his work.

1

Rhondda: 'The most active and thriving community in Great Britain or the World'[1]

There was a moment of real and profound intimacy, unexpected and short-lived like a glimpse of some everlasting, of some saving truth.

Joseph Conrad[2]

All Rhondda's chroniclers, be they novelists, artists, historians or simply inhabitants, have been confident that through their works and their lives they have been permitted to enjoy glimpses of 'some everlasting, of some saving truth'. To Gwyn Thomas, this most famous of all south Wales valleys was 'a more significant Chicago'.[3] To Hywel Francis and David Smith, Rhondda was 'the greatest coal-producing valley in the world' and 'one of the crucial emblems of the whole world's industrial history . . . a rich articulation of the possibilities available for humankind'.[4] Figures from this rewarding, bruised, and iconographic past thought in similar terms: the miners' leader, syndicalist and ultimate 'organic intellectual' Noah Ablett struggled to realize his visions at the level of the Rhondda No.1 District of the South Wales Miners' Federation (SWMF) precisely because he believed it to have global centrality: the Rhondda No.1 District was the largest district of the largest regional federation of the largest trade union of the first industrial society. Plans laid in the Aberystwyth Restaurant, Tonypandy could be thought to have the potential to change the course of world history. Even if that project was not realized, Rhondda nevertheless stood on the cutting edge of the Welsh industrial and political experience throughout the period covered in this work. Its historical development repeatedly wrenched Welsh society from one form into another over the course of a century, and in so doing it bore messages of relevance not only for the Welsh but for other rapidly urbanized and industrialized peoples throughout the world.

The first sale-coal operations in Rhondda were opened by Bridgend tanner Walter Coffin at Dinas in 1809.[5] In 1990, coalmining in the area came to an end with the closure of the last colliery, at Mardy in Rhondda Fach. Between those dates, Rhondda was first transformed from a pastoral idyll to the heart of the late-nineteenth-century Welsh industrial revolution, and was then transformed again into the quintessential 'valley of unemployment' as the fortunes of the steam-coal industry plummeted during the inter-war decades. After the Second World War the coal industry was nationalized and revived, before undergoing a lengthy period of 'rationalization' that ended only in its death, albeit not without momentous struggles on the part of its workers and their communities. During the post-war decades Rhondda's industrial base was somewhat diversified, whilst its future became closely linked to the more prosperous south Wales coastal belt. But if Rhondda's future is henceforth to be without coal, there is no doubting that its past, during the period 1885–1951, was coal, in production or out.

At the beginning of the nineteenth century the Rhondda valleys were covered by extensive tracts of woodland, were sparsely populated by yeomen, tenant farmers, and agricultural labourers, and were largely untouched by industrial production. Visitors such as Benjamin Heath Malkin in 1803 could praise Rhondda for its 'union of wildness and luxuriance, and of sublimity with contracted size and space'.[6] Such characteristics continued to be associated with the upper Rhondda valleys during the next half-century, for such industrial development as occurred was confined mainly to the lower reaches of Rhondda Fawr and Rhondda Fach, where between 1809 and 1855 twenty-six coalmining undertakings were opened. These workings were small-scale levels or shallow pits, producing bituminous (household or 'house') coal, carried to its markets perhaps by the Glamorganshire Canal or, from the 1840s, by the Taff Vale Railway, which was extended to Cymmer in the lower Rhondda. By this time, however, it was the neighbouring Cynon valley that was witnessing the most rapid and extensive exploitation of the deeper-lying reserves of 'steam' coal so suitable for use at sea as steam power superseded sail. Rhondda's vast industrial expansion, centred as it was upon large-scale steam-coal collieries, did not begin until 1855, when the first steam-coal pit was worked at Cwmsaerbren, Treherbert, on land belonging to the Bute estate.

The proving of the existence of the Aberdare Four-Foot seam heralded a new era in Rhondda's history. Between 1855 and 1922 no fewer than forty-four steam-coal collieries were opened in the two

Rhondda valleys.[7] By 1875 Rhondda was producing more coal than the Cynon to the east, and by 1884 the area was producing over one-fifth of all coal brought to the surface in the whole of the south Wales coalfield. Accompanying the steam-coal collieries were many bituminous-coal workings, and four major railway lines that conveyed the resultant produce to the main ports of Cardiff, Barry, Newport and Swansea, and thence to markets world-wide. In 1884–5 the area's coherence was reflected in the creation of the new parliamentary constituency of Rhondda under the Liberal Government's Third Reform Bill, whilst in 1896 the transformation of the area's identity was signalled by the decision of the recently formed Ystradyfodwg Urban District Council (YUDC) to rename itself the Rhondda Urban District Council (RUDC) on the grounds that the former name was not known in commercial and financial circles whilst the name Rhondda 'has acquired a reputation in both circles, owing to the exceptional quality of its steam coal, which has gained a world-wide reputation as "Rhondda Coal".'[8]

Such coal was worked overwhelmingly by hand, and predominantly by the 'longwall' method as the twentieth century opened. Although the rapid expansion of the industry precluded the operation of any apprenticeship system, coal-getting was by no means an unskilled task. There was a place for simple labouring in and around the mines, but most miners drew upon years of experience as hewers, hauliers, timbermen or repairmen. Although levels of acquired wisdom, age, strength, manual dexterity and indeed remuneration varied amongst this differentiated work-force there is little evidence of any resultant behaviour patterns that might be thought characteristic of an 'aristocracy of labour'. A more likely and continuing source of differentiation was instead the wide range of occupational experiences dependent on the size of the pits, the nature of the seams worked, the peculiar geological conditions thereof, and the differing managerial customs and practices encountered. Employment in the Crown level, at Treorchy, alongside a maximum of ten other workers in 1906, was a different prospect altogether to being one of the 1,800 miners descending the Cambrian Colliery No.3 pit down at Clydach Vale.[9] Coal might be mined from the Rhondda No.2 seam, which could be less than fifty yards below the surface, or it might have to be won from the Gellideg seam, perhaps as much as five hundred yards below ground. Ultimately however, with miners often working in half a dozen or more concerns in the course of their working lives, it was the arduous nature of colliery employment and its attendant unrelenting threat of injury and death that made for a relative cultural homogenization and a common occupational identity.[10]

In comparison with other manual workers of the late Victorian and Edwardian era, albeit in scant compensation for the awful dangers they faced, coalminers were well paid, and those of south Wales better paid than most of their British counterparts. Demand for labour in what was a labour-intensive industry expanded in tandem with the sinking of deep mines and, in Rhondda, resulted in nothing less than a demographic revolution. The higher wages and shorter hours of Rhondda mining attracted agricultural labourers from south-west England, and other iron and coal miners from the earlier-developed 'north crop' settlements such as Merthyr Tydfil and Tredegar. Within the confines of the Rhondda valleys they together forged a new society.

The relative stagnation of Rhondda's early-nineteenth-century economy is illustrated by the fact that between the censuses of 1801 and 1851 the population of Ystradyfodwg parish increased from only 542 to 951.[11] Yet by 1871 the same parish numbered 16,914, and by the turn of the century no fewer than 113,735 people were resident in the Rhondda Urban District on census night.[12] By 1921 Rhondda was the second-largest urban settlement in Wales after Cardiff, and had a population larger than all Welsh counties excepting Glamorgan, Monmouthshire and (just) Carmarthenshire.[13] As with many colliery districts where the age structure of the population was relatively young, Rhondda exhibited a higher-than-average fertility rate: 36.4 during the years 1904–13 compared with the England and Wales average of 25.7.[14] Nevertheless, Rhondda's enormous growth in population was due overwhelmingly to in-migration, as is indicated by Table 1.1. On the basis of Philip N. Jones's study of the Ogmore and Garw in 1881, which analysed the occupational, residential, marital and religious patterns of these growing coalfield communities, it seems likely that Rhondda's population of diverse origin was socially assimilated in all areas, except that of language, well before the onset of the First World War.[15]

Occupationally little differentiation was possible, ethnic or otherwise, given the overwhelming domination of the coal industry. The 1921 census found that 67 per cent of males aged twelve and over were engaged in mining, with 'commerce, finance and insurance' the next largest occupational category, at under 4 per cent. The other

Table 1.1: Distribution of birthplaces of Rhondda inhabitants,
1901 and 1911[16]

Location	1901	1911
Glamorgan	61.8	61.0
Monmouth., Carms., Pembs.	12.4	3.5
Brecon and Cards.	7.1	10.9
Rest of Wales	5.3	5.8
ALL OF WALES	86.6	81.2
South-west England	9.0	11.2
Rest of England	3.1	5.4
ALL OF ENGLAND	12.1	16.6
Remainder	1.3	2.2

industries that existed in the locality were either subsidiaries to mining (such as coal carbonization plants), or were intimately related to the growth of the mining population (such as brickworks, quarries, and breweries).

This mono-industrial society was also a society where women enjoyed few opportunities for waged work. In 1901 only one-seventh of Rhondda's female population was recorded as in employment and, of that number, over four-fifths were young, unmarried women, for whom paid employment was one stage in the life-cycle that heralded marriage, childbearing and quite possibly an early widowhood. Accepting the imperfections of a census that frequently ignored home-work and penny capitalism at the very least, 'separate spheres' was a reality in the south Wales coalfield. Domestic service accounted for approximately half of women workers, and shop work, teaching or dressmaking for the bulk of the remainder.[17]

The fact that there were very limited occupational opportunities available for women is of major importance in understanding the uncelebrated and often marginal role played by women in the history recounted in this work. Of course there were female political activists, and even though a majority of those played a supportive and supplementary role there were a few who articulated their beliefs (sometimes their concern with 'women's issues') in predominantly male environments, and who forged successful political and representative careers. Thus Elizabeth Andrews, born in 1882 in Hirwaun and a dressmaker in her early years, rose through the Women's Co-operative Guild and the Labour Party to become the Labour Party's Women's Organizer in Wales in 1919.[18] But in the absence of a strong and independent economic base, and with only the teaching profession exhibiting meaningful traditions of trade unionism, most women were defined by their multiple status as daughter, sister, wife and mother. Male activists paid little attention to the concerns of their womenfolk, despite the pointed remarks of 'Matron', a contributor to the *Rhondda Socialist*, who observed that 'if working-class women are ever to be anything else than a subject class, they must work out their own social and political salvation from within. This is particularly true with regard to the wives of working men. While progress is being recorded all round, they are still in a primitive state of domestic slavery.'[19] With women in mining districts quite possibly working at home for up to seventeen hours a day, few opportunities were forthcoming for participation in political activity. Considerations of occupational and class interest so dominated the ethos of the local Labour movement as to exclude almost completely any sense of gender, even to the extent that the campaign for pit-head baths took until the inter-war period to make much headway. In most respects the Labour movement duplicated the patriarchal society from which it sprang.

At its economic and social peak in the early years of the twentieth century, then, Rhondda was both a coal society and a man's world. Standing at the centre of 'Imperial South Wales' it was supremely confident of its present contribution and its future prospects. When, in June 1912, the King and Queen paid a visit to the valley, the Loyal Address, with characteristic false modesty, stated that:

> We make no pretence to be other than a purely Mining community of recent growth and rapid development, yet we nevertheless pride ourselves on the fact that our District with its population of nearly 158,000 persons and its annual output of over 8,000,000 tons of coal is closely and materially connected with the well-being of every part of your Majesties' Dominion.[20]

The 'rapid development' of the area was evident in the domination of the landscape by the many collieries and works with their attendant engine houses, winding sheds, pit-head gear and spoil tips. The extraction and exportation of coal set the rhythms of daily life, punctuating it with the rumble of trucks to-ing and fro-ing between pit and port, leavening the air and polluting the watercourses with dust and smoke. Amongst such obvious manifestations of industry were crammed the people of the district: row upon row of terraced houses climbing the mountainside at ridiculous angles, or competing for space on the narrow valley floor with railway line, road and river. Overcrowding in these five or six-room terraces was substantial: in 1911, Glamorgan had the highest density of population of any county in England and Wales except London and Lancashire, whilst the district of Mid-Rhondda had a density more than ten times the national average.[21] In an industrial society dependent upon the labour of young men, often single in-migrants, lodging was a regular practice, and although owner-occupation was increasingly common (approximately two-thirds of miners were estimated to own their own homes around the time of the First World War), great demand for rented accommodation stimulated very high rents.

To write of 'Rhondda' is, of course, to write of a composite settlement. No two districts within the two valleys were exactly alike. Inhabitants of Rhondda Fawr generally considered themselves to be a cut above those of Rhondda Fach. Some settlements, like Blaencwm, bore the mark of their origins as single-pit villages, whilst others, like Ystrad, managed to exude a sense of detachment from the materialistic hurly-burly proceeding around them. Junction towns like Treorchy and Porth developed as commercial centres, whilst Mid-Rhondda, that conglomerate of Clydach Vale, Llwynypia, Tonypandy, Trealaw and Penygraig, offered a high concentration of recreational establishments from public houses to music-halls to sports grounds. The notion that Rhondda, like the rest of the south Wales coalfield, was for a time a 'frontier society' remained most tangible in the upper Rhondda Fach, where the greatest settlement occurred on the western slopes of the valley. For most of the twentieth century, inhabitants of Ferndale or Tylorstown have been able to look across the river to Blaenllechau or Stanleytown, lonely outposts of halted expansion whose geography reminds the observer both of the frantic economic imperatives of growth that made such house-building feasible and of the later desolation of decline. Rising above the human settlement of the valleys were the blunt tops of the mountains, themselves marked first by paths and then tracks and finally roads as the area's residents travelled for both business and recreation across those obstacles to communication. Split into two unequal parts, the greater valley nearly ten and the smaller less than seven miles in length, with the few miles below Porth before the river joined the Taff effectively drawn into the orbit of the market town and 'gateway to the coalfield' of Pontypridd, Rhondda had no fixed centre. With its parish church at Ystrad largely an irrelevance, and its council offices at Pentre through convenience not logic, 'Rhondda' was an identification whose complexity was not always apparent to outsiders. The geographical loyalty of a Rhondda resident was first to his or her particular settlement, often conceived at sub-ward level: Dinas, Cymmer, Llwyncelyn or Trebanog rather than simply Porth; Ynyswen, Cwmparc or Blaenrhondda as much as Treorchy or Treherbert. Only by starting with these small building-blocks could the edifice of a Rhondda identity be constructed. The 1917 Commissioners of Enquiry into Industrial Unrest believed that the absence of 'municipal centres and centralised institutions' retarded 'the development of the civic spirit and the sense of social solidarity' in the area; but this view was derived as much from social idealism and a failure to recognize what was geographically possible in these narrow valleys as it was from a complete understanding of the society in question.[22]

Indeed, an examination of the sort of society that Rhondda was at its peak, in the years before the First World War, gives the lie to the view that 'community sense' was lacking, for this was a society marked by a high level of cultural, recreational and associational activity, with a strong sense of its own identity, however contested that was. For a start, Rhondda was physically and ideologically marked by religion, and by Nonconformity in particular. The two valleys were littered with places of worship: Anglican, Methodists (Primitive, Wesleyan and Calvinistic), Congregational, Baptist, Catholic, Forward Movement and Salvation Army, most with both English- and Welsh-language variants, running services often three, four or more times a week, and supplementing formal worship with Sunday schools, bible classes, prayer meetings, and the Band of Hope. For some there is no doubt that the chapel was the centre of their social world: indeed for many women it provided the only respectable and organized outlet for such leisure time as they enjoyed.[23]

Women and adolescents were to the fore in the Evan Roberts-inspired 1904/5 Religious Revival, which swept through Rhondda as through much of the rest of the south Wales coalfield.[24] This transitory phenomenon captured the attention of all, and the minds of some; but although, during the climax of the Revival, it was reported that colliery horses 'seem to wear a surprised air . . . that the oaths and blasphemies of the pit haulier are no more', and that prominent rugby players had been 'saved' and had given up the game, the death of thirty-one miners in an explosion at Clydach Vale in March 1905 restored an air of sobriety and was held to mark the end of the Revival's appeal locally.[25] Despite the fact that the Revival still awaits its historian, it seems unlikely that it diverted the longer-term trends of secularization and marginalization. Indeed, the historian must beware of overestimating the cultural power and centrality of Welsh Nonconformity, particularly as the new century developed and, with it, alternative forms of social organization and leisure activity.[26] H. S. Jevons, writing just before the First World War, pointed out that in so far as 'religious fervour' remained a characteristic of Welsh miners it was of the older generation, with a 'distinct falling off in attendances at the chapels' having been noticed in the twentieth century.[27] The Royal Commissioners of 1910 observed that religious 'accommodation is largely in excess of any reasonable expectation of attendance'.[28] Nonconformity's attempt to dominate the public discourse of late Victorian and Edwardian Wales was subject to challenge from other religions and even from the 'new religion' of socialism; but a more widespread popular response could be one of simple indifference and passivity.[29]

Rhondda inhabitants, and men in particular, be they religious or otherwise, could choose from a wide range of secular opportunities in their leisure time. There were plenty of public houses, hotels, working men's institutes and libraries (one for each self-respecting miners' trade union branch, or 'lodge' as they were known) and many clubs and societies to use them: friendly societies, Conservative Clubs, Labour Clubs, a Marxian Club, temperance societies, a Professional and Businessman's Club, a Hibernian Club and even some Odd-fellows.[30] Rhondda's demographic cosmopolitanism was exemplified by the presence from the 1890s of Italian or 'Bracchi' cafes and temperance bars.[31] For entertainment of a more occasional kind there was the Grand Theatre in Pentre, the 'Opera House' at Treherbert, the Empire Theatre in Tonypandy, or the Judge's Hall, Trealaw – all venues for films, concerts, and public meetings.

The domain of spectator sport was colonized primarily by rugby football, although it was perhaps unsurprising that in this area so manifestly devoted to the pursuit of wealth the charge of professionalism should have been rife. In 1897, Newport's Arthur Gould led Wales to victory against England at Rodney Parade, a victory won by 'Rhondda valley forwards', and at this time clubs such as Llwynypia, Treherbert, Penygraig and Treorchy were amongst the leading representatives of the Welsh game.[32] Rugby was not the only sport to command support: association football had its adherents, Rhondda producing teams such as the Scotch Albions (Trealaw), the Ton Strollers, Porth and Hafod.[33] Cricket clubs were formed up and down the two valleys; Llwynypia also had its quoits.[34] In this period Rhondda and Pontypridd produced famous boxing champions, with Tom Thomas of Penygraig, Percy Jones of Porth and Jimmy Wilde of Tylorstown heading the rankings: they emerged from a culture that staged prize-fights in hotels, on mountainsides and at fairground booths.[35] Outside the realm of organized leisure and beyond the pleasures of allotments and gardening (limited by space and poor soil in Rhondda) there were also the public parks and the mountainside, suitable for rambles and 'fornication'. Finally, residents of this crowded, bustling and vigorous community could reflect upon all of this and plenty besides in their weekly newspapers, such as the *Rhondda Leader, Glamorgan Free Press*, and *Glamorgan County Times*, and the *Porth, Mid-Rhondda*, and *Rhondda Fach Gazettes*.[36]

As such titles suggest, by the early twentieth century English was the predominant language of Rhondda people. Both the 1901 and 1911 censuses reported that over half the population were able to speak Welsh, but Welsh monolingualism was insignificant, and the younger generations of Rhondda residents were growing up without the language of their parents.[37] English in-migrants arriving by this time were no longer being drawn into bilingualism, and their language was increasingly that of most public domains, with the exception of Welsh-language chapels. English predominated in the council chamber and the miners' lodge, as the 'language shift' documented by Tim Williams for Pontypridd in an earlier period came into effect for Rhondda as well.[38]

The Anglicization experienced by this 'American Wales' extended the range of identities open to Rhondda people in the years before the First World War. The presence of a popular press, of valley-wide organizations, and of a strong, distinctive economic image created a self-consciously modern society, confident of its future. What the links might be with the wider world, and what direction that future might take, were matters of speculation and debate. For members of the middle class, be they coal magnates, shopkeepers or professionals, the most common identity was that of a Nonconformist, capitalist liberalism, centred upon the fortunes of the coal trade, operating in a

Welsh context that knew no necessary conflict with the wider structures of the British state and empire. This 'world-view' emphasized the inherent democracy of its society, and the opportunities open to all who trod the roads of education, respectability, piety and self-improvement. When the Rhondda Urban District Council secured control of secondary education provision within its boundaries in 1913, following over a decade of campaigning, it was seen as a triumph for all its citizens, the Liberal-dominated authority having abolished tuition fees in 1904.[39] Upward social mobility could only be a minority experience, however, and increasing numbers of Rhondda's working class conceived of themselves not as participants in the communal myths of Edwardian Wales, but as engaged in a collective endeavour, still linked to the coal industry, to raise themselves and others like them in Britain's coalfields and industrial districts. One of the most distinctive features of this self-projection was the thirst for knowledge and the value placed upon it that led Labour councillors to prioritize the teaching of Latin and French in their schools above that of Welsh, that led observers to wonder at the casual familiarity of Rhondda miners with Einstein and Balzac, and at the same time led many young men into the works of Marx, Dietzgen, and the unyielding political economy characteristic of the Central Labour Colleges and the Plebs' League.[40] Exaggerated but telling was the assertion of the *Rhondda Clarion* in 1936 that in Rhondda 'almost everybody has made some kind of effort to understand the problems of the modern world'.[41]

These overlapping but ultimately competing 'definitions of community', both descriptive devices and analytical tools, structure considerations of the trajectories of politics later in this work, but can be illustrated here by two different individual experiences.

Rhondda as an enabling, liberal, beneficent society, as an appropriate arena for great talents, is exemplified by the personal history of Sir Walter Nicholas. Born at Brynamman to the owner of the Amman Iron Company, perhaps appropriately in that Liberal political *annus mirabilis* of 1868, Walter Nicholas trained as a solicitor in offices at Neath and Newport before taking First Class Honours and the Law Society Prize in 1894. A County Councillor before he was thirty years old, Nicholas joined the Cardiff-based firm of Morgan and Bruce in 1897 as a partner, and became solicitor to the newly-formed SWMF in 1898. Liberal in his politics, Anglican in his religion, in 1901 he took over as clerk of the RUDC from fellow-partner Walter H. Morgan, and during the next two decades established himself as 'King of the Rhondda', dominant on the RUDC in many respects, and performing a wider role as chairman of the Urban District Councils Association of England and Wales. Knighted in 1919, Sir Walter Nicholas died aged only fifty-eight in April 1926, too soon to witness the dreadful hammer-blow that was to fall upon his community and its aspirations in that fateful year.[42] A man assisted by a privileged background, yet of considerable talent and ability, Walter Nicholas and the Rhondda valleys merited each other at the time of their greatest achievements.

An alternative trajectory with differing allegiances was also available in the same period to those who made Rhondda their home. Thus Thomas Isaac Mardy Jones, born in 1879 at Ferndale, his father killed when he was six, went down the mines at the age of fourteen, lost an eye in a mining accident, but nevertheless was able through his own efforts to win a place at Ruskin College, Oxford, and to return to his native valley as checkweigher at the Mardy Collieries from 1907. Parliamentary and registration agent for the SWMF from 1909, he won the Pontypridd seat for Labour in the general election of 1922, sitting for nine years. Mardy Jones was something of an intellectual, a Fellow of the Royal Economic Society, and the author of many books and pamphlets: his views were to be influential within the ranks of the Labour movement as it developed in the early twentieth century. His arena, like that of Sir Walter Nicholas, was Rhondda, but his future was conceived in terms of the rise of all members of his class, be they in the south Wales coalfield, in the cotton mills of Lancashire, or the East End of London. Thus his Rhondda identity was submerged in the collective bargaining structures of the SWMF, of the Mineworkers' Federation of Great Britain (MFGB), of the Trades Union Congress (TUC) and of the Labour Party.

It would be wrong to suggest that Walter Nicholas and Mardy Jones inhabited separate worlds. When, in 1912, a debate was staged in the Judge's Hall, Trealaw between George Barker and Ted Gill (for the nationalization of the coal industry) and Noah Ablett and Frank Hodges (against), Walter Nicholas sat in the chair. In the 1920s both Nicholas and Mardy Jones pleaded with central government to show their locality some economic mercy, but to no avail. Walter Nicholas was, in his time, the official SWMF solicitor; Mardy Jones, later in life, was official lecturer to the newly formed National Coal Board. Both were practical, and intelligent men, and both rose with Rhondda and the wider coalfield as it crashed into the twentieth century.

Whatever the benevolent rhetoric of coal trade harmony, there is little doubt that during the first decade of the twentieth century south Wales took on the appearance of a class society. By the eve of the First World War coal-ownership in the Rhondda valleys was concentrated in a handful of joint-stock companies, such as the Ocean, Cory Brothers, Fernhill, Cambrian, Naval, Lewis Merthyr, Locket's Merthyr, United National and David Davis and Sons. Uniting some of these and sitting atop the pile was the Cambrian Combine, owned by Lord Rhondda, David Alfred (D. A.) Thomas, which by 1916 controlled two-thirds of Rhondda's coal output. Facing the coal-owners was the resilient and aggressive SWMF, which gradually formed its own 'combines' to parallel the power of capital. With productivity falling and wages under pressure, the battle-lines between employers and employees were drawn with increasing clarity down to the inferno of the Cambrian Combine dispute and the attendant Tonypandy riots in 1910–11. Although defeated in this momentous struggle, Mid-Rhondda miners had led the way to the successful conclusion reached following the first national strike of British coalminers in pursuit of a minimum wage in 1912. The Liberal ethos of a community united in pursuit of material wealth and civic rewards crumbled in the face of harsh economic realities.

It is perhaps the seemingly naked 'class war' of the period of the 'Great Unrest' between 1910 and 1914 that has given historians so many problems when examining the generally enthusiastic response of the organized working class, even in proletarian south Wales, to the First World War. Unravelling the puzzle must begin by denying any straightforward alignment of labour militancy with internationalism and 'revolutionary defeatism', whilst simultaneously observing that a patriotic 'will to win' is not equivalent to anti-socialist jingoism.[43] Patriotism and labour trenchancy were as compatible for the majority in the south Wales coalfield as they were for the majority in both France and Germany.[44] In south Wales, resistance to perceived exploitation was at the heart of the 1915 strike, whilst a satisfaction with the concessions won, aided and abetted by a respect for the sacrifices of fellow workers, accounted for its settlement.[45]

But if the clashes between capital and labour in south Wales up to the Armistice were predominantly over the share of the industrial spoils to be claimed by profits or by wages, in the inter-war period they became about the preservation of the miners' hard-won standard of living, about the solidarity of the British trade union movement, and about the right to have a trade union at all.

The fortunes of the steam-coal trade, and particularly of those coalfields heavily reliant upon exports, plummeted after the First World War. Critical to the decline were the progressive replacement of coal by oil as a power source for world shipping in the inter-war decades, within a more general context of the rise of other alternative energy sources such as electricity; the rise of competing and more competitively priced coalfields in central and eastern Europe and in America; and a foreign-exchange policy that further enhanced the costs of exported coal. On top of this, and indeed determined by it, the forces of capital and labour worked against each other in a series of bitter conflicts.

Denied nationalization by Lloyd George's perfidy in 1919, and subjected to savage wage cuts in the aftermath of decontrol in 1921, the miners were finally defeated in the herculean struggles of 1926. Thereafter the SWMF, threatened with extinction by both the coal-owner-backed company unionism of the South Wales Miners' Industrial Union and the hostile economic environment, fought a rearguard battle. In Rhondda, from the end of 1924, and particularly after 1926, production and employment went into a prolonged slump as the community fell from grace, a fall welcomed by a few outsiders, but experienced tragically by Rhondda people.[46] First to close were many of the coal levels, usually employing smaller numbers than the steam-coal pits. But then the pits themselves began either working short-time or closing altogether, perhaps functioning as pumping stations for years at a time. By 1939, coal production in Rhondda pits was one-third of its 1913 level.[47] Employment in mining fell from just under 40,000 in July 1927 to under 20,000 by July 1936. Without other local industries to take up the slack, unemployment, measured amongst the insurable male labour-force, rose to a peak of 53 per cent in 1932.[48]

This inter-war world was very different from that of Edwardian Rhondda. For those in work, mechanical coal-cutters made relatively little impact in the south Wales coalfield, only being responsible for 24 per cent of all coal cut by 1937. However, mechanical conveyors to take the coal away from the face were increasingly common, carrying 39 per cent of all coal by the same date.[49] The pace of work underground changed, new grades of worker emerged and tensions over job control resulted from this shift away from traditional practices. Miners frequently complained that, in the haste to produce coal, the older skills and techniques were being lost, and the dangers of work intensified.[50] Wages fell markedly from the highs of the immediate post-war boom: average earnings per shift sliding from over twenty-one shillings in January 1921 to a low of under nine shillings in October 1933.

The collapse of the export coal trade had disastrous demographic consequences for Rhondda, rendering it one of the most heavily depressed areas in the coalfield. Although fertility exceeded mortality to provide a net natural rate of population growth of 8.5 per cent during the period 1921–31, at the same time out-migration ran at 23.4 per cent, and Rhondda's population went into a decline from which it has never recovered. Between 1921 and 1951 the total number of people living in the two valleys fell by no less than 36.1 per cent, from 162,717 to 111,389.

For all the spirit and determination of those who stayed, depopulation denuded the area of some of its finest talents. Those seeking to make their careers on the national stage were best advised to start from a different place, and over a third of the population aged between fifteen and twenty-nine were estimated to have left Rhondda between 1921 and 1931.[51] Admittedly, they were to have their own impact, particularly in the developing industrial towns of southern England and the Midlands. Such was the cultural prominence of emigrants that there was identified a 'Rhondda Valley' section of Coventry, whilst in Oxford ex-miners dominated the local Transport and General Workers' Union branch and provided an important stimulus to the growth of the local Labour Party.[52]

Meanwhile Rhondda suffered. Many local businesses, so dependent upon the buoyancy of coal, now went into catastrophic decline, with resultant closures and bankruptcies. The annual turnover of Rhondda's Co-operative Society fell from £88,000 in 1920 to £15,000 in 1927.[53] Sporting activity took a dive, with Treherbert Rugby Football Club shutting down in 1929, following the path taken earlier by Mid-Rhondda and Cwmparc Association Football Clubs.[54] In boxing, it was the indomitable and courageous, but still defeated, Tommy Farr who now epitomized Rhondda's spirit: there were to be no further world champions.[55]

More serious were issues of health and welfare. South Wales had a mortality rate 31 per cent higher than the south-east of England in the years 1937–9. Maternal mortality, infant mortality, the incidence of malnutrition, rickets, diphtheria, tuberculosis, pneumonia: all were higher in the depressed coalfield than in the prosperous 'South', and particularly high amongst women and children.[56] Rhondda, identified by the nation as synonymous with 'conflict, gloom and despair', was awarded 'problem status'.[57] This attracted sociological and governmental investigations, alongside voluntarist activities.[58] Quakers William and Emma Noble established the Maes-yr-Haf Educational Settlement at Trealaw, which became one of the centres of the unemployed and social-service club movement in the coalfield. Backing Maes-yr-Haf was A. D. Lindsay, Master of Balliol College, Oxford, who 'adopted' the two valleys and brought idealistic students (including the later Home Secretary, Henry Brooke) with him. All such bodies, however, appealed only to a minority of the unemployed, who were equally likely to be involved (albeit intermittently) in the activities of the National Unemployed Workers' Movement.[59] For an even smaller minority, the avenue of collective advancement through education might now offer an individual escape lane in the form of Coleg Harlech.[60]

Rearmament at the very end of the 1930s and then the onset of the Second World War (which troubled Rhondda's political conscience relatively little) led initially to a revival in the demand for coal, and Rhondda's economy began to pick up.[61] Although export growth was halted by the fall of France, internal demand stimulated by the exigencies of war meant that coalminers were once again in short supply. But despite the revival of coal during the Second World War, Rhondda's leaders could no longer have so much confidence in the industry's ability to sustain their society, and plans for post-war industrial reconstruction and diversification were laid.[62] Measures included the further development of the Treforest trading estate below Pontypridd, to which Rhondda workers could commute, and the opening of the Polikoff clothing and EMI electrical equipment factories at Treorchy, as well as a series of smaller local factories.[63] As a result of these developments employment opportunities for women increased, although the male, mono-industrial culture remained dominant. As for coal, the National Coal Board assumed control of twenty-five colliery enterprises when it came into being on 1 January 1947, and although a number of these had not been worked for years and were never to be opened, nevertheless new projects were developed at the Fernhill complex at the top of Rhondda Fawr, and at Mardy at the top of Rhondda Fach. Coal remained an important employer: in 1957 it accounted for 55 per cent of the male labour force aged fifteen and over, and a longer-term future was predicted for it than eventually transpired. With the nationalization of coal in 1947 and with industrial diversification, with the introduction of the Welfare State and with government commitment to full employment, it was perhaps appropriate for the Rhondda miners to title their souvenir programme in 1947 *Rebirth of the Rhondda*.[64] In the light of the closure of Rhondda's last colliery, at the top end of Rhondda Fach in December 1990, and with the parallel emergence of the Rhondda Heritage Park and its 'Black Gold Experience' on the site of the old Lewis Merthyr Colliery below Porth, the motto of the Rhondda Borough Council that replaced the old Urban District Council in 1955 might be thought even more appropriate: *Hwy Clod na Golud* (Fame Outlasts Wealth). The subject of this work is the political fame won by Rhondda's Labour movement, and it is the subject of its origins and subsequent progress, enacted within the social and economic context outlined in this chapter, to which attention now turns.

2

The rise of Labour, 1885–1910

Introduction

The Miners trained people to vote Labour before there was a Labour Party.

W. H. Mainwaring[1]

This chapter examines the political history of the Rhondda valleys between the first parliamentary election for the Rhondda constituency in 1885 and the onset of the Cambrian Combine dispute in 1910. Through a detailed examination of electoral and organizational, parliamentary and local politics it generates a new perspective on the political history of the time, shedding light in particular upon the dynamics of late Victorian and Edwardian Welsh Liberalism and Lib-Labism, and upon the ideological and organizational underpinnings of the 'rise of Labour' in the south Wales coalfield.

The first half of the chapter investigates both the parliamentary history of the constituency, and the Liberal domination of the structures of local government. Prevailing historical orthodoxy identifies these as complementary dimensions of 'Lib-Labism': the supposed unity of the middle and working classes in advocacy of the agenda of 'old Liberalism', with the 'rights of Labour' – the interests of the organized workers – finding an appropriate berth amidst the avowed ideological harmony of the 'Nonconformist nation'.[2] William Abraham, or Mabon, Rhondda's MP during this period as well as leader of the south Wales miners, has his place in this orthodoxy as the personification of a Welsh Lib-Labism that retained its hold upon the majority of Welsh voters down to the First World War.

In this work a significantly different picture is drawn not only of Mabon but also of the reality and longevity of Lib-Labism. It is argued that the importance of Mabon's 1885 victory, when he stood

as a 'Labour' candidate against the representative of official
Liberalism, has been understated in historical accounts too ready to
assimilate it to the superficially conciliatory Lib-Labism outlined
above. Furthermore, the unity supposedly epitomized by Mabon did
not exist at the lesser levels of representative government and political
organization. Labour leaders, far from being allotted their niche in
the Liberal polity, found themselves marginalized within the local
Liberal organization and facing considerable Liberal competition
when attempting to gain representative office. The artificial reality of
Lib-Labism drove Labour leaders (be they believers in Gladstonian
Liberalism or the programme of the Independent Labour Party (ILP)
– it mattered little) to demand independent organizational support,
forthcoming predominantly from the trade unions that had, in the
first place, conferred their status upon them. It also led them to
articulate a supportive language of loyalty to the Labour movement
and to the wider working class.

The development of an independent working-class politics is the
subject of the second half of the chapter. This makes possible a new
understanding of the 'rise of Labour'. The historical orthodoxy of
Welsh Liberalism outlined above demanded that the Lib-Labs, from
Mabon down, be seen as having retarded the maturation of the Labour
movement. Such a perspective was embraced by historians of that
movement as much as by historians of Liberalism. Mabon's victory in
1885, and all Lib-Lab successes thereafter were thus of little relevance
to the emergence of a Labour Party.[3] The milestones of Labour advance
were instead threefold: the strike of 1898 that gave the opportunity for
the introduction of socialist doctrines into the coalfield and that
witnessed the development of the ILP in south Wales; the South Wales
Miners' Federation (SWMF) ballots on the question of affiliation to the
Labour Party in 1906 and 1908 that indicated a majority preference for
independent working-class politics, and that led to the affiliation of the
Mineworkers' Federation of Great Britain (MFGB) in 1909; and the
industrial relations turmoil of 1910 onwards that destroyed the
conciliatory tenets and personnel of Lib-Labism and replaced them
with the aggressive views of syndicalism and syndicalists, socialism and
socialists. All these developments were important, but the new
perspectives generated here on Lib-Labism and on the ethos of the
'rights of Labour' reinterpret such events in the context of the evolution
of the logic of independent working-class politics over a much longer
period. They also bring forward the timing of the 'death of Liberalism'

and its replacement by Labour, in the Rhondda valleys at least. There, Labour, with its claims already established at parliamentary level (albeit ambiguously), challenged Liberal domination in the sphere of local government with mounting success. The 'rise of Labour' is given a new chronology springing from a different set of emphases, emphases which gave priority to organizational independence over the rhetorical devices of Welsh Liberalism.

'Mabon' MP

> Mabon is as respected at St. Stephen's as he is beloved and appreciated in his own constituency. He has done excellent work, and his sane, practical efforts will be given an honourable place in history.
>
> *Rhondda Leader*[4]

William Abraham, also known by his bardic name 'Mabon', was MP for Rhondda from 1885 until 1918, and for Rhondda West from 1918 until his retirement in 1920. He was secretary of the Rhondda miners from 1877 until 1898, vice-chairman of the Sliding Scale Committee from 1875 until 1903, and president of the SWMF from 1898 until 1912. Until the MFGB affiliation to the Labour Party in 1909, Mabon took the Liberal whip in the House of Commons, and was backed locally from 1886 by the Rhondda Labour and Liberal Association (RLLA) which he had created following his elevation to parliament. If any Labour leader during the late nineteenth and early twentieth centuries deserved the label 'Lib-Lab' it was Mabon. He was the ultimate consensual public figure in industrial south Wales. And yet Mabon was simultaneously aligned with a very different tradition, a tradition that, whilst perhaps sharing in the wider objectives of Gladstonian Liberalism, demanded a voice for the workers, and a place for their representatives in the arena of politics and government. It is true that Mabon was content if he, and he alone, provided that voice; but notwithstanding his relative lassitude in this matter, other Labour leaders were prepared to thrust themselves forward, utilizing the language of the 'rights of Labour' pioneered by Mabon himself, but not necessarily sharing his Liberal faith. It is only by understanding both dimensions of Mabon's long parliamentary career that his ambiguous position as a Lib-Lab can be revealed.

That parliamentary career first began to be mooted in 1883, when the annual demonstration of the Rhondda Steam Coal Miners' Association (RSCMA) considered advancing a parliamentary

candidate under the new electoral system being constructed by
Gladstone's Liberal ministry.[5] Expecting Rhondda to be constituted a
separate parliamentary division, and the franchise to be extended to
many working men, RSCMA leaders believed it would be within their
power and the limits of justice to return their own nominee.[6] Mabon,
having by this time served as RSCMA secretary for six years, no mean
feat for any workers' leader in such an unpropitious climate for trade
unionism, was the obvious candidate.[7]

Gathering support during 1884, by January 1885 RSCMA delegates
representing twenty-two lodges voted in favour of Mabon as a
'Labour' candidate.[8] With this mandate a conference was convened of
delegates from all pits, with thirty-three lodges totalling over 16,000
miners being represented. The conference decided to support Mabon
financially, and resolved that each colliery committee should form
itself into a 'parliamentary committee' and 'invite all local tradesmen
and artisans to take part in their proceedings', whilst a Parliamentary
Executive Committee (EC) of ten was chosen to co-ordinate the
campaign at divisional level.[9] The practice of a trade union's
advancing its own candidate at a parliamentary election was not
unknown in south Wales – Thomas Halliday, one-time leader of the
Amalgamated Association of Mineworkers, had stood unsuccessfully
in the Merthyr Boroughs constituency at the general election of 1874
– but neither was it to go unchallenged.[10]

Also in January 1885 a Liberal Association (or 'Three Hundred')
had been formed for the Rhondda division, composed of five groups
of sixty representatives elected at district meetings. Conflict between
the Liberal Association and the RSCMA arose almost immediately,
and arose upon lines of class interest. At the first meeting of the
Three Hundred the validity of the elections was questioned by one of
their number, David Lawrence of Treorchy, also a member of the
miners' Parliamentary EC. The RSCMA had protested at the 'hurried
manner' in which the district meetings of the Three Hundred had
been convened, and at the 'great disproportion of the representation
given to colliery officials to the disadvantage of the workmen thereat'.
Consequently, the RSCMA had decided not to abide by any decision
regarding parliamentary representation made by the Three Hundred.
Lawrence attempted to raise these matters with the Liberal meeting,
but his protest was quashed by the Chairman with the comment that
they had 'other things to discuss besides parliamentary
representation'![11] The Three Hundred then elected its officers, and

whilst it was natural that the coal-owner Lewis Davis of Ferndale, president of the now defunct Pontypridd and Rhondda Liberal Association, should be appointed president of the new association, the omission of Mabon from the list of five vice-presidents was surely unwise. In its very composition the Rhondda Liberal Association (RLA) proclaimed its supposed independence from, and lack of interest in, the working class of the district.[12] In comparison, Mabon was more politically astute, receiving a letter of thanks from Gladstone for a miners' resolution of sympathy with his government and their continued confidence in him following the fall of Khartoum, and following this up with personal endorsements from Lord Aberdare, Glamorgan MPs Sir Henry Hussey Vivian and C. R. Mansel Talbot and the Lib-Lab MP Henry Broadhurst.[13]

Eventually four nominees placed themselves before the Three Hundred as candidates for the Parliamentary Division, including Mabon and Lewis Davis.[14] Following a special meeting at which candidates answered test questions on key Liberal issues such as free education, disestablishment and the reform of the House of Lords, the voting took place and resulted in the victory of Davis over Mabon in the final round by 143 votes to 51.[15]

Lewis Davis commanded business operations for D. Davis & Sons from Bryndderwen House, Ferndale, close to the huge Ferndale collieries. A Wesleyan Methodist, he called himself an 'advanced radical' in political matters, believing in the Liberal touchstones of free trade and disestablishment. His views on Labour representatives were that they were acceptable providing they had more general knowledge, but he did not think that 'Labour, simply as Labour, should be specially represented in an Assembly which has to deal with the multifarious concerns of a large kingdom'.[16] However, despite his victory in the ballot, Davis declined the invitation of the RLA to stand as their candidate, on the grounds that his business responsibilities were too weighty, and instead suggested that his 22-year-old son, barrister Frederick Lewis Davis, be considered.[17] Accordingly the RLA determined that it would hold a fresh ballot, and planned it for June.[18]

However, by this time there was growing concern over the validity of the original election of the Three Hundred back in January. As the *South Wales Daily News* observed:

> . . . there is clearly a party in the Rhondda Division who persist in

maintaining that the Three Hundred were not fairly elected, that they were not properly chosen, that certain interests predominate much beyond their legitimate proportion, and that consequently the selection which was made when Mr. LEWIS DAVIS was adopted by a large majority was not the choice of the electors.[19]

The RLA response was that the procedures had been correct: that placards had advertised the public meetings at which each district 'sixty' had been elected, and that the meetings had been announced at places of worship and at many collieries. Furthermore, Mabon had allowed his name to go forward for consideration despite any perceived bias.[20] Mabon's supporters contested these points: one dissident member of the Three Hundred pointed out that the initial meeting at the beginning of January had been held in mid-afternoon, when the miners were in work. Few miners had seen any placards, and reading out notices from the chapel pulpit was not 'the surest way of finding the ears of many of the colliers'.[21] Additionally it was claimed that the Three Hundred was dominated by 'a self-elected clique' and 'overburdened with colliery management and preachers' influence'.[22] With the second ballot in sight, relations between the camps of the major contenders became increasingly bitter, with Lewis Davis speaking out against Mabon, claiming that he would not represent the electors of the Rhondda, that 'the majority of the colliers do not want him', and that the other electors would prefer 'a man of another stamp.'[23] His son's cause was in turn assailed by E. A. Rymer, miners' agent from the Forest of Dean, who accused Nonconformist ministers of turning their own chapels into 'synagogues for the preaching of the political ascendancy of the coalowners'.[24] It was amidst mounting controversy, therefore, that the Three Hundred balloted again in June, and this time F. L. Davis defeated Mabon by 125 votes to 56.[25]

In due course F. L. Davis received and accepted the invitation of the RLA to contest the division, and it was announced, none too wisely given some sensitivity regarding his age and lack of experience, that 'in order to make himself more conversant with the actual wants of the mining community he intends . . . taking the earliest opportunity of going underground in one or more of the Ferndale Collieries'.[26] In spite of this second defeat, Mabon stood firm. He had informed the RLA that he would be contesting the division whatever the result of the ballot, as he had been nominated by the RSCMA, and mass meetings in June and July reaffirmed this backing.[27] The stage was now set for a contest between William Abraham, miners' agent, and F. L. Davis, coal-owner's son.[28]

In terms of policies there was little to divide the candidates. Both claimed to be radical Liberals, expressing support for Chamberlain's 'Radical Programme'.[29] The only notable difference was that Davis did not favour the payment of MPs, whilst Mabon did: a division that spoke for class background as much as anything.[30] The issues that superficially dominated the campaign were minor and local, arising in the first place from the controversies surrounding the selection process. The Davis camp argued that Mabon had no right to contest the seat, as he had twice been rejected by the Three Hundred.[31] The 'Mabonites', in reply, continued to argue that on the one hand the Three Hundred had been improperly constituted, and on the other that the RSCMA had every right, a 'moral' right even, to put forward its own candidate. Mabon maintained 'that the Rhondda Miners Association had held mass political meetings in the district long before there was any sign of activity among the Liberal organization'.[32] To the charge that his occasional writing of articles for the Tory *Western Mail* impaired his Liberal credentials, Mabon countered that he wrote not on political issues but on matters concerning the coal trade only. His supporters also levelled personal comments at the 'almost infant' Davis, attacking his youth and inexperience.[33] The campaign became marked by outbreaks of violence, many of Davis's meetings being severely disrupted; and when Mabon visited Ferndale he was assaulted by a stone-throwing mob.[34] Mabon's supporters were accused of intimidation: boycotting, even threatening tradesmen who supported Davis or who refused to give funds to Mabon; but the intimidation was on both sides – when Mabon took part in a procession in his honour from Porth to Ynyshir, it was headed by a Cardiff brass band. A local band had been scheduled to perform, but had been threatened with dismissal from their colliery employment if they had done so.[35]

The single most important issue of the campaign, and the key to its comprehension, was that of class. Davis represented capital, the employers; Mabon represented Labour, the workers. Voting along class lines under the reformed franchise would have produced an overwhelming victory for Mabon. Deference and perceived self-interest were to drain somewhat his reservoir of support, but it was always in Mabon's interest to portray the contest as a capital–Labour conflict, whilst Davis attempted to assert that 'the contest was between Labour and capital, hand in hand, on one side, and Labour on the other'.[36] Davis found himself troubled at meetings by questions over hours and pay at the Ferndale collieries, and when at Ynyshir it was asserted that his family had done 'great deeds of philanthropy' the speaker was answered with cries of 'with our money'.[37] Davis's cause was not aided by the local depression in the coal trade, which forced many collieries into short-time working.[38] A study of the composition of the rival camps lends support to the suggested importance of the capital–Labour distinction: Mabon found the bulk of his support amongst his colleagues – men such as David Lawrence and Howell Ajax, who served on the RSCMA Parliamentary EC, but also Thomas Davies, proprietor of the Windsor Castle Hotel, Ton Pentre (known as Thomas Davies 'Windsor', a man who married three times and fathered fifteen children), who held office in the RSCMA as Treasurer, and John Morgan of the Rhondda House Coal Miners' Association (RHCMA). There was scarce advocacy of his cause from other classes: solicitor Walter H. Morgan ('the colliers' lawyer' of Morgan and Bruce, and clerk to the Ystradyfodwg Urban Sanitary Authority (YUSA), later the Urban District Council), the grocer, baker and confectioner T. Pascoe Jenkins, and the miller, grocer and draper Aneurin Cule. The only minister to support Mabon was the Congregationalist John Salisbury Edwards. In contrast, Davis found resonant support amongst tradesmen such as boot merchant Richard Lewis and builder David Williams. The influential headmaster Tom John also backed Davis, as did three Nonconformist ministers: Congregationalists Evan Richards and Morgan Charles Morris, and the highly respected William Morris ('Rhosynnog') of Noddfa Baptist Chapel, Treorchy. What is noticeable about the allegiance of coal-owners and their functionaries is that many remained publicly neutral. In Rhondda Fach, although the Davis family and firm claimed the support of Ferndale notables, the rest of the valley proved not to be so loyal. In fact the local record of the Davises as employers was something of a liability during the campaign itself.

On polling day Davis toured the district in a carriage accompanied by female friends, whilst Mabon came up the valley on foot, soon being carried on assembled shoulders. Despite the forced closure of the area's pubs, the violence of the campaign reasserted itself when a crowd attempted to stone Davis supporter Dr James, the medical officer of the Ferndale Collieries. There was fighting in the streets in Pentre and the police station was attacked. The day's excitement was finally ended by rain late that evening, and both parties retired to await the result the following day.[39]

Table 2.1. Result of the 1885 Parliamentary Election[40]

William Abraham	Labour	3,859	(56.3%)
Frederick Lewis Davis	Liberal	2,992	(43.7%)
Majority		867	
Total votes cast		6,851	
Total electorate		8,210	(turnout 83.5%)

Upon the declaration of the result, and amid great enthusiasm, Mabon was taken in a man-drawn carriage on a tour of the valley, the procession stopping outside Ystradfechan House in Treorchy to cheer Ocean Coal's general manager, 'the Squire of Ystradfechan' William Jenkins, for not bringing pressure to bear upon the electors to vote against Mabon, despite his own preference for Davis.[41] This had undoubtedly been a clear and a popular victory for Mabon, Rhondda's first, and Labour, MP.

Rhondda's first parliamentary election closed, therefore, with an explicit division between official Liberalism and Labour that had been marked by bitter rhetoric and minor outbreaks of violence: little evidence of any harmonious Lib-Lab polity. It might have been expected that this division would be perpetuated in separate political organizations and subsequent parliamentary contests. However, before the end of 1885 the 'Mabonites' had formed a new political organization – the RLLA – which, by the end of February 1886, had absorbed the RLA of the Davis camp, and which was organizational proof of the existence of Lib-Labism.[42] Such developments testified to the spirit of reconciliation prevalent in both camps once the fury of electioneering was over, and although another general election was called for February 1886 the Davis family made it known that they had no intention of challenging the now securely-placed Mabon, and he was the sole nominee for the Rhondda division.[43]

Why was such reconciliation possible and indeed desired by the two camps? From Mabon's viewpoint, there was little to be gained in estrangement from official Liberalism. He had made his point in winning the election, and could afford magnanimity in victory. His own politics differed little from orthodox Gladstonian Liberalism, and a unification of the two camps would make his parliamentary tenure secure: financially, and against any future challenge. Mabon's experience as a trade unionist told him that in times of depression the ability of miners to support those elected to act on their behalf could falter, whereas the coffers of Rhondda's middle class offered security. As for the RLA, it had been clearly defeated, and knew that overturning the result would be difficult. Reconciliation was an attractive option, since within a reunited Liberal organization it was their money, social leadership and political style that would be most likely to prove dominant, whilst the shock to their class sensibilities of being represented by a working man could be mitigated by employing him as an icon of their progressivism. An examination of the subsequent history of parliamentary representation suggests that both Mabon and the RLA gained much from their unification in the RLLA.

Throughout the eight general elections from 1885 to December 1910, Mabon remained Rhondda's MP. When he was forced to fight an election campaign, he did so with great success, in both 1900 and January 1910 receiving the largest majorities in any constituency in the country; but he went unchallenged in each of the general elections of 1886, 1892 and 1895, albeit in 1892 facing the prospect of opposition right up to the date of nomination. At that time his would-be opponent was schoolteacher and restaurateur County Councillor Richard Morris, three times a Liberal sub-agent in parliamentary elections in Denbighshire and, since coming to Rhondda in the mid-1880s, involved in the RLLA both on its EC and as its County Council representative.[44] He was something of a radical, and his opposition to Mabon stemmed from the latter's mounting unpopularity as a supporter of the Sliding Scale.[45] Morris was approached by a deputation of local miners in May 1892 and accordingly floated the idea of his candidature.[46] However, lack of funds, and widespread confusion over the rationale behind the candidature rendered it hopeless from the beginning.[47] The Rhondda Conservative Association (RCA) had itself hoped to challenge Mabon, but opportunistically decided to throw its meagre strength behind Morris, thus leading to Morris's inaccurate branding as a 'Radical Unionist' and 'Tory Puppet' by the Liberal press.[48] Mabon meanwhile received the explicit backing of the Liberal Party establishment.[49] When the RLLA formally adopted Mabon as its candidate 'a large number of speakers were those who, in 1885, were among Mabon's opponents, and 'ardent supporters of the candidature of Mr. Fred L. Davis'.[50] With the result of the election never in doubt, Morris withdrew on nomination day.[51] The 'non-election' of 1892 demonstrated the strength of both Mabon and the Liberal establishment in which he had become grounded. It also indicated the marginality of opposition to that establishment, be it from left or right. In 1895, Mabon was returned unopposed, the RCA deciding that to force a contest would be pointless.[52]

In 1900 the RCA determined to put Mabon to the test, and Cardiff Councillor Robert Hughes fought a campaign focusing upon the issues of the Boer War, and Mabon's alleged duplicity in camouflaging his radicalism through advocacy of the claims of Labour.[53] Neither theme proved effective. Although in May 1900 the relief of Mafeking had been celebrated in spectacular fashion by Rhondda residents, the glory of the conflict had faded by the time of the election, and Mabon was able to blame the Tories for causing the war in the first place.[54] As for the second issue, Mabon argued that Labour and radicalism were inseparable.[55] With the result presumed a foregone conclusion, Mabon's supporters treated the campaign as an opportunity to demonstrate personal loyalty to the Liberal cause. The RLLA selected Mabon as 'a Labour representative and a Liberal representative of the most stalwart type . . . true to the Liberal flag', whilst the inhabitants of Ferndale maintained their rowdy tradition by giving Hughes an uproarious welcome.[56] Come polling day and Mabon was able to mark the largest majority in the kingdom (see Table 2.2) with a rendition of 'Hen Wlad Fy Nhadau'.[57]

Table 2.2. Result of the 1900 Parliamentary Election

William Abraham	Liberal-Labour	8,383	(81.7%)
Robert Hughes	Conservative	1,874	(18.3%)
Majority		6,509	
Total votes cast		10,257	
Total electorate		12,549	(turnout 81.7%)

In 1906, with the national mood much less propitious, the RCA did not attempt a challenge, but by the election of January 1910, they were better prepared, having decided in 1908 to contest the seat.[58] Their candidate, Cardiff solicitor Harold Lloyd, began an intensive campaign in December 1909, speaking at public meetings throughout the constituency, and winning respect for his courage and persistence in the face of hostile audiences.[59] On the other side Rhondda No.1

District of the SWMF appointed its EC as Mabon's election committee, whilst the RLLA adopted Mabon as its candidate, and pledged co-operation with the District in the forthcoming campaign.[60] The pattern of the 1900 election was thus repeated; and yet there should have been one crucial difference between the two campaigns. For in 1909 the Mineworkers' Federation of Great Britain (MFGB) had formally affiliated to the Labour Party, and from then on Mabon, in common with his fellow SWMF-sponsored MPs, was a Labour MP taking the Labour Party whip. Any connection with the Liberal Party had, in theory, been severed but, in 1910 the calculation was made by the Liberal establishment that, despite Mabon's *de jure* position as a Labour MP, *de facto* he was as 'true to the Liberal flag' as ever. Mabon did nothing to disabuse his old friends, and took pains to present himself in as traditional a light as possible. Although he had been compelled to dissolve his ties with his own political creation, the RLLA, he was nevertheless eager to receive their valuable and influential support. Thus in December 1909 he wrote to them asking for that support in order that he might be returned to Parliament as 'a true Labour representative, who will also stand for Welsh Nationalism and all that is progressive in practical politics, side by side with my friend, colleague, and fellow-countryman, David Lloyd George'.[61]

The RLLA was happy to oblige, on the distinct understanding that such support as was given was not for 'Socialism in the future'.[62] Liberals held public meetings in support of Mabon across Rhondda in January 1910. At Ferndale he was supported on the platform not only by SWMF colleagues T. I. Mardy Jones, Tom Evans and Tom George (the last two both representatives on the SWMF EC), but by Liberals Revd Evan Richards (at that time president of the Mid-Rhondda Free Church Council), solicitor Horatio Phillips, and builder Morris Morris (himself chairman of the Ferndale Free Church Council).[63] Elsewhere he was backed by Liberal 'worthies' including Sir Samuel T. Evans, the Liberal MP for the seat so coveted by Vernon Hartshorn and the most 'advanced' sections of the SWMF – Mid Glamorgan.[64] Mabon presented himself as the 'Labour and Progressive candidate', stressing that he represented not only a Labour standpoint but 'everything that appertained to Welsh nationalism and every progressive measure, wherever it might come from'.[65] His published election address was careful to avoid mentioning any political party by name, instead concentrating on the popular theme of 'People versus Peers', whilst his 'election song' went even further in expressing progressive unity:

Mabon's 1910 Election Song

Rhondda men be strong in action,
We must rout the Tory faction,
And to win in this Election,
Mabon is our man.
The Tories' rule is Autocratic,
We must have it Democratic;
Therefore, with voice emphatic,
House of Lords must go.
Nought but tribulation,
Give they to the nation;
The People's votes and not the Lords'
Must govern legislation:
Vote for Freedom, no Protection,
Vote for Progress, no defection,
Vote for Mabon, next Election –
Strike a Free Trade blow.[66]

Further demonstration of this unity came in the shape of Mabon's nomination papers, signed by coal-owner William James Thomas, and seconded by miners' leader George Dolling.[67] Mabon, in his keenness to enlist Liberal support, did not forget the miners, but they tended to take a lesser role, and in terms of campaign issues the perilous state of industrial relations in the coalfield did not surface at all.[68] On polling day the result was another record majority in national terms.

Table 2.3. Result of the January 1910 Parliamentary Election

William Abraham	Labour	12,436	(78.2%)
Harold Lloyd	Conservative	3,471	(21.8%)
Majority		8,965	
Total votes cast		15,907	
Total electorate		17,640	(turnout 90.2%)

Whilst superficially this represented a victory for the Labour Party, in fact the Liberal hegemony that had been established after 1885 remained in place.[69] But progressive harmony was not an enduring characteristic of 1910 Rhondda. In September there began the dispute over 'abnormal places' at the Ely pit of the Naval Colliery, Penygraig, a dispute which was to mushroom into a full-scale strike/lockout centred on Mid-Rhondda and involving all Cambrian Combine concerns, and which was to encompass both the notorious and celebrated rioting of 8/9 November and the sending of troops to the district by Liberal Home Secretary Winston Churchill. By the time of the December 1910 general election, Mabon was regarded in a far less favourable light by many Rhondda workmen than he had been a year earlier, and his continuing connections with the RLLA and with many of the Rhondda tradesmen who had been on the receiving end of the November rioting were coming under greater scrutiny.

For a while it seemed as if Mabon might face opposition not only from the right (Harold Lloyd having consented to try his hand once more) but also from the left.[70] There were reports that local socialists were attempting to find the candidate and the money to mount a challenge to Mabon's tenure.[71] By early December a list of possibles was being circulated, including Victor Grayson, Tom Mann and Ben Tillett.[72] Both the Mid-Rhondda ILP and the local Social Democratic Federation (SDF) combined in the variously named Rhondda Socialist Society (RSS) or Rhondda Socialistic Propaganda Organization in an attempt to muster sufficient resources for a candidature, but in the end it was decided not to mount a challenge, ostensibly owing to a lack of funds.[73] Nevertheless, Mabon had to be sensitive to charges that he had neglected the Combine workmen and that he had failed to represent his miners adequately in Parliament.[74] His position as a Labour MP was not aided by the continuing allegiance of the RLLA, which in adopting him as 'their candidate' this time commended him as a 'staunch advocate of Liberalism'.[75] Again, his platforms were crowded with Rhondda's Nonconformist ministers and tradesmen, the Liberal bourgeoisie shoulder to shoulder with Labour miners, and again his message was one of Progressive unity. But the whole event was overshadowed by the industrial dispute. Rhondda voters, whether through apathy, disapproval of Mabon, or, as Mabon's supporters claimed, bad weather on polling day, turned out to return their MP to Westminster, but with a reduced majority (see Table 2.4).

December 1910 was the last parliamentary election at which Mabon faced open challenge. From the reconciliation of 1886 through to his retirement from the Commons in 1920, Mabon was warmly regarded and supported by Rhondda Liberals, despite his last decade as a Labour Party MP. He was seen by them as a mark of their progressivism, as a token of the ideal of (dominant) Liberal/middle-class and (subordinate) Labour/working-class unity. As such an

Table 2.4. Result of the December 1910 Parliamentary Election

William Abraham	Labour	9,073	(71%)
Harold Lloyd	Conservative	3,701	(29%)
Majority		5,372	
Total votes cast		12,774	
Total electorate		17,640	(turnout 72.4%)

influential icon his significance redounded beyond Rhondda and into the wider coalfield, where his Liberalism united with the beneficent image provided by his conciliatory industrial leadership.[76] In general, Mabon played a non-assertive role within the Liberal parliamentary matrix, and this has encouraged a view of him as totally assimilated within the Liberal polity, as a classic Lib-Lab.[77] But such a view, whilst in keeping with the established historical orthodoxy of Welsh Liberalism, fails to address the very important sense in which Mabon was a 'Labour' MP, in his advocacy of the 'rights of Labour', and his readiness to assert its place within the Liberal universe, even when such assertion might lead to conflict.

Mabon's 'Labourism' can best be found in the language he employed during the campaign of 1885, and it became a central ideological pillar of working-class political representation from that point on. The starting-point for this Labourism was a keen sense of pride in manual work, and an emphasis upon its inherent dignity. Manual labour was seen as in no way inferior to non-manual or intellectual labour, but as a wealth-creating process. As Mabon put it, Labour created 'the sinew, the bone, the marrow, the life, and the prosperity of the community at large'.[78] This awareness of the immutable value of Labour was of course rooted, in Rhondda, in coalmining. It was natural that it should be paralleled by a profound consciousness of the exploitation and danger located in the very processes of that industry, and of the need for action, often legislative, to remedy the worst of the injustices suffered.[79] There existed a work-rooted sense of a Labour interest, very much a miners' interest, conceived of as being set apart from other interests such as those of the industrialists, the wealthy, the landowners, the privileged – interests often subsumed under the general heading of 'capital'.[80] F. L. Davis was begging the question when he asked amidst the 1885 campaign if it was likely that the Liberal organization 'would select for candidature one who had not and would not have the interest of the working man at heart?'[81] Davis's own ignorance of mining matters and his status as the son of a major coal-owner stood in contrast to Mabon, a man elected by the miners themselves to represent them, a major figure in the coalfield who had an intimate knowledge of the problems and difficulties they faced, and who also played a substantial part in community life. Mabon, it was alleged, was 'as capable of representing the mining communities as any gentlemen nobs from the universities', for he had found his 'college in the coal-pit' and his 'tutor in the mandril'.[82] In total, this class consciousness asserted itself in a belief that it was both desirable and legitimate for the miners to organize themselves both industrially and politically, and that, given the new status of many of them as electors, it was in accordance with the principles of justice that their view, being the majority view, should prevail in the choice of an MP. The ideological coherence of this Labourism in 1885 supplied both the motivation and the rationality for the overthrow of the feudal claim of the Davis family, and its definite replacement at the highest level by the Rhondda's own personification of independent working-class political representation. Mabon's first parliamentary victory was achieved by miners for miners, his campaign being organized by those he represented, and he being elected by their votes. But this was more than a triumph for the miners alone: it was the resonance of the interests of Rhondda miners with the wider claims of Labour that allowed the development of a belief in both the probability and the propriety of a working-class candidature.[83] This belief remained sufficiently firm to be capable of shrugging off rebuffs at the hands of the Liberal organization; including those of the selection process, but more importantly, those implicit in the initial establishment and orientation of the RLA itself. Looking back at 1885 it can be seen that what from the outset was an unashamedly middle-class Liberalism took no account of the desires of the new electorate. Its assertion of the identity of interest between capital and Labour was impossible to sustain given its successive choice of coal-owning candidates; and Mabon's victory stamped upon the consciousness of the south Wales coalfield the potential power of organized Labour, forcing Welsh Liberalism to take cognizance of this new challenge.

Although 1885 provides the strongest evidence of Mabon's Labourism, later in his career he was occasionally prepared to speak out against what he considered to be damaging infringements of the 'rights of Labour'. One such issue was the 'National Question', centred upon the rise of Cymru Fydd, an organization aiming to revive the structures of Welsh Liberalism with a long-term aim of winning some form of Home Rule for Wales.[84] At its inception in 1884, Mabon had warned the supporters of Cymru Fydd that 'Welshmen were working men first of all. They subsisted by their daily toil, and they could not be expected to give an unqualified allegiance to any party if that party forgot industrial questions.'[85] And whilst he was undoubtedly only too pleased to play up his Welsh identity and language in Westminster, Mabon saw a danger in the lack of attention paid by Cymru Fydd to Labour. He felt that if it was not careful, 'the Welsh party of Wales' as he termed it, would alienate 'the working people of Wales'. Mabon recognized that for 'his people' working conditions and wages were far more immediate and material than questions of national identity and spiritual destiny. A decade later, Mabon remained suspicious of what he saw as the domination of Cymru Fydd by groups lacking roots in the industrial democracy of south Wales and consequently lacking adequate concern for Labour questions. He allowed that 'the North may be allowed to follow its inclination after localism, nationalism, and sentimentalism, or any other "ism" they think proper; but we in the South must look after the bread and cheese of the people, also protecting their lives and limbs in the shape of useful and practical legislation . . .'[86] When the Cymru Fydd controversy arrived in Rhondda in 1895 Mabon came out in explicit opposition to its objectives, organizing his own meetings to counter those of Lloyd George and Cymru Fydd in the locality, and aligning himself with D. A. Thomas and the camp of the 'Newport Englishmen'.[87]

Mabon's political career therefore has more than a hint of ambiguity about it. On the one hand he could be a forthright champion of the interests of 'Labour', and on the other, a rather timid and conformist Liberal. It is this latter characterization that has proved most attractive to historians, themselves aware of the much more industrially and politically militant working-class leaderships that were to succeed Mabon in the twentieth century.[88] After all, as the economic and industrial relations climate worsened Mabon's advocacy of conciliation and moderation in matters of the coal trade was undermined by the imperatives of direct action. But this is not the only way in which Mabon can be viewed, and when the language of Labour and class he deployed in 1885 is observed in the context of the local structures of Lib-Labism, the ambiguity and indeed growing falsity of that hybrid unity is clearly revealed.

Liberal domination

> . . . the Welsh Liberal world was one run by a series of small, locally-
> based, self-perpetuating middle-class elites, linking the world of
> municipal government, local politics, the chapels, and unofficial social
> leadership in a democratic, face-to-face community.
>
> Kenneth O. Morgan[89]

Rhondda's representative politics may be analysed at four major
levels: the parliamentary, as has been seen, was created in 1885 in the
shape of the Rhondda constituency. The second tier of representation
was the Glamorgan County Council (GCC), created by the County
Councils Act of 1888, to which Rhondda returned ten representatives
(until 1910, when the number was increased to twelve), supplemented
by a varying number of Aldermen. The Local Government Act of
1894 added a further layer with the creation of the Ystradyfodwg
Urban District Council (YUDC – in 1897 retitled the Rhondda Urban
District Council, RUDC), and 1894 also saw the reorganization of the
Pontypridd Board of Guardians (PBG), Rhondda delivering over
twenty Poor Law Guardians along with those from the adjacent areas
of Pontypridd, Llantrisant, Caerphilly and Mountain Ash. In this
study it is these four major levels of representation that receive
greatest attention, although it is important to note the prior existence
of the Guardians, the existence from 1877 to 1894 of the Ystradyfodwg Urban Sanitary Authority (YUSA), and the existence, until
1902, of the Ystradyfodwg School Board (YSB).[90]

The most important point to make about this evolving and
expanding political structure is that, from the 1880s through to 1910,
middle-class Liberals were dominant at all levels. Not until 1910 did the
Liberal share of Rhondda local-government seats fall below three-
quarters, and even then the Liberals remained well clear of their nearest
challengers, Labour (Appendix Tables 1–2). This domination is even
more extensive if one considers that on most local government issues
Liberal and Labour representatives were likely to vote together, given
the seeming acceptance of Liberal ideology by substantial numbers of
Labour representatives, at least up until the middle of the first decade
of the twentieth century. Thereafter, with Labour becoming more
socialist than Liberal and posing a mounting threat, the Liberals could
often rely upon Conservative assistance in attempting to maintain their
grip on local government. Of equal significance was the domination of
local government by the middle class: again no less than three-quarters

of all representatives could be so categorized (Appendix Table 3). This evidence is superficial in that it must not be assumed that different occupational groups, despite sharing a common class-identity, should necessarily behave in essentially similar ways. But it remains a fact that the other political party attempting to call upon a middle-class constituency (the landed classes making no impact upon Rhondda politics), the Conservatives, were marginal to Rhondda's electoral history, a factor that had implications for the vitality of Rhondda Liberalism.[91] At the level of the individual authority, the most noticeable contrast with the general picture is that of the rise of Labour on the RUDC in the first decade of the twentieth century; by 1910 it held nine of the thirty available seats. In contrast Labour made little progress on PBG until 1910, and remained marginal on the GCC throughout this period (Appendix Tables 4–8).

Ultimately more significant than the total numbers of representatives classed as belonging to various political groups is the material documenting the political complexion of the competition for seats on the various representative bodies (Appendix Tables 12–14). Where this material can be interpreted unambiguously it indicates that a substantial proportion of elections were fought out between candidates identified by themselves and by their electorate as Liberals. That this was more likely to be the case on the GCC than on the RUDC might be explained by the fact that there was greater prestige and appeal in the County Council honours than in those of the District Council for Rhondda's bourgeoisie. Becoming a County Councillor marked one out on a wider scale than could service on the District Council. Competition was thus likely to be greater. For the Labour movement, however, the District Council offered more immediate, tangible results, and so Labour competition was much greater here than anywhere else. What is suggested by this evidence is that Rhondda Liberals were as likely to be competing against each other for local government office as they were to be fighting members of other political parties. It might be thought necessary for a political party to have attempted to limit the number of candidates of a similar persuasion to one per available seat, in order to avoid splitting its support and providing any opportunity of victory to a candidate of a different ideological persuasion. This the Rhondda Labour and Liberal Association (RLLA) patently failed to achieve – a situation that necessitates an investigation into the activity of the RLLA at the level of local government politics.

As has been noted, the RLLA was established in 1885, and was joined by the RLA in 1886. Its first officers bore the mark of its origins in all being Mabonites, the secretary and vice-president both miners. But in becoming representative of the full range of Rhondda Liberalism the RLLA took in men with considerable political experience and influence who had been actively involved in campaigning against Mabon, and who rapidly overshadowed their old adversaries.[92] Subsequent fund-raising was dependent not upon support from the RSCMA but rather on the donations and subscriptions of Rhondda's middle class. Mabon was uncomfortable with this situation, but one early attempt to goad the miners into taking a more active part in funding the RLLA yielded no results.[93] The RLLA became a middle-class organization after the pattern of so many other Liberal Associations at that time. Details of its structure, officers and activities are scarce, and as a result it is difficult to be precise about the extent of its operations, but it seems that it led an intermittent and gradually declining existence.[94]

The RLLA's original function was to provide organizational and financial support for Mabon as Rhondda's MP. Organizational support was only required in the event of a parliamentary challenge to Mabon, and as there was none until 1900, no mobilization on the part of the RLLA was required for fifteen years. Thereafter, no further challenge was forthcoming for a decade. Financial assistance was readily provided by the subscriptions and donations of individual RLLA members and external supporters. The RLLA seems not to have indulged in fund-raising events. Occasionally, propaganda drives incorporating public meetings or rallies were organized, but there was little urgency or regularity about these efforts. A meeting at which Liberal opinions and values were aired was as likely to be a miners' annual demonstration or a local club or association banquet as to be an event held under RLLA auspices.[95] The only sphere in which the RLLA acted with effect was in the registration of voters.[96] In spite of these organizational inadequacies, Liberalism remained successful. The contention that Liberal Party organization was largely an irrelevance to the fortunes of Liberalism can be upheld, in particular with regard to the Conservative parliamentary challenge.[97] But the Rhondda Conservative Association (RCA) was hardly a worthy opponent, and it was precisely the absence of any sustained and serious Conservative political threat that meant that there was no imperative to organize or to present a common front at any level of political representation. The

RCA had been established in 1884, had disappeared, and had re-emerged in 1886.[98] It was easy for the Liberal press to assert that 'it never had an existence beyond tap-room precincts', as the Conservative clubs were the only proof of the tenuous survival of the RCA. By May 1895 there were six such clubs in the Rhondda, and by 1912 fourteen.[99] These were popular and financially profitable institutions, but their success was not readily transferable to the political arena.[100] On the other hand, whether the weakness of the RLLA assisted its relationship in the twentieth century with an increasingly organized Labour movement is more questionable. Liberalism, despite its lack of organization, dominated the sphere of local politics; but it did so not by regulating its candidacies, but by leaving local coteries and individuals to advance their own candidatures in a way that actually obstructed the upward progress of Labour leaders within its own ranks – an obstruction that resulted in the emergence of an independent tradition of Labour organization at local level, much as the RLA had forced Mabon into independence in 1885.

Only in the GCC elections of 1889 did the RLLA organize on a Rhondda-wide basis, advancing a slate of ten candidates, one per seat.[101] That the camps of Mabon and Fred Davis had been united under the RLLA banner was proved by the campaign. In the Treherbert and Treorchy Ward, for instance, candidate William Morgan (a farmer, magistrate and 'retired gentleman'; also the father of Walter H. Morgan) had been a Davis supporter in 1885, whilst Revd John Salisbury Edwards had backed Mabon. Now they campaigned together, and Mabon and his trade union colleagues were prepared to speak in their joint favour.[102] Other RLLA candidates included Penygraig headmaster John Jones Griffiths, secretary of the RLA in 1885, and F L. Davis himself. It could be argued that the process of reconciliation had gone too far in the direction of those defeated in 1885, as not one working man appeared as a Liberal candidate. The only role such men seemed to have at this stage was to chair public meetings in support of their bourgeois counterparts.[103] The RLLA slate was overwhelmingly successful, with nine out of its ten nominees being returned. Even the unlucky candidate, David Evans (manager of D. Davis & Sons' Ferndale No.3 pit at Bodringallt) in Pentre and Ystrad, was beaten by an unofficial Liberal, his fellow colliery manager, William Jenkins.[104]

In 1892, in anticipation of the triennial GCC elections the executive committee of the RLLA decided not to attempt any Rhondda-wide

action or advance any Rhondda-wide slate. Instead, RLLA ward
committees were to be left with the power to decide whether to
contest or not. Subsequently, nominations revealed a substantial
degree of disunity amongst members of the RLLA, although it is
impossible to discern whether this was the result or the cause of the
executive committee's decision.[105] In Treorchy a dispute had broken
out within the RLLA committee over the choice of a successor to the
recently deceased Revd John Salisbury Edwards. Eventually the
committee chose another Baptist Minister – William Morris
'Rhosynnog'; but another candidate in the field was Mabon's close
associate T. Daronwy Isaac, local miners' agent and representative on
the Sliding Scale Joint Committee. Isaac's political stance? He was
President of the RLLA![106] In Pentre, sitting member and RLLA
nominee in 1889, Richard Morris, found himself at odds with the
RLLA local committee, which selected estate agent Elias Henry
Davies to oppose him, whilst there was a third Liberal in the field in
the shape of Daniel Eynon.[107] In the Tonypandy and Trealaw Ward,
the RLLA nominee, bookseller William Gwrtydd Williams, found
himself opposed by the old Mabonite T. Pascoe Jenkins, recently
retired president of the RLLA. The results of this confused situation
provide no simple message as to the significance of official backing:
the unofficial candidates Isaac and Richard Morris, won in Treorchy
and Pentre, whilst in Tonypandy it was Williams who triumphed
against unofficial competition.[108]

A hypothesis that the degree of inter-Liberal competition reflected
the reality of political disharmony finds no support within the
available evidence. During the 1892 GCC elections there was an
attempt to claim that rival denominational slates were in operation
under the blanket label of 'Liberal', but this was no more than
malicious gossip.[109] No national issues seem to have filtered through
to local government elections in ways that make sense of the
numerous inter-Liberal contests. Liberal politics were instead
distinguished by the politics of personality, the politics of the 'public
man', and the message borne by the Liberal 'public man' had also to
be borne by Conservative and, in part, by Labour contenders, were
they to stand any chance of electoral success.

The initial, and potentially most significant reference point for this
version of representative suitability was the occupation of the
candidate. At the peak of the social pyramid were the major coal-
owners, but these were less and less involved in local politics. F. L.

Davis, for example, sat as Alderman on the GCC for only six years before retirement from local politics altogether. The only substantial coal-owner to retain a local political profile was Clifford J. Cory of Cory Bros., County Councillor for Ystrad from 1892 until 1910 as well as a magistrate and Deputy Lieutenant of Glamorgan. In any case the wealth and power that large-scale coal-ownership indicated could alienate as well as attract the voters. The major colliery companies therefore tended to push forward their managerial staff, who had the virtue of actually residing in the locality. The Ocean Coal Company, for example, supplied Rhondda with two highly important figures in local politics – William Jenkins and W. P. Thomas. Jenkins had joined the Ocean Coal Company in 1871, had managed the Bute Merthyr Colliery near Treherbert, and had risen to become general manager of the company before his retirement in 1915. He served in local government from the late 1870s onwards, on the YSB, the YUSA, the RUDC and (as an Alderman) on the GCC. W. P. Thomas was Jenkins's protégé, serving as an office boy, a clerk and an accountant in the company before becoming Jenkins's secretary. Eventually he inherited Jenkins's post, and with it the general manager's residence, Ystradfechan House, strategically placed between Treorchy and Cwmparc. He also played a prominent part in local politics as an Urban District Councillor for twenty-four years, his supporters claiming that his initials stood for 'Winning, Persevering, Triumphant'!

The very position of colliery managers could alienate many voters. But managerial office provided an opportunity for cultivating a reputation for honesty and fair judgement as well as for profit-seeking and disregard for human life. Colliery managers were much-respected local figures, and the fact that they were salaried limited the extent to which they could be accused of making vast profits from the naked exploitation of the men over whom they presided. Lesser coal-owners did not have the option of employing their managers as substitute politicians. For men such as brothers-in-law William Henry Mathias and William James Thomas, who owned only one colliery each, the only way to ensure a voice in local affairs was to stand for election oneself, which these two did with considerable success. Mathias sat for forty-two years on the YUSA/YUDC/RUDC and thirty years on the GCC, as well as having a stint on the PBG, whilst Thomas (as owner of the Standard Colliery) represented Ynyshir on both the latter bodies.

In a more favourable position than those directly involved in the
management of the coal industry were professionals, especially
doctors. Although they were often colliery doctors, and thus served
the interests of the colliery company as much as ever they did those of
their patients, nevertheless they had a very wide range of social
contact, respect and influence. In Porth, doctors such as Ivor Ajax
Lewis (a pioneer of baseball in the area as well as father of eleven
children) and the brothers Evan and Henry Naunton Davies
dominated local representation in the 1890s, the latter also serving as
medical officer to the PBG. In Ystrad, a long-standing politician was
Dr William Evans Thomas, the Cory Bros. surgeon, on the RUDC
from 1894 to 1933, and on the GCC from 1910 to 1930. Thomas
enhanced his popularity by his readiness to supply medicines and
sick-notes to his patients![110] As for other professionals, there were
notable successes, such as architect Rhys Samuel Griffiths (RUDC
1894–1912 and also consulting architect to the GCC), and solicitor
William Thomas Davies (RUDC 1906–15, son of Henry Naunton
Davies); but these were isolated cases from occupations lacking a
particular political profile. The teaching profession supplied men
such as John Jones Griffiths, Richard Morris and Thomas Charles
Morgan ('Y Scwlyn' of Cwmparc, also a shareholder in the Ocean
Coal Company); but such a prominent figure in the profession as Tom
John (the headmaster of Llwynypia schools, one-time president of the
National Union of Teachers (NUT) and editor and director of the
Rhondda Leader) was defeated on both occasions he challenged for
the RUDC.

Nonconformist ministers were barely in evidence. There were a few
who filled local office; but a larger number tried and failed, including
William Morris ('Rhosynnog'). Possibly the appeal of Nonconformist
ministers was limited by denominational rivalries and chapel
parochialism, although this was barely articulated. Other restraining
factors may have been a reluctance to mix so obviously religion and
politics, whatever the content of their weekly sermons, and the
practical fact that many were itinerant, and therefore could not
commit themselves to holding local office for more than a few years at
a time.

As for shopkeepers, they had unrivalled opportunities to meet and
charm potential voters, but because there were so many of them, and
because they lived on a precarious balance between customer loyalty
and resentment of prices and profits they did not have the electoral

security of other bourgeois. Furthermore, despite the best efforts of their publicity, it was difficult for a grocer or a draper to present himself simply as a servant of the community – the wealth he made could employ few and could really only be seen to benefit himself, whereas the teacher or doctor was immediately marked out in a serving and humane capacity (whatever the reality). As for the coal-owner or manager, it was relatively easy for them to pose as creators and benefactors of the community at large. Without their enterprise and skills, it could be argued, Rhondda would not exist as a human entity. They employed thousands, and it was upon their achievement that Rhondda's world-wide reputation rested.

The 'shopocracy' could try to compensate for this relative disadvantage: their representative status could be generalized through local and valley-wide Chambers of Trade. Morris Morris (RUDC 1894–1903), a builder and contractor, and David Smith (RUDC 1899–1911), a draper, both held the position of chairman of the Ferndale Chamber of Trade. Other *petits bourgeois*, such as publicans and hoteliers, tended to have a less ambiguous public persona to maintain, albeit one that needed to avoid the censure of Nonconformist teetotalism. And on the border between traders and professionals were estate agents, land agents and auctioneers, who as they rose in wealth and age could elevate their status to that of businessmen or professionals. It is difficult to provide secure generalizations about the electoral 'cash-value' of occupational identities, but they played an important part in determining the possibilities of political ambition and influence.

Related to, but distinct from, occupational identity were the predominantly middle-class qualities of suitability for a representative post in local government. One point working in favour of tradesmen in particular was their thrift, their reputed skill in handling money. All the occupations referred to above were considered to possess their quotas of expertise, be they in mining engineering or in pill-peddling. Reference to a candidate's 'experience' was one way of implicitly excluding working-class candidates, considered inherently less thrifty and trustworthy, whatever the realities of trade union responsibilities. If it was natural enough to work down the mines in the Rhondda valley, then to do something different could mark one out as 'above par', could imply superior intellect, talent, wealth and vision. One reason that eventually Labour was able to combat and defeat the Liberal bourgeoisie at the local level was that it was able to put forward as candidates its crop of 'above par' products – the miners' agents, lodge secretaries, and checkweighers – men who could justifiably claim that all their progress (if they were to conceive of it in individual terms at all) had been the result of their own efforts, and not of birth into a moneyed or established family, as was the case with at least some of those they struggled against.

A further dimension to the 'politics of personality' was that of the relationship between a candidate and his locality, his ward. Particular candidates could be identified as emanating from one part of a ward – thus candidates were fielded ostensibly to attempt to represent the interests of, say, Dinas within Ward Seven (dominated by Penygraig) or of Cwmparc within Ward Two (dominated by Treorchy). The most common convention was that applied in the Upper Rhondda Fach Ward, Ward Ten of the RUDC, where it was accepted that two of the three seats be filled by Ferndale men and the other by a Mardy man. This was adhered to throughout this period, and when the Mardy seat fell vacant, as it did in 1902, and again in 1908, only candidates from Mardy came forward to contest it.

Individuals were thus 'representative' in a variety of ways. But they also brought their own personal qualities and interests to the hustings. Successful candidates for local office often played out a social role that extended beyond the boundaries of their occupation or of the business of local politics itself. Many were involved in the religious life of the community: Treorchy resident and Abergorky Colliery accountant William Thomas Jones, for example (RUDC 1894–1916, GCC 1901–16), was a Welsh Congregationalist deacon, taught in Sunday school, and was a member of the local Free Church Council. There he joined mining instructor and *Rhondda Leader* director John Samuel (RUDC 1899–1901), who was deacon and treasurer of Noddfa Baptist Chapel, and Samuel's friend W. P. Thomas (RUDC 1904–28), deacon, trustee and secretary of the same chapel, and treasurer of the Welsh Baptist Union. Such a close interweaving of political and religious connections was found across the denominations and across the valley.

Equally significant might be participation in the leisure activities of the community. Treherbert grocer and prominent Calvinist Enoch Davies (PBG 1898–1904, GCC 1901–28), who was the son-in-law of local butcher and one-time County Councillor Evan Davies, was an eisteddfodwr and member of the Gorsedd; Fernhill colliery manager Daniel Richard Jones (RUDC 1903–12) was a festival conductor and president of Fernhill Workmen's Institute; whilst William Thomas Davies (RUDC 1906–15) founded the Porth Carnival, as well as assisting in the spread of the Workers' Educational Association (WEA). Later, the grocer William 'Corona' Evans, 'the Prince of Porth' (GCC 1910–34), donated land in the Porth area sufficient to create a public park, whilst also sponsoring the local YMCA and serving as captain of the Porth Fire Brigade.[111] Involvement in community self-help organizations such as friendly societies was also quite common. Thus, grocer James Evans (GCC 1898–1928) was treasurer of the Cambrian Welfare Association and William Thomas Davies a leading member of the Ivorites, Foresters, Oddfellows, Hearts of Oak, and Philanthropic societies. John Jones Griffiths endeared himself only to part of the community as secretary of the Rhondda Valley Temperance League.

Perhaps the clearest indication of the importance of the 'politics of personality' comes in the Pentre and Ton Pentre area, where representation on both the GCC and PBG during this period was dominated by two men: estate agent Elias Henry Davies and butcher Elias Thomas Davies. Elias Henry Davies was the more powerful of the pair – he had been active in Rhondda local government from the 1870s, and been nominated as a potential Liberal parliamentary candidate in 1885. He continued to act as a Guardian after the reorganization of 1894, and sat until his death in 1915. He also represented the ward on the GCC, first as County Councillor (1898) and, again after 1901, as Alderman, until his death. He was partnered on the PBG by Elias Thomas Davies from 1898 until 1913, and succeeded by him as County Councillor from 1902 until 1913. An active Congregationalist, a freemason, and president of Rhondda Cymmrodorion Society, Elias Henry Davies was of sufficient merit as a public figure to be included by J. Vyrnwy Morgan in his 1908 volume *Welsh Political and Educational Leaders of the Victorian Era*.

Without any effective, integrative party organization, Rhondda politics were dominated by the 'politics of personality'. This politics of notability was sufficiently strong to withstand the feeble challenge of Conservatism, but its very success led it away from any negotiation with the working class. The absence of such a threat stimulated only lassitude in 'old Liberalism'. Working-class leaders below Mabon were excluded from representative office by the unstructured and status-ridden mechanisms of local Liberal domination. Liberal politics were thus class-based, not merely in their objective

composition, but also in the way in which they assumed the
inevitability of certain forms of social and political leadership, and
the exclusion of others. Kenneth O. Morgan's characterization of 'the
Welsh Liberal world' is appropriate for Rhondda in all but one respect
– its democracy. These 'self-perpetuating middle-class élites' existed in
a political world all their own. If it was a 'face-to-face community',
only middle-class faces were visible. The incorporation of the
working class into this world of 'public men' was minimal. Although
in many respects Labour candidates still had to play this same game,
they were always on a different team. There was no real unity between
the classes or their political representatives. The dominant middle-
class Liberal vision of 'community' in south Wales did not force the
integration of the working class, but assumed it, an assumption that
was questionable from 1885, and increasingly questioned in the early
years of the twentieth century. It is the political trajectory of
Rhondda's working class that must now be traced.

The fragility of Lib-Labism

> Labour measures must of necessity always be progressive, and their
> tendency uplifting: and so the more Labour makes its power felt, the
> better for unspecious Liberalism.
>
> 'H', 1902[112]

It is possible to argue that, before 1909 and the affiliation of the
Mineworkers' Federation of Great Britain to the Labour Party, Liberal
and Labour politics in many mining constituencies were indistin-
guishable: that they can best be treated as 'Lib-Lab' politics. To write
of 'Labour politics' as essentially separate from those of Liberalism
might therefore be considered to impose a retrospective and distorting
distinction upon this political history. This important objection can
be answered on two levels. The more elevated answer is that to
identify the actual affiliation of the MFGB to the Labour Party as the
important turning-point is to misunderstand the dynamics of politics
altogether, is to see the form of politics as being more important than
its content. If one sees affiliation to the Labour Party as important
either in ideological terms (the adoption of a new party programme
differing in some respects from that of the Liberal party), or in terms
of the organizational independence of political parties nationally, one
fails to grasp that ideological and organizational divisions can emerge
within localities, within organizations and within superficially

successful Lib-Lab alliances. These divisions can make the separation of political experience as vivid and as real as if it were enshrined in the organizational independence of two national political parties. It is only through an appreciation of the content of politics that the distinction can be made between its Labour and its Liberal forms, a distinction that forces their separate consideration.

This is manifest in the second level of answer: that of the Rhondda experience of Liberal and Labour politics. A number of points have already been made that have bearing upon the nature of contemporaneous Labour politics, and upon this central question of why it was that Labour politics grew outside the Liberal fold.

Mabon's 1885 victory was an individual act, not part of a general pattern at parliamentary or local level. There was no sustained drive for political representation by the Rhondda miners during the two decades after 1885, and Mabon himself was financially supported and largely neutered by middle-class Liberalism. There were only isolated cases of groups of miners or other workers giving their chosen candidates support. Despite the decisiveness of Mabon's 1885 victory it was no small task for Labour men to follow him, even at the levels of local government. One problem faced by all working-class candidates was the sometimes fierce and almost totally unstructured nature of political competition, in which the RLLA barely interfered. There was no sustained organizational impulse behind Labour candidates, and they were forced to come forward very much as individuals competing on a political terrain normally occupied by men of a higher social class, and were forced to challenge these men on their own terms. Once, in 1892, an *ad hoc* organization, the Porth Labour Committee (PLC), lent its support successfully both to miner Moses Moses (GCC 1892–98) and to Ynyshir Lodge Secretary Morgan Williams (GCC 1892–1925), but at subsequent elections it failed to reappear.[113] The only time that trade unions entered the fray was in 1896, when the executive committee of the Cambrian Miners' Association approved the candidature of its sub-agent, 'Mabon Bach', William Evans.[114] It was generally impossible for Labour candidates to be able to depend upon the organized assistance and conferred legitimacy with which Mabon had been provided by the RSCMA, and particularly by its Parliamentary Committee in 1885. Mabon himself made no attempt to spawn a political power-base or to set a tradition, beyond the establishment of the RLLA which fell swiftly under the control of his ex-opponents. This was due to his failure to recognize that the interests of Labour required more than representation by himself alone. Mabon, although championing the cause of Labour, did not conceive of it dominating all spheres of political life. Nothing was to be gained in his opinion by replacing Liberal support with working-class, Labour identities – Mabon believed in the Liberal programme, providing it was suitably modified to take account of the Labour interest. Mabon came to signify more the general acceptance of the political status quo than he did any continuing progress towards working-class self-emancipation.

Without organizational backing in the last two decades of the nineteenth century, Labour candidates rose or fell depending upon their personal characteristics and their embodied representative significance, factors combined with the quality or otherwise of the opposition. The majority had no explicit political differences with any Liberal competitors. On the whole they were already playing out representative roles within the confines of their work – as miners' agents or checkweighers – but some still found the time to join the chapel diaconate on a Sunday, or to help run the co-operative stores. They were thus in a better position to compete with the tradesmen and colliery managers who made up the bulk of the candidates and who could call upon economic power as well as social influence. What could distinguish Labour candidates from their 'betters' was their Labourist significance. Their essential and distinctive message was similar to Mabon's in 1885: to vote for a working man was to vote for someone who understood the hopes and needs of members of his class and who would work to see these satisfied. Contests frequently touched on the theme of class consciousness, upon 'us against them', the 'bottom dog' against the wealthy, privileged and powerful. When the sitting Labour RUDC member, checkweigher Daniel Evans, faced opposition in 1897 from publican Henry Williams, Evans's election committee made a public statement that if working men were to vote for Williams they would 'betray the very class to which you belong'.

There was no Liberal tradition of allowing any Labour candidates an unopposed run in those seats that were available. Only on two occasions did Labour candidates stand without having to face Liberal opposition: elsewhere contests were frequent and hard-fought. Although Labour men were Liberal in their political beliefs, their political practice taught them the virtues of self-reliance and class identity, securities against the seductions of their supposed allies. Labour candidates in the period 1885–98 needed to combine the assured persona of a 'public man' with the guarantees of class identity and loyalty if success was to be glimpsed.

Nor at the more routine levels of political activism did Labour men find Liberal acceptance or influence easily forthcoming. The RLLA became dominated by ex-RLA bourgeois activists, and in other ways Labour men played an incidental or token role – at public meetings for middle-class candidates they might be found on the platform speaking in support, chairing the meeting, or perhaps working behind the scenes as agents.

As for socialism, this was marginal before the strike of 1898. Until 1896 the only activity in the district took the form of 'missionary' expeditions by Sam Mainwaring and by the Cardiff branch of the ILP.[115] There is little evidence that the 1893 strike led to the spread of socialist ideas in the area, although there was by this stage some dissatisfaction with Mabon's advocacy of the Sliding Scale.[116] A visit to the area in 1896 by Tom Mann sparked interest, and by 1897 the *ILP News* was recording a branch at Mardy.[117] In the same year ILP propagandist Enid Stacey delivered a series of lectures on socialism, and by December 1897 the Mardy branch secretary, Hugh Lloyd, could report a membership of twenty.[118] The Social Democratic Federation (SDF) also seems to have established a foothold in the area, following a Tonypandy meeting.[119] But these were, as yet, minor developments. Socialism was barely on Rhondda's political agenda: no candidates for local honours proclaimed themselves socialists, and the word 'socialism' was absent from all electoral propaganda.

Without a serious alternative the political allegiance of the working class was to Liberalism. But neither the RLLA nor the local Liberal cliques provided any means whereby a reasonable number of local working-class leaders could obtain influence on local governing bodies, nor did they assign to them anything more than a marginal role on the organizational front. Liberalism smothered anything but isolated working-class involvement. This Liberal 'definition of community' denied an inclusive role for working-class leaders by defining leadership in a naturally middle-class sense; but those leaders and the interest they represented were at the same time playing an increasingly important part in determining the industrial success of the coalfield. *De facto*, the independence of Labour was a reality. In terms of Westminster politics, the Liberal hegemony was a success, but in terms of gut politics and the very important area of the manner in which politics was conducted, that hegemony was false. Liberals probably underestimated the importance of this *de facto* independence because of ostensible ideological harmony and they were therefore organizationally ill-prepared to withstand the Labour challenge when it finally emerged.

The rest of this chapter concentrates upon the emergence of that challenge. In part it returns to the familiar landmarks outlined in the introduction: the 1898 strike and the introduction of socialist discourse into the area on a more substantial scale; the 1906 ballot upon the question of MFGB affiliation to the Labour Party; the rise of the ILP as a local political force; the 1908 ballot and actual affiliation in 1909. Some of the material presented here in relation to the two ballots challenges existing historiographical assumptions, but the most challenging aspects are found in the accounts of neglected areas: the evolution of a commitment to local political action by the Rhondda No.1 District of the SWMF, the structure of Trades and Labour Councils (TLCs), and the blending of a resilient political Liberalism with strong and independent Labourist loyalties to produce a Labour politics in advance both of any Labour Party organization and of the affiliation of the MFGB to the Labour Party in 1909.

1898, Socialism and the SWMF

The history of the South Wales miners did not begin in 1898 but that year did signal the start of what would be a profound shift of emphasis in their own lives of continuing struggle.

Hywel Francis and David Smith[120]

Labour politics until 1898 were largely static, cast in a highly restrictive Liberal mould. What broke this deadlock was the 1898 strike, which altered industrial and political configurations. The struggle and eventual defeat of the miners gave birth, in October 1898, to the South Wales Miners' Federation, the organization upon and within which the area's subsequent political reputation was built. The more immediate political development was the introduction of socialist discourse into the coalfield on a scale hitherto unknown.

The 1898 dispute originated in a desire by the south Wales miners to revise the Sliding Scale arrangement for determination of wage-rates, although the 'gathering climate of conflict' was also spurred on by recent controversies regarding the Workmen's Compensation Act 1897, the failure of efforts to secure a scheme to control output (and thereby prices and wages), and by attempts by the coal-owners to impose the discharge note.[121] Such negotiations as there were during the dispute itself were conducted in an acerbic manner by the owners, determined not to concede anything to the men, and to revise arrangements in their own favour. They were finally able to impose a humiliating defeat upon the men, but in the process of doing this radicalized the latter's attitudes, and the attitudes of their leaders, regarding the Sliding Scale, so that the termination of the Sliding Scale and its replacement by a Conciliation Board became a major objective of the new union. The latter was itself a direct product of defeat: effective organization being seen as the way to avoid such catastrophe in the future. In all these developments Mabon remained prominent. In certain aspects his industrial leadership was weakened by the dispute. He had originally argued against the demand to end the current Sliding Scale, but a ballot of the men that autumn had resulted in a large majority in favour of handing in notice. Second, he and his fellow leaders found the prolonged controversy over whether they had plenary powers to negotiate particularly humiliating. Worst of all, the final terms of settlement included the abolition of the monthly holiday known as 'Mabon's Day'. And yet the magnitude of the defeat seems to have united the south Wales miners in a manner previously unknown. Mabon himself had learned that despite years of cautious, moderate leadership, the coal-owners had 'insisted on their pound of flesh', and was amenable to the reappraisal of trade union organization that led to the establishment of the SWMF in October 1898, and its affiliation to the MFGB in January 1899. Mabon's appointment as President of the SWMF renewed his claim to leadership of the coalfield's working class, and, as SWMF membership figures grew during the first years of its existence, enabled him to speak with greater authority than ever before.

As for socialism, 1898 was the first strike in south Wales to attract substantial attention from socialist propagandists and press. The Social Democratic Federation (SDF) held a number of meetings in Rhondda in April and May, but a lack of interest in industrial problems combined with the lack of a full-time organizer limited the SDF's appeal, and its success was minor and temporary in comparison with that of the ILP.[122] The latter appointed Willie Wright as south Wales organizer in May, and his efforts at meetings, combined with the interest shown by the *Labour Leader* in the dispute and the more positive ILP attitude towards trade unionism led to massive gains in support.[123] By the end of the dispute there existed ten new ILP branches in Rhondda, to complement the one already in existence at Mardy.

The strength of the socialist movement was, however, transient. With the end of the dispute the ILP lost momentum. Willie Wright fell ill, and without his guidance branches floundered through lack of money, organizational inexperience, and underdeveloped political education.[124] He recovered to represent Welsh ILP branches at the 1899 annual conference, but by then his representation may have been nominal, 1899 seeing the virtual elimination of ILP organization in Rhondda.[125] Only the Mardy branch managed to survive into 1900, and that disappeared during the following year. The ILP had flowered only briefly.[126]

Although socialist success was momentary, it was significant. Socialism had won converts in the teeth of hegemonic Liberalism. The ILP had challenged the authority of the RLLA to speak for the miners, as much as the miners' leaders had been reminded of the need to pay attention to the wishes of those they represented. After 1898, Rhondda Liberalism could no longer depend upon the long-term absence of effective opposition: socialism had been placed upon Rhondda's political agenda.[127] Yet when that opposition came, in the middle of the first decade of the new century, its greatest strength derived not from the socialism of the re-established socialist societies, but from the Labourism of the Federation lodges, from a Labourism that ideologically had more in common with the Liberalism it threatened than with the socialism it befriended.

The radical impact of 1898 in the development of Labourism and the spread of socialism was not immediately reflected in the political arena. Only gradually did the increased class and political conscious-ness of Rhondda's working class force itself into political recognition. The defeat of 1898 sapped energies and morale: a period of recovery had to be anticipated. Beyond that was the need for organization, for the discovery of suitable men to advance into the political arena, and for the nuances of the triennial term system to be negotiated. Even more important was the fact that administration of local governing bodies was hardly an exciting prospect in comparison with a strike. Momentum, enthusiasm and commitment had to be built gradually.

Change did come, however, and the numbers of Labour councillors and candidates grew throughout the first decade of the new century. What was of equal significance was that this growth in numbers was paralleled by a development of widespread organizational backing for candidacies. Whereas, up to 1898, organizational support had been the exception, by 1910 it was the rule. Neither the gradual augmentation of Labour representation nor the growth of the Labour movement were unilinear developments: until 1911 no Rhondda-wide Labour Party existed. Instead the responsibilities of the nascent political Labour movement were divided in unequal, changing measures between the SWMF, the TLCs and the socialist societies and groupings, and it is to this variegated pattern that attention must now turn.

The SWMF was organized by each pit, or occasionally group of pits, possessing its own trade union branch – the lodge. There were approximately fifty Rhondda lodges during the first decade of the twentieth century, ranging from the small single-pit (Ynyshir House in 1908 had forty-seven members) to the large single-pit (Abergorky had 1,816), and on up to the multi-pit (the Cambrian totalled 3,183). Lodges were grouped into districts, of which there were a total of nineteen in the south Wales coalfield. Of all the south Wales districts, the largest was Rhondda No.1 (31,000 members in 1908). Rhondda was covered by two districts – the main Rhondda No.1 District, and the smaller Pontypridd and Rhondda (also known as Rhondda No. 2). On the whole, Rhondda No.2 District consisted of lodges from the lower Rhondda, between Porth and Pontypridd.[128]

Each lodge held annual and general meetings that all members were entitled to attend. These general meetings were responsible for determining issues of principle and for electing the lodge committee, which held executive power and usually met weekly. The size of the lodge committee varied with the size of the union membership and total work-force, but numbers of twenty were not unusual. Control of the lodge committee was seen as vital by competing political factions. Practices differed according to individual lodges, but frequently one committee office was of greater importance than others. In some this was the secretaryship, in others the chairmanship. Some bigger lodges went so far as to elect, usually *sine die*, their own miners' agent. Whatever the particular balance, lodge committees encapsulated the leadership and talent of the work-force, and often demonstrated such leadership and responsibility in spheres far beyond the coal-face.

District organization was similar. Each lodge sent a certain number of representatives to the monthly district (general) meetings, based on lodge membership. These meetings were responsible for the election of the district executive committee, which met weekly. The most important single figure was the miners' agent, supported by his deputies as agents and officers of the district. Each district then not only sent delegates to SWMF conferences, but also a certain membership-related number of delegates to the SWMF executive committee.

During the first few years of the SWMF's existence survival was its preoccupation: in Rhondda no interest was evinced in local or parliamentary politics. As the 1900 general election approached, a deputation from the RLLA attended a Rhondda No.1 District meeting to solicit financial aid for the contest and for Mabon's presumed subsequent expenses. The deputation pointed out that the miners had not given money for two to three years, and that most of the money collected had been from tradesmen; and ultimately it was agreed, at the prompting of district agent Dai Watts Morgan, that the district donate £200.[129]

Watts Morgan was a central character in the development of the Federation's attitude towards organized political involvement. Born in Skewen in 1867, living and working in Wattstown from 1880 onwards, Dai Watts Morgan rose from checkweigher at the National Colliery to district miners' agent in 1898, and followed in Mabon's footsteps in his political Liberalism, serving on the EC of the RLLA and speaking at RLLA meetings and banquets.[130] By 1903 he was being talked of as a possible Lib-Lab parliamentary candidate for the South Glamorgan constituency. When in 1899 the Porth and Cymmer GCC seat fell vacant, Watts Morgan was a reasonable candidate from both Liberal and Labour standpoints. Backed by the RLLA and by sitting Labour Alderman Morgan Williams, Watts Morgan was surprisingly defeated at the by-election by David Jenkins, a timber merchant.[131] Jenkins, however, declined to stand for re-election a year later, and thus Watts Morgan must have been particularly annoyed at the decision of the district committee to refuse to allow him time off from his agent's duties to contest any local government vacancy.[132] Colleague James Baker (who had succeeded Watts Morgan as checkweigher at the National colliery) filled the seat without encountering any opposition, backed by the newly-formed Ynyshir Labour Committee.[133]

With such initiatives coming from the grass roots, Watts Morgan continued to push at district level for a greater political role for the 'Fed'. This task had be undertaken with subtlety. At a 1902 monthly meeting he attempted to explain the 'Pickard scheme':

He strongly repudiated that they had ever talked politics or done anything politically at any of the meetings of the district, and the £200 that was voted annually to Mabon MP, was given not for his services to the Liberal party, but for his services to the Labour cause. To the Rhondda miners Mabon was distinctly a Labour representative. It was distinctly understood that if any Labour measure beneficial to the workers was introduced into Parliament, Mabon was to support it irrespective of whether it was brought in by a Liberal or a Conservative Government. That was the connection between Mabon and themselves, and as a district they had nothing whatever to do with the Rhondda Liberal and Labour Association [sic].

The money which was to be raised by the Federation for a Parliamentary fund would be used independently of all political parties, and those who would be nominated – whether they were Liberals, Conservatives, Socialists or Democrats – must first and foremost be Labour men.[134]

Only a few days after this meeting James Baker died at the age of forty-one, leaving seven children and a vacancy on the GCC. This time Watts Morgan was permitted to advance as a Labour candidate and was returned unopposed.[135] Opinions within Rhondda No.1 District were gradually shifting towards sponsorship of political action. Observing that 'the bulk of the District Council was composed of capitalists', the Cymmer and National lodges advanced an important motion at district in 1903:

That with a view of increasing the number of Labour Representatives on our Local Governing Bodies, we ask the Lodges of the No.1 District to adopt a scheme for the purpose of returning and maintaining a fair number of Labour Members in each Ward. We think this can be done by grouping together a number of collieries for such purposes.[136]

A year later this scheme was brought forward as the Labour Representation Fund for district approval. Five geographical areas had been mapped out: Porth, Ferndale, Treorchy, Mid-Rhondda and Ystrad, each to have a committee responsible for propaganda and meetings. In its advocacy Watts Morgan provided his most sustained justification of local political activity:

I have told you before that my position as your servant entitled me to a large amount of consideration in various quarters, but I have never received anything like the consideration I do now, because I have a voice in the carrying out of matters belonging to the County, and I get an insight into and a direct knowledge of matters pertaining to your affairs and interests. And if you select proper men you will directly benefit by having your own views and claims on local matters voiced in the deliberations of the various local authorities by one of yourselves.[137]

Watts Morgan considered that it was as much the duty and the policy of the SWMF to look after the general welfare of its members as it was to watch over wages:

He was not speaking as a Liberal, but they had a Labour Party. The proposal was something intended to work in connection with the Federation and yet apart from it altogether – that on the public bodies there might be more men to look after matters affecting the interests of members of the Federation. Their members were bound by whatever was done in the administration of the Poor Law by the Board of Guardians, and by the administration of the Local Government Act by the County Council and District Council, and where they formed fully nine-tenths of the population, it was only fair for them to get a voice in the raising and spending of the rates.

The scheme was adopted in principle, but its actual implementation was patchy, with only Porth and Ynyshir areas spawning 'Labour committees'.[138] There is no record of a Rhondda-wide network being established, and those committees that did come into existence in practice behaved much like Trades and Labour Councils (TLCs). Not until 1907–8 was an efficient scheme implemented for Labour representation sponsored by the Rhondda No.1 District.

A few weeks later Watts Morgan was back to speak to the District upon this subject. He had been prompted to do so by the experience of fighting for and retaining his County Council seat against the challenge of local Liberal solicitor, William Thomas Davies:[139]

. . . if you allow a candidate to come out in the name of this Federation, I say it is full time for us to make it impossible for any other nominee to have a ghost of a chance to oppose our nominee. We ought to be able to poll two-thirds of the electorate in every division that we have in the Rhondda valley.[140]

Watts Morgan had become a firm advocate of the general principle of Labour representation, in part no doubt through his own conviction, but also through his experience of having to fight for his local government seat, and to fight as much against those with whom he was considered to share his wider political beliefs as against any of a more different hue. In so doing he expressed, by his actions as much as by his words, an independent trajectory of Labour representation. Watts Morgan was an avowed Liberal, but neither his Liberalism nor his RLLA involvement was of much assistance in retaining his seat. Assistance was to be found not amongst Rhondda's bourgeoisie, but from his fellow-workers, via the Rhondda No.1 District and the Labour Committee.

When the possibility of an extra parliamentary seat for the district was raised, Watts Morgan agreed that Labour was entitled to any such seat 'rather than a Liberal capitalist', because the area's prosperity rested upon the miners:

> Take away the mining population from the Rhondda and where were, or would be, the rest? They were all practically depending upon the miners for their upkeep. The miners' living was got from the coal which they imperilled their lives to get, and that in itself should be a sufficient inducement to the other classes to see that the condition of the miners was of the highest standard, and tending to the uplifting of character, and leading to the happiness of the men who were the life of the district.[141]

There was no hint of compromise, of possible arrangement with the RLLA. Rhondda No.1 District decided, in tune with SWMF directives, that it was to fight any new seat. Miners' leaders whose Westminster-related politics were essentially Liberal, were deriving strength from a Labourist perspective and increasingly found that the logic of their position was one of independent working-class politics.

During 1898 socialism had been seen as more than a missionaries' creed, rather as a legitimate choice that a politically conscious individual could make, distinct from Liberalism and Conservatism. By 1901 more than one local newspaper was running weekly columns explaining 'socialism' to its readers, as 'an endeavour to aid in the evolution of a better social order'.[142] The first organization to benefit from this heightened awareness was the National Democratic League (NDL), which had some success in Rhondda as in other parts of the south Wales coalfield.[143] From April 1901 onwards, it held meetings in the district, and by the end of August there were reported to be no less than seven NDL branches locally.[144] Yet these disappeared during the following winter, and although there was a revival during the summer of 1902, in common with its national fortunes the Rhondda NDL had vanished by the end of that year, a victim of its complete neglect of industrial issues.[145]

More hardy and ultimately more influential were the socialist societies that began to re-establish themselves at the beginning of the new century. By the end of 1902 a revitalized ILP branch had been established at Ferndale, followed by branches at Porth and Penygraig and accompanied by an SDF branch at Blaenclydach. In May 1905 the first 'all-Socialist' demonstration was organized, promoted by the Marxian Club, speakers including Ben Tillett and Charlie Stanton.[146]

It is within the context of mushrooming political awareness that the 1906 ballot by the MFGB to decide the question of affiliation to the Labour Party should be viewed, for the accompanying campaign provided in south Wales a unique opportunity for miners' leaders to express their political convictions.[147]

Rhondda No.1 District, being the largest SWMF district, was naturally a centre of agitation and interest. But its centrality within the debate was also due to the fact that it was the home of the leading opponent of affiliation, Mabon, who had begun the controversy in south Wales by refusing to use his casting vote from the chair of the Federation executive committee on whether or not to recommend affiliation to the union membership.[148] An examination of the Rhondda campaign thus sheds light upon political sensibilities in the coalfield in general.

Opposition to affiliation has been seen as the preserve of a reactionary Liberalism or Lib-Labism, as expressed by the older, more cautious and timid leaders.[149] No doubt there is some truth in this view: Mabon, seemingly content with his place within the Welsh Parliamentary Party, had ideological and personal objections to association with the partially-socialist Labour Party. And the prominent advocates of affiliation, such as James Winstone, Noah Ablett and T. I. Mardy Jones, were all ILPers. But whilst it is acceptable to say that elements of opposition to affiliation were politically derived, Rhondda evidence indicates that a more comprehensive view might stress the miners' Labourism as important in forming oppositional attitudes. Support for such a view can be found in the language of the campaign. For although the ideological gulf between Mabon and his deputy Watts Morgan on the one hand, and the ILPers on the other, was certainly considerable, there was a common unity behind the rhetoric: a set of shared assumptions about the rights and needs of Labour.

The 'Yes' campaign was led by the local ILP. During May and June 1906, ILP branches, soon operating through the newly established general purposes committee, held public meetings and invited speakers such as James Winstone, Vernon Hartshorn and Charlie Stanton to hold forth on subjects ranging from 'The Need for Labour Representation in Parliament' to 'The Hypocrisy of the Liberal and Conservative Parties'.[150] The 'Yes' campaign stressed the need for unambiguous Labour representation and commitment to advancing the interests of workers, unclouded by any attachment to Liberalism, Lib-Labism or Tory democracy, and unrestricted in its application to the whole working class by any specifically occupational loyalties. 'Worker' expressed this class rather than occupational consciousness in his criticism of the 'Pickard scheme':

> The present Federation plan is politics of the mere 'bread and cheese' class. The miners stipulate a representative type that knows all about the coal industry, and, therefore, is expected to be legislatively alert to all points that will improve the working conditions of the miner . . . it is a very narrow programme politically, because it reduces the choice of representatives to men who are colliers in tradition and experience. This has made the term of Labour representation limited, and every other worker who is not a member of the Federation, has not the remotest chance of ever being a Parliamentary representative.[151]

Joining forces with major trade unions to provide a united working-class vote, it was argued, was preferable to associating with Tories and Liberals who could often be found arrayed against the miners in the Commons.[152] Mardy Jones argued that:

> The basis of the LRC is wide enough to embrace the interests of all workers of hand and brain, and is strong enough to attack all the unfair privileges which our landlords and capitalists extort out of the wealth created by the toil of the workers of the country. The narrow view of trade representation must give way to the broad view of common interests of all classes of workmen. The cause of Labour is the cause of the nation.
>
> For generations the miners have been diffident in their attitude towards all industrial interests outside direct mining questions. In the strength of their natural advantages for organization they have allowed their trade interests to blur their outlook on the wider problems of Labour politics. Happily they are now beginning to realize that the miners of the country cannot secure a higher standard of life, of work,

and of wage unless there be also a concurrent improvement in the social conditions of the mass of the people. Workers of all trades have inter-dependent interests.

The industrial conditions of our lives as workers are controlled by the laws made in Parliament by the very men who do not hesitate, as employers, to grind the last penny out of our toil. This is why Labour representation, if it is to be effective, must also be independent. That is, the best interests of Labour are best served by all the Labour members uniting to form a distinct political organization of their own, with distinct political principles and ideals of their own . . . By owning no allegiance to any other party, the Labour Party stands out clearly, and it is in a stronger position to influence Parliament to carry out social reforms.[153]

The opposition to affiliation was headed by Mabon and Watts Morgan, Mabon being at his most politically active since the general election of 1900.[154] The grounds for opposition rested in part upon anti-socialism and a mistrust of what was seen as the domination of the Labour Party by middle-class intellectuals whose experiences were far removed from those of the working class, and who could not have the interests of the working class at heart. Instead the expressed preference was for a 'Labour first' or trade-union-only Labour Party – an authentically working-class party. It was also argued that affiliation would lead to isolation. A 'Yes' vote would damage the Liberal government, acting in the interests of working people. There was in the language of both advocates and opponents of affiliation a common emphasis upon the interests of Labour. The primacy of the latter was not in dispute: disagreement focused upon how best to protect and advance those interests. The result when it came, although clearly a victory for the 'Yes' campaign both in the Rhondda and in south Wales (although not in Britain as a whole), could not be seen as an endorsement of socialism: for that had been underplayed by the ILPers. Once the campaign has been placed within the context of a variety of local political initiatives, it can be seen that what was emphasized above all was the enduring Labourism of the miners and of their leaders.

Although neither the campaign nor the result indicated a mass conversion to socialism, the ILP derived great benefit from their success in winning the debate and from the momentum of victory.[155] In the wake of the result, the round of ILP meetings intensified.[156] By the beginning of 1907 the branches at Porth, Ferndale and Penygraig had been joined by one at Pentre.[157] In May the general purposes committee of the Rhondda ILP launched a summer propaganda campaign, lasting until September, with large meetings being held at different venues each week and with prominent south Walian socialists as speakers.[158] Branch membership made 'rapid strides' and the *Glamorgan Free Press* acknowledged the campaign's success: 'Socialism is much more popular in the district than it has ever been. Its popularity is undoubtedly due to the untiring efforts of the branch members and officials of the ILP.'[159]

As winter approached, the ILP went indoors, holding fewer, but more ambitious, meetings, attracting such figures as Ramsay MacDonald and Victor Grayson.[160] The year 1908 saw an expanded campaign, with over two hundred meetings being held, and over eight hundred members being organized into thirteen branches. Ideas to establish a weekly ILP paper for the Rhondda, a 'scout corps' and a Labour church were bandied about, and news of the efforts being made reached the Yorkshire paper *The Worker*, which exclaimed excitedly: 'The only Valley that would run the Yorkshire Valley close was the Rhondda Valley in Wales through which the fiery Cross of Socialism was rapidly spreading.'[161]

Understandably, some of the branches had weak roots. The AGM of the Rhondda ILP held in January 1909 counted 550 members in thirteen branches, some of which were 'doing splendid work', others of which had 'had a hard struggle'. However the 'scouts' had been established, and an increasing number of women members was reported.[162] Propaganda work continued throughout the following year: preparations were made for a socialist newspaper, and two new branches were established.[163] The AGM of 1910 counted 223 meetings held throughout the year, with eleven extant branches; and for the first time a Rhondda delegate attended the ILP annual conference.[164] The ILP had become an important part of the Rhondda Labour movement during the years after the 1906 ballot.

It is important not to overstate the influence of the ILP. Undoubtedly, from 1906 onwards the volume of socialist propaganda in Rhondda outweighed that of any other political creed. But this could only be partially related to political power and representation, and to give ILPers and socialists all the credit for the eventual attachment of the miners to the Labour Party is to misunderstand both the meaning of that attachment and the ways in which modes of thought conducive to the same could arise. The political configuration of Rhondda's working class was altering before the campaign of 1906, and to comprehend the 'rise of Labour' one must go beneath surface appearances and national ideological alignments, to 'read' instead the behaviour of men such as Watts Morgan, and the contribution to political independence of Labourist modes of thought. Independent political representation arose from the blending of both socialism and Labourism, and from the combination of the vigour of the ILP with the organizational power and communal resonances of the SWMF and of various TLCs.

Labour and local government, 1898–1910

The very first duty to be performed next to convincing yourself of the need of a change, is to give expression to your conviction by electing men to your governing bodies who will devote themselves to the service of the disinherited. Don't neglect the local bodies, the District Council, and the Board of Guardians in particular. Your emancipation depends more upon those than upon the Imperial Parliament, although, of course, it is very essential that you should be properly represented there.

John Morgan[165]

It was at the level of local politics, in the absence of change at parliamentary level, that the dynamics of political independence were worked out. Immediately following 1898 the patterns of local Labour politics remained much the same. Candidacies were few: only two Labour men stood for the thirty places in the 1899 elections for the reconstituted RUDC. Many Labour leaders continued to play supportive roles to Liberal notables.[166] Those candidates that did come forward might have organizational backing, such as that provided by the Porth Labour Committee, or have little option other than to stand alone on the basis of their public personae and their representative significance. That was not always sufficient when matched against 'the monied fraternity', as Samuel Jones of Ferndale noted:

The working classes of these Valleys – more especially the miners – are a most servile and inconsistent body. A smile, a nod, or a handshake from an official is sufficient to secure a vote for the candidate whom that official may favour. To prove this we have only to glance at the constitution of our local governing bodies. Is it possible to conceive of a state of things more deplorable? This is a district which is notorious for its powerful Labour organization. Yet, Labour representation is conspicuous by its absence.[167]

The perception of such a problem was indicative of the increasing degree to which class consciousness intruded upon electoral proceedings. In the harsher economic climes of the new century it became more regular and prominent. In 1901 the chairman of the Porth Labour Committee, miner and undoubted Liberal supporter Ben Davies, stood against three tradesmen for the Porth vacancy. A supporter informed the *Glamorgan Free Press* that 'every collier who votes for a tradesman in this contest will be a traitor to his class. Let him be branded as such by his fellows.'[168] Davies himself hailed his subsequent election as 'a signal victory for the cause of Labour. The result of this election proves what can be done by united action on the part of workmen.'[169]

Alignments and allegiances might be more complex than those of political party or class identity: an example being the unsuccessful 1903 RUDC Ward Eight candidacy of John Hughes. Hughes was, in many respects, an ideal Labour candidate. Thirty-six in 1903, he had worked in Llwynypia and the United States before settling in Cymmer, and was checkweigher and lodge chairman at Cymmer Colliery. He attended Tabernacle English Baptist Chapel, Porth, and served on the management board of the Porth Cottage Hospital. He was undoubtedly a Liberal in his party political sympathies.[170] Hughes's opponent was also a Liberal: sitting member Joseph Brooks, fruiterer and director of the *Rhondda Leader*. On the face of things, this was not a problem: representatives of the working class and of the bourgeoisie regularly clashed in local elections despite sharing a similar party-political creed. Thus when the Porth Labour Committee (PLC) met to select a Labour candidate it rejected the appeal of a deputation of 'Liberals and Nonconformists' for united action, pledging itself to return 'a Labour man'.[171] Problems arose, however, at three levels. First, Brooks was an exceptional bourgeois. He had been sympathetic to the miners during the 1898 strike, and he was the only tradesman to back Watts Morgan in his 1900 GCC contest with David Jenkins. 'Let us fight our enemies and not our friends' was one call.[172] Second, the Porth area already had two Labour representatives on the GCC (Morgan Williams and Watts Morgan), and one on the RUDC (Ben Davies). To attempt to gain another seat was felt by some to indicate greed, 'starting a new era in the Labour Party aspiration in the Rhondda'.[173] Finally, Hughes's candidature suffered from a problem that was to bedevil the Labour movement – that of internal disharmony and parochialism. Hughes, a Cymmer man, had won the nomination of the PLC against Henry Loxton, miner and candidate of the Lewis Merthyr Lodge. Lewis Merthyr was very unhappy at the furtherance of Hughes's name, and resigned from the PLC in protest, publicly criticizing Hughes as polling day approached.[174] Despite the support of Watts Morgan and Ben Davies, Hughes suffered defeat at the hands of Brooks by 928 votes to 797. Labourist aspiration had therefore temporarily overreached itself – but the margin of defeat was not large, and the significance of the contest was not that Labour suffered from division and doubt, but that Labour was prepared deliberately to oppose a sitting and obviously popular Liberal representative.

In these circumstances no Liberal Councillor could regard his seat as invulnerable. In 1904 Labour's Tom Evans defeated the sitting Liberal Councillor in Penygraig, Dr Evan Naunton Davies, to increase Labour representation on the RUDC to five.[175] Two years later, railway guard Griffith Evans came second in a four-horse race behind sitting Liberal Councillor Daniel Richard Jones in the first contest to be supported by the new Treherbert TLC, of which Evans was a founder and the secretary. This was more than merely a Labour–Liberal challenge. Not only was Evans not a miner, but he stood on an explicitly Labour Party platform, making no concession to traditional Liberal policies.[176] Although unsuccessful in 1906, Evans was back the following year, challenging the 'Grand Old Man' of Treherbert, William Morgan, who had represented the area on the RUDC since 1894, and who was also up for re-election that year on both the GCC and the PBG. Treherbert TLC advanced nominees: Evans for the RUDC, and miner William Eveleigh for the PBG.[177] Both Evans and Eveleigh won their seats with three-figure margins, and the success of Treherbert TLC in challenging entrenched Liberal representatives pointed the way forward to a new era of Labour organization and independence.[178]

From 1898 to 1907 a heightened combativity on the part of Labour can be noticed in contrast to the earlier political pattern. Then, conflicts between Liberals and Labour had arisen when a Liberal decided to challenge the tenure or acknowledged 'right' to a vacancy of a Labour man. Now, in what was a qualitative change, Labour men were prepared to challenge the continued tenure or 'right' of their social betters. A second change was the degree to which Labour candidates came forward as representatives of organizations. The haphazard nature of Labour organization prior to 1898 has been illustrated already, as have the attempts of the Rhondda No.1 District to establish a structure for advancing local government candidates – attempts that were to come to fruition in 1908. By this time, however, there were in existence a number of TLCs, some of which were advancing Labour candidates, and the district's attempts to a greater or lesser degree were bound up with these bodies, which provided a second tier of the Labour movement beneath the SWMF.

Rhondda TLCs functioned as electoral organizations, propagandist bodies, and focuses for both trade union co-operation and community concern. Before the First World War there were five: at Porth (founded as the PLC in 1892), No.9 Ward (1904), Treherbert (1905), Mid-Rhondda (1905), and Pentre (1908).[179] To begin with they were simply electoral organizations. The PLC arose in 1892 to back Moses Moses and Morgan Williams, and re-emerged in 1900 and 1901, when it assisted Watts Morgan and James Baker.[180] The PLC was the model for the 1904 Labour representation fund scheme advanced by Rhondda No.1 District, which was to establish five 'Labour committees' in different areas of the Rhondda. The stated objects of the one committee that was definitely established, known as the Labour Representation Committee (LRC) No.9 Ward, bear out this electoral emphasis:

(a)   To promote the extension of Labour principles among the working classes, for the purpose of securing Labour representation on the following boards, namely, County Council, Urban District Council, and Board of Guardians.

(b)   To raise funds for the purpose of defraying both election and attendance expenses incurred by its members on the various boards.

(c)   [To do so] By means of subscriptions from colliery workmen and others who are in sympathy with the movement.[181]

The objective of a TLC operating in electoral mode was to secure sufficient public support for the Labour candidate. To achieve this, and to ensure a broad choice of candidates, it was necessary to enrol as many local trade union organizations as possible under the TLC banner.[182] Treherbert TLC included not only five large lodges, but also local branches of the Amalgamated Society of Railway Servants (ASRS), the Printers, and the Shop Employees. This heterogeneous pattern was also followed by both Mid-Rhondda and Pentre TLCs.[183] By 1909 the PLC embraced, along with the miners, the Surface

Craftsmen, ASRS, NUT, Rhondda Class Teachers' Association (RCTA), Insurance Agents' Union, Hairdressers, Municipal Employees' Association (MEA), Shop Assistants' Union (SAU), Gasworkers' Association and the Tramwaymen's Union.[184] Whilst the miners' lodges remained dominant within all TLCs, the existence of a broader organization spread their influence and provided some for the weaker trade unions.

TLCs regularly advised and criticized the RUDC. Common matters of concern were the state of Rhondda's housing stock and drainage, the pay, hours and working conditions of municipal employees, the water supply, and urinals.[185] Two areas of the Rhondda were not served by a TLC. Treorchy had to wait until 1916 to be so provided, whilst the other, the Upper Rhondda Fach, was controlled by the miners' lodges alone. There were rumours that a TLC was to be formed, but this never occurred.[186]

The existence of an organizational framework as provided by the TLCs was an invaluable contribution to Labour's strength. The everyday work of TLCs put Labour activists in constant touch with the conditions of life in the area, at a level at least equal to that activated by the leadership of miners' lodges, and TLCs also permitted workers from a variety of occupations to co-operate: a vital corrective to the predominance of coalminers. TLCs thus provided the launching pad for what, in 1908, was the largest and most ambitious electoral sally in the Rhondda since 1885.

This in itself was the product of a reappraisal by Rhondda No.1 district of the significance of local political representation, and of the difficulties encountered by Labour candidates in local elections. At a District meeting in August 1907, in the midst of a discussion of Rhondda's housing problems, Councillor Tom Evans suggested that that part of the parliamentary levy intended for local purposes should be used for propaganda work, as it was only if more resources were devoted to increasing Labour representation that progress in matters such as housing could be anticipated. The district committee was urged to formulate an appropriate scheme.[187] The Labour representation scheme that was this time put into full operation allowed for 4*d*. from the shilling levy to be set aside for the purpose of supporting Labour members on local governing bodies. The allocation was to be £20 per ward per member, with the proviso that if a ward did not use any such funds the surplus could be redistributed to more 'progressive' areas. Funds were also available to assist with election expenses for unsuccessful candidates providing they had been ratified by the district committee.[188] The news of the scheme was welcomed in the press by railway signalman and president of the Pentre TLC, Tom ('T.C.' or 'Top Cat') Morris:

> Those who have long desired to see local government become a more efficient lever of social reform than it has hitherto been . . . welcome this far too long delayed step of the miners to secure their rightful share of local representation. Too long have these bodies submitted to have dumped upon them representatives of capitalism, landlords, jerrybuilders, self-seekers and cliques . . . Instead of it [local government] becoming the expression of democracy it becomes the citadel of an arrogant autocracy, and that, alas, being made so by the apathy amongst the working classes towards local elections. If the measures of social reform now vested within the administrative powers of District and County Councils were put in force, they would to a very great extent mitigate the evils of unhealthy environment which surrounds us to day . . . working class opinion has never been focussed truly upon the functions of local governing bodies . . . They have allowed official and sectarian cliques to choose candidates for whom they are asked to vote for, and the workers have simply allowed it to continue until local government has appeared a farce . . . Here we have the most democratic institution at our very doors which can be made a powerful lever for social reform through its administrative powers, being allowed to become the preserves of the reactionary forces. . . . At last the dawn of better days has arrived. Now that the workers have taken upon themselves the duty of securing Labour representatives, the day of the reactionary and 'nice-man' councillor is at end, and none too soon. I trust he [the working-class voter] will be wisely guided in his selection, and thus lift local government out of the morass which it has got into. After all it is only to the extent that we secure efficiency in local affairs that we can secure efficiency in national affairs.

Morris singled out three areas for local-government-led social reform: the Housing Acts, the Feeding of Children Act, and the municipalization of public services.[189] Social reform, wrote Morris, had been little present: ' "Efficiency and Reform" has been the old-time formula, which assumed the shadow in the seat of the contest, and minus reform after.' But 'an awakened democracy will not be fooled as it has been in the past . . . If it is to secure the full benefits of Acts of Parliament passed on to the administrative bodies, it must see that democracy is fully represented.'[189]

The adoption of the scheme in December 1907 resulted in stimulating the sponsoring of candidacies as, for the first time, local bodies could count on financial and propaganda support across Rhondda, rather than being forced to rely upon their own resources and to campaign in a vacuum. By March 1908 candidates had been selected for no less than seven RUDC seats, the largest Labour 'slate' to date. The campaign marked a departure in its valley-wide organization and in its vigorous pursuit of electoral success. The candidates stressed the 'right' of Labour to seek representation on the RUDC, to be represented by 'one of their own colour' and 'to share in their own government'.[190] Mid-Rhondda candidate George Burton told a public meeting that: 'A friend had told him on the street that he must have been possessed of superabundant audacity to contest this Ward . . . He however, although only a checkweigher, claimed as much right to contest the ward as a butcher, a draper, or a grocer.'[191] Echoes of 1885 could be found in the words of another Labour supporter: 'the time had arrived that they should be directly represented by their own fellows, men who had borne the same trials, troubles and burdens as themselves, and who would always be approachable to working men, and in full sympathy with their aspirations.'[192]

The predominant theme of the Labour campaign was thus one of Labourist loyalty to class and to the Federation. The central figure in the campaign was Watts Morgan, who spoke up and down the Rhondda in support of his men, and who put out circulars on behalf of Rhondda No.1 District backing all candidates and appealing 'to Miners and other Workers' for their loyalty.[193]

Given the amount of effort invested in the campaign the results, two victories against five defeats, were considered somewhat disappointing.[194] Explanations, general and particular, could be found. The two successful candidates, William Herbert Morgan and Tom Harries, were both substantial figures. Morgan was a checkweigher at Fernhill colliery, secretary of both the Workmen's Institute and Treherbert ILP, vice-president of the Ton Co-operative Society and a founder of the Treherbert TLC. Having been a representative on the Federation's executive committee since 1903, he would also become financial secretary of the Rhondda No.1 District in 1908, and was tipped for great things. Harries was a checkweigher at the Tylorstown collieries and secretary of LRC No.9 Ward, and he also had served on the SWMF executive committee since 1903.[195] As for some of the defeated candidates, it was felt that the candidacies of

Mardy Jones, of checkweigher and fellow Ruskin product Noah Rees, and of George Burton had been damaged by their reputation as socialists and atheists.[196] Mardy Jones was also hindered by the fact that Labour already filled two of the three Ward Ten RUDC seats: 'If the general public and the fair-minded miner get to think that there is no limit to Labour aspirations, and that monopoly and not an equable share in administration work are the aims, then disappointment is bound to come. "Shoni Fair Play" is not dead.'[197]

In retrospect the 1908 results did not look quite so bad. In what were mainly two-cornered contests, the seven Labour candidates had polled nearly 45 per cent of the votes, and Labour had strengthened its position on the RUDC, bringing representation up to eight. As 1908 had been the first occasion upon which a Rhondda-wide campaign had been fought, there were grounds for medium-term optimism.

After a lull due to lack of finance in 1909, things began to warm up again in 1910.[198] Finance remained a problem, as the Osborne Judgement stifled the distribution of the parliamentary levy, and TLCs and lodges fell back on their own resources.[199] Nor was the freshness associated with the 1908 campaign present, as a number of sitting Labour representatives happened to be up for re-election, but the triennial elections of the GCC and PBG, along with the annual RUDC elections, enabled Labour again to make its presence felt on polling day. On the RUDC, all four sitting Labour Councillors were returned without difficulty, and were joined by Labour's eisteddfodwr, Congregationalist deacon and Pentre TLC secretary, James James ('Iago Penrhys') who defeated colliery manager William Dundas Wight, assisted by the latter's locally unpopular stance in the Pentre colliery dispute, and a thorough door-to-door canvass.[200] The greatest Labour advance in 1910, however, came on the PBG, where Labour returned five of its seven candidates.[201]

Labour representatives had now made substantial inroads in two of the three local governing bodies in the Rhondda. On the RUDC sat nine Labour councillors (30 per cent of the total), on the PBG five (22 per cent). Labour representation on the GCC (between 2 and 12 per cent) left much to be desired, but it could be argued that this was the least relevant body of the three, and could await its quota of Labour men. The Liberal hegemony was breaking up. The composition and orientation of the Labour contingent nevertheless remained traditional. Miners dominated: fourteen out of the sixteen Labour public representatives were directly connected with the coal industry, whilst one other, Edward Jones, had only recently left his post as miners' librarian and caretaker to become an insurance agent. All but two of the fourteen miners already occupied positions of acknowledged leadership and responsibility, such as checkweighers, agents and secretaries. Examining the political beliefs of the Labour representatives one finds that, once one goes beyond their loyalty to 'Labour', no fewer than nine were Liberals, and only three could be termed unequivocal socialists.

Paradoxically, the 'rise of Labour' was in part the result of Liberal dominance. Working-class leaders, even politically Liberal ones such as Watts Morgan, could not gain acceptance within the Liberal polity, and were thus forced to find it outside, on the basis of what turned out to be superior organizational strength and class consciousness. Had it been interested, the RLLA could have noted the signs of change that arose in the early years of the 1900s, the shift in attitudes that allowed the *Rhondda Leader* to point out that the 'Labour Party in the Rhondda' was not 'excessive in demanding to have ten members, an average of one for each ward' on the RUDC.[202] But no allowance was forthcoming and, in frustration, the 'aspirations' of Labour grew to mirror the preponderance in Rhondda society of the class they represented. That level of aspiration was, before 1910, to prove problematic for the Labour movement: even a Labour Councillor such as Tom Harries could say that 'he would not favour a monopoly of Labour on any Council or body, but he desired to see a fair representation of all classes'.[203] Although by the second half of the 1900s it provided a sustained and organized political challenge to its Liberal 'betters', the Labour movement had yet to command the public arena, and had yet to dominate it with its municipal or ideological agenda. Whilst a number of subsequently highly important Labour leaders were mentally prepared to assert Labour's hegemony before the Tonypandy riots and Cambrian Combine strike altered the political sensibilities of south Wales, Labour was still perceived by many as attempting to find its rightful place within the conventional Liberal public matrix. Labour was, therefore, both publicly and to some extent in its own consciousness, an 'interest' to many. The events of 1910 were to transform that consciousness and that public perception, and recast the ambitions of the Labour movement in a hegemonic form equal in its ideological span to the Liberalism it replaced, and superior in its organizational underpinning. The Labour movement was to mesh class and community identities in such a way as to make its dislodgement an impossibility, but was also to experience a fierce struggle over the control of its future direction, and of the future direction of the society it came to represent.

Conclusion

> Throughout the valleys of Glamorgan we can see the class-consciousness of working men assuming political form. But it is a story that requires detailed, almost fragmentary, presentation against the background of local pressures and animosities in each constituency.
>   Kenneth O. Morgan[204]

This chapter began with an investigation of the election of Wales's first 'Labour' MP, and has ended with the depiction of a Labour movement on the verge of mounting a serious challenge to the hitherto hegemonic control of Rhondda Liberals on the RUDC. Such a challenge had an organizational depth delivered by the commitment of the major local trade union in the shape of the SWMF, by five TLCs that drew most local trade unions together, and by eleven ILP branches that added propagandist fervour and an intellectual edge manifestly sharper than anything being offered by rival political groups. It has been the central argument of this chapter that it is this organizational independence that is the key to an understanding of the dynamics of Liberal and Labour politics in the Rhondda valleys, for beneath the variable application of party political labels such as 'Liberal', 'Lib-Lab', 'Labour' and 'Socialist' the activist element amongst Rhondda's working class shared in a unity initially forged by their exclusion from the Lib-Lab polity, and shared in a language of occupational and class interest that proved to be increasingly successful in appealing to the broader political constituency.[205]

Both the dynamics of Labour's rise and its attendant chronology differ markedly in this study from the general historical orthodoxy. Mabon's victory in 1885, rather than being immediately written into the evolution of Welsh Liberalism, has been identified as a key moment in the articulation of working-class political consciousness in the south Wales coalfield, an articulation that necessitated the invention of a class-harmonious 'Lib-Lab' politics. The 'democracy' of Welsh Liberalism has been debunked, revealed for its petty snobbery as well as for its remarkable, chaotic structure. The evolution of a Labour challenge, often misunderstood as hampered by a Lib-Lab/socialist struggle, has been shown to have employed a common language, a common set of perceptions. And the local government arena, with its regular contests and challenges, has been identified as a dimension critical to the understanding of all these features. To a degree, the implications of the study for the understanding of the politics of industrial south Wales are manifest: the view of Mabon provided here may strike chords with portraits of other prominent Lib-Labs, but his significance as coalfield leader immediately extends his importance beyond the confines of the Rhondda valleys.[206] In so far as Rhondda was the largest, most populous, most important part of the coalfield, a new understanding of this part must change the understanding of the whole. More importantly, what has been documented here both in the dissection of local Liberalism and, the anatomy of working-class political initiatives, suggests that historians will have to go beyond the stock images of the ideological hegemony of 'old Liberalism' and of its human counterpart, the cheery, head-in-the-sand Lib-Lab, wherever they may search. Undoubtedly, K. O. Morgan's 'local pressures and animosities' will demand their detailed, fragmentary presentation, but in amongst the detail and the local specificity the theme of the 'rights of Labour', increasingly understood as the rights of the working class, may transcend the physical boundaries of each and every valley.

3

Labour in command, 1910–1927

Introduction

... from the point of view of making history the Cambrian strike was an epoch-making event ... This strike was no failure from the point of view of the development of the working class, but was the awakening of that spirit which carried the South Wales miners into the van of the international working class.

Ness Edwards, 1938[1]

... whereas the [Cambrian Combine] strike was a catalytic agent for the [Tonypandy] riots, the latter had other and deeper causes, which were expressive of a social crisis, heightened in mid-Rhondda but permeated throughout a South Wales whose history, in the last quarter of the nineteenth century, differed in a number of respects from that of Britain.

David Smith, 1980[2]

It is from the Tonypandy riots, and from the Cambrian Combine strike that surrounded the riots, that one can date the political collapse of the Liberal edifice in the Rhondda valleys. These were events of immense importance in the development of the south Wales coalfield. Ness Edwards was correct to see the Combine strike as 'epoch-making', for it laid bare the absence of any economic common ground between the forces of Labour and capital in the coalfield, and it dealt a devastating blow to the Mabonite approach of conciliation and compromise in union matters. In its place it generated within the SWMF alternative, more combative leaderships that aimed not merely for recognition and equal status within the coal industry, but for the control of the industry as a prelude to a very different future for society as a whole. Of equal significance has been the history of the Tonypandy riots of 8–9 November 1910, rewritten in recent years by David Smith. Prior interpretations had written off the riots as the unfortunate by-product of the Cambrian Combine strike, and/or as the futile result of frustration and disappointment on the part of the 'mob'. Such analyses were vanquished by the insights spilling out of a new methodological perspective that uncovered the 'semiology of riot': the logic of the crowd's behaviour.[3] More ambitious but no less persuasive was the argument that the Tonypandy signposts directed attention to the whole of south Walian society: Mid-Rhondda fracturing the Edwardian illusion of a Liberal consensus. As Labour activist Tom Morris observed in 1912, 'Instead of Liberalism embosoming the rights of Labour, it has challenged them by policeman's truncheons, fixed bayonets, and ball cartridge.'[4] This 'social fracture' not only shattered the mirror glass of the tradesman's ethos, the 'politics of personality', which had proved so important in the evolution of local politics, but also gave great impetus to the advance of working-class political representation, as well as to the industrial struggles led by the SWMF. From 1910 the Rhondda Labour movement extended its ambition, its organization, and its success: it seized the political initiative, and retained it until it was in full command of local representative institutions. The implications of the 1906 and 1908 miners' ballots in favour of affiliation to the Labour Party were taken up as substantial unity was forged between the movement's Labourist and socialist currents. This chapter deals with the 'external' history of the Labour movement from 1910 until 1927: Labour's outward success at parliamentary and local political levels, its relations and struggles with Liberals, Independents, and Tories, and the deepening of organizational and cultural dimensions to the movement – dimensions that nurtured and sustained its growth.

Parliamentary domination, or 'left unchallenged'

In the Rhondda sentiment has wisely ruled to give the veteran 'Mabon' an unopposed return. He has had a great record of close identification with the progress of democracy. He has helped, as few men have, to give the miners of Wales the power of self-expression, and we must not throw dirt into that fountain of which we have drank. In politics like all else there must be gratitude. However, it must be clear that the Rhondda Seats must not be understood as likely uncontested seats perputuity [sic]. Major Watts Morgan in East Rhondda is left unchallenged because of his general broad democratic views.

Rhondda Leader, 21 December 1918

After the December 1910 election, and alongside Mabon's

marginalization as an industrial leader, it became necessary to contemplate his impending retirement.[5] Some of this contemplation stimulated the formal organization of the Rhondda Labour Party, but although Mabon's intention to retire at the next election was announced at the beginning of 1913, the intervention of the First World War thwarted the expected general election of 1915, and the altered political climate of 1918 led Mabon to decide to re-present himself at the 'Coupon Election'.[6] Rhondda had, under the Representation of the People Act 1918, been awarded two constituencies – East and West. The SWMF decided to claim both as miners' seats, and Mabon, for Rhondda West, and his long-standing deputy Dai Watts Morgan, for Rhondda East, were returned as Labour MPs to Westminster without challenge.[7]

The absence of any Liberal candidate mounting a challenge in either constituency demands explanation. Despite Mabon's appearance as an official Labour Party candidate, local Liberals could accept him as they had done in 1910: in anticipation of his retirement, out of respect to his long service and in recognition of his sympathies with traditional Liberalism. He could continue as a nostalgic artefact of the glossed days of class harmony and political unity. Watts Morgan's return was less easy to stomach: whilst he was no socialist, and had been involved with the Rhondda Labour and Liberal Association at the turn of the century, he had also been responsible for building up an autonomous political organization sponsoring the return of working men to local government bodies, often in competition with middle-class Liberals. Furthermore, to allow Labour to claim both seats without opposition would set an awkward precedent, and make the reclamation of either a formidable task for local Liberals. There is evidence that some within the RLLA favoured contesting Rhondda East, but nothing came of it.[8] The Liberals were in a highly confused and disorganized state: the long-standing weaknesses in their political machinery were now blatantly evident. Further cause for Liberal bemusement was the prevalent rumour that both Mabon and Watts Morgan were in receipt of the Coupon, that they were in some way still part of the 'progressive coalition', and that thus neither the RLLA nor the Rhondda Conservative Association were under any obligation to challenge the Labour men.[9] The rumour was exaggerated but did have a factual base, for, quite apart from the moderate political views of Mabon and Watts Morgan, both regretted the breaking of the Coalition and both were looked upon favourably by Lloyd George.[10] The rumour became so strong, with both the RCA and the RLLA announcing they were not challenging the Labour men for this reason, that eventually the Labour Party had to issue an official denial, after securing guarantees from the candidates themselves that they were, indeed, Labour candidates.[11]

One other consideration that must have been influential in deterring opposition was Watts Morgan's personal war record. For over four years he had been the archetypal patriotic Labour leader: he had volunteered for military service as a private soldier within days of the war breaking out, had been rapidly commissioned and set in charge of recruiting within north Wales, and as early as 1915 was being praised and honoured for his services to 'King and Country'.[12] Regularly making known his opposition to 'peace cranks' who were 'insulting the boys of whom we are all so proud', he capped his reputation with a Distinguished Service Order for bravery on the Western Front, having led his pioneer unit in a counter-attack against German troops breaking through British lines around Cambrai. His impressive military career finished with his earning a letter of thanks from the king for his work in assisting the demobilization programme, and a retiring promotion to lieutenant-colonel.[13] To challenge a man who had very obviously 'done his duty', and whose political views could hardly be considered offensive, was barely conceivable, and it is no surprise that potential Liberal candidates refused this task.[14]

Two years later, parliamentary politics intruded again, Mabon finally announcing his retirement from public life in February 1920 for reasons of ill health.[15] The selection by the Labour Party of William John, Rhondda No.1 District agent, as his successor, was completed by August.[16] Again no Liberal candidate was forthcoming, and this time it was a two-horse race between John for Labour and local builder Gwilym Rowlands (son of the manager of the Naval colliery and later MP for Flint) for the Conservatives.[17] If in 1918 the absence of Liberal opposition was understandable, though unfortunate, in 1920 it was surely fatal for its long-term credibility. The RLLA had withdrawn from the political fray, and had left parliamentary representation in the hands of the Labour Party, which could not seriously expect to be troubled by the paltry resources of Rhondda Conservatism.

The Conservatives fought an imaginative campaign.[18] Gwilym Rowlands styled himself a 'Coalition Labour' candidate 'representative of combined moderate opinion', and stressed his allegiance to the principles of trade unionism and class co-operation. He found support in telegrams from Bonar Law and from Lloyd George, having the latter's message printed on his posters, whilst some local Liberals also spoke in his favour.[19] Rowlands claimed that the 'progressive alliance' was now defunct and that Labour was presenting its true 'socialist' colours, whilst recent municipal election voting behaviour showed the increasing amount of anti-socialist common ground between Liberals and Conservatives: 'the issue before the electors is the one great issue of Constitutional Government versus Direct Action and Bolshevism'.[20] Rowlands's posters contrasted the Union Jack with the Red Flag. The problem with this approach was that it was, in practice, difficult to portray the seemingly reasonable and level-headed Will John as a 'wild man Bolshevist' – 'the fact remains that amongst the leaders of the South Wales coalfield Mr. John is regarded as belonging to the moderate section'.[21] Or, as the *South Wales News* put it:

> . . . 'direct-actionists' are comparatively few in number, and although noisy, their influence is negligible. It is safe to say that the outstanding revelation of this bye-election is the fact that the bulk of the miners of this populous area look askance at the revolutionary proposals of the extremists, and are solid for a sane Labour policy, as enunciated by Mr. William John.[22]

John, forty-two at the time of the by-election, had a record of long service to the miners and the community more generally. A checkweigher and then lodge secretary at Llwynypia, he had played a critical role in 1910–11 as chairman of the Cambrian Combine committee. Imprisoned briefly along with John Hopla during the turmoil of the dispute, on his release he took the posts of district financial secretary and representative on the executive committee of the SWMF, before becoming district agent in 1912. He was also a stalwart of the Baptist cause, serving variously as deacon and secretary of Moriah Chapel, Tonypandy.

Although Rowlands could find little mileage in the 'extremist' theme, a more difficult campaign problem for John to handle was that of the issue of state control of the liquor traffic.[23] John, in supporting this, was in line with official Labour Party policy.[24] But whereas both John and Rowlands were opposed to the Temperance (Wales) Bill, Rowlands opposed the question of local veto and state control, and played up his image as 'the anti-prohibition candidate'. In so doing he was expected to draw support from the working-men's clubs, even Labour clubs.[25] But Rowlands's gamble did not pay off. On the one hand he was attacking John as a revolutionary, on the other as a dogmatic Nonconformist. Whilst these attitudes might be reconcilable, Rowlands could not make them appear so, and his populist approach did not reap the expected benefits. John won the unqualified support of the local Nonconformist churches; and his staunch adherence to his principles may have attracted as well as repelled voters, as, when he toured the Labour and working-men's clubs to explain his attitude, each of the clubs visited passed resolutions approving his candidature.[26] Contemporary opinion was that miners' wives, exercising their parliamentary vote for the first time in a Rhondda constituency, were also exercising influence over the voting choices of their husbands![27]

Although this one important issue of the election was dear to the heart of traditional Welsh Liberalism, the Labour campaign had little in common with the general election campaigns of 1910. The prominent speakers for John were all Labour Party figures, including Jimmy Thomas, J. R. Clynes, and Frank Hodges.[28] John stressed the failure of the Coalition government to fulfil its 1918 election promises and the repulsive nature of profiteering, whilst the Rhondda No.1 district claimed that every vote against Labour was a vote for the smashing of trade unionism. John's election address included the slogan 'For or against our Federation' alongside 'beer or progress', and the executive committee of the SWMF put out a circular asking voters to show John 'the same degree of loyalty in the political field' as in the industrial.[29] Finally, Mabon appealed to 'all the progressive forces in West Rhondda to spare no effort to secure his [John's] return by a record majority . . .', and 'to all my friends of the old Labour and Liberal Association . . . [to be] as loyal to him now as you have been to me . . . hold steadfastly the fort we won for Labour five and thirty years ago this very month of December.'[30] Mabon might have, in his dotage, overlooked the fact that many of his friends from the RLLA had opposed him in 1885; but his remembrance of that success is striking. Rhondda's second generation of parliamentary leadership, in Watts Morgan and John, had now come to the fore. Continuities with the moderate style of Mabon, and particularly with his ability to be accepted by a constituency wider than that of the miners alone, were obvious; but neither of the two new MPs relied on Rhondda's middle class or upon the RLLA: the SWMF and the Labour Party provided them with their strength, and their community was essentially working class. The result of the by-election was as shown in Table 3.1.

Table 3.1. Result of the 1920 Parliamentary Election in Rhondda West[31]

William John	Labour	14,035	(58.5%)
Gwilym Rowlands	Conservative	9,959	(41.5%)
Majority		4,076	
Total votes cast		23,994	
Total electorate		34,203	(turnout 70.2%)

Although this was not as emphatic as Mabon's victories in 1900 and in 1910, John had won comfortably. With two relatively young sitting MPs, the Labour Party's parliamentary future appeared more than secure.[32] That this was the case was made evident by the general elections of 1922, 1923 and 1924, at each of which Rhondda returned its two Labour MPs, contested for the first two elections, but uncontested in 1924.

The closest result was that of Rhondda East in 1922, when the National Liberal Frederick William Heale, managing director of a firm of London accountants, put up a brave fight against Watts Morgan, the latter having to mount a campaign for the first time. But Watts Morgan romped home the following year, remarking of his opponent that 'the Orchard did not appear to bear much fruit'. Labour's campaigns were much the same upon each occasion. The candidates were endorsed without hesitation, each presented as 'The Labour and Rhondda Miners' Federation Candidate', and their personal records of service to the union (and in Watts Morgan's case, to the County Council and in the Great War) were mentioned. Watts Morgan had a handbill for 1923 that termed him 'Trusted, Tried, Faithful and True'.[33] In terms of policies the candidates pursued their own favourite themes: Watts Morgan stressed the failure of reconstruction, John played on the link between the Labour Party and Welsh radical traditions of nationality, land reform, and Noncon-formity. At root, both candidates emphasized the opposition between labour and capital, and the importance of returning men with knowledge of coalmining. At neither election was it considered necessary to draft in 'big names' from the Labour movement nationally, both seats being looked upon as unshakeable strongholds.

As for the opposition, this was poorly co-ordinated, with the

Table 3.2. Result of the 1922 Parliamentary Elections[34]

	RHONDDA EAST		
David Watts Morgan	Labour	17,146	(55.0%)
Frederick William Heale	National Liberal	14,025	(45.0%)
Majority		3,121	
Total votes cast		31,171	
Total electorate		38,516	(turnout 80.9%)
	RHONDDA WEST		
William John	Labour	18,001	(62.1%)
Gwilym Rowlands	Conservative	10,990	(37.9%)
Majority		7,011	
Total votes cast		28,991	
Electorate		34,632	(turnout 83.7%)

Table 3.3. Result of the 1923 Parliamentary Elections[35]

	RHONDDA EAST		
David Watts Morgan	Labour	21,338	(71.9%)
Alfred John Orchard	Conservative	8,346	(28.1%)
Majority		12,992	
Total votes cast		29,684	
Total electorate		39,802	(turnout 74.6%)
	RHONDDA WEST		
William John	Labour	18,206	(65.4%)
J. R. Jones	Liberal	9,640	(34.6%)
Majority		8,566	
Total votes cast		27,846	
Total electorate		35,462	(turnout 78.5%)

Liberals and Conservatives switching seats and candidates in consecutive elections. The Conservative Gwilym Rowlands seemed to think that he had a chance to improve upon his 1920 showing in 1922, but despite styling himself as a 'Unionist-Labour' candidate his performance declined.[36] His successor to the challenge of Rhondda West was the Liberal First World War hero J. R. Jones MC, who had even less impact. In Rhondda East, Heale's encouraging 1922 result was not followed up by local Liberals, and local hotelier and ex-Glamorgan county cricketer Alfred Orchard took over in 1923 for the

Tories, promptly dissipating Heale's base of support. Orchard was officially endorsed by the Liberals, but his advocacy of free-trade policies alienated some Tories, and no influential Liberal figure, nor the Liberal press, was prepared to speak for him. Even these rather pathetic efforts lapsed in 1924, with both Liberals and Tories murmuring about their intentions to challenge Labour, but failing to come up with any candidates, the Liberals giving as an excuse their 'lack of organization'.[37] Perhaps against these solid Labour candidates opposition seemed futile. Liberal and Tory candidates alike might rail at 'Socialism, Bolshevism and the Red Flag', 'the arming of the proletariat', 'the preaching of sedition', and 'the spirit of Communism that was coursing through the valley', but it served them little, and the failure to produce contests in 1924 when Labour nationally was, if not in retreat, at least on the defensive, was significant.[38]

The assertion of local control

Rhondda Labour . . . has in its greedy strides for power nearly brought about the total elimination of our practical men from its local council.
Rhondda Leader, 27 March 1920

Returning two MPs, admirable though it might be, was hardly seen as the climax of the Rhondda Labour movement's electoral efforts. Of equal significance to party activists was the attainment of control in local government, particularly on the RUDC, but also on the GCC and PBG. Looking at all three bodies together, the Liberal dominance of 1910, when they had returned over 60 per cent of Rhondda representatives, was only slightly weakened by 1913 (down to 54 per cent), and it was not until 1919 that their majority hold was removed. However, when the ousting of the Liberals came it was brutal, with Labour taking as firm a grip on public representation as the Liberals had earlier possessed, with an average of around 60 per cent of all representatives. The Liberal position faded still further by the end of the 1920s, whilst Rhondda Conservatism, although not insignificant in 1913, only retained a toe-hold after the First World War. Both Liberals and Tories were superseded by the category of Independents, but these last never seriously threatened Labour's Rhondda-wide hegemony (Appendix Tables 1–2).

Labour's advance was most marked and rapid on the RUDC, where Labour was equal in strength with the Liberals by 1912, and the largest single party by 1915. Emphatic control was gained in 1919, support peaked in 1920, with Labour returning two-thirds of the council, and, although in the mid-1920s Labour was unable to maintain an absolute majority on the council, the handful of Independent Labour councillors worked with the Labour Group on most issues, enabling it to combat a minor resurgence amongst Conservative and Independent representatives. The Liberals remained on a plateau from 1921 to 1925 within the context of long-term decline, and 1926 saw a return to unqualified Labour domination (Appendix Tables 5–6). On the Glamorgan County Council, Labour took the majority of Rhondda seats in 1919 and did not relinquish that majority, the whole County simultaneously going over to Labour (Appendix Table 4). As for the Pontypridd Board of Guardians (PBG), Labour dominated the ranks of Rhondda representatives after the First World War, but had to contend with a substantial minority of Independents who received considerable support from others within the Poor Law area (Appendix Tables 7–8).

In occupational terms, the rise of Labour is paralleled, hardly surprisingly, by the rise of the working-class representative, overwhelmingly from the coal industry (Appendix Tables 3, 9–11). There are far fewer ministers, farmers and colliery managers and associated staff to be found in representative office, with tradesmen and professionals constituting the bulk of middle-class representatives. So dominated by miners was the Rhondda Urban District Council by 1921 that there was press comment that it had become a stereotyped 'miners' council', with detrimental consequences for its vision and representative nature.[39]

Analysis of the political complexion of competition for local government office reveals a significant transformation from a political society before 1910 in which inter-Liberal competition was frequent, to one after 1910 in which competition was predominantly between Labour and those to its political right (Appendix Tables 12–14). In contrast to the glorious free-for-all of Liberal Rhondda, Labour exercised considerable discipline and organization over its activists, and left-wing conflict was, in electoral terms, rare during these years. Labour's domination seems to have had a sobering impact upon the other parties, for there was very little duplication of 'anti-Labour' forces at local as well as at parliamentary level.

The domination of Rhondda politics by the Labour Party during the period 1910–27 is thus not in doubt. Behind the statistics, however, lie the events: the petty chronology of advance and retreat, the squabbles over candidates and the occasionally vibrant electoral rhetoric. For the majority of Rhondda people, and for many party and trade-union activists, this was the tangible history of the growth of Labour politics. An investigation of that history reveals the themes of class loyalty and occupational solidarity rooted in the years before 1910, blending with a new vision of a socialist future.

The dramatic events of Tonypandy 1910 had an immediate impact upon local politics. An RUDC by-election in Mid-Rhondda, held as the broken glass of the riots was being swept up, afforded local voters the opportunity to record their disaffection in more sedate ways. In normal circumstances it might have been thought that the seat was safe for the forthcoming Liberal candidate Tom John, who also happened to edit the most successful of the local papers, the *Rhondda Leader*. But, amidst the current 'social fracture', with the *Rhondda Leader* exhibiting hostility to the strikers, Cambrian Colliery checkweigher, ILPer and eisteddfodwr Evan Joshua Roderick swept home by 1,143 votes to 702, and Labour possessed a full third of the seats on the RUDC.[40]

Ambitions to make further advances in 1911 were dealt a severe blow, however, by a railway accident at Hopkinstown on 23 January, in which three sitting Labour District Councillors died. William Herbert Morgan, Tom Harries and Tom George were all members of the Federation executive committee and were on their way to one of its meetings. Will John, Cambrian Combine committee secretary Mark Harcombe, and Naval lodge secretary Tom Smith were also in the train, but were travelling in a different compartment and escaped injury. Mabon had intended to accompany his colleagues, but had changed his plans and travelled the previous day. The loss to the Labour movement, in Rhondda and in the wider coalfield, was considerable nevertheless, as Morgan in particular was considered 'one of the leading young men of the Federation'. Although other, more radical leaders were to emerge within the Federation, the sudden removal of three sitting Labour representatives not only placed a considerable burden on the local movement which now had to try and fill the resultant vacancies, but also deprived it of an equal number of potential candidates for local office who might otherwise have tried their luck against Liberal or Conservative opposition. It is reasonable to suggest that, had Morgan, Harries and George survived, Labour might well have been in a position of control on the RUDC by 1912.[41]

As it was, the years before the First World War saw Labour make further efforts to improve their standing on this body, and by 1914 they held fourteen of the thirty-three seats. Although progress was not evenly spread across the two valleys, and although veteran Labour men occasionally retired, leaving vacancies to be filled and elections to be won simply to maintain Labour's standing on the RUDC, the fact was that Labour had built up a position of considerable strength on the District Council, was proving that it could be elected and re-elected, and was gradually moving into a position of absolute control.

Labour's campaigning trademark was the organization of concerted Rhondda-wide campaigns, with its notables speaking at a series of meetings in the contested wards. Policy statements and electoral promises varied to a degree from candidate to candidate and from area to area, but encompassed general themes of loyalty, to class and to the Federation. A circular stressing precisely this quality was produced for the November 1910 by-election, stating:

> 1. That every checkweigher, committee-man, etc. in the Miners' Federation who fails to give his active support to the Labour candidature is unworthy of the confidence of his fellow-workers, and should be removed from office immediately.
> 2. That every member of the Miners' Federation who opposes the Labour candidate by silence, voice, or at the ballot box is guilty of treachery to the workers' cause – is a traitor.[42]

On top of this traditional and solid, if emotive, appeal to class was placed, after 1910, a more distinct Labour conception of the purposes of local government, laying stress upon the extension of municipal responsibilities.

The general lineaments of Labour's progress are clear, but the local patterns vary considerably. Labour's centres of strength in these years were in Treherbert (where by 1915 it held two of the three seats), Upper Rhondda Fach (two of four), and in Mid-Rhondda (seven of nine). It was at its weakest in Treorchy (no seats and no TLC either) and in Porth (one seat of four and little activity). Various reasons may be advanced in explanation of this uneven spread of success. One factor, previously apparent throughout local politics, might be the strong personal support attracted by individual non-Labour sitting councillors, such as general-store proprietor and prominent Congregationalist Thomas Thomas of Ystrad, who was able to repulse Labour challengers in 1908, 1911 and 1914. Personal characteristics remained highly pertinent to the reception of Labour candidates: when in 1913 two such individuals stood in adjacent wards, the success of Ben Davies was ascribed to his being 'a sane and moderate Labour member' whilst miner Tom Rees's failure was judged due to his being 'an extremist'.[43] Elizabeth Davies was one Labour candidate who found it impossible to overcome her identity as a woman, twice being unsuccessful in RUDC elections. She was considered to have fallen victim to male prejudice, which had weakened her support within both the electorate at large and the local Labour movement.[44]

Personal characteristics were not everything to the electorate: in 1911 the secretary of the Cambrian Combine committee, Mark Harcombe, began a long and highly influential political career by defeating the sitting Liberal Councillor and local hotelier David Charles Evans, vice-chairman of the RUDC, who, had he retained his seat, would have led the Council for the year 1911–12.[45] Labour, tapping the source of class solidarity and trade union loyalty, was adding organizational vitality to candidates with political and community profiles lower than those that had been previously accepted, and in doing so was overturning the certainties of Liberal domination.

Much was dependent upon the attitudes of the local Trades and Labour Councils and ILP branches. Mid-Rhondda TLC was particularly combative, pushing forward candidates at nearly every opportunity.[46] Treherbert and Pentre TLCs were also ambitious, although the latter struggled to find success. Porth TLC, on the other hand, had a record of apathy and of shrinking away from a fight. In 1911 it refused, not for the first time, to challenge the Liberal Cymmer colliery manager Thomas Griffiths, whilst at the same time Mardy Lodge held a pit-head ballot that voted against putting up a Labour candidate against the sitting Conservative Councillor and the colliery's manager, Henry Edward Maltby.[47] Some of the reasoning behind such restraint was financial, but there was also a lack of confidence in Labour's ability to find candidates equal to the task of challenging well-established and highly respected public figures who might also be in positions of considerable industrial power.[48] Other weakening factors were local jealousies and rivalries, as in Porth and the lower Rhondda Fach, and the absence of a Labour organization or tradition, as in Treorchy.[49] Indeed, the Treorchy Labour movement's first breakthrough in local politics, as well as its first TLC, was to be delayed until the war years. After spring 1915, elections were suspended, and when public representatives died or retired it was up to the relevant authority to co-opt a replacement. On the whole the procedure was to co-opt an individual of the same political colour as the previous representative, although when Abergorky checkweigher John Minton had been co-opted on to the RUDC following the resignation of the Liberal Councillor and Abergorky colliery manager David Rees Morgan, Treorchy had found its first Labour representative, albeit by the back door.[50]

At the end of the First World War, and immediately before the spring 1919 local-government elections, Labour returned fifteen councillors out of a total of thirty-three to the RUDC; to the GCC it returned four out of a total of seventeen representatives; and to the PBG it returned six out of a total of twenty-three representatives. The effect of the 1919 elections was dramatic: Labour advanced to twenty of thirty-three and majority control on the RUDC, and to returning eleven of seventeen GCC representatives, and twelve of twenty-three guardians. Labour had, in one fell swoop, achieved a grip on the local levers of power that was not to be removed during the inter-war years.[51]

The party certainly started the post-war period with a fierce, even monopolist, intent, fielding twenty-two out of a possible twenty-three candidates for the PBG in 1919, and not letting one seat on the RUDC go unchallenged in that year. The party's campaigning message had a dual emphasis: on the one hand the recommendation of certain policies and administrative changes, on the other the stress on service to the Labour movement and to the wider community. For the first, the Rhondda Borough Labour Party (RBLP) formulated a uniform policy for all Labour candidates, and produced an official manifesto for the RUDC entitled 'An Appeal to Working Electors', in which it promised to provide mothers' pensions for widows with children and to agitate for the shifting of the burden of rates to the coal-owners and absentee landlords. Others added the need to improve the housing situation and to provide free education and the introduction of direct labour by the RUDC to relieve unemployment.[52] The second approach was left in the hands of individual candidates themselves. One of the PBG candidates, secretary of the Maindy Lodge, stalwart of the Pentre TLC, and father to fourteen children, John Thomas Davies, gave this message:

> During the last twenty years I have taken a very active part in the Spiritual, Social and Industrial life of the Community, am conversant

and in full sympathy with the needs and aspirations of the inhabitants, and have at all times endeavoured to uplift my fellow-workers by alleviating distress and suffering in the Locality.[53]

Labour's opponents were very much on the defensive, and tried to twist the meaning of 'Labour' away from that of the Labour Party and back to the old idea of representing the working class as a whole. Thus Alfred Orchard wrote that 'Labour's just claims and demands have always had my sympathetic support and attention', whilst Gwilym Rowlands claimed 'I have strongly supported all just claims of Labour and all movements for the amelioration of the conditions of workers.' Dr William Evans Thomas's address of 1924 is even more telling than these examples of Tory double-talk. A long-standing Liberal, Thomas asserted: 'I carry no label, but as a Worker I appeal to the Workers, Ladies and Gentlemen, to again return me to the Council to look after the interest of every Resident in the Ward, irrespective of the Religious or Political views they hold.' He ended 'Vote for the man who has always acted "Labour", even though he may not brandish the label.'[54] Much of this rhetoric was meaningless, and Labour candidates could always go one better in stressing their identity as 'Workers'. Thus in 1925 James James countered some bitter attacks from his opponent by pointing out in his election address that: 'James is a collier – one of yourselves. Workingmen be true to your own class. Vote like Men for Your Own Man. Do not be misled by your enemies. What they say of him they think of you. Vote for James James – The Workers' Champion and retain the Only Labour Seat in the Ward.'[55]

Labour was not always able to finance a full range of candidates. A low rate of contested elections in 1922 was partly due to Labour's successes three years previously, and the lack of response from its opponents, who were increasingly reluctant to challenge sitting Labour representatives, but preferred to await vacancies caused by death or retirement.[56] A shortage of funds might also be a problem. LRC No.9 Ward had been experiencing financial problems from 1919 onwards, and approaching the 1920 RUDC elections it decided not to forward a candidate at all. But Tylorstown United Lodge very much desired a contest, and was prepared to accept the financial responsibility. It put up checkweigher Llewellyn Jones, who was duly elected, and later that year was recognized as an official Labour representative by LRC No.9 Ward.[57] A continuing difficulty was the relative timidity of the Labour movement in Porth. Porth was the only ward where Labour did not forward a full complement of candidates for the 1919 PBG elections; it also failed to challenge William 'Corona' Evans for the County Council seat from 1919 until his death in 1934, and it frequently shrank from contesting RUDC seats.[58]

It was precisely this lack of determination and commitment that provided space within which 'unofficial' and Independent Labour candidates could flourish. This is a particularly complicated topic, as one must distinguish between those who were essentially Conservatives or Liberals or simply Independents but who were hijacking the label of 'Labour' in an attempt to attract extra votes, and those who were generally in sympathy with the Labour Party and of a similar background to Labour Party candidates, but who had not received or sought official approval for various reasons. There were perhaps twelve of these latter, genuine Independent Labour candidates who appeared at various times during the 1920s. Many happened upon 'Independent Labour' status rather than directly seeking it. Thus checkweigher Tom Ayton Jones, elected as a guardian with the support of Mid-Rhondda TLC (of which he was secretary) in 1919, was forced to lose that support and his official status when he left the coal industry to become a telephone operator, as he was no longer a trade-unionist. Others were forced out not by circumstances but by the emergence of a political challenge, usually from the left. Gwilym Lloyd, Secretary of Hendrewen Lodge, one-time vice-president of the Rhondda Labour Party and District Councillor from 1921, was deselected in 1924 by Treherbert TLC, and compelled to defend his seat (successfully as it happened on the first occasion) as an Independent Labour candidate, against the challenge of Central Labour College product Jack 'Bolshie' Williams, the favoured son of the Fernhill Lodge, the largest and most powerful constituent organization of the TLC.[59] When in 1921 LRC No.9 Ward refused to advance an official candidate for the RUDC, no fewer than four candidates appeared, all claiming plausibly to be Independent Labour. The successful candidate was John Hughes, a long-serving stalwart of the local Labour movement, but compelled to operate throughout his eight years on the Council in this anomalous position. Only one man, butcher and association football *aficionqdo* Morgan 'Mog' Benjamin of Ynyshir, took the decision to leave the Party and stand as Independent Labour, prompted not by deselection but by disagreements with those he termed 'Communists' inside the local party.[60] Independent Labour candidates were essentially similar in their beliefs and policies to those of the Labour Party proper, and when conflicts arose between Independent Labour candidates and their left-wing challengers they were rarely products of the former's shifting political stance, but rather of the rise within the Labour Party of a combative left-wing that was seeking pretexts to challenge those it regarded as moderates or right-wingers.

Party organization

The rank and file do not understand what the Labour Party really means. When the thing is clearly explained it is surprising how the workers rally round their own class and Party.

Cornelius Gronow, *Rhondda Socialist*, 1911

Labour's mosaical advance was the predominant feature of Rhondda politics between 1910 and 1927, politics that are best seen as an unequal battle between Labour and its opponents. Much as before 1910, an organizational framework facilitated Labour's development, both at parliamentary and local levels. This framework effectively united the SWMF, the TLCs, ILP branches and the Labour Party itself in a hegemonic form as broad as the community it sought to represent, but was distinguished from that previously obtaining by the formation, albeit over many years, of an official and recognized Labour Party.

Following the affiliation of the MFGB to the Labour Party at the beginning of 1909, conferences of all Rhondda TLCs had been held to deal with issues such as the appointment of Labour magistrates and the housing question.[61] Then, in June 1910, the Cambrian Lodge, prompted by W. H. Mainwaring, called upon the Mid-Rhondda TLC to call a joint conference of all Labour organizations in Rhondda to form an LRC.[62] This was duly done, but what gave these minor moves impetus was the local character of the general election campaigns of 1910.

The SWMF executive committee had resolved in November 1909 that the Rhondda constituency should be contested by 'a Labour candidate under the auspices of the Labour Party', but there was no existing Labour Party organization in the locality to manage the campaigns, which instead were dominated by Liberal notables.[63] The attempt to field a 'genuine' Labour candidate in the December 1910 election was proof of left-wing dissatisfaction with Mabon's behaviour, political and industrial, and although the candidacy fell through for financial reasons it was stressed that there had been no withdrawal in favour of Mabon. The call instead from the four ILP and two SDP branches, 'together with unattached Socialists', was for mass abstention as a protest against the MP.[64]

Such dissatisfaction with the existing state of affairs was not confined to the socialist societies. LRC No.9 Ward passed a resolution protesting at the way in which the campaign had been conducted and suggesting that in future Rhondda's TLCs should take responsibility for its organization.[65] Similar criticisms were repeated throughout 1911. The *Rhondda Socialist* looked forward to the day when the anomaly of a 'so-called "Labour" member returned by the efforts of Liberal campaigners' would be ended, and when 'certain hybrid politicians will taste of a dish likely to somewhat disagree with their refined political palates'. ILPer David Evans ('Dai Evans, The Bomb') of Clydach Vale went further:

The last Parliamentary elections were not run on anything like satisfactory lines from a Labour point of view. The selection of candidate was not made in a democratic manner. No Trade Union other than the Miners' Federation, was consulted at all, and only the Executive Council of that body! As for the Elections he would be a keen man indeed who would detect that the candidate was a Labour nominee. Liberal literature, and photographs of the candidates issued from the Liberal headquarters and adorned by the names of the Welsh National Liberal leaders of the past, including several lords. Such was the stuff offered on behalf of the Labour candidates. And the meetings again! Liberals in the chair, Liberals as speakers, with some exceptions. The Liberal Party was referred to as our party, the Government was praised, and Mr. Lloyd George was worshipped. Labour was not be heard even on the 'second fiddles'. It only came in to pay the piper. Many of Labour's bitterest opponents were amongst the most prominent speakers – men who before and since have denounced Labour candidates at local elections and have slandered us with their lying shrieks of 'Atheism', 'Free Love', etc.. These men should not have been aided in their hollow hypocrisy and their pious pretences to be the friends of Labour.[66]

Added to the desire to avoid a repetition of such events was an awareness that Mabon was by now quite elderly, and would most likely be stepping down from Parliament within a few years. In such circumstances it was felt important for Labour to have an efficient

Party organization in place were it to stand a chance of retaining the seat.[67]

Thus, in June 1911, Mid-Rhondda TLC convened a conference to consider the formation of a Rhondda Labour Party. Two months later, officers were elected, rules and a constitution drawn up and adopted. On 31 October 1911 the Rhondda Labour Party was formally launched, and it was immediately decided to affiliate to the national Labour Party. The stated object of the Rhondda Party was 'to unite the forces of Labour in order to secure the election of Labour Representatives on all National and Local Governing Bodies'.[68]

Once the Party had been established the task was to ensure that all relevant organizations affiliated, and men such as T. I. Mardy Jones toured the area 'with the zeal of a missionary movement' speaking to mass meetings, lodge meetings and TLCs, with the purpose of educating and organizing 'the workers of the Rhondda valleys into political and industrial solidarity as the bedrock of their social salvation'.[69]

At this stage the Rhondda Labour Party had an executive of twenty members, one from each polling district, nominated by general meetings of all local Labour organizations. There was also a plan to form local committees in polling districts. Voting at conferences, the sovereign body within the local Party structure, was to be one vote per hundred members or fraction thereof of each affiliated organization, thus ensuring the predominance of miners' lodges. At this stage the relationship of the Party to the rest of the local Labour movement was left open. The priorities were to ensure maximum affiliation and the preparation of the electoral machinery required for parliamentary contests. Only then could the Party 'go on to consider its function in relation to Labour Representation on local public bodies. That is, whether it should supersede existing Trades and Labour Councils in this work, or supplement them only.'[70]

This start, on paper, was impressive: affiliations were received from a number of local organizations, and at least one local committee, or ward party as it became known, was established.[71] But, without a parliamentary election in the offing, and given the superfluity of the Party in organizing Labour's local government efforts, what with the strong SWMF scheme already in place, the Rhondda Labour Party's early vitality and ambition seems to have ebbed away. At the beginning of 1913 the 'state of organization' was thought by some 'deplorable', the blame for this being placed upon the 'cool reception'

afforded to the new organization by the Rhondda No.1 District.[72] By
the end of the year it was being argued that the Rhondda Labour
Party existed only as an Executive Committee.[73] And yet in July 1913
Mardy Jones had claimed that 'there is a Labour committee at work
in every polling district. Ask the secretary of your trade union branch
about it, or your checkweigher, or any of the Labour Councillors and
Guardians.' The most likely explanation of such seemingly
contradictory evidence is that these Labour committees were active
purely for registration purposes, but that they played no greater role
in co-ordinating the local Labour movement.[74]

The war years saw the Rhondda Labour Party EC try to co-
ordinate the work of all TLCs and local socialist societies, and hold
conferences of all Labour bodies, but it was aware that the Party had
yet to reach a position whereby it embraced all political activities of
the local Labour movement.[75] In 1917 it began to canvass the idea that
the Party would become a federation of existing TLCs. This would
formalize the *ad hoc* relationship between the Rhondda Labour Party
EC and the TLCs, remove the need to establish local committees, and
make policy more consistent throughout the area without reducing
the efficiency of the TLCs in dealing with ward matters.[76] Plans for
reorganization were drawn up, but their implementation was delayed
until the national Labour Party's new constitution had been adopted
and the outcome of constituency redistribution was known.[77] Then,
on 12 April 1918, the revamped and renamed Rhondda Borough
Labour Party (RBLP) held its inaugural meeting, at which the
delegates represented forty thousand people.[78] But again the Party
failed to take the initiative in restructuring the local Labour
movement or in sinking deep roots in the wards. This was probably
because both Rhondda constituencies went uncontested in the
'Coupon Election': contests would have galvanized the Party and the
TLCs into working out and implementing joint campaigning
arrangements – as it was, preparations were made for the necessary
co-operation, but in the event were not required.[79]

When the Rhondda West by-election came in 1920 there were
observations that the Labour Party's preparations had been hurried,
and as late as October 1922 Will John could report to the Federation's
executive that 'there was no political organization of any description
in the Rhondda East or Rhondda West Divisions'.[80] From the beginning of that year, however, the district organizers had been preparing
a reorganization scheme, a process that ended in May 1923 with the

adoption of a new constitution by a conference of the reformed Party, and the beginning of a new process of financing local government politics whereby the Rhondda No.1 District would supply the RBLP directly with the money rather than handing it over to TLCs or lodges, thus giving the RBLP greater central financial and political control. The RBLP would become the central TLC. There was a specific decision to have one organization for Rhondda, with separate formal structures for the two constituencies, rather than split into two separate parties.[81]

The year 1923 saw an orthodox Labour Party structure established in Rhondda, with its core attribute of financial control, and with its position as sovereign political body within the local Labour movement acknowledged by the SWMF. But, as has been seen, the growth of the Labour Party to a position of local hegemony had already taken place, and organizationally it had been the continuing structures of the SWMF, TLCs and ILP that had nurtured and fuelled this growth, rather than what was, from 1911 to 1923, a floating and rather powerless Rhondda Labour Party. It is important, therefore, to explain how these Labour organizations performed, and what the relationships were between them and the Rhondda Labour Party.

The SWMF continued to play a very important part in the political organization of the Rhondda Labour movement. The Labour representation scheme of the Rhondda No.1 District continued, with the district endorsing and financially supporting local representatives and candidates through the TLCs (and in the cases of Mardy and Ferndale, through those lodges) until 1923.[82] 'Political' matters were thus still discussed by the district, although certain matters would be referred to the Rhondda Labour Party.[83] By 1919, at a parliamentary level the SWMF maintained three political agents throughout the coalfield, who worked in conjunction with the Labour Party and who each had charge of a group of constituencies: for Rhondda, T. I. Mardy Jones was the man.[84]

There was obviously considerable overlap between the now long-standing political activities of the Federation and the ostensible sphere of influence and operation of the newly-formed Rhondda Labour Party. However, it is difficult to substantiate the allegation that this resulted in the district's giving the Party a 'cool reception' that put a damper on the latter's progress.[85] There is no questioning the political sympathy of the union for the Labour Party in a broad sense; but it is possible that, in the midst of the considerable industrial strife of 1911 and 1912, the attention of the Rhondda No.1 District was not upon the Rhondda Labour Party.[86] Without a general election campaign, and given the prior existence of a proven structure for succouring local government offensives, activity in this area by the Rhondda Labour Party may have been regarded as superfluous. It is difficult to argue that there was any greater fissure within the Labour movement between the Labour Party and the district. After all, many of the new Party's officials were prominent miners' leaders, whilst the Party was not seeking to trespass upon what was regarded as the district's territory in the control of local government representation. If the district could coexist with the TLCs with relative ease, as it had done for a number of years, the Rhondda Labour Party was not likely to appear particularly threatening. Moreover, there is evidence of considerable co-operation between district and Party within a few years of the latter's establishment. In July 1914 the district agreed to hold a series of meetings jointly with the Rhondda Labour Party on 'political and industrial questions'. The district continued to send delegates to the Labour Party conference, and gave financial support to the South Wales Association of Labour Members.[87] Finally, when the proposed constitutional rearrangements that took place in 1923 were mentioned, only a few lodges complained at the withdrawal of political control from the Federation, and there was no resistance recorded by the district. Perhaps Rhondda's miners recognized that their domination of the local Labour movement was hardly likely to be overturned, whether formal control lay with them, the TLCs or an RBLP executive.[88]

As for the TLCs, from 1910 up to the formation of the inclusive structure of the RBLP in 1923 their activities were extended in a number of different ways, all of which reinforced their importance within the Labour movement locally, and contributed significantly to advancing Labour's place within Rhondda's political matrix. First the range and the depth of TLC coverage were extended, with Treorchy establishing its own TLC in 1916.[89] In 1921 the Upper Rhondda Fach managed to organize its own body, albeit with little encouragement from either the Ferndale or Mardy Lodges, which preferred to keep political matters very much in their own hands.[90] As for those TLCs already in existence, they aimed to attract a wider range of trade unionists to their ranks, and did so with great success in the years leading up to the First World War. The Mid-Rhondda TLC drew in teachers, municipal employees, tailors, butchers, railwaymen, clerks, insurance collectors, the National League of the Blind and (vitally) the Amalgamated Musicians' Union (Rhondda Branch)![91] Treherbert drew in plasterers, life assurance agents, and the discharged soldiers and sailors, Porth the shop assistants, bakers, gasworkers and tramwaymen.

Such a broadening of the representative base of the TLCs extended their relevance across the community at large, something borne out by the range of topics they considered and acted upon. TLCs continued to bring many matters to the attention of individual Labour Councillors and to the RUDC as a whole, such as the housing problem, the need for maternity centres, the state of the water supply, the administration of the poor law system, the appointment of new Magistrates and so on, and provided a forum for stewardship reports by Labour representatives. As Paul O'Leary has written: 'The Trades Council was clearly an institution of central importance in the attempt to assert proletarian control over community life by the continuing process of redefining class identity.'[92]

TLCs made their greatest impact, however, during the First World War, as bodies both capable of assisting with the heavier administrative demands placed upon local authorities, and of acting as conductive mechanisms for popular discontent and protest sparked by the difficult conditions of home-front existence. Regarding the first function, TLCs were responsible, for instance, for forwarding representatives to serve on the Naval and Military War Pensions Committee established in 1915.[93] Merged with this 'official' role was their unofficial agitation over food prices. From the end of 1916 onwards there was mounting tension in the district over food shortages and rising prices, with complaints arising over the fair distribution of food, queuing, and suspicion that retailers were deliberately hoarding supplies to inflate prices. By the beginning of 1918 mass meetings and 'stop days' were being held to express discontent more vigorously, and to protest that the RUDC-established Rhondda Food Control Committee was not performing eponymously. The TLCs became involved in the agitation, not only in holding meetings and discussing grievances, but also in forming vigilance committees to take a greater active part in drawing attention to abuses and in solving problems. Treherbert TLC's Vigilance Committee put up posters in its locality advertising its role as an information-gathering and protest-coordinating body, whilst the Food Control Committee took notice of such activity and co-opted TLC activists to assist with its work.[94] Similar levels of TLC concern and involvement were found regarding rents and rates. Mid-Rhondda and Treherbert TLCs had been busy organizing meetings in protest at the raising of rents as early as October 1915, but it was not until early in 1918 that this became a 'warm' issue, vigilance committees being formed by TLCs and lodges alike, and proceeding to advise people of their rights and to survey the current situation of rent increases. In September 1918 a conference was held representing Labour and Co-operative organizations in the Rhondda, Pontypridd and Mountain Ash areas, which decided to advise tenants to pay the usual rent but to withhold payment of rent increases. One month later an agreement with the Rhondda Valley Property Owners' and Ratepayers' Association was reached which produced a scale of 'fair' payments and increases.[95]

Whilst TLCs affirmed their importance to the community and their relevance to a wide range of trade unions, they did not neglect their electioneering and propaganda roles either. Especially after the First World War TLCs held public meetings in much the same way that the ILP had done before 1914, establishing propaganda committees and running summer campaigns. At the same time they polished up their machinery for canvassing and for getting the vote out on election day, as well as standardizing the mechanisms for filtering candidates and approving them for contests.[96]

In another way TLCs were coming to adopt similar practices to Ward Labour Parties. Directly political rather than trade union organizations were afforded space on TLCs: in May 1919 the Mid-Rhondda TLC resolved to change its rules to allow all bodies capable of affiliation to the Labour Party to join it, this being followed by the arrival of the ILP and the Women's Co-operative Guild as well as the Rhondda Socialist Society (RSS).[97] The transition from a strictly Trades and Labour Council to a Ward Party identity, when it came in 1923, was therefore, not traumatic. The only significant operational change was that direct intervention in municipal and trade union affairs was much reduced, with these 'trade council' functions passing upwards to the RBLP itself.[98] Possibly the TLCs were relieved to find themselves part of an overall Labour Party structure: there is evidence that they were afflicted by long-term serious financial problems, and to change to being Ward Parties, directly funded by the RBLP, would have been a great relief.[99] Such problems were largely due to the cost of municipal elections and to the cost of maintaining public representatives: activities that, it seems, were not fully funded by the Rhondda No.1 district's grants. Treherbert TLC decided to cut down on postage by sending letters of protest only when they could be backed up by some threat![100]

One other development centred upon Rhondda's TLCs which deserves mention at this stage is that of the organization of a Rhondda-wide Council of Action in 1920. This was an attempt to co-ordinate an industrial and political body throughout the area, bringing together TLCs with socialist societies and taking the active facilitating and organizing role that the Rhondda Labour Party was not, at this time, filling. Because the Council failed to establish itself permanently, it is more interesting for the ambitions and conflicts that it reveals within the local Labour movement; but its appearance at all suggests that there was room for a more vigorous and inclusive organization working above the individual TLCs.[101]

The ILP continued to contribute to Rhondda's Labour organization in the years leading up to the First World War, although many branches flowered for a season and then disappeared, before perhaps being revitalized a year or so later.[102] The peak of ILP activity locally was 1911: thereafter both the numbers of branches and of meetings and members were all recorded as being in decline.[103] Certainly after 1918 the ILP suffered from competition with the Labour Party's new constitution, which allowed the establishment of branches of individual members and which, in the Rhondda, saw TLCs beginning to step into the propaganda role once filled by the ILP.[104]

Finally, Labour organization in the Rhondda was extended by the appearance, after 1918, of women's sections and of Women's Co-operative Guilds. Many of these were formed, and although some were short-lived, they added much in particular to Labour's strength at election times. The one woman behind much of the progress made at this time was Mrs Elizabeth Andrews, who was the Labour Party's Welsh women's organizer from 1919 onwards, and who lived at Ton Pentre. She worked to establish women's sections, and to run programmes of lectures and political education for them. She also ensured that a central women's section within the new RBLP was established.[105]

The foundation in 1923 of the reconstituted Rhondda Borough Labour Party standardized and regulated many of the organizational accommodations and *ad hoc* practices that had characterized Rhondda Labour politics since the turn of the century. As at least some of the political conflicts of surrounding and later years were influenced in their development by the organizational form of the new RBLP, it is necessary to explain briefly the principles of its operation.[106]

The decision was taken to retain the overall structure of the party as a Borough Party, covering both Rhondda West and Rhondda East constituencies, rather than split into two separate parties, for it was felt that the constituency division was artificial and that an all-Rhondda structure was more appropriate to deal with the business of local government.[107] Power was certainly held at the level of the borough, and the divisional/constituency parties (DLPs and CLPs) were largely skeleton organizations acting as transmission belts from the wards to the borough.

The RBLP, Rhondda East DLP and Rhondda West DLP operated in a similar fashion. Each had its own officers and executives, which met regularly, and were responsible to 'conferences' or general meetings which met monthly (every two months for the RBLP). Executives were composed of one representative from each ward, plus one woman (two, one for each division, in the case of the RBLP) elected by a joint meeting of women's organizations, a representative from the East Glamorgan Labour Women's Advisory Council, the secretaries of the various Labour groups on local government bodies, and the officers of the party (*ex officio*). Conferences received delegates, one from each trade union branch, ILP branch, women's organization, Co-operative society or other 'Labour and Socialist organization', each with one vote for every hundred members or fraction thereof.

As for Ward Labour Parties, these operated in essentially the same way, albeit on a smaller scale, and were held responsible for maintaining efficiently the electoral organization, securing 'adequate' Labour representation in local government, and carrying out propaganda work. They were to receive stewardship reports from their representatives, as the DLPs and RBLP were from representatives of the Labour groups and the MPs. Perhaps most significantly, the Labour Party was now placed in full control of the selection process for parliamentary and local government contests. Each affiliated organization could nominate a candidate, and the choice would be made at a 'conference' or general meeting before being endorsed by the EC of the Ward Party, DLP, CLP or RBLP. Nominees had to sign a form declaring that they would stand 'exclusively' as the official Labour Party candidate, and would 'advocate the Party's Programme and Policy during the Contest', as well as promising that if elected they would 'faithfully support the Labour Party Group on the above Body, and will adhere to the policy and decisions which that Group may from time to time agree to'.[108]

This party structure remained in place throughout the inter-war years and beyond, with only a few alterations.[109] Its operation was not the subject of heated debate or of proposals for major reform, and it had little to distinguish it from the general pattern of Labour Party organization throughout the country. The organizational variety characteristic of the pre-war years was finally superseded in 1923 by a standard party 'machine', efficient in its electoral objectives, and content to maintain Labour's position of overwhelming domination of public representation.

A Labour culture

> Class conscious we are singing,
> Class conscious now are we,
> For Labour now is digging,
> The grave of the bourgeoisie!
> > Labour League of Youth, May Day 1920[110]

Organizational strength, if not coherence, was of obvious importance in the development of Labour politics in the Rhondda. But the life of a Labour Party activist, member, sympathizer, or merely potential voter, did not always have to centre upon meetings and elections. At least for a few years, from the industrial strife of the 'Great Unrest' period into the early 1920s, the Rhondda Labour Party managed to sustain a range of social, cultural and educational activities that complemented and encouraged its hard-nosed political advance.

Some of these activities derived from or were associated with existing forms of political work. For instance, in 1911 the Clydach Vale branch of the ILP 'carried on a vigorous campaign by open-air and indoor lectures, distribution of literature, etc.', and at the same time started a male voice choir.[111] Political meetings, talks and lectures were very much in the mainstream of Labour politics, and it was possible to lend these events greater colour by turning them into debates, or perhaps by providing musical accompaniment.[112] Another tactic was to string together some lectures on a theme. Any 'outsider' who happened to visit Tonypandy on 5 May 1918 might have been attracted to the Karl Marx Centenary Celebrations, which included contributions from some of the Rhondda Labour movement's most notable intellects: co-authors of *The Miners' Next Step*, Noah Ablett and W. H. Mainwaring; teacher, Central Labour College (CLC) lecturer and author of *Help to the Study of Capital*, William G. Cove; CLC product and Mardy checkweigher, Ted Williams; Tom Morris and Noah Tromans. Had such outsiders been present a year earlier they could have taken part with the CLC classes and ILP branches in a ramble to Llanwynno, where speeches were heard from Arthur James Cook, George Dolling and Ted Williams, or joined one travelling in a different direction, as reported in the *Pioneer*:

> The Rhondda boys had a ramble last Sunday to Tonyrefail, and spent a very pleasant afternoon with the Tonyrefail and Gilfach comrades. In the evening Comrade Mainwaring delivered one of the series of lectures on the Chartist Movement, which proved, as usual, both instructive and interesting. After singing the 'Red Flag' we marched home through the rain.[113]

This blending of ordinary leisure pursuits with political education was a common tactic. Another 1918 event was an eisteddfod at the Judge's Hall, presided over by Will John and Jack Hughes (who was both Llwynypia Lodge secretary and president of the Williamstown Male Voice Choir), which included traditional musical competitions along with a prize for an essay on the subject 'Labour Policy For After The War Problems' and one for a review of Mark Starr's *A Worker Looks at History*.[114] For those activists less gifted academically, one could play rugby union or act, both pursuits available under the aegis of Jack 'Bolshie' Williams's CLC class up at Fernhill.[115] But, of all the 'extra-political' activities sponsored or spawned by Rhondda Labour politics during these years, four stand out for particular considera- tion. The first, the provision of independent working class education, is well known and well documented, and it will be presented only in outline here.[116] A second long-term development was that of Labour Clubs, whilst the others – the youth movement and the Treorchy 'mock parliament' – were early 1920s affairs, but no less interesting for that.

The origins of the workers' education movement as it developed in south Wales, lie firmly in the Rhondda valleys. One pioneer of both independent Labour politics and working-class education was T. I. Mardy Jones, a one-time Ruskin College student who led a successful campaign in the Rhondda No.1 District to establish scholarships for miners to attend that particular seat of learning. The district sent

men such as Noah Rees and Tom Evans to Ruskin, whilst Mardy
Jones was able to obtain RUDC sponsorship for him to teach local
classes in economics.[117] In contrast, efforts to establish a WEA
presence locally were spurned by the Labour movement, and failed to
take root.[118] A great impetus was given to the cause of independent
working-class education by the events of the Ruskin College strike,
and the foundation of the Plebs League in south Wales in January
1909, leading on to the decision by the Rhondda No.1 District in
January 1910 to back the Central Labour College.[119] The latter's
reputation as a breeding-ground for syndicalists, industrial unionists
and later Communists is legendary; in Rhondda terms it confirmed
the promise of many of the district's 'young men in a hurry', and even
attracted the support of moderates like Watts Morgan. In the
coalfield its ethos permeated the Plebs League and its classes, which
were often established and taught by the returning products of the
CLC. These classes grew, despite the onset of war: five running in
1912–13, twelve running in the Rhondda No.1 District in 1917, and
eighteen supported by both Rhondda districts by the end of that year.
It was reported that over three hundred men were attending classes in
the Rhondda in 1916, and the spread of their proletarian doctrines
caused alarm amongst ruling and coal-owning circles, sufficient to
warrant recognition by the 1917 Commission on Industrial Unrest.[120]
After the war the movement entered its 'golden age', with the Labour
College itself drawing in a generation of students of great talent and
later importance. For many political and trade union activists the
independent working-class educational experience, whether sampled
locally or in London, was a formative one. And for the majority who
did not attend classes the impact of this young tradition could still be
felt in the new quality of analysis and discussion that filtered through
to the institutes and the lodges, and to the Labour Party itself.

Less intense and less directly political was the proliferation of
Labour Clubs throughout the two valleys. Conservative Clubs were a
pronounced, if ineffective, feature of pre-1914 Rhondda
Conservatism.[121] Labour Clubs began to appear in numbers before
the First World War, and by the summer of 1914 there were six. Of
course many of their activities were social, but often the inspiration
was political. The Ystrad Rhondda Labour Club, for instance, was
opened in March 1912 when the local ILP branch decided that they
needed a meeting-place that could not be denied them by hostile
Nonconformists. They bought and converted a block of five cottages,

and when the club was opened it had a library, with newspapers and journals, and held concerts, May Day galas, and classes. The club, like others, joined the appropriate TLC, and hosted political debates and lectures as well as actively canvassing for Labour candidates in local elections. They might also involve themselves in the relief of distress: providing dinners for the poor or assisting with the feeding of necessitous schoolchildren during an industrial dispute. In the summer of 1914 they all formed the Propaganda Committee of Labour and Socialist Clubs of the Rhondda, organized a series of open-air meetings and helped to register voters. The Labour and Progressive Club went further in sponsoring a candidate for the RUDC elections in 1911, against the wishes of the Mid-Rhondda TLC! On the whole the Labour Clubs were a positive addition of institutional depth and occasional colour to Rhondda Labour politics.[122]

Classes and clubs were permanent features of the Rhondda Labour movement, but there was also room for transient manifestations of cultural politics. For instance, 1920 saw the brief flowering of a Junior Labour League in Rhondda. The League had seventy-five members, and held talks on Bolshevism, on the lessons of Jack London's *White Fang* for the Labour movement, and on J. Bruce Glasier. A May Day concert was held at Ton Pentre Workmen's Hall, at which both boys and girls dressed in white with red ribbons and rosettes and mottoes proclaiming 'Workers of the World Unite' and 'The Children Are The Hope Of The World'. Various songs were sung, including 'The Red Flag' and 'Class Conscious We Are Singing'. The summer season of activities ended with a charabanc outing to Newport. Although this organization seems to have lapsed, youth activities did continue on a small scale for a few years, being substantially revived in the 1930s and again in the 1940s.[123]

Finally, at the beginning of 1924 a 'mock parliament' was established at the Sports Pavilion, Ystradfechan, Treorchy, in imitation of one running in Cardiff. It ran for over a year, and held debates on a variety of subjects ranging from 'The Capital Levy' and 'Imperial Preference' to 'The Preservation of Welsh Place-Names' and 'The Descent To Barbarism of Present-Day Young Women'. Much of its business was naturally light-hearted: cabinets and governments were formed and dissolved, with sometimes the 'Tories' and 'Communists' working together to keep 'Labour' out of office. But there was a serious side to the parliament: in the opinion of the

Glamorgan Free Press and Rhondda Leader it acted as a safety valve, a place where 'young men in a hurry' (of which Rhondda always had many) could let off 'hot air'. Analysis of its membership shows it may have served as a training-ground as well, for many future political and union activists could be found in its chambers, including one MP (Iorrie Thomas) and a number of County and District Councillors. Furthermore, the experience gained in the 'mock parliament' could be put to immediate use in local elections, as happened in 1925. Miner Roman Pritchard stood for Labour in Ward Two, and was attacked for his opinions by the local paper. Replying on his behalf the officials of RBLP No.2 Ward (also members of the 'mock parliament') pointed out that for the past two years Pritchard had been able to express these opinions in the mock parliament, 'which is open to men and women of all parties and capacities, and ideas, subjected to the test of debate'.[124]

Interesting, amusing and obviously very important to some activists though they were, it must be considered doubtful whether the range of social, educational and cultural activities discussed above constituted either an alternative culture or the politicized life-style reputedly offered by Continental socialist parties. In an area of high unionization, with the miners' lodges offering community as well as industrial leadership, the Labour Party was going to add to the breadth of social activities on offer rather than supplant or reorder them. The Labour Party was primarily an electoral organization: cultural activities were optional extras – attractive, useful, but never vital. Labour's progress, especially from 1910 into the early 1920s, was assisted by choirs, clubs, debates and rambling trips, but was not dependent upon them. Thereafter they seem to have faded: the Labour Party enjoyed a cultural renaissance in the mid-1930s, largely in response to the Communist threat, but it was the latter party that was increasingly innovative in the range of politico-recreational activities it sought to provide. Possibly, once firm control of local government had been established in the early 1920s, and the optimistic mood of industrial relations had been reversed, cultural efforts were felt to be either unnecessary or irrelevant to the major struggles ahead. Obviously the Labour Party's progress was not built simply upon superseding Liberal, middle-class leadership in the community: it involved greater organization and a fundamental stress upon class consciousness and class loyalty. And yet it did not involve a wholesale rejection of traditional mores and patterns of behaviour.[125]

For those that wanted to build an alternative culture, eventually the Communist Party was to prove an attractive home; but, once in charge, Labour was more concerned to make the existing culture its own than to demolish it, as the complicated relationship between the Labour movement and organized religion in the Rhondda indicates. Labour enjoyed an ambiguous relationship with the area's religious institutions, particularly those of a Nonconformist character. For some time the most prominent members of chapel society were hostile to Labour; but eventually that society conferred its approval upon working-class social and political leadership. At the same time, both individuals and the Labour movement in general drew considerable inspiration from religious sources.[126]

In 1885 the vast majority of Nonconformist ministers had backed F. L. Davis against Mabon, and throughout the three succeeding decades the Labour movement continued to be regarded with considerable hostility by substantial sections of the Church and of the chapel establishment. Some Nonconformist ministers were quite prepared to speak out against Labour candidates for local office, whilst others accused Labour men of atheism or of 'free love'.[127] Liberal and Tory candidates played up their own religious beliefs: in 1912 the *Rhondda Socialist* caustically suggested that the RUDC prepare a hymn- and tune-book for retiring councillors' electioneering meetings![128] Worse were the occasional expulsions of Labour Party or trade union activists from chapels for their activities and beliefs. Nonconformist hostility could, on occasions, be more noticeable than that of the Anglicans: the Nonconformists had their Liberalism to protect, after all, whereas for the Anglicans the defence of Toryism was not an issue.[129] 'Demos' of the *Rhondda Socialist* felt the need for some plain speaking when, in July 1912, he addressed 'An Open Letter to Rhondda Ministers':

> You know the conditions of the workers. You are well aware that they do not get the wages they are entitled to. Surely you understand that the Capitalist system – the exploitation of Labour by the owning class – is responsible for this? Have you denounced and exposed the system to your congregations? It is no use crying 'No politics in pulpit,' and then preach sermons on Education Bills, Disestablishment, Lloyd George Budgets, etc., for and against, as the case may be, the 'Free Churches' on the one side, and the Established Church on the other. For many years the Nonconformist churches of the Rhondda have been sending delegates to Liberal conventions and demonstrations. But when you are

asked to take up the case of the workers against the tyranny and oppression of their masters you say that you cannot interfere, that it is your work to preach 'the Gospel', as if that was something that has nothing to do with justice and human rights. In cases of a trade dispute – a strike – you are 'neutral' . . . In local elections, as a rule, you break your professed rule of neutrality, and take sides – AGAINST THE WORKERS . . . If the candidate happens to be a Socialist, you generally make the shallow and hypocritical pretence that you oppose him because of his economic creed; but if the Labour man is only a trade unionist, you are ingenious to find some excuse for appearing on his opponent's platform. The fact of the matter is, you oppose the idea of Labour representation, and you seem to regard the workers' cause with hatred and contempt . . .[130]

If there was one issue that focused the question of the attitude of Rhondda Nonconformity to Labour then it was the practice of holding political and trade-union meetings on Sundays, a day that was, after all, the only realistic time to hold most meetings, given colliery working patterns.[131] At the beginning of 1909 Glamorgan Nonconformists circularized public authorities in the county seeking to enlist their co-operation in prohibiting the holding of secular meetings, concerts and entertainments on the Sabbath, amidst a more general assault on Sunday trading. The initial response of the RUDC was that the only restriction they could enforce was to require licensed buildings to be closed on Sundays to the performance of stage plays. But, at a special meeting in December 1910, at a time of great industrial unrest, the RUDC voted sixteen to eight to close all licensed halls, including workmen's halls and institutes, for all purposes on Sundays.[132]

The reaction of the Labour movement to this development was vigorous. The Mid-Rhondda TLC called a conference of all TLCs and socialist bodies locally, which then sent a deputation to the RUDC to reverse the ban, which affected even Sunday concerts aimed at raising money for the relief of distress occasioned by the Cambrian Combine and Gelli colliery disputes. Noah Ablett put the point of the Labour movement to the Council thus: 'It is financially impossible for the Socialist Party to deliver their message except on Sundays. Chapels are not available for the purpose, and because we cannot get a hall to put our news before the people we say freedom of speech is interfered with.'[133]

But the Churches had also mobilized support, this time in favour of the ban, and they presented as many petitions to the RUDC as the various Labour organizations. In an attempt to compromise, Dr William Evans Thomas proposed that, until the end of the industrial disputes at the Cambrian and Gelli, sacred concerts on Sundays at licensed halls in aid of the distress funds be permitted; but this did not carry support from his fellow Liberals, and was defeated. The ban continued (reaffirmed in October 1911), and had a dampening effect upon the holding of Labour and socialist meetings for some considerable time.[134] Only during the war did the regulation fall into a measure of disuse. In March 1916, Evan Joshua Roderick put forward a motion to repeal the ban, but this was defeated by the Liberals. Pressure from the Labour movement continued to be applied, however, and in November 1916 the Sunday opening of licensed halls was permitted for 'emergency bonafide workmen's meetings on conditions relating to their employment'. Finally, in November 1919 the ban was fully repealed by the now dominant Labour group. Rhondda churches did not again attempt to intervene in local politics against the Labour Party.[135]

As for the more 'positive' aspects of the relationship between Labour politics and Christianity, these were both ideological and individual. Ideologically, the greatest blending between the ideals of the Labour movement and those of the Christian Church was to be found in the 'new theology' of J. R. Campbell, and there was some minor support for this in Rhondda. Eight branches of the Progressive Theology League were formed locally, but the League, facing Free Church Council opposition, was refused the use of chapels and had to resort to Unitarian meeting-places.[136] Later, the National Brotherhood Movement made an appearance and found support amongst a number of Labour leaders.[137]

More generally favoured was the idea that socialism was 'practical Christianity', a stress upon the common ideals of the Church and the Labour movement. Some Christian ministers expressed this attitude directly. The Revd William Meredith Morris BA, the Anglican minister at Clydach Vale, preached sermons on the Labour unrest, denounced landlordism and capitalism, condemned private ownership, and declared in favour of collectivism. He earned the tag 'the socialist cleric' to go alongside his fellowships of the Royal Historical Society and of the Royal Society for the Arts. Others included the Revd T. Eric Davies, who shared platforms with ILPers, and wrote a regular column for the *Rhondda Socialist*, and Labour

District Councillor, Baptist minister and ILPer the Revd James Nicholas.[138] Below the clergy there were many Labour men and women who were practising Christians, holding various positions of responsibility within local churches: lay preachers, church secretaries, deacons, stewards, Sunday school teachers. One was Labour District Councillor John Minton, deacon and lay preacher at Hermon Welsh Congregational Chapel, Treorchy. Indeed, the anti-socialist vigilante W. F. Phillips accused the Rhondda Labour Party of blatant hypocrisy in its selection of candidates for local government elections:

> In several Wards in the Rhondda, the Socialists have taken care to select men who are members of churches and actively engaged in religious work. The object of that is to secure the votes of church members who will not vote for men who are Socialists and outside the churches. In plain language, this is simply a Socialist dodge . . . every vote for a nominee of the Trades and Labour Councils is a vote in favour of the desecration of the Sabbath.[139]

Religious motivation did not, however, lead to the fruition of ideas for the establishment of a Labour church, possibly because the opposition of the chapels to Labour was neither one-sided nor everlasting. Mid-Rhondda Free Church Council, advocate of the old theology rather than the new though it might be, and opponent of Sunday opening of halls, nevertheless was chaired in the 1920s by the 'firebrand' Owen Buckley, chairman of the Llwynypia Lodge, and had been prepared in 1909 to nominate lay preacher and Labour candidate Mark Harcombe for the RUDC. Local churches were also happy to help assemble petitions for the reduction of the sentences upon Will John and John Hopla in 1912. As Labour assumed a position of leadership throughout the community it advanced its standing within organized religion, and many of its leaders spoke regularly from the pulpit, either as lay preachers or simply as guests.[140]

But no single denomination dominated Labour ranks: indeed it must be noted that many Labour activists had no recorded religious affiliation, a characteristic that seemed to become more prevalent in the 1930s and after. In religion, as in society more generally, Labour, from a position of subordination, progressed neither to one of wholesale acceptance of existing social patterns nor to one of total rejectionism with the concomitant forging of an inclusive 'alternative culture'. Labour's development, rather, straddled both positions and overlapped the boundary between consensual and oppositional behaviour.

Conclusion

The working class of mid-Rhondda in 1910 did not, could not, own its own self as yet, but it was, as it demonstrated through industrial struggle and social crisis, its own self. And with this self-knowledge new definitions of community could come.

David Smith, 1980[141]

Labour took political power in Rhondda between 1910 and the early 1920s, backed by strong organization and in the context of the literal shattering of its opponents' world: locally in 1910, and internationally from 1914. The First World War provided Labour with further occasion to demonstrate its validity as an instrument of political representation and social change, and the Party found its electoral efforts complemented by a cultural dimension that, although not all-inclusive or standing in total opposition to existing society, nevertheless offered variety and enlightenment in the service of the Labour cause. Labour, engaged in the process of redefining its community, did so in a way that removed the centrality of organized religion whilst continuing to draw some support and inspiration from its ethos. At the same time, the Gladstonian Liberalism that had provided ideological inspiration for many Labour activists wilted, as it was outstripped by political reality and subjected to unrelenting challenges from competing doctrines of the left. By the 1920s, with the odd exception, Labour activists saw themselves as socialists, although there remained much disagreement over the content of that socialism. The Labourist appeal to class identity remained at the heart of Labour's relationship with its constituency, but it found in its relationship with socialism a harmony that had frequently been absent in its earlier Lib-Lab incarnation.

The redefinition of the Rhondda community that legitimated Labour's replacement of the Liberals commands an attention that spans the rest of this work. Labour might dominate, it might accede to local political power, but the meaning of that power, the purpose of holding it, the vision of the society to be sought after – these were yet unresolved questions. Subsequently, differing definitions of community were to emerge, with divergent political strategies springing from them. The Rhondda Labour movement, externally so secure, was to experience an internal crisis that was to tear it in half, and lead to the resuscitation of two-party politics in the area from the late 1920s, as the Communist Party challenged Labour for the leadership of this community.

4

Labour in crisis, 1910–1927

Introduction

Any kind of Labourism that doesn't contain Socialism, or any kind of Labourite who is not a Socialist, is much like a nut without a kernel.

Rhondda Socialist, 12 April 1913

From 1885 onwards Rhondda's working class possessed an ideological perspective distinct from that of the area's middle class, despite their both sharing a commitment to political Liberalism. This 'Labourism', though often subterranean and unsophisticated, informed both opponents and proponents of affiliation to the Labour Representation Committee (LRC), and provided much common ground in their striving for first political representation and then political power. With Labour making rapid strides in local politics by the end of the 1900s and with the question of the miners' affiliation to the Labour Party settled in 1908, any tension that had existed between Lib-Labs and socialists as separate political groups in the Rhondda valleys eased. This was demonstrated not only by the formation of a Rhondda Labour Party, but also by the advocacy of various pragmatic goals for Labour in local government: goals that could appeal to both socialists and non-socialists within the Rhondda Labour movement. At the same time, rivalry over industrial leadership was coming to the boil: from 1910 onwards one can see not only the psychological victory of more combative industrial relations strategies over what was regarded as Mabonite timidity, but also the origins of a rejectionist political strategy. The best-known manifestation of such rejectionism was a syndicalism that, in its pure form, wished to bypass political, and particularly parliamentary-oriented, activity altogether; but this was only the tip of an ideological iceberg, and was not adhered to consistently by more than a fraction of Rhondda socialists. More significant and representative rejectionism was found in an attitude that could be fiercely critical of 'conventional'

behaviour by Labour representatives, and sought to demarcate clearly
the differences between working-class and middle-class politics.
Before full control of local administration was gained in 1919 this
rejectionism was expressed largely with aggressive gestures – gestures
that continued to be made by Labour left-wingers into the 1920s, and
by Communists thereafter. However, from the end of the First World
War the real struggle in Labour politics was over the actual
management of local administration. The pragmatic strategy was to
work the system to maximum advantage, but to recognize the limits
of power (particularly the financial limits), the coercive mechanisms
open to a hostile central government, and the responsibilities that the
Labour movement had to its constituents. The rejectionist strategy
was far less tolerant of constraints upon policy, and in rhetoric at
least was prepared to carry the struggle to central government and
force it to act repressively against a democratically elected body
fighting for working-class interests.

The dividing lines between these two strategies were frequently
blurred, and it should not be imagined that there were two distinct
groups of activists permanently arguing over the correct policy to be
adopted. A more accurate characterization of these strategies would
be to see them as poles around which individuals and groups might
gather over one particular issue, but whose alignment might change
over the next. By definition, the rejectionist line included pragmatic
aims such as the use of power to maximum effect: the conflict
between them arose only when such use conflicted with other aims or
forces, such as financial stability or central government directives. A
further qualification is that the circumstances within which a
rejectionist line was first adopted might alter to make the continued
adherence to such a policy no longer sensible: even hard-liners had to
be prepared to make compromises, or might, in the midst of a
particular struggle, realize that rejectionism was no longer the correct
option. The boundaries and limits of the different strategies were
therefore fluid not fixed, and cannot be taken to coincide in a
simplistic fashion with clichéd couplets such as revolutionary/
gradualist socialisms. Nevertheless, this specific, administrative
history provided one arena within which different visions of the
political future were suggested, verified or discredited, and was at the
heart of the later split in the Rhondda Labour movement that saw the
emergence of a distinct Communist Party challenge.

The outlines of a distinctly 'Labour' municipal strategy only became clear from 1910 onwards. To some extent this was because it was only from this date that the attainment of local power was a strong possibility; but the delay could also be put down to the progressive nature of the RUDC administration under the Liberals. Even the Tory *Western Mail* had to admit that 'its record is a progression of great and greater schemes in the interests of the teeming population of those world-known valleys . . .' and that it was the model of efficiency, with low rates and low borrowings. The RUDC could be praised for its educational and cemetery provision, for its 'high quality tramway system', its foresight in purchasing its own gasworks in 1898, its extensive sewerage system and its plans for extending the electricity supply.[1] In these circumstances, Labour's early municipal advance owed more to a desire to establish a working-class presence denied it by conventional Liberal political mechanisms than to major divergences in municipal manifestos.

However, the events of 1910 and after gave Labour's plans for the future a distinct edge, as it sought to advance the idea that local-government bodies should utilize more of the powers made available by central government: E. J. Roderick fought the Clydach Vale RUDC by-election of November 1910 on a platform that included the adoption of the Feeding of Necessitous School Children Act, highly relevant in the context of an extended industrial dispute.[2] And Labour's ideas were not limited to emergencies, but encompassed a housing policy that aimed to provide 'well-built, healthy and low-rented houses' in place of those jerry-built and rented at exorbitant rates; a commitment to paying municipal employees a 'living wage' and to shortening their hours; and desired to extend medical provision, particularly in the form of school inspections, and to improve the accessibility of secondary-school education. As T. I. Mardy Jones wrote:

> A number of laws very beneficial in operation for the poorer classes are allowed to be unutilized. The colliery villages could be better planned, better lighted and kept, be made more ornamental with trees; they could have more parks, libraries, gymnasiums, play-grounds, and very much else if the Council so decided. But the local Council does not so decide, because the workmen permit the Council to be manned by ratesavers; that is, persons whose concern seems to be the saving of the rates instead of using their powers for the public advantage.[3]

Labourites asserted that the progressive period of Rhondda

Liberalism had come to an end in terms both of Council administration and of social leadership.[4] The radical mantle had to be taken up by a Labour Party 'adopting a definite programme of municipal reform'.[5] Thus, in the years after 1910, the Rhondda Labour movement formed its own conception of the purpose of local government. It was not breathtakingly radical, and in many ways it represented an extension of the progressive attitudes of the Liberals towards municipal responsibilities; but it was serious and sincere in its desire to work the system to maximum advantage for the community as a whole. It was also a conception shared, in so far as it went, by the many Rhondda syndicalists and the 'hotter' sort of socialists.

Syndicalism and rejectionism

Some of the boys here think that it [the appointment of Labour Magistrates] is the only way to bring some measure of democratic administration to the Bench. Others think it the wrong policy altogether for the Labour movement to have anything to do with such a Capitalist concern as the administration of Capitalists' law . . . These views belong to those who don't believe in political action, and as the Bench is a purely political institution they fail to see what good can come of any industrial worker meddling with these out of date Capitalist concerns.

Merthyr Pioneer, 8 September 1917

The relationship between syndicalism and political action was not as straightforward as might be implied by Noah Ablett's famous cry, 'Why cross the river to fill the pail?' Whilst for some such as Ablett, Will Hay and Charlie Gibbons political action was 'futile' and irrelevant to the crucial struggle by trade unions, this approach was not typical even of leading syndicalists.[6] One man who is credited with a major part of *The Miners' Next Step* was Noah Rees: at the same time as he and his co-authors met to hammer out the final draft of the historic pamphlet, he had just begun to serve a term on the RUDC as a Labour Councillor.[7] So whilst industrial struggles took priority over political ones, the latter were not necessarily shunned on principle. The 'Programme' of *The Miners' Next Step* declared that:

. . . Political action must go on side by side with industrial action. Such measures as the Mines Bill, Workmen's Compensation Acts, proposals for nationalizing the Mines, etc., demand the presence in Parliament of men who directly represent, and are amenable to, the wishes and instructions of the workmen.[8]

As for the *Rhondda Socialist*, the 'Bomb', the aim of this publication was to work at 'consolidating the Trades Union and Socialist forces of the Rhondda, together with spreading the light of knowledge in the interest of the workers', and it was issued from August 1911 onwards under the control of a committee of Rhondda ILP branches.[9] Its editorial of 15 March 1913 is revealing for the broad range of strategies that it was prepared to embrace:

> We are out for the bottom dog. We will advocate the return to Parliament and Municipal bodies of Labour men. We will support unattached out and out socialists; we will preach Industrial Unionism, the Federation of Trade Unions. We will uphold the policy of the general strike; any means and all means if we are satisfied that we shall be doing something to uplift the down-trodden and oppressed. We know its imperfections, but we also know that Socialism is the next stage in the evolution of society, and that it will be infinitely preferable to the present state of capitalist society. But we refuse to be bound to any one policy of emancipation; we will take advantage of all the avenues which lead to freedom, and whereby we may make a sortie on the besieging camp of capitalism. We, therefore, call to our side all rebels, whether they be ILP, or BSP, or Syndicalism, or Trades Union, or Suffragist. First and last we are rebels! Rebels! Rebels! Rebels![10]

Further evidence that a blanket hostility to political action did not typify all syndicalists is provided by an analysis of the composition of the Unofficial Reform Committee's identifiable Rhondda supporters. Although these included some hostile to political action, they encompassed many more who had already participated in municipal politics, or who would do so during the next few years. One example, another possible author of *The Miners' Next Step*, was Thomas Rees Davies of Tonypandy, an ILPer, a correspondent for the 'Bomb', president of Mid-Rhondda TLC, and, for forty years from 1915, a Rhondda Urban District Councillor. When, in 1916, the Rhondda Socialist Society was recast as the Rhondda and Pontypridd Districts Socialist Society it made an explicit commitment 'to secure the return of an independent working class representation upon all legislative and administrative bodies'.[11] Rhondda syndicalism did not automatically signify a refusal to engage in political activity, as this activity could be seen as complementary, if supplementary, to the industrial struggle.

Equally, the adoption of a rejectionist strategy in local politics was not a direct trade-off from syndicalist antipathies, Labour's municipal policy being broadly accepted across the Rhondda socialist movement. Instead, before Labour attained full control of local representative institutions, rejectionism was found in attitudes and gestures aimed at targets within the scope of political and electoral activity.

These targets were united by one central question: the degree to which the leaders of the SWMF and of the Labour Party – the leaders of Rhondda's working class – should accept existing social and political practices. One example was the appointment of 'Labour' magistrates. Labour had struggled for many years to secure even minimal representation on the bench, but in the aftermath of the Tonypandy riots it had been suggested by some in authority that the appointment of more working-class JPs could have a beneficial effect upon working-class attitudes towards law and order.[12] Some moves were made in this direction, but at the same time radical elements within the Labour movement began to argue against representation, on the grounds that the magistracy was an institution opposed to the working class, was reinforcing the system of private property, and would turn Labour Magistrates into 'hirelings and watchdogs' of capitalism.[13] The issue that most clearly expressed such divisions within the Labour movement was, however, the First World War.

The majority response from the Rhondda Labour movement to the war, at least in its first years, was one of support, even enthusiasm. Prominent Labour leaders, including Mabon, and of course Dai Watts Morgan, appeared on recruiting platforms.[14] Mabon served as president and T. I. Mardy Jones as secretary of the Rhondda Parliamentary Recruiting Committee, working also to raise funds for troops and equipment.[15] In directly militaristic ways, as well as in assisting with the expanded administrative burdens of war, Labour was playing an increasingly important role in the public life of the locality. Admittedly, as the war progressed, the emphasis upon drumming up enthusiasm was replaced by a stress upon mitigating the worst effects of the hostilities and attempting to ensure that working-class families did not suffer in comparison with their social 'betters'. But throughout, the amount of active pacifism or 'revolutionary defeatism' remained dwarfed by more conventional attitudes within the Labour movement.[16] What began to produce conflict was an awareness of the increased cost of living, of the maximization of profits by colliery companies, and the resistance with which what were felt to be reasonable requests for wage increases were met. Against this background of growing war-weariness, the February Revolution in Russia and the alternatives to a 'victory or bust' attitude canvassed by the calling of the Stockholm Conference evoked greater interest and a greater sense of possibility than the scattered anti-war meetings of a few activists and, although the movement was divided over these issues, by the end of the war a substantial fraction of the Rhondda Labour movement was consistently adopting a line critical of British government policy and of those who gave it unqualified support.[17]

This attitude assisted the challenge posed by T. I. Mardy Jones to Dai Watts Morgan when the SWMF made its selection of parliamentary candidate for Rhondda East in 1918. It was precisely the qualities of patriotism and moderation that made Watts Morgan such a fine choice as a Labour candidate designed to avoid a contest with the Liberals which repelled a substantial portion of Rhondda miners. Three ballots were needed before Watts Morgan defeated Mardy Jones, winning only 52 per cent of the vote. 'Possibly his views are more imperialistic than some of his constituents like' suggested the *Rhondda Fach Gazette*.[18] The anonymous far-left commentator 'Demos' saw Watts Morgan as 'reactionary . . . both industrially and politically . . . He apparently has no conception of the economics and ethos of socialism.'[19]

As the war drew to a close, Demos went on to launch a spectacular attack upon Labour's local government performance, contrasting the recent appointment of Noah Ablett as miners' agent for the Merthyr District with:

> . . . the floundering empiricism which leads the Labour members on the Rhondda Urban District Council no-one knows whither. Many a Councillor imbued with a flaming zeal to abolish for ever the damnable conditions under which some of the inhabitants of the Rhondda live, has sacredly vowed to do 'his bit' in the attainment of such a desirable consummation. But on entering the Holy Temple of Mum a seal is set on his lips, and on entering into the Great Presence he is struck by the awful silence which all and sundry observe, and he is initiated into the great policy of 'Hush', and henceforth he sees what few others see on the portal of the Temple, in flaming letters of gold, the heaven-inspired message of 'Nothing Doing'.
>
> And so we have 'nothing doing' in health, maternity, welfare, education, food and soldiers' and sailors' allowances – nothing but the

jog-trot of official routine. The Councillor will complain that he is over-burdened with work, but there is a remedy. He is over-burdened with work, but the average Councillor, Labour and anti-Labour, has not the intelligent foresight into the realities of public administration which it is desirable that he should possess, and therefore officialdom holds sway. 'Will you walk into my parlour?' said the spider to the fly, and the innocent flies walk like lambs to the slaughter. If a Councillor finds that his public duties are burdensome what should he do? The answer is obvious: Give them up, Let somebody else try. There is a remedy. There is probably no authority in the Kingdom so inefficient, so over-ridden by officialism, than the Rhondda Urban District Council. There is no Labour group which has so sadly disappointed its supporters and so satisfactorily pleased its one-time opponents. There are one or two notable exceptions among the group which do not deserve so severe a stricture, but on the whole, viewed even from the most sympathetic viewpoint, the achievement is lacking. Therefore let us see whether it is not possible to again enthuse (if there be such a word) our elected representatives, to put forth further effort to clear away the old stagnating conventions and the secret diplomacy and the nauseating cant and the sickening humbug. Oh, for a Bolshevik, a Lenin, or a Trotsky.[20]

Given Demos's position on Rhondda's political spectrum, one has to treat these words with caution. What is interesting is that, once one strips away the glorious polemic, Demos did believe in the purpose of political action in the sphere of local government. His manifest rejectionism did not spring from an ultra-syndicalist denial of the value of political work. Demos was not alone in speaking out at this time, and it is conceivable that a combination of war-weariness with a new awareness generated by international developments, particularly in Russia, was providing a climate conducive to the circulation of far-left views.[21] This view is given added weight by Demos's last line, and one must agree that the 1918 Labour group on the RUDC did not possess one flamboyant, revolutionary personality to stand any comparison with the reputations of the Russian revolutionaries. In defence of Labour, one has to say that the RUDC was hardly the place for budding revolutionaries to pass their time, worthy though its contribution might be in the long run. And one wonders to what extent Demos's broader criticisms were fair: it is possible that convention, tradition, precedent, and the sizeable presence of Walter Nicholas all had a dampening effect upon the radicalism of individual Councillors; but Labour had yet to attain a full majority on the

RUDC, and could not be expected to have achieved a great deal, especially in the distracting and demanding circumstances of war. Overall, what is important is that there were some left-wing critics frustrated by Labour's slow progress and expecting more. Their expectations were heightened once Labour took full control of local government in 1919, and the remainder of this chapter examines the tensions and conflicts occasioned by that control through to the termination of the industrial dispute in 1926. Initially, Labour administration was marked by divisions over the teachers' strike of 1919, and over the attempt to resolve Rhondda's housing crisis with the issue of housing bonds in 1920, both of which raised the question of the degree to which Labour's public representatives were answerable to, and representative of, the wider movement. Subsequently it centred upon the political significance of the vital struggles over unemployment and the poor law.

Power: in the hands of the worker?

The Labour Movement was a movement seeking to materialize ideas through forms of social organization, ideas which would concede human rights and industrial justice to those who labour by hand and by brain. He cited William Morris – if the workers only had the intelligence to conceive, the courage to will, and power enough to compel, much that is unjust could be swept away – But people have to be consciously alive to the conditions, and desire a new social order before reconstruction can come. Transformation would be peaceful, through political power. To shout 'revolution' will not bring down the Capitalist system like blowing the trumpets at the wall of Jericho. There is no short cut to the millennium. 'We cannot go faster than those who form the vast majority of our people are prepared . . . Our work is educational and the propagation of ideals. There are abundant signs that the nemesis of the present social system has been reached. Our urgent mission is to prepare for the time when power will pass into the hands of the worker.'

Tom Morris, reported in the *Rhondda Leader*, 18 November 1920

The Rhondda teachers' strike of 1919 was concerned primarily with the level of teachers' salaries, and essentially took the form of a struggle between the Rhondda Class Teachers' Association (RCTA), which represented both certificated and uncertificated teachers, and the Education Authority of the RUDC.[22] The latter's new salary scale, announced in December 1918 after two years of negotiations, was rejected by a ballot of the teachers, and in March the following year 1,130 teachers struck for one month.[23] The dispute was resolved only with the intervention of Mabon and the Board of Education, and with the issue of a salary scale which in most respects satisfied the teachers' demands. The relevance of the dispute to the local Labour movement may be explained by the fact that although Labour did not take full control of the RUDC until April 1919, by which time the strike was over, its existing Councillors dominated the committees that had dealt with the teachers throughout the negotiations, and were largely responsible for repeatedly ignoring the claims of the RCTA.[24] This stance alienated much rank and file opinion within the Labour movement. David Evans of Ynyshir accused the RUDC of sweated labour and appalling conditions in its schools, whilst another commentator wondered whether the Labour Councillors 'have ever been workers at all'. Arthur Cook claimed to be ashamed of the Labour Councillors' actions in 'assessing the teachers' salaries at starvation rates', and pledged the support of the miners for the uncertificated teachers in particular.[25] During the dispute, RCTA public meetings tapped further support by inviting representatives of the SWMF, the National Union of Railwaymen, churches and chambers of trade to stand on their platforms whilst they sent delegates to union and TLC meetings to explain their case.[26] The teachers articulated their strongest case through the language of trade unionism: here in a mining area, it was argued, Labour Councillors were denying teachers trade union rates of pay and defending the interests not of Labour but of colliery proprietors, property owners and shopkeepers. A perceptive analysis of the situation came from 'A Labour Teacher', who argued that the Labour Councillors were allowing themselves to be hemmed in by prevailing financial orthodoxies and restraint. Commenting on the strength of resolve of the RCTA, he acknowledged that:

> The intelligent thinking young men amongst the miners, especially those who have been to the Labour colleges, and those who attend the educational classes, are giving their support ungrudgingly, even though the relics of the Victorian era, some of whom are on the Council, may be against us . . . The trouble is that there is no more difference between the Labour members and the others as there is between Tweedledum and Tweedledee. The Labour members are lacking in vision and have compromised their principles. I cannot see the difference between the colliery proprietor and the coal-miner, the brewer and the checkweigher.

The future Labour man, however, is going to be of different calibre. Having studied the classics of Labour he will have confidence in himself, and the bluff of officialdom and the unholy unction of officialdom alike will have no effect on him. The future rests with Labour. Our only hope is Labour. If we cannot have our demands conceded through Labour, our case is hopeless.[27]

Although the actions of Labour Councillors during the teachers' strike provoked considerable criticism from younger and more radical elements within the Labour movement, at this stage the full dimensions of rejectionism were not apparent in the critique of existing Labour practices: the money was there as the Board of Education demonstrated, and it was simply a case of Labour Councillors opening their eyes to the possibilities of the system. The more critical struggles came when the limits of the system were encountered, as with the housing question in 1920.

As the First World War ended, the RUDC had faced a serious housing crisis. Building activity had fallen consistently from its peak in 1909, whilst the war had retarded private building through increases in the price of materials and the scarcity of labour.[28] The situation became desperate in 1919, when building activity ground to a halt and there was a net decrease in the available housing stock. For Dai Watts Morgan, delivering his maiden speech in the House of Commons in April 1919, housing conditions were 'the chief cause of the industrial unrest. People have been herded together, and that is the reason why there is so much unrest in our district at present.'[29]

As Labour had been stressing the housing question for many years, often through the TLCs, it was only to be expected that they should be aware of the problem and hopeful of finding a remedy for it when they came to power in 1919. The major problem they faced, however, was that of finance. There was no possibility of directly funding a house-building programme from the rates, whilst the Ministry of Health and the Treasury refused to consider supplying local authorities with central government money. Two of the new Labour Councillors considered the situation impossible: Arthur Cook and Owen Buckley argued that unless central government supplied the necessary finance the RUDC ought to resign *en bloc*. As Cook said: 'If the Council cannot get the necessary reforms carried out you ought to resign. Be men!'[30] The majority of Councillors were not prepared to take such a suggestion seriously; but the only pragmatic measure open to them was to attempt to raise the money (as much as £300,000) through the launching of local municipal housing bonds, which they agreed upon in spring 1920.[31]

The adoption of this measure proved immediately controversial in Ferndale, where at the beginning of May 1920 a lodge meeting carried a motion proposed by Charlie Gibbons, instructing its representatives on the RUDC 'to oppose the system of Housing Bonds', demanding instead 'that the whole financial responsibility be placed on the profits of industry', this being the official policy of the SWMF.[32] In protest at this resolution and at being treated like 'a delegate' the lodge treasurer, one-time lodge chairman and District Councillor John Williams, resigned from the RUDC.[33] The other Ferndale Labour Councillor, miner Abel Jacob, at this time chairman of the RUDC, appealed to the lodge to renew its support for the scheme, and refused to resign. But the lodge, led by Noah Tromans, opposed Jacob and endorsed the initial stance.[34] Jacob refused to back down, speaking at meetings promoting the scheme, and so the Ferndale Lodge on 30 June withdrew his financial support.[35]

However, such drastic action was quickly proved unnecessary, at least over the housing question. Of the £300,000 the RUDC had hoped to raise, only £18,420 had been forthcoming by July, investors finding the low rates of interest and the depreciating value of the stock involved unattractive. Needing to proceed with even an attenuated building programme the RUDC attempted to raise the finance by way of loan or overdraft. But progress was slow: it was not until April 1921 that £25,000 was received from the Public Works Loan Board for the project, and this still left the RUDC needing to find nearly £45,000 in what was an increasingly difficult financial climate.[36] Labour's plans for solving Rhondda's housing crisis dissolved, and only with the full turn of the economic tide around 1924–5 did pressure on the housing market begin to lessen.[37] The Ferndale Lodge rescinded its motion discontinuing financial support for Abel Jacob in January 1921. Noah Tromans, critic of Jacob the previous year, now stated that as the Lodge's public representatives were part of the RUDC Labour Group, they might reasonably consider themselves bound by this body's decisions, which in this case had been to back housing bonds.[38]

During both the disputes outlined above, there had arisen the important question of the degree to which the actions of Labour's public representatives should be controlled by the political organizations that financed their tenure. In the teachers' dispute the

Labour Councillors had come in for considerable criticism for what was an implied breach of the unofficial code of trade-unionism, whilst with regard to housing bonds the Ferndale Lodge had felt the need to attempt to discipline its wayward Councillors. This problem asserted itself in other areas, with Porth and Pentre Trades and Labour Councils asking the RUDC, in 1920, for each affiliated organization to be supplied with copies of the Council agenda before each meeting. Moderate Labour Councillors rejected such a course of action as an attempt to 'sovietize' the District Council. James James attacked the 'Mad Mullahs' of the TLCs, declaring that he 'was not going to be a mere gramophone to any particular body; as [his] individuality had to be preserved'. In the light of such strained relations existing between TLCs and public representatives it was decided to convene a conference of all Rhondda TLCs to consider policy on this issue of control.[39]

The conference, held in September 1920, decided to establish a Council of Action to represent all workers. All existing local councils would be replaced with one for all Rhondda, which would then affiliate with those of Merthyr, Aberdare and Cardiff. Mass meetings would choose miners' representatives from the different localities, whilst other bodies would have one or two representatives also chosen at mass meetings for the valley as a whole.[40] The scheme occasioned opposition on the grounds of the preservation of local autonomy and existing institutional structures, and eventually it was decided to have a Rhondda Council of Action that would accept delegates taken from the TLCs and other organizations, which would themselves remain untouched.[41] In the event the Council of Action functioned only until the defeat of the miners in 1921, but it illuminated the problem of the movement's control of public representatives, and indicated the gap that had yet to be filled by any valley-wide political structure.[42] Its collapse accompanied the end of the 'Labour emergency', as the coal industry was returned to private ownership amidst swingeing wage cuts throughout the south Wales coalfield, and from this point the Labour movement, in local government as much as in industrial relations, was forced to fight a rearguard action. In these circumstances the ways in which striking miners and their families might be treated by local government agencies during major industrial disputes were a subject of great relevance throughout the community, and the high levels of unemployment surrounding both events ensured that this relevance was permanent and widespread.

These issues stimulated intense and bitter political debate within the Labour movement, and the struggle over the strategy to be adopted in handling the crisis exacerbated existing internal tensions to the point at which, in 1927, the local Labour Party was split in two.

For the RUDC, 1921 saw an exacerbation of its financial difficulties, as the three months' lock-out forced the authority to extend the feeding of needy schoolchildren and the supply of milk to infants, a practice that had to be prolonged beyond the termination of the industrial dispute owing to the unemployment and distress prevailing in the district.[43] In an attempt to conserve resources all Council committees were ordered to suspend new projects in May 1921, a small number of staff were made redundant, appointments were frozen and efforts were made to collect outstanding rates, whilst loans were secured both from the Council's bankers and from the Ministry of Health.[44]

In these circumstances, it was apparent that any attempt to institute measures to relieve local unemployment would have to rely upon external sources of finance.[45] The major source was the Unemployment Grants Committee (UGC), but the grants offered were small and hedged around with difficult clauses regarding the rates of pay and conditions of employment of those taken on.[46] Nevertheless a programme of public works was drawn up, largely concerned with road building and maintenance, at an estimated cost of £155,000, and, of this, work to the value of £96,000 was approved by the UGC at the end of December 1921.[47] By May 1922, over three hundred of the local unemployed were receiving work on various projects, and although this barely scratched the surface of the local unemployment problem, new schemes continued to be advanced in subsequent years.[48]

The major problem facing the RUDC remained that of financial solvency. In 1922 it was decided to establish a Special Staffing Committee (SSC) to institute economy measures, chaired by Mark Harcombe. It managed to secure a cut of 10 per cent in the pay of RUDC employees, justified on the grounds of a fall in the cost of living, and agreed with local trade unions.[49] The SSC then turned its attention to rates arrears, which had mounted since the 1921 coal dispute.[50] A bailiff was appointed and collecting procedures were tightened up, but this did not solve the problem of arrears, the causes of which were very largely beyond the RUDC's control.[51] The SSC was powerless to prevent the authority's overall financial position worsening, whilst simultaneously making few friends for the ruling Labour group amidst its working-class constituency.[52] With the economic situation continuing to deteriorate, pressure from that constituency mounted for the authority to institute an expensive programme of feeding necessitous school children.[53]

If the problems confronting the RUDC were substantial, those facing the PBG from 1918 onwards were both monumental and tragic. The dependence of large numbers of people upon outrelief was not a phenomenon confined to substantial industrial disputes: expenditure for the half-year ending in March 1920 (during which there was no major coal strike) topped £100,000 for the first time, whilst after the 1921 dispute had ended, expenditure nevertheless remained at a very high level. It had long been acknowledged by local and central authorities that such outgoings were problematic. As early as 1910 the Local Government Board Inspector covering the Pontypridd (Poor Law) Union had reported that:

> For some years, especially in industrial centres, there has been an entirely new spirit on the Boards of Guardians, the personnel of the Boards having changed, and the Labour members, who are paid for their attendances at the Board meetings by their societies, predominate on the above Boards, and they advocate a policy of more generous if less legal relief. They boldly proclaim for . . . instituting a system of relief more elastic than that based on the legal standard of destitution, and are more ready to afford relief to cases of apparent hardship . . . They overlook the great aversion with which the improvident applicants for outdoor relief regard the workhouse with its restraint and discipline, and the supposed stigma attached to it, for which reasons they will only enter it in case of absolute destitution, whereas they feel no compunction whatever about receiving outdoor relief so long as it does not interfere with their liberty.[54]

More specific, less party-political weaknesses in the administration of Pontypridd poor relief were tabulated, ranging from the inexperience and inefficiency of relieving officers, to the collection of incomplete information regarding earnings and household income. Such deficiencies were repeatedly remarked upon in later reports.[55] But the major problem was the lack of a uniform policy in handling outrelief applications. Frequently Guardians dealt with applications from persons in the parish or ward that they represented, and it could be in their electoral interests to be generous. Many Guardians also received and dealt with applications on a personal basis, rather than following the rules and turning all applications over to relieving officers.[56] The year 1919, however, saw changes in PBG administration, with the adoption of an outrelief scale across the Union, and some of the earlier criticisms of Labour members could no longer be seen as appropriate, as Labour representatives Noah Tromans and John Treharne (checkweigher at Coedcae Colliery) were in the forefront of these moves.[57]

Such reforms satisfied the PBG's inspectors, and made the level of weekly expenditure more predictable, but did not manage to keep it down. By May 1920 the scale of outdoor relief originally set in April 1919, had been forced down from ten shillings per adult and eight shillings per child, to nine shillings and sixpence per adult and seven shillings per child.[58] Such trimming could not reverse the tide, far beyond the PBG's control, and an even greater crisis ensued with the onset of the 1921 coal dispute. In the quarter ending June 1921 the PBG faced a 77 per cent increase in the cost of its outrelief compared with the equivalent quarter a year earlier.[59] In preparation for this heavy burden the PBG had cut its outrelief scales further at the beginning of April 1921, down to seven shillings and sixpence per adult and five shillings per child.[60] Again such a measure was largely futile, as the PBG still had either to obtain a loan or else start to exclude large numbers of applicants (predominantly single men) from outrelief.[61] With the PBG's bankers proving unhelpful, the Ministry of Health had to be approached for assistance, and a condition of the loan they provided was a further cut in outrelief scales, enforced in May 1921. Nevertheless the Board continued to supply outrelief to able-bodied men, supposing that it was granting outrelief by way of loan and thus continuing to side-step the spirit of the law.[62]

Once the 1921 dispute was over the PBG, like the RUDC, stood in a parlous financial state, with little prospect of substantial central government assistance. Simultaneously it had to acknowledge the necessity of returning to a state of solvency, and the general inadequacy of the level of relief it provided. Its response was to try and recover relief granted by way of loan during 1921, whilst slowly pushing the scales of relief upwards. By the late summer of 1923, adult provision, of twelve shillings and sixpence, was higher than ever before.[63] As for the outrelief granted by way of loan during the 1921 dispute, eighteen months was allowed to elapse before the Board began to force recovery of the money owed, but then, with as much as half the debt outstanding, it was felt that it was necessary to use legal channels if further resistance was encountered. The process was complex and unsatisfactory through the practical difficulties of collecting from bad and disappeared debtors, but was not without sensitivity to individual needs. Investigators ascertained the earning capacity of the debtor, then tabulated this information and placed it before a sub-committee, which decided what weekly sum would be paid. If the debtor was too poor, repayment would be adjourned or, if the breadwinner was unemployed, the debt might be written off completely. Despite these safeguards, thousands of orders for payment had to be issued within the Union area from 1923 onwards, and a major political storm accompanied the process.[64]

Loans assisted the partial recovery of the PBG, and presented an image of responsibility to the Ministry of Health, but few other benefits were forthcoming: resolutions calling for direct financial assistance from the ministry were passed and ignored, and financially the PBG remained in varying degrees of difficulty through to the beginning of the 1926 dispute. As politically significant, however, were the debates within the local Labour movement over this strategy of attempted financial probity.

Poplarism and pragmatism

Mr. Richards pointed out that there were two schools of thought in South Wales . . . One school says that we must get all we can out of society as it is today. The other says that we cannot get anything unless we destroy Capitalism . . . If we agree that we must concentrate all our activities on overthrowing capitalist society then for God's sake adopt it. If you are satisfied that you cannot do it now, then sit down and try and get the best out of it for our men. I am a Federationist said Mr. Richards, with no other ists attached. As things are today we are rent in twain because we are always intriguing against each other.
Tom Richards, reported speaking to the SWMF Conference, April 1925[65]

It is necessary to delve more deeply into the political debates and divisions surrounding the substantial local government problems of the immediate post-war period, for these not only had great significance in determining Rhondda's party politics from the mid-1920s onwards, but were also seen as having some national relevance.

In November 1921 the Relief Advisory Committee of the PBG received a deputation representing the unemployed. Tom Young of

Tonyrefail spoke on its behalf: 'Well there is a limit to the action which you as Guardians can take. I know there is a limit, and personally I don't agree with the Ratepayers being burdened with this out relief. I would rather see the Board of Guardians declare themselves bankrupt.'

Chairman Noah Tromans replied:

> This statement was made at the last meeting of our Board of Guardians, and it has been pressed on several occasions . . . on various Public Platforms in South Wales. I am one of those who believe that it will not be an advantage. Governments do not move quickly enough to save all the suffering which would be entailed. Your proposal would bring discredit upon the Representatives who were appointed for a specific purpose in unemployment.
>
> Our purpose in getting power was to relieve what you get across here, the worn out soldier of industry, also at Llwynypia [hospital] and down at the Cottage Homes with two hundred and sixty children. In the Infirmary tonight there are a considerable number of our fellows injured in the battle of life. Outside a great Army, and that was the function for which we came into existence, and your appeal is to leave these people. It is not fair to ask the men to do that. If we take South Wales as a whole, organized Labour lacks power, lacks strength. You are asking us to create revolution. I can not be a party to what you suggest. I am prepared to do all I possibly can within limits.[66]

This exchange indicates the dilemma facing Labour in its administration of local government at this time. Tom Young spoke for a version of the Poplarist approach, Noah Tromans for a more cautious pragmatism.

When discussing the options open to Rhondda Poplarites (those on the left advocating what has been termed a rejectionist strategy concerning the Poor Law) it is necessary to note the merely marginal presence of Poplarites on the PBG, which made the Rhondda situation clearly different from that obtaining in Poplar itself. From 1920 until 1922 the only Poplarite Rhondda Guardian was the Communist John Bowen of Ferndale, miner at the Ferndale colliery and one-time chairman of the Ferndale Lodge, whose only impact was to start a few shouting matches.[67] In 1925 there was an attempt to gain a Poplarite foothold, also emanating from Ward Eleven. Here there was a convention that one of the three seats available in the ward was reserved for a representative from Mardy, and two for representatives from

Ferndale. Initially in 1925 it seemed likely that tradition would be followed: with one sitting Guardian drawn from Mardy (John Morgan, an Independent, albeit one-time Labour), the convention determined that only two Labour candidates should be presented by Ferndale, and Ferndale Lodge decided to put up its two sitting candidates, Noah Tromans and Thomas Owen Evans. Mardy Lodge, however, decided to challenge John Morgan by advancing its chairman, the Communist Dai Lloyd Davies, as its candidate, against the wishes of the local Labour Party. Davies, presented himself as 'the Official Labour Candidate of the Mardy Lodge' and issued an uncompromising manifesto:

> To the charge that I am a Communist, there is but one reply. I am a Communist, and for this I do not apologize. I submit a Test. Is the following programme preferable to the empty nothingness of the Conservatives, or in any way inferior to the seductive shibboleths of other nostrum-chasing opportunists? Who, more than the Communists, fight in the interests of the Working-Class? Because I have always fought for my Class, I am a Communist, and, because I am a Communist, I shall always fight for my Class.

The programme was as follows:

> Uncompromising opposition to Repayment of Relief from locked-out Workers. For Strikes, Lock-Outs, or Unemployment through depression in Trade, consequent upon Capitalism's failure to properly administer industry, the Workers are not responsible. Again, Capitalism must feed its 'hands' as it does its horses – it is entitled to no return. For that which it gives it must previously have taken from us.

The remainder included a call for a full scale of relief; adequate provision for maintenance of widows and orphans; extra grants and supplies of milk and other foods to sick children, invalids and expectant mothers; and the reorganization of the Poor Law to place more of the burden upon the national exchequer and to cut out rating inequalities. Davies was careful not to alienate Ferndale support, calling upon electors to vote for himself along with Thomas Owen Evans and Noah Tromans, and against John Morgan, 'the Coalowners' Candidate'; but he still came bottom of the poll.[68]

Without any presence within the PBG, the left had to apply external pressure. This took the form of regular deputations, marches and petitions, and was centred upon a campaign for improved outrelief allowances (themselves based upon the official scale of the

National Unemployed Workers' Committee Movement, later the National Unemployed Workers' Movement – NUWM): eighteen shillings allowance per adult, five shillings per child, with a range of other benefits. Increasingly this was supplemented by calls for the extension of school feeding. Of course, calling for such measures was not confined to Poplarites or to the left, and supporting such calls did not necessarily mean support for the NUWM or the Communists. The RBLP, Rhondda No.1 District and the NUWM often formed a combined deputation, whilst differing on other important issues such as the repayment of loans.[69]

The distinctiveness of rejectionism was therefore not so much in the methods employed in day-to-day agitation as in the attitudes adopted towards public representatives, and in the supposed long-term objectives of the Poplarites. Although the latter were never explicitly stated in a coherent manner, opponents assumed that the general idea was to force central government to assume a much greater financial responsibility for the Poor Law, possibly by pushing the PBG into bankruptcy or by operating at such high levels of expenditure that the government would have to step in. It was also suggested that this was part of a long-term strategy to undermine capitalism and the state, a stepping-stone to revolution. But given its representative weakness Rhondda rejectionism was focused not upon what it could achieve with the instruments of local government, but rather upon the more pragmatic attitudes, policies and individuals that it opposed.

If there is one figure who personifies the pragmatic strategy followed by the vast majority of Rhondda's Labour Party public representatives in the years following the First World War, then it must be Noah Tromans. Tromans was a member of the PBG from 1908 until his retirement in 1925, sitting for Mountain Ash until 1923 and for Rhondda Ward Eleven thereafter. As, in 1919, he had been appointed wage agent and general secretary of the Ferndale Lodge his political roots were from that point on located more in Rhondda than in Cynon. Tromans served as vice-chairman of the PBG during part of 1921, and then as chairman from the latter part of that year until 1924. He played an influential part in the adoption of a consistent outrelief scale in 1919, and his voice was a powerful one in the PBG, Ferndale, the Rhondda No.1 District and the Rhondda Labour Party.[70] The history of the debates and dissension of the period 1921–5 is in many ways the personal history of Noah Tromans, who stood at their centre throughout.

Tromans gave a firm indication of his political views in a debate with Charlie Gibbons at a Ferndale Lodge meeting in 1922, which considered the question of political action, particularly regarding local government. Gibbons was against involvement, Tromans for, and although this debate is of interest largely for the differences of opinion that it displays over the question of political and parliamentary struggle, it is also of note for Tromans's justification of involvement on specific policy grounds. He believed that local authorities, under Labour control, could be used effectively 'in the interests of the Workers'. He identified the Feeding of School Children Act as one instrument used in the workers' interest during the 1921 strike. Later in the debate he pointed out that £120,000 had been spent by the PBG during the previous sixteen weeks to relieve the distress among the unemployed, and that 'there need be no real suffering during an industrial conflict as long as you have a strong body of Labour Representatives on Local Governing Bodies'.[71]

Tromans's views and actions were the focus of much heated argument over the succeeding years, as he was a motive force in the strategy adopted by the PBG during the 1921 dispute, and in the policy of attempting to reclaim payments 'by loan'. This policy immediately produced dissent very close to home. From 1923 onwards Tromans was complaining that he was the victim of organized persecution and malicious rumours, facing opposition within the Ferndale Lodge from Charlie Gibbons and John Bowen, and from Mardy the combined talents of Arthur Horner and Dai Lloyd Davies.[72] Horner argued that: 'It was about time that the Labour Guardians were called to boot, and made aware that they were representatives of the working class, and had not been sent to administer those institutions which were the expression of Capitalist Society, which we intend to exploit.'

From 1923 on, Horner and Davies pressed for an official reversal of the repayment policy. Initially this was unsuccessful: Lewis Merthyr Lodge, for instance, felt that repayments were necessary, and the Rhondda No.1 District committee voted not to oppose repayments in 1924, although it was prepared to speak out against what it perceived to be unfairness towards individuals.[73] Similarly, the Rhondda Labour Party had difficulty in composing a policy to satisfy either Poplarites or pragmatists. Rhondda East DLP managed to forward a resolution to the 1924 Labour Party Conference that desired that Poor Law authorities be forced to 'give an adequate scale of relief in all cases of distress', and would have made the reclaiming of relief illegal. But at the same time the RBLP conference voted in favour of the repayment of loans, simultaneously passing a vote of censure upon the RUDC for its policy on nursing, school feeding and clinics.[74]

In Mardy, Horner himself refused to repay relief granted by way of loan, and was prosecuted, whilst those being investigated were 'advised' by Mardy Communists not to respond to the PBG's 'means-test' style methods. This was a source of great irritation to Tromans, who condemned his opponents.[75] Reductions in the poor rates, he observed, augmented the wages of miners. Mardy 'Advisors' advising people not to make repayments would be responsible for their making court appearances: 'the Board could only grant money by way of loan, and if a person borrowed money he must accept the obligation and honourably repay the money as soon as he could'.[76]

Gradually Tromans found opposition growing. Rhondda No.1 District came round to opposing the repayment of loans and, at its meeting in February 1925, Tromans found himself on the receiving end of a motion of censure, moved by Horner, and aimed at the Labour Guardians. Tromans argued that the Labour Guardians had not defied the instructions of the district not to repay the loans, as such instructions had been merely advisory. As for the Mardy prosecutions, Tromans said he had persuaded the clerk to the PBG, William Spickett, to adjourn summons for two months, and, in response to a deputation consisting of Horner and Davies, the PBG had instigated an investigation into the ability of individuals to repay, aimed at avoiding causing undue hardship. The motion of censure was rejected. Despite this, in October 1925 the RBLP finally committed itself to a substantial part of the NUWM programme. Then, at a special conference, it demanded the raising of allowances for boots, clothing and rent, for payment to boys thrown off the Labour Exchange, and for the subsidizing from the rates of the wages of men working short-time. Although Tromans pointed out that this was impossible, the conference by a very large majority accepted it.[77]

Simultaneously Tromans faced a crisis of his authority within the Ferndale Lodge, as internal conflict came to a head over the issue of the left's support for Dai Lloyd Davies at the PBG elections, condemned both by the RBLP No.11 Ward, and by the Ferndale Lodge itself. Tromans and his colleagues sought to force the resignation of a number of left-wing committee-men and other officials over this issue, and a political storm ensued: in August 1925

Tromans was branded 'an able administrator of capitalism' for his work on the PBG by CLC product and Mardy NUWM Secretary Dan Richards, who was using the unofficial 'pit paper' *Red Dawn* to attack Tromans. Tromans's furious response was to attack Richards as 'a youth, with much book-learning and little or no experience; whose egotism prompted him to angle for the following of the Ferndale workmen'.[78] The conflict was raised in SWMF executive meetings, and an investigation was instigated by Rhondda No.1 District. Its conclusions were that the exclusion of Tromans's opponents had been 'extremely harsh', framed under a rule not initially written 'for the purpose of punishing members guilty of political irregularities'. The report recommended that the lodge reconsider the exclusion in the interests of unity.[79] Following this the left went on the attack: Ferndale CPGB secretary and lodge committee-man Frank Williams attacked Abel Jacob and the PBG for defying Lodge instructions to increase the scale of relief, claiming that 'they had betrayed the workers'. Tromans replied by saying that the RBLP had agreed to support a demand for increased relief, but other Labour representatives could not be controlled. At the conference, the non-binding decision was to try and get a new scale, but at the group meeting, only the Rhondda Labour members were favourable. Tromans said that he had been loyal but he was opposed to any increase in the scale because he believed there to be enough problems already in collecting the rates, and the new scale would have necessitated raising Rhondda rates by a third, considered to be an impossible amount. The RBLP, he felt, had been placed in this difficult situation by CPGB pressure.[80] Tromans also came to the conclusion that he was in an impossible position, and at the beginning of December 1925 resigned from his post.[81]

Meanwhile, the battles over loans had been replicated in the courts with a test case on relief granted by way of loan being taken up by the PBG, backed by other Boards of Guardians from around the country. In the spring of 1925 the PBG brought before Pontypridd County Court claims for repayment of relief against a David Jones, but the judge found for the defendant. An appeal was framed by way of proceedings against Sammy Drew, a colliery labourer of Charles Street, Porth, whose case was regarded as typical of many whose objections to repayment were that they signed no document declaring personal liability and were not led to understand that the money granted was in the form of a loan. (Drew also just happened to be a

Communist and the Rhondda secretary of the NUWM!) As there had
been no formal communication of the PBG's decision of March 1921
that relief was to be given in the form of a loan to the defendant, the
judge found against the plaintiff. Beneath this technical ruling there
may have lurked a political motive not to encourage Boards of
Guardians to grant large amounts of outrelief on loan (which
recipients might refuse to repay), such grants proving injurious to the
financial stability of the said authorities. If there was no prospect of
recovering outrelief, then the Guardians would have to be more
cautious in the amount they granted.

The case was taken to the Court of Appeal, but in June 1926 the
original decision was upheld and the PBG dropped the matter. The
national significance of the case was curtailed, however, as although it
had previously been held that a Board had a common-law right to
recover relief, the case was decided sufficiently early to give ample
warning to Boards of Guardians that if they intended to recover relief
they must make it quite clear that it was granted as a loan. This the
PBG did throughout the 1926 dispute. The major import of the
decision was to injure further the financial health of Boards of
Guardians that had thought themselves to be granting relief by way of
loan in 1921.[82]

The crisis of 1926

The serious unemployment in South Wales, largely due to exhaustion of
coal seams, provided an opportunity for driving one or two [Poor Law]
Unions to the verge of bankruptcy by the encouragement of extravagant
relief.
>   Ministry of Health, 'The Effect Upon the Poor Law System of the
>   General Strike and Coal Dispute 1926'

Before examining local government administration during 1926, the
attitude taken by central government institutions, notably the
Ministry of Health, towards the Poor Law during the General Strike
and miners' lockout needs clarification.[83] The Conservative
government and its civil servants were overwhelmingly hostile to the
miners. Consequently they were deeply suspicious of attempts by
local government bodies to ensure that miners and their families
could avoid being 'starved back to work'. The supply of what were
considered to be generous levels of outrelief, for instance, was
construed as 'a deliberate attempt to break the financial stability of

local government areas with the object of forcing the Exchequer to accept responsibility for the relief of unemployed persons generally'.[84] Accordingly, from the start the Ministry set its face against any attempt to 'finance an industrial dispute from the poor rates', but acknowledged that it was very difficult to enforce the provisions of the Merthyr Tydfil judgement, which denied outrelief to strikers but not to their families. Only where authorities sought either the Ministry's sanction to raise loans or sought loans from the Ministry directly could greater supervision be exercised, over the levels of outrelief as well as over the terms of their application. Such borrowings allowed full financial scrutiny of the efficiency of the local administration, and were the most effective means of bringing pressure to bear upon individual bodies.[85]

What the Ministry deemed sufficient and necessary for outrelief was set out in Circular 703, issued on 5 May 1926, and the Ministry took pains to point out that where the recommended scales were exceeded borrowing would be refused. The Ministry was keen to keep an eye on those local government bodies that were considered to be particularly significant because of their history, politics or size. The Pontypridd Union was the second most populous in the country. It had a history of financial difficulties; and its administrative record was far from spotless. It covered one of the most politically volatile and threatening areas of the kingdom, and so it was understandable that the Ministry should take a special interest in its affairs at this time.[86]

The Ministry was considerably aided in its efforts to control the PBG during the 1926 dispute by the precarious financial state of the Board over preceding months. In March 1926 the PBG, desperately in need of financial assistance, had applied to the Ministry for the sanction of a further overdraft. The Ministry granted this, but at the cost of imposing a cut in the outrelief scales offered by the Pontypridd Board.[87] This had occasioned a hostile reaction to the cut from many quarters of the local Labour movement, and, at a demonstration of the unemployed at Porth, speakers including Arthur Horner and Lewis Jones criticized the PBG for their 'inhuman treatment' of the poor.[88] But by this stage the *de facto* control which Noah Tromans had managed to exercise over the PBG on behalf of the Labour Party had vanished, and at the start of May 1926 there were only twenty-three Labour Guardians on the PBG compared to twenty-nine non-Labour Guardians, whilst the chairman, Ivor Thomas, was an

Independent.[89] Thus, at the beginning of the 1926 dispute, the Labour Group on the PBG was not able to defy central government instructions concerning the relief of strikers and their families, and simultaneously faced a momentous task in attempting to relieve a very large number of people at what was a very high weekly cost for the duration of the dispute.

For the first two months of the dispute, the PBG had to deal with three major issues: its handling of the relief of strikers and their families; the relief it provided to the 'permanent poor' (those receiving relief before the dispute); and the balance that it could strike, along with the RUDC, between the relief of children through necessitous feeding and the cost of such relief. With regard to strikers and their families, the PBG did not attempt in 1926, as it had done in 1921, to evade the terms of the Merthyr Tydfil judgement. No relief was given directly to males on strike, and no relief at all was thus within the reach of single men. In Circular 703 the Ministry of Health made its judgement quite clear, and the PBG conformed with it.[90] Moreover, the PBG immediately followed the Ministry's advice as to the scale of outdoor relief to be given to strikers' families: Circular 703 recommended maxima of twelve shillings for wives of strikers and four shillings for each child – the PBG simply implemented the scale of relief in existence before the dispute, of eleven shillings and sixpence for wives, all such relief to be granted by way of loan.[91] However, whilst the Ministry recommended that at least 50 per cent of such relief to wives be given in kind (to avoid the likelihood of the money's being pooled between ineligible striking husband and eligible wife), the PBG determined that all relief be given in the form of money.[92] The scales of the 'permanent poor' continued to be those implemented at the beginning of April.

More complicated were the arrangements for the feeding of children, both those of strikers and those of the 'permanent poor'. The RUDC acted swiftly to implement the feeding of the schoolchildren of strikers as the dispute began, and the PBG followed this lead by deciding that relief to all children (of strikers or 'permanent poor') should be provided in the form of meals at school, or feeding through the Maternity and Child Welfare (MCW) Committees of the District Councils.[93] The PBG predicted that if it was required to relieve adults and children together then the cost could be as much as £50,000 per week, a sum it could not bear.[94] By relieving the majority of necessitous children through the schools and

MCWs the PBG would save itself on average four shillings per child per week.[95] However, although the PBG hoped thus to divest itself of a major financial burden the RUDC did not appreciate having to shoulder this alone. Recognizing that if it should cease school feeding its costs would also end, and the PBG would have to relieve children at four shillings per week, the RUDC decided to try and come to some agreement with the PBG over the sharing of costs, whilst retaining feeding that was considered to be nourishing and more beneficial than the provision of four shillings.[96] As a result it was decided in early June that feeding (and the provision of milk) should be continued, with the PBG subsidizing such provision to the tune of two shillings per week per schoolchild (payable to the Rhondda Education Authority) and one shilling and threepence three-farthings per week per child up to eighteen months (payable to the MCW). Each child aged between eighteen months and school age would receive two shillings weekly from the PBG directly.[97]

But if relations between the PBG and RUDC were clarified by mid-June, relations between the PBG and the Ministry of Health were not. Despite the PBG's adoption of a scale for strikers' families below that recommended in Circular 703, the PBG remained in great financial difficulty. Its overdraft had risen from £30,000 at the end of March to £80,000 in May, and by the beginning of June it was necessary for the PBG to apply to the Ministry for sanction of further borrowing. The Ministry had no compunction in using this opportunity to demand that the PBG review their scale of outrelief, particularly to the permanent poor, and impose a maximum per household of thirty-two shillings weekly.[98] The Labour Group on the PBG, with a few others, resisted these suggestions. Over a quarter of those being relieved by the PBG fell into the category of 'permanent poor': families who might have been receiving outrelief for some considerable time, and who might thus be considered to be more in need of sufficient relief than strikers' families. It was felt that the PBG had done quite enough already to comply with the Ministry's 'strike-smashing' instructions, and that no more major concessions could be made. At a meeting of the PBG on 8 June, attended by a deputation from the Rhondda No.1 District, it was decided, by twenty-nine votes to twenty-seven, not to alter the scale of relief for the permanent poor, whilst permitting a reduction in the scales for strikers' families from eleven shillings and sixpence to ten shillings for the wife, from four shillings to three shillings for children between eighteen months and school age, and from six shillings to five shillings for children aged between fourteen and sixteen.[99]

The Ministry was unmoved by this show of defiance. It refused to meet a deputation from the PBG appealing for financial assistance and repeated its decision that the PBG had to reduce its relief substantially along the lines earlier suggested. With its bankers refusing any further overdraft without the sanction of the Ministry, the PBG met again, on 14 June, and this time voted twenty-nine to twenty-three to accept the Ministry's conditions.[100] With this act the resistance of the PBG to central government dictates was broken, and throughout the remainder of the dispute the PBG did largely as it was told. The comment of the Ministry at the end of the year was that 'The administration of the Guardians is not subject to serious criticism.'[101]

The burden of resistance now passed largely to the RUDC where it also was hampered by a precarious financial position. Towards the end of June it was necessary for the RUDC to obtain the Ministry's sanction for a loan of £100,000, and although the Labour majority on the RUDC was committed to the retention of school feeding during the dispute, they were eager to trim costs where possible and decided to only feed half the children of 'permanent poor' families in each week. This naturally aroused opposition from the left of the Labour Group, Communist and non-Communist.[102]

The widespread support on the left for the PBG's early June 1926 resistance collapsed once the PBG capitulated to the Ministry. Since the Labour Group did not control the PBG, and had voted against capitulation on 14 June, this was an unfortunate development, because Labour Guardians were now automatically tarred with the reactionary brush. On 7 July at Ynysangharad Park, Pontypridd, nearly five thousand people from the Pontypridd Union area demonstrated against the low relief scales. A deputation was received by the PBG, and demanded increases in the outrelief scales. A Conference of Trades Councils from East Glamorgan 'instructed' the Labour Group on the PBG to hold firm for a higher maximum scale, but all to no avail. Although the attention of most miners involved in the 1926 dispute was elsewhere at the time, divisions over outrelief and school feeding within the Labour movement were becoming greater.[103]

For the last six months of the dispute it was the RUDC that, despite its financial difficulties, did most to mitigate the hardship of the time.

Its efforts were concentrated upon school feeding and the provision of milk for infants. The arrangements for both, with the RUDC providing the service and being granted per capita sums by the PBG, have already been detailed. The political significance of these arrangements, however, was that the RUDC was able to provide services of greater value than the charges taken from outrelief provision to account for them. An estimate in May of the value of two meals per day per child for one week came to no less than three shillings and sixpence, yet the outrelief scale was only being reduced by two shillings per week. Subsequent investigations indicated that the percentage of children considered to be suffering from subnormal nutrition declined during the period of large-scale feeding, and the Rhondda's school medical officers claimed that 'the large scale feeding of school children at the schools, under the conditions obtaining during practically the whole of the period of the suspension of work in the district, was markedly to the physical advantage of the children fed'.[104]

Much the same tactic was used concerning the supply of milk to infants by the Rhondda MCW, although here the Ministry repeatedly refused requests to allow milk to be supplied without reducing outrelief to take account of this, and refused to make a grant for the supply of milk.[105] Deputations to the Ministry did obtain finance for an experimental boot-centre under the auspices of the PBG, which was granted £200 per month for the purchase of leather.[106]

Despite the RUDC's struggles to mitigate the worst effects of the dispute upon its children, when the dispute ended at the end of November 1926 the question of whether the authority could afford to continue providing large-scale feeding had to be faced, and it was this that, amidst the desolation and bitterness of the failure of the miners' strike, finally forced the rift between left and right in the Rhondda Labour Party.

At a meeting of 3 December 1926 the Central Canteen Committee (CCC) of the RUDC recommended that, given the 'general resumption of work', the provision of meals for necessitous schoolchildren be discontinued from 17 December. The decision of the RUDC, in the light of both the substantial unemployment and poverty prevalent in the valley, and the beneficial nutritional consequences of feeding, was to refer this back to the CCC for further consideration; but on 21 December this body again recommended the cessation of feeding, with effect from 30 December. The Education

Committee then adopted this recommendation by fifteen votes to four, and at a special meeting of the full Council it was passed by ten votes to five.[107] Accordingly, mass school feeding ceased, but the issue did not retreat. Once it was discovered that the PBG could not grant financial relief instead of feeding, the question returned. At a meeting of the Education Committee on 11 January, the Labour moderate Abel Jacob, seconded by the Liberal Dr William Evans Thomas, moved that meals be provided 'for those necessitous children in respect of whom no unemployment benefit or relief from the Guardians was received by the parents'. An amendment was then moved by David Evans and Dai Lloyd Davies that the authority undertake to deem necessitous all children in families where income was less than seven shillings per head plus rent. Fascinatingly, the Labour Group on the RUDC then divided: nine votes in favour of the amendment, all Labour and including Mark Harcombe, James James, Tom Smith, Tom Rees, Llewellyn Jones and Thomas Rees Davies along with known 'left-wingers' like Jack 'Bolshie' Williams, David Evans and Dai Lloyd Davies; and nine against: Labour representatives Rhys Morgan Rees, Eliza Williams, William Wells, Abel Jacob, Samuel Hedditch and John Hughes siding with Liberals Dr William Evans Thomas, John Talwrn Jones, and the Tory George Newman. With the result a tie, the Labour chairman of the committee Tom Owen had to cast his vote to decide the issue and voted against the amendment. The substantive motion of Jacob and Thomas was then passed by exactly the same margin, ten to nine. The battle moved to the Special Meeting of the full Council, where the recommendation of the Education Committee survived by ten votes to eight a motion by Dai Lloyd Davies, seconded by James James, to refer it back.[108] Considering the financial difficulties of the RUDC, and the decisions of the Board of Education and Ministry of Health to oppose any resumption of large-scale feeding, this was perhaps the prudent line; but it left the RUDC open to the Communist charge of 'starving the children'. Rhondda No.1 District petitioned the CCC for a return to large-scale feeding without success, and when the RBLP held a conference to review the situation it was first adjourned and then subject to a walkout by all but three Labour Councillors following a vote of censure upon the Labour Group for allowing the restriction of feeding.[109]

On 9 March 1927 there followed another effort to reverse the decision to stop feeding, but the motion moved by Dai Lloyd Davies and seconded by David Evans was defeated seven votes to nine at a meeting of the full council at which twenty-five Councillors plus the chairman were present. The clerk to the Council argued that if large-scale feeding were resumed then the authority would be at the mercy of its bankers and that there was every likelihood that a Government administrator would be appointed. The Rhondda Labour movement was in a state of division, chaos and paralysis, and it was following the RBLP's vote of censure that the national Labour Party moved in to purge the Communists and the disaffiliation crisis began.[110]

Conclusion

> We were threatened with supersession, and in the face of that threat we prefer to keep our poor under our own care and do what we can for them rather than hand them over to an arbitrary Commissioner from whom they could expect little humanity.
>
> West Ham Public Assistance Committee, 1932[111]

It remains to be considered whether a more aggressive stance by the PBG and the RUDC, especially during 1926, would have yielded greater rewards. The Bedwellty Board of Guardians took such a stance, its Labour majority maintaining high levels of outrelief until superseded by a commissioner appointed by the Ministry of Health.[112] But Labour did not have a majority on the PBG, and there was only a marginal Poplarite presence on the authority. So a Bedwellty-style operation was impossible. In any case, whether such a policy would have proved beneficial must be highly doubtful, as the consequences of supersession for local populations reliant upon the Guardians were drastic.[113] So rather than seeking to vilify Labour public representatives for failing somehow to turn defeat into victory, it should be recognized that they were in an impossible position, and that both the PBG and the RUDC reacted to events rather than controlled them. This was understandable: the magnitude of the social and financial crisis those bodies faced was unparalleled and, realistically, there was little they could do to mitigate its disastrous effects upon their systems of finance and administration were they to continue to provide any services at all. Trimming of scales and rules of eligibility was futile in terms of the money it saved, but unavoidable if central government financial support was to be sought. At the same time such actions alienated the more radical wing of the Labour movement. Yet such radical critics could not produce an acceptable solution of their own. They spoke about 'forcing' central government intervention, but such actions could not be relied upon to improve Poor Law services. There was little likelihood that central government would be any more generous, and the delay in transition from local authority to the man from the Ministry might also have unfortunate consequences. Finally, it was unacceptable to most non-Communist Labour representatives to consider such action, which they saw not as an act of political aggression but as tantamount to surrender. To attempt to wreck the administration of local government bodies could be considered politically suicidal. Better to stay and fight for the best deal one could obtain for one's people than to desert them in pursuit of a revolutionary chimera.

5

The left divided, 1927–1951

Prelude: Disaffiliation

In accordance with the Liverpool conference resolutions regarding the
Communist Party . . . it was RESOLVED: 'That the following parties be
disaffiliated: Rhondda Borough Labour Party; Rhondda East Labour
Party; Rhondda West Labour Party.'
National Executive Committee of the Labour Party, 23 February 1927

The deterioration of relations between the Rhondda Borough Labour
Party and the Labour Group on the RUDC led to the paralysis of the
Rhondda Labour Party, specifically over issues arising from the 1926
dispute. However, this conflict took place in the wider context of the
attempt by the Labour Party at national level to clarify its relationship
with the Communist Party of Great Britain.[1]

In 1920 the Labour Party rejected for the first but not the last time
the affiliation of the CP, a decision supplemented in 1921 by one
rejecting affiliation of CP branches to local Labour parties. Such
decisions were unambiguous and relatively simple to enforce; but
problems arose once attempts were made to restrict access to the
Labour Party by individual Communists. The 1922 Labour Party
Conference accepted the NEC recommendation that every delegate to
the party had to accept its constitution and principles, and that one
could not be a delegate if also a member of any organization having
for one of its objects the return to Parliament or any local government
authority of any candidate other than one endorsed by the Labour
Party. However, these were toothless resolutions, and the second
clause was rescinded in 1923, allowing Communists to run as official
Labour candidates should they be selected. At the same time, the
Conference decided that Communists were ineligible to join the
Labour Party as individual members. The difficulty with this
decision, however, was that a member of the CP refused admission as
an individual member of the Labour Party could nevertheless

legitimately secure election as a delegate from his or her affiliated organization and thus continue to attend Labour Party meetings. In an attempt to remove such anomalies the NEC established a sub-committee on Communist candidatures in 1924, which resulted in the NEC decision that individual Communists were permitted to have individual membership of the Labour Party and indeed to serve as delegates, but were not eligible to be Labour Party candidates. However, any clarification was short-lived as, although the 1924 Labour Party conference accepted the NEC recommendations, it also passed the resolution of the Sutton Divisional Labour Party (DLP) that prohibited any member of the Communist Party from being eligible for membership of the Labour Party.

In response, the NEC had again to establish a sub-committee to study the ramifications of these decisions, and its recommendation, endorsed by the NEC, was that the Sutton resolution be applied so that no Communist could become or remain an individual member of the Labour Party, and that trade unions should, when electing delegates to Labour Party Conferences or meetings 'refrain from nominating or electing known members of non-affiliated political parties including the Communists'. These 'interpretational resolutions' were passed at the 1925 Labour Party Conference. The NEC recognized that these decisions might well be unpopular with a number of local parties, and intimated that it would be prepared to act to enforce them, if necessary by disaffiliation.

Such powers were needed, for as many as fifty local Labour parties refused to operate the decisions of the 1925 Conference, coalescing around the Left Wing Movement established by the Greater London Left Wing Committee in January 1926. Beginning in February 1926 with the Battersea and Bethnal Green parties, by the time of the Rhondda disaffiliation no less than eighteen local parties had met the same fate, largely concentrated in London and in Glasgow.[2]

How do the RBLP and its constituency partners fit into this story? Given its history of radical left-wing opinion exemplified by the Unofficial Reform Committee (URC), Rhondda Socialist Society (RSS) and South Wales Socialist Society (SWSS), it was perhaps unsurprising that Rhondda should be the area of greatest Communist support in south Wales after 1917, although this support did not translate either immediately or unequivocally into support for the CPGB.[3] The SWSS, RSS and URC were complemented by a Workers' Suffrage Federation branch operating in Mid-Rhondda from the end of 1917 onwards, and by left-wing elements within the ILP.[4] From amidst this *mélange* of groups emerged a general sympathy for the formation of a single Communist Party, albeit one internally divided over the questions of affiliation to the Labour Party and the efficacy of parliamentary and electoral activity.[5] Divisions over such issues led to the resignations of Will Hay and David A. Davies from their positions as chairman and secretary of the South Wales URC and SWSS in June 1920, and their replacement by Arthur Horner and Charlie Gibbons. David A. Davies went on to convene a conference in Cardiff in September of all Communists opposed to affiliation to the Labour Party and to parliamentary action, which led to the formation of the Communist Party (British Section Third International), also known as the Communist Party of South Wales, which had Edgar T. Whitehead as its secretary, and which was supported by Arthur Cook and George Dolling in its early days. The URC also remained in existence as the Rhondda Workers' Committee, with Tom Thomas as its secretary.[6] But it was the CPGB that held centre field in Rhondda by the early 1920s, with nine branches established.

The strength of the CPGB can be understood best if it is not seen as a highly distinctive group within the local Labour movement. Communists at this stage were not seen as entryists, and their attitudes often overlapped with those of non-Communist Labour Party members upon such issues as necessitous feeding, Poor Law policy, and the disaffiliation crisis.[7] In the early 1920s the proliferation of Communist activity was barely a problem for the Rhondda Labour movement. Of course there were differences of opinion, but the importance of these lay in themselves and in the debates they represented, quite distinct from the formal question of an individual's membership of the CPGB. This became an issue because of developments at national level, and because it was a convenient way for moderates and right-wingers to counter opposition from the left.

Friction with NEC and Labour Party Conference decisions first arose in 1923, with the RBLP determining not to accept the 1922 conference resolution that excluded CPGB members from being delegates to the Labour Party.[8] More serious developments were the holding of an unofficial Left Wing conference in September 1923 in Rhondda, at which two hundred delegates from twenty-five Rhondda pits were present, and the decision in November 1924 by the RBLP to ignore the recommendations of the 1924 Labour Party Conference until the NEC interpretations were known.[9] Less ambiguous defiance followed: in 1925 the RBLP held a special conference that voted in favour of the affiliation of Rhondda's CPGB to the RBLP (12,090 votes to 5,668), in favour of Communists being allowed to stand as Labour candidates (11,367 votes to 4,437), and unanimously in favour of Communists being allowed to be individual members of the Labour Party. There was also a vote in favour of the affiliation of the prohibited National Unemployed Workers' Movement (NUWM) by 15,879 votes to 1,312.[10] By the beginning of 1926 the Rhondda situation was being identified as a problem by the national agent in his reports to the NEC.[11]

The margin of votes in favour of pro-CP decisions gives the lie to press suggestions that a minority of activists entrenched in key positions within the Rhondda Labour Party were thwarting the honest desires of rank-and-file members to conform with national Labour Party decisions.[12] Of course there were power struggles for key positions; but the point that many non-Communist organizations and individuals were resistant to exorcizing Communist influence in the way envisaged by Labour Conference decisions is reinforced by the opinions expressed by the moderate Oliver Harris in the SWMF newspaper, *The Colliery Worker's Magazine*. Harris considered the decisions of the 1925 Conference to be a 'serious blunder':

> A large number of local Labour parties, trades councils, etc., have refused to carry out that decision, and have declined to ban members of the Communist Party, who usually are among the most active supporters of the cause of Labour . . . The Labour Party should be broad enough to accept all schools of thought that support the policy of emancipating the workers from the grip of Capitalism. It is already tolerant enough to accept many politicians of reactionary tendencies, whose adherence to the Labour cause is merely one of expediency, and if we can accept men of that type we should have no difficulty in also accepting men like Tom Mann, Pollitt, Page Arnot and others, who have rendered yeoman service for many years to the cause of the workers . . . Rigidity of this kind is fatal to any cause, and progress can only be secured if it is fed by fresh and virile ideas engendered by various schools of thought.[13]

But, in the tense and strained circumstances of 1926 and 1927, tolerance and broad-mindedness, amongst men and women of both parties, was at a premium, and so it was that, after the motions of censure passed by the RBLP upon the Labour Councillors, the NEC acted to purge the Rhondda Party of its Communists and their supporters.

The NEC approved the disaffiliation of the Rhondda Labour Parties on 23 February 1927. Official notice of this decision was conveyed at a Porth meeting on 12 March, when RBLP Chairman Mark Harcombe declared the decisions of the Liverpool Conference to be operative, and said that in future the Party would consist only of those affiliated bodies who were prepared to subscribe to the Labour Party constitution in its entirety. The Party was to be reaffiliated, with left-wingers (those unprepared so to subscribe) excluded. The left was somewhat nonplussed by these developments: they had anticipated the wholesale resignation of officials from the Labour Party that would leave them in complete control, and had already printed and distributed leaflets for a public meeting to be held at the Judge's Hall, Trealaw the following evening, referring to 'the efforts of the Right wing to smash the Rhondda Borough Labour Party'.[14]

The reconstituted, official RBLP moved to consolidate its position, on 18 March holding a conference to endorse candidates before the municipal elections.[15] But the RBLP (Disaffiliated) retained considerable residual support at this time, with many non-Communist individuals and organizations far from automatic in their desire to toe the official line. The newly elected chairman of the RBLP (Dis.) was Dick Lewis, non-Communist ex-chairman of Rhondda West DLP, whilst George Dolling was president of the Rhondda East DLP (Dis.); and Labour Councillors Jack 'Bolshie' Williams and Mrs Eliza Williams were also numbered amongst the supporters of the renegade organization. A majority of RBLP executive members remained with the disaffiliated party, as did as many as twenty of the twenty-six affiliated miners' lodges. Known supporters of the official party until April, however, were limited to the National Union of Railwaymen, the General and Municipal Workers, three EC members and the Abergorky Lodge.[16] Quite possibly much of this division of support was owing to inertia and confusion.

With hindsight it is easy to view the disaffiliation crisis as marking a distinct parting of the ways on the left, with the splits of 1927 being hardened over the next two years as the CPGB moved into the 'Third Period' (the so-called 'Class Against Class' strategy) and into a policy of uncompromising opposition to the Labour Party. But the CPGB had not, in Spring 1927, yet ditched the Left Wing Movement, and in this national context the moves that were made over the rest of that year in Rhondda to effect a reconciliation between left and right were not wholly futile. Talks about talks began in July, and in October the two RBLPs met, delegates having been instructed to support efforts to reach an amicable settlement. Mark Harcombe and Will John suggested that the CPGB should drop its demands for affiliation in return for allowing individuals to take positions in the party and in local government, and, in 1928, Horner was mandated by the Mardy Lodge to attend a 1928 RBLP (Dis.) conference and to support a fusion of the two parties. Desire for such a move was present within other lodges, but although the spirit was willing, the flesh was weak. No restoration of unity was possible in the end, as the CPGB adopted the New Line, severing links with the Labour Party and terminating the Left Wing Movement, leaving non-Communist left-wingers and some wavering lodges with little option but to drift back to the Labour Party.[17] Therefore, in retrospect, the split can be seen as marking the beginning of a new phase in Rhondda's political history. From 1927 onwards, in local and parliamentary elections, the hegemony of the Labour Party was punctuated, if not punctured, by the challenge of the Communist Party of Great Britain.

Rhondda's political mosaic, 1927–1951

The forthcoming Parliamentary Elections will provide further proof of the SINCERITY of the Communist Party in its desire to unite the working class. We stand for the return of a Labour Government pledged to preserve peace, oppose the development of Fascism, and better the conditions of the working class.

Rhondda Vanguard, August/September 1935.

Until the disaffiliation crisis of 1927, the results of Rhondda parliamentary contests had been determined largely by the selection procedures of the Rhondda Labour Party rather than by the issues, campaigns and personalities of the candidates presented before the electorate. As long as the Labour Party remained united its Rhondda fortunes seemed guaranteed, whatever the political climate elsewhere. The splitting of the party into two marked the beginning of a new phase. Of the thirteen parliamentary elections that took place in the constituencies of Rhondda East and Rhondda West between 1929 and 1951, eight saw the appearance of Communist Party candidates. And in 1933 and in 1945 in Rhondda East, Labour's percentage margin of victory was reduced to single figures by such candidates. Indeed, in 1945 Harry Pollitt came within one thousand votes of defeating the sitting Labour MP W. H. Mainwaring. No other party, be it Liberal,

Conservative, or Plaid Cymru, was able to match the challenge that the Communists posed to Labour, and although Labour's control of parliamentary representation remained intact, and was barely troubled in the Rhondda West constituency, nevertheless it did have to take cognizance of the Communist presence.

The first opportunity for the Communist Party to throw down the gauntlet to Labour's parliamentary domination came at the 1929 general election. By this stage the split between the parties was over two years old, and unlikely to be mended in the near future given prevailing international and national conditions. Rhondda's electorate had been enlarged by the effects of the Representation of the People Act 1928, and was bound to be somewhat changed since the last time it had been given a chance to vote, six years earlier in 1923. The result in Rhondda West was largely a formality. Both Will John's opponents were barristers: R. Moelwyn Hughes, the Liberal (later Labour MP for Carmarthen, 1941–5) selected as candidate for the seat in 1927, fought the election campaign whilst on his honeymoon; Captain Wilfred A. Prichard MC had only been selected as Conservative candidate a month before polling day. The Tory in Rhondda East, J. Francis Powell (another barrister), was similarly inconsequential, and spent most of his time attacking the well-known Liberal and ex-Treorchy, Llwynypia and Ystrad scrum-half, Porth headmaster Dr R. D. Chalke. Chalke had been selected to fight the seat back in 1927 and had been very active in the area since: consequently he put up a spirited challenge to Watts Morgan, polling more votes in Rhondda East for the Liberals than any other of Labour's rivals.[18] Nevertheless, it was the candidacy there of Arthur Horner for the Communists that aroused the greatest interest during the campaign. For the first time Labour was faced by a candidate on its left, and the experience was uncomfortable.

Arthur Horner was selected as CPGB candidate in June 1928 and was given support by the Mardy, Ferndale and Tylorstown Lodges, as well as by the local NUWM. Horner conducted a vigorous and energetic campaign and hoped for as many as ten thousand Communist votes.[19] For Labour, Watts Morgan had been ill during the early months of the year, but roused himself to attend the Ferndale May Day demonstration.[20] Discovering that he was sharing the platform with Horner, Dai Lloyd Davies and Arthur Cook, Watts Morgan left the platform and heckled Horner's speech from the floor. He carried on an aggressive, anti-Communist campaign, claiming that he was 'fighting Communism with the gloves off' and that Horner was 'the emissary of the blood-stained Comintern of Russia . . . working to break down the democratic Government and Trades Union organization of this country'. He stressed that constitutional action, rather than 'bayonets, bullets and bombs' was the answer, and made inquisitive and suggestive noises about the sources of Communist finance.[21] Watts Morgan's victory, when it arrived, was no surprise, but the CPGB could be pleased that it had at least dipped its toe in the electoral waters (see Table 5.1).

Table 5.1. Result of the 1929 Parliamentary Elections

RHONDDA EAST			
David Watts Morgan	Labour	19,010	(50.2%)
R. D. Chalke	Liberal	10,269	(27.0%)
Arthur Lewis Horner	Communist	5,789	(15.2%)
J. Francis Powell	Conservative	2,901	(7.6%)
Majority		8,741	
Total votes cast		37,969	
Total electorate		44,834	(turnout 84.7%)
RHONDDA WEST			
William John	Labour	23,238	(65.1%)
R. Moelwyn Hughes	Liberal	9,247	(25.9%)
Wilfred A. Prichard	Conservative	3,210	(9.0%)
Majority		13,991	
Total votes cast		35,695	
Total electorate		41,161	(turnout 86.7%)

In 1931 the Communists decided to try their luck at both seats, and again put forward Horner in Rhondda East, with Jack Davies (founder member of Rhondda CPGB and Chairman of both the Llwynypia Lodge and the Cambrian Combine Committee) in Rhondda West. Liberals and Conservatives decided not to contest, and so the campaigns were simple Labour versus Communist affairs, focusing mainly on national issues with a fair share of 'ballot not bullet' and 'Moscow Gold' sloganizing thrown in for good measure.[22] Whilst Will John easily defeated his challenger in Rhondda West, in Rhondda East Arthur Horner made a considerable advance, particularly in the total number of votes polled.[23] It seems likely that many Liberals and Conservatives who voted in 1929 abstained in 1931, and those that did vote plumped understandably for Watts

Morgan, whilst some Labour votes may well have gone to the Communist camp. Even so, Watts Morgan's majority remained substantial (see Table 5.2).

Table 5.2. Result of the 1931 Parliamentary Elections

RHONDDA EAST			
David Watts Morgan	Labour	22,086	(68.1%)
Arthur Lewis Horner	Communist	10,359	(31.9%)
Majority		11,727	
Total votes cast		32,445	
Total electorate		44,039	(turnout 73.7%)
RHONDDA WEST			
William John	Labour	23,024	(84.3%)
John Leigh Davies	Communist	4,296	(15.7%)
Majority		18,728	
Total votes cast		27,320	
Total electorate		40,950	(turnout 66.7%)

Watts Morgan's death in February 1933, however, raised the political stakes. Maintaining the continuity of miners' representatives the Labour Party decided upon Rhondda No.1 District agent W. H. Mainwaring as its replacement; the Liberals selected collier's son William David Thomas, a District Councillor and solicitor; whilst the Tories once more abstained.[24] Labour ran an energetic campaign, emphasizing Mainwaring's Welsh credentials, and giving him the credit for the reopening of Mardy colliery.[25] The Communists brought in Tom Mann and Harry Pollitt to work for Arthur Horner, who stressed his belief in united action and in the example of the Soviet Union and argued that Labour and trade-union leaders had betrayed and surrendered the vital interests of the workers. He contended that Mardy colliery's reopening had been a well-timed electoral gesture by the colliery company, and that the only reason people were prepared to vote for Mainwaring was to get rid of him as district agent![26] Mainwaring responded by labelling Horner as 'a wrecking candidate', offering 'tactics that would lead the workers to disaster'. This critique was usually rounded off by an attack upon the CP for its advocacy of violent revolution, civil war, and ultimately 'fascist dictatorship'![27] The result, when it arrived was closer than Labour had predicted, but not as close as the Communists had hoped (Table 5.3).

Table 5.3. Result of the 1933 Parliamentary Election in Rhondda East

William H. Mainwaring	Labour	14,127	(42.6%)
Arthur Lewis Horner	Communist	11,228	(33.8%)
W. D. Thomas	Liberal	7,851	(23.6%)
Majority		2,899	
Total votes cast		33,206	
Total electorate		44,311	(turnout 74.9%)

The verdict at the time was that Mainwaring's uncomfortable margin of victory was due in part to the difficulties he had faced in his role as miners' agent during some very troubled times, and to a rather unwelcoming and uncharismatic personality, thrown into sharp relief by the mercurial brilliance of Arthur Horner.[28] Retrospectively, the result is often seen as a triumph for the Communist Party, as Labour's majority was cut to under 3,000 votes. But comparing the 1933 result with that of 1931, the vote for Horner rose by only 869, and a major reason for the cut in the Labour majority must be considered the appearance in 1933 of the Liberal candidate.

Two years later, at the general election of 1935, Mainwaring faced another challenge, although this time Arthur Horner, now miners' agent in the anthracite coalfield and thus unable to flout SWMF rules forbidding a challenge by any Federation official to a Federation candidate, was replaced by Harry Pollitt. There was no challenge to Will John in Rhondda West, and the Liberals decided to abstain this time in Rhondda East.[29]

Mainwaring's campaign attacked Pollitt for supposedly masking his Communism behind beliefs characteristic of 'an extremely tame Labour man', and attacked the CPGB for the disruption their activities caused to trade unionism specifically and political organization in general.[30] Jim Griffiths, the president of the SWMF, spoke for Mainwaring, and the SWMF put out posters urging loyalty to the Federation and thus to the Labour candidate.[31] A Labour slogan of 'Socialism by ballot, not bullet' was countered by a Communist slogan of 'Rhondda needs a leader, POLLITT is the man'![32]

Pollitt's campaign was certainly eye-catching. It utilized a motor car complete with microphone, and cheekily asked that the Labour candidate be withdrawn in the interests of working-class unity.[33] The central thrust of the campaign was against non-unionism, topical because of the stay-down strikes, with other issues stressed including

Abyssinia, the means test, and unity versus the coal-owners and the national government.[34]

The CPGB reported that it had recruited one hundred and fifty new members during the campaign, apparently quadrupling their membership.[35] They did not hope to do as well as in 1933, but the result was a great disappointment to them, given Mainwaring's large majority and given recent local government successes (Table 5.4).[36]

Table 5.4. Result of the 1935 Parliamentary Election in Rhondda East

W. H. Mainwaring	Labour	22,088	(61.8%)
Harry Pollitt	Communist	13,655	(38.2%)
Majority		8,433	
Total votes cast		35,743	
Total electorate		44,243	(turnout 80.8%)

However, following the amended verdict on the 1933 result, 1935 should be reappraised as moderately successful for the CPGB. Although Mainwaring's majority rose to eight and a half thousand, the Communist total vote was increased by two and a half thousand, and the percentage vote (38.2 per cent) was the highest yet achieved. Liberal votes went to Labour, whilst some Labour voters shifted left to the Communists. The Communists might not have been able to threaten Labour's hold on Rhondda East, but they were building up one of very few large repositories of Communist support in the country.[37]

It was to be a decade before Rhondda witnessed another parliamentary contest, at the July 1945 general election. Yet again Rhondda West went uncontested, but Rhondda East was the site of the valley's closest parliamentary contest since 1885 (Table 5.5).

Table 5.5. Result of the 1945 Parliamentary Election in Rhondda East

W. H. Mainwaring	Labour	16,733	(48.4%)
Harry Pollitt	Communist	15,761	(45.5%)
James Kitchener Davies	Plaid Cymru	2,123	(6.1%)
Majority		972	
Total votes cast		34,617	
Total electorate		41,832	(turnout 82.8%)

A good part of the explanation for this extraordinary result has to be sought beyond the confines of Rhondda itself: in the general leftward shift found in the country as a whole and in the wave of popular support for the Soviet Union from 1941 onwards.[38] Initially the CP had been put in an awkward position by being forced to oppose the Second World War as an 'imperialist war'.[39] Press criticism had been heavy, and difficult to deal with, membership of the Rhondda CP was reported as 'almost stagnant' in February 1941; and the Labour Party locally was happy to make as much political capital as possible out of the CP's line.[40] Thus, when Hitler invaded the Soviet Union and the CP could change line, south Walian activists such as Dora Cox found their position much eased:

> . . . we almost heaved a sigh of relief, although it was a terrible thing, when Russia was invaded. And we were in it then, you know, we were in it. And it did make an enormous difference to our Party, of course, because . . . a great deal of the increase in membership for our Party was really showing support for the Soviet Union. [41]

A variety of different campaigns, organizations and meetings sprang up: Aid for Russia, the Anglo-Soviet Movement, the Help for Russia Fund, the Second Front, and 'Salute the Red Army'. In general, Labour and Communists backed these meetings, as did the SWMF and individual lodges, although tension and rivalry between the political parties remained.[42] It was the Communist Party that benefited most from this change in public opinion. Membership had risen by 75 per cent locally by the end of 1941, and the CP was able to combine moves to strengthen Anglo-Russian ties with pressure for building a united Labour movement, and a national anti-fascist front, all goals that could also serve the cause of the Party.[43]

Personalities remained important, set within this national and international context. Harry Pollitt had continued to nurse the Rhondda East constituency throughout the war years, spending at least one weekend in every month in the valley, and doing a considerable amount of public speaking on his visits.[44] In 1945 he ran an extensive campaign: 201 meetings in five weeks, with the candidate himself speaking at ninety-nine of them, and estimated to have reached an audience of 22,000.[45] Labour could not match the verve and spirit of the Communists, least of all with Will Mainwaring, a candidate whose popularity remained open to doubt. Cyril Gwyther relates that the Communist campaign was 'more forceful and positive':

> Mainwaring, you see, was not a popular candidate . . . I spoke at a meeting for him on the night before the election, up in Penygraig, and

Mainwaring came in at the end and spoke, and his attitude astonished me. It was a case of 'Well, if you think I'm your man vote for me, if not vote for Pollitt.' . . . He was very detached, non-committal, 'Well here I am, I've offered myself to you.' Pollitt had a unique opportunity to sweep the board. [46]

Pollitt came very close, but Mainwaring held on to win, against Communist expectations. Two factors were subsequently believed to have made the difference between victory and defeat. One was the issue in the constituency of an election leaflet calling upon voters to vote Labour. The special character and contribution of this lay in the fact that it was issued by the South Wales Area of the NUM, and signed by its president, Arthur Horner. It had been prepared for distribution throughout all south Wales coalfield constituencies apart from Rhondda East, where it was to be withheld to avoid conflicting loyalties. However, the RBLP managed to obtain a supply of these leaflets, and distributed them throughout the constituency two days before the poll, presumably taking votes away from the Communists owing to the appeal to loyalty from the 'Fed' and to the confusion sown by Horner's signature. The second factor was the delayed arrival of the forces' vote, the forces being insulated from domestic struggle and the CP campaign.[47] The precise contribution of these factors to the result is impossible to measure; but were particularly stressed by the bitterly disappointed Communist camp. Labour was relieved merely to have held the seat.[48]

The CP never again came so close to victory in Rhondda East, and at the general elections of 1950 and 1951 its challenge receded. The turn of the political tide against the CPGB was discerned soon after the excitement of 1945, with a Cold War effect obvious in local election results, and with the defeat for the first time at the 1946 conference of the NUM (South Wales Area) of a motion in favour of Communist affiliation to the Labour Party. With the spread of popular anti-Communism the CP's identification with the Soviet Union was now proving to be a liability, and membership plummeted across Wales.[49] As the 1950 general election approached, therefore, few commentators gave the returning Pollitt much chance of victory. Mainwaring had been much more assiduous in cultivating the constituency since 1945, especially with his work on the theme of reconstruction, and the Labour government's record seemed to vindicate the loyalty the constituency had shown towards the Party during the inter-war years. Pollitt, on the other hand, was unable to repeat his brilliant personal campaign of 1945, suffering from a prolapsed disc. On top of these handicaps came the national spectre of a Conservative victory, which only concentrated support for the Labour candidate.[50] The result was a catastrophic drop in the vote for Pollitt, and few could predict any subsequent recovery for Communist fortunes in the constituency.[51] Labour seemed to have taken virtually all the votes lost by the Communists, whilst losing some to the Conservatives, a pattern repeated in the 1951 general election, which saw a change in the Communist candidate, south Wales district secretary Idris Cox (originally from Maesteg) coming forward to replace the ailing Pollitt. Again the Communist campaign lacked impact, and the result, which saw the Conservative ex-Grenadier Guardsman Oliver Stutchbury beat Cox into third place, was further confirmation of the collapse of Rhondda Communism (Tables 5.6 and 5.7).[52]

Table 5.6. Result of the 1950 Parliamentary Elections

RHONDDA EAST			
W. H. Mainwaring	Labour	26,645	(75.9%)
Harry Pollitt	Communist	4,463	(12.7%)
George Nicholls	Conservative	2,634	(7.5%)
David Davies	Plaid Cymru	1,357	(3.9%)
Majority		22,182	
Total votes cast		35,099	
Total electorate		40,124	(turnout 87.5%)
RHONDDA WEST			
Iorwerth Thomas	Labour	27,150	(82.4%)
J. P. Driscoll	Conservative	3,632	(11.0%)
James Kitchener Davies	Plaid Cymru	2,183	(6.6%)
Majority		23,518	
Total votes cast		32,965	
Total electorate		37,384	(turnout 87.9%)

The Labour–Communist challenge was no longer the full story, with Rhondda West experiencing a poll for the first time since 1931 in 1950, repeated in 1951, and with Plaid Cymru and the Conservatives supplying the opposition. Plaid presented no more of a serious challenge in 1950 or 1951 than they had in 1945, although the new Labour member Iorrie (Iorwerth) Thomas enjoyed making anti-nationalist statements.[53] Thomas, who had been on the RUDC since 1928 and whose power-base was the Park Lodge, brought some fresh air

Table 5.7. Result of the 1951 Parliamentary Elections

RHONDDA EAST			
W. H. Mainwaring	Labour	27,958	(81.2%)
O. P. Stutchbury	Conservative	3,522	(10.2%)
Idris Cox	Communist	2,948	(8.6%)
Majority		24,436	
Total votes cast		34,428	
Total electorate		40,270	(turnout 85.5%)

RHONDDA WEST			
Iorwerth Thomas	Labour	26,123	(81.0%)
Emrys Simons	Conservative	3,635	(11.3%)
James Kitchener Davies	Plaid Cymru	2,467	(7.7%)
Majority		22,488	
Total votes cast		32,225	
Total electorate		37,315	(turnout 86.4%)

to parliamentary politics when he arrived in 1950, putting much work initially into his campaigning and general service to the constituency and to the Labour Party.[54] In his election campaigns he was outspoken in his condemnation of the Conservative Party and its record, supplying an uncompromising message of 'Vengeance on the Tories':

> Do you trust them? Don't you remember the fate of Rhondda from 1926 up through the lean, hungry and hard years of the 1930s under Tory rule? Those years of Soup Kitchens and Boot Funds – when the children of the Rhondda were wrapped up in cast-off clothing; when Rhondda mothers and fathers went without the things they needed for the sake of their children.
>
> You cannot forget those bitter years; your sad memories recall only too well that it was a Tory Government that inflicted all this hardship on Rhondda.

The history of the Tonypandy riots complemented the memory of the Depression, and a positive gloss was given by the record of the Labour government.[55] In 1951 the message was much the same, as was the convincing margin of victory.

As for local government, Labour remained in almost total control throughout this period. On the Glamorgan County Council (GCC) the 1931 elections heralded the beginning of blanket domination that was to remain intact until the end of the period studied. Liberal and Independent representation collapsed, and only one Communist appeared on Labour's left (Appendix Table 4). As for the RUDC, here a different pattern emerged. Labour began the post-disaffiliation period without a large majority, and facing opposition on both its left and right. The latter went into a long, slow decline. If one lumps Liberals, Conservatives and Independents together then one sees that they were able to muster about ten representatives until the early 1930s, but by the end of that decade this had fallen to only four. The post-war period saw them being further squeezed, until only one remained in the early 1950s. As for the Communist challenge, there was an early showing in the late 1920s, but this collapsed during the Third Period. Then there was a rapid climb to a maximum of seven Councillors by 1935, but the impetus could not be maintained and by 1939 Communist representation fell to five. In 1946 and 1947 numbers held up, but thereafter the collapse was abrupt, and by 1949 there were no Communist Councillors left on the RUDC. Labour, therefore, steadily consolidated its position during the early 1930s, rising to a peak of twenty-seven Councillors in 1932. But by 1936 it was down to twenty-one, and although there was recovery in the years before the outbreak of war, it was not until 1947 that Labour could again count twenty-seven Councillors. Thereafter, its supremacy was unchallenged, Labour holding every seat but one on the RUDC from 1951 onwards (Appendix Table 5).

Competition for local government office was rather higher in the 1930s than it had been in the 1920s, but then it fell markedly after 1946 and 1947. By the 1950s many seats were left uncontested on a regular basis. Competition for seats was strongest on the left of the political spectrum, and the form this took was overwhelmingly that of Communist–Labour contests. Labour Party discipline, such a feature of the 1910–26 period, remained in place throughout the 1930s and post-war years (Appendix Tables 12–13).

The remainder of this chapter examines the political dynamics of Labour's domination of Rhondda politics. Initially the decline of the right-wing opposition to Labour from the end of the 1920s onwards is summarized, but the bulk of the analysis focuses upon the significant challenge proffered by the CP, particularly in the mid-1930s.

The collapse of opposition from the right

I do not know what is the experience of Plaid members throughout the country – but I know that it is a matter of banging against the wall here.
                           J. Kitchener Davies to J. E. Jones, 8 February 1941[56]

The heart had disappeared from Rhondda's Liberal and Conservative politics by the early 1920s. Continuing opposition to Labour that adopted the labels of Liberal and Tory was very much an individual affair: there were no concerted 'drives' for office by these political parties, and in part this explains the lapse in terminology from 'Liberal' to 'Independent' as it became applied by the local press and, eventually, by many candidates themselves. A new organization that had some success in the late 1920s was the Ratepayers' Association, its objectives being to secure 'economy with efficiency' in local administration and to return 'candidates of independent views pledged to govern impartially for all the community'. Its base was the Porth Ward, which became by 1927 the only ward to return a majority of non-Labour Councillors to the RUDC.[57] But the desire to re-establish local administration on a sound financial footing was not a policy unique to the Ratepayers' Association, as Labour's sober management proved, and instead they had to fall back on anti-Communism as their main plank. It could never be much more than a localized, lower Rhondda Fach nuisance to Labour, who faced rather more heavyweight political opponents further up that valley.[58]

The only other Independent presence worthy of lasting note was that of the Pentre Councillor Glyn Wales. Wales was a railway clerk who represented Ward Three for forty years from 1934 on the RUDC, and from 1946 until 1974 on the GCC. Essentially sympathetic to Labour, his not being in the mining industry was considered something of a bar to his progress, and so he stood as an Independent, supported by the Ystrad branch of the NUR.[59] From 1943 he was joined by Glyn Elias, another railway clerk, who represented adjoining Ward Four, but who in 1950 joined the Labour Party, and served until 1974 in its ranks.[60] Interesting though these characters were, they were isolated, and fresh Independent candidatures at local elections were increasingly seen as futile.[61]

It remains only to mention the growth in Rhondda of the Welsh Nationalist Party, Plaid Cymru, significant not so much for its local candidacies (and barely for its general electoral sallies) as for what it was to become in the 1960s. The first official meeting locally of Plaid Cymru was held in 1928 in Ton Pentre, but regular activity was not seen until the early 1930s, with the holding of meetings at a number of venues throughout the valleys. By the end of 1932 four branches had been formed, with much focus upon cultural and literary debate.[62] In 1933 Morris Williams, editor of the *Welsh Nationalist*, became the first official Plaid Cymru candidate in south Wales at a local government election, coming last in Ward Six. Although enthusiastic about the campaign, Plaid Cymru members locally realized that victory was not within their grasp, and some 'felt that it would be a waste of our energy, our time and our money to attempt to unseat councillors because of the grip of the Labour Party on the minds of the people'.[63]

Plaid Cymru had two major problems in Rhondda. First, it was run by a very small number of people, some of whom wearied of the struggle after a few years.[64] And more generally, its policies and attitudes were not calculated to appeal to the Rhondda electorate. Kitchener Davies, its most important local ideologue and its regular parliamentary candidate, saw the Labour Party and Communism as complementary rather than distinct forces, and viewed his nationalism as part of an anti-Communist crusade. His offensive and tactless argument for a 'depopulation and deindustrializing' of Rhondda could hardly be expected to win him votes, and nor could Plaid's official hostility to the United Front protest of 1935.[65] In these circumstances it was a simple task, if an almost unnecessary one, for Labour to dismiss Plaid as an anti-Semitic, pro-fascist rabble.[66]

Plaid revived a little after the Second World War, with vehement public attacks being made upon the Labour Party, but with support and personnel spread extremely thinly, Plaid had a long way to go before it was to be taken seriously as an electoral force.[67] With the collapse of opposition to it on the right, Labour's serious long-term opposition from the late 1920s into the late 1940s was coming only from the left.

The wellsprings of Communism

During the last few weeks Communism has been spreading through the Rhondda Valley with the force of an epidemic. It is one of the sad and amazing features of the whole situation prevailing, that during the last few weeks . . . Communism is becoming a real active force in the life of the Valley; and I should like to say that it does not spring from any definite knowledge of the philosophy of Communism but that it is caused purely and entirely by the conditions and the adversity prevailing amongst the people.

Revd T. Alban Davies, 9 April 1935[68]

Occasionally, support for the CPGB has been seen as a direct product of unemployment and poverty.[69] But it is no simple task to demonstrate the necessary connection between such conditions and political choice, as neither political nor social radicalism are inevitable correlates of either unemployment or poverty.[70] Furthermore, it is wellnigh impossible to demonstrate precise linkages at this level of specificity, for to attempt to tie shifts in parliamentary or local politics to levels of unemployment, standards of living, real wages or the infant mortality rate would be a problematic exercise, even if reliable and unambiguous data for all of these measurements could be obtained. There is a gap between the objective reality of socio-economic circumstances and the casting of votes in an election: the gap is in truth between the perception of those circumstances and the act of voting. Even if it were possible to comprehend mass attitudes in the Rhondda valleys towards unemployment and poverty there could be little certainty placed upon the intelligibility of links between such attitudes and voting.

Given this disclaimer, how might the Communist Party have attracted support? Although there must be no determinism about unemployment and poverty, nevertheless the social and political circumstances created in inter-war Rhondda, combined with the industrial struggles at their heart, did create political space within which it was possible for Communist attitudes to flourish. During 1926, for instance, CPGB membership throughout Britain rose, particularly in south Wales, the Communists being seen by some as providing the most effective defence of the miners' interests and the most inspirational leadership in times of difficulty. Thereafter, Communists were frequently leading struggles against unemployment and the draconian regulations surrounding it, and against the threats of fascism and of war at home and abroad, defending and supporting Republican Spain whilst keeping a suspicious eye on the motives of the British government. At the same time Communists were backing the campaign to rebuild and restructure the SWMF, and taking leading roles in the battles against the threats of non-unionism and company unionism. The Communist Party could be perceived as a pure repository of revolutionary hopes, as the ideal vehicle for the conduct of the struggle against fascism, war and unemployment. Communist support might develop for some as a distinct commitment to the Communist Party's viewpoint, as a conviction of the correctness of the Marxist interpretation of history, or as a resolve to use whatever means were available to struggle against oppression and injustice.

Archival material rarely provides direct confirmation of such feelings and attitudes. The local press focused upon parochial not international events, and was generally suspicious of or hostile to Communism. One way in which a representative understanding of the mentality of Communist support could be gained would be by oral history, but, unfortunately, the generation that experienced the vital years of Communist struggle is now largely beyond reach. Nevertheless, into this generality of both approach and geographical coverage may be inserted those identifiable factors that can be treated with a measure of originality based upon the unique nature of the primary source material.

Four such factors stand out. The first two concern the reasons for the Rhondda Labour Party's loss of support to the Communists after 1927: the financial policies followed by the RUDC, which alienated many voters, and the allegations of corruption and nepotism aimed at the Labour Group on the RUDC, which climaxed in the mid-1930s, and led to a major contrast being made between a tarnished Labourism and a Rhondda Communism unsullied by the temptations and responsibilities of office. These factors, taken together, led to a general shedding of support for the Labour Party. Some of that lost support, particularly that motivated by corruption, divided between more right-wing and more left-wing candidates, but most moved to the Communist camp, however briefly. The third and fourth factors are more to do with the Communist Party itself. On the one hand, the distinctive political culture offered by the Rhondda Communist Party to its adherents and supporters was much more vigorous and inclusive than that being offered by the Labour Party. On the other hand, the brave, bold and imaginative leadership offered by the Communists in the struggles of the 1930s, and especially in the struggles of 1935 against the means test, was a crucial factor.

The burdens of office

If the Minister of Health contends that the district council of the Rhondda is solvent, let us consider at what a cost. At the present time, the report of the medical officer of health for the Rhondda certifies that there is a large number of children in the Rhondda area suffering from malnutrition because of a lack of nourishment, and a large number of children are absent from school because they have no clothing or no boots in which to attend school. The Rhondda education authority are neglecting the provision of clothing and food for the children because they have not got the money to spend in those directions.

Will John MP, 1928[71]

The serious financial problems that had faced both the RUDC and the PBG during 1926–7 did not disappear with the restoration of industrial 'peace' and the termination of the widespread feeding of necessitous schoolchildren. The Pontypridd Board of Guardians had but a short life, as with the passage of the Local Government Act 1929 it was to be replaced by Public Assistance Committees (PACs) run from the County Councils in 1930.[72] During the remainder of its time it concerned itself largely with stabilizing its financial position, restricting expenditure, and attempting to recover the outrelief loans provided during 1926, whilst resisting any pressure to improve its scales. The Guardians remained in an impossible position, in debt to the tune of over a quarter of a million pounds, and wholly dependent upon the Ministry of Health to sanction their actions.[73] Politically the control of the PBG was a non-issue: to win a seat on it could have no impact on its twilight administration.

The RUDC was a very different matter, and throughout the remainder of the 1920s and the 1930s the struggle between Communists and Labour was concentrated at this level. Rhondda Communists did not make substantial efforts to win seats on the GCC: although they might consider themselves capable of winning two or three from the Rhondda quota, they would undoubtedly be overwhelmed by Labour, whose dominance in most other mining areas was unchallenged from the far left. The RUDC was the main arena, and its administrative and political history during these years was largely determined by its financial position.

That position was as critical as that of the PBG, with in April 1927 the RUDC having an overdraft of £186,000 and owing loans of over £155,000.[74] The Ministry of Health decided that it would not demand immediate repayment of the Goschen Committee loans, but extend the period of repayment on condition that the RUDC would put up the rates and cut its expenditure by at least 5 per cent. This the RUDC agreed to do, establishing a Special Estimates Committee to effect the economies.[75]

Some of the economies instituted were fairly minor matters: the discontinuation of scholarships to summer schools; of grants for teachers entering training colleges; the curtailment of the travelling undertaken by school inspectors and the postponement of salary increases for chief officials. Others were more significant: the cutting of money for the maintenance of schools, the discontinuation of medical inspections for secondary-school pupils, a freeze on teaching appointments and a reduction in the numbers of supply teachers. Maternity and Child Welfare (MCW) clinics that were to have been established at Treherbert and Mardy were deferred, whilst the overall MCW budget and the budget for scavenging were cut.[76] Most politically explosive however, was first the continuing problem of necessitous feeding, given added emphasis by the disaffiliation episode, and second the attempts that were made to recover the RUDC's arrears of rents and rates.

Pressure for the reinstatement of widespread school feeding remained high throughout 1927 and into 1928, emanating from a wide range of organizations within the local Labour movement.[77] There was an admission by the Labour majority on the RUDC that feeding was desirable, but also a recognition that such a programme was impossible were the Council to be forced to rely upon its own resources. Repeated approaches were made to the Ministry of Health for assistance in this matter, without success. Nor was the Board of Education prepared to fund expenditure on a scale approaching that of 1926. In these circumstances frustration and conflict on the RUDC were exacerbated.[78] The Labour majority resignedly accepted central government decisions, whilst some on the left (the Communists, occasionally supported by some Labour Councillors) struggled against it and against what they saw as complacency.[79]

There were investigations into the condition of Rhondda school-children to assess the need for feeding, and in November 1927 it was estimated that 2,500 children were suffering from malnutrition. There was an attempt to institute feeding for them without this being taken into account by the PBG when it set outrelief scales, but this was disallowed by the Ministry of Health.[80] In spring 1928 it was possible to arrange for a small number of children to be fed without offending central government policy, although this was seen as unsatisfactory by Labour, Communists and the medical officer of health alike, and protests, deputations and demonstrations for a more extensive system continued.[81]

Necessitous feeding was superseded during 1928 and 1929 as the major focus of conflict in local government by the RUDC's policy of attempting to collect rates and rents arrears. Rates collection had fallen heavily during and since 1926, and by March 1928 the RUDC faced arrears to a total of £239,876. A sub-committee with plenary powers was established to consider its plan of attack.[82] A campaign to recover rental arrears from tenants in Ferndale had already been instituted, proving controversial and leading to violent clashes in the Council chamber.[83] It had not been very successful: in January 1929, of the 234 tenants under the RUDC only twelve were clear of rental arrears.[84]

The RUDC began to take firm action against those in arrears. Selected tenants were served with notices to quit, whilst some rentals began to be adjusted downwards to take account of the difficult economic circumstances. Protests were frequent, but direct action was absent until the Mardy eviction disturbances of November 1931.[85] Mardy was as sensitive an area for the collection of arrears as it had been for the recovery of outrelief earlier in the decade, and when the RUDC Finance Committee decided it was time to send in the bailiffs against defaulters, upper Rhondda Fach members (Ferndale and Mardy) anticipated trouble. This they got when Arthur Horner led Mardy residents in thwarting a bailiff's attack upon a Mardy home, for which action he was convicted of unlawful assembly, along with twenty-eight others.[86]

It is difficult to be precise about the political impact of the Labour-controlled RUDC's policy on both arrears and school feeding. There were other issues that could not but present Labour in a poor light with the majority of its constituents: demands for public-works schemes to relieve unemployment, for better housing provision, and for the extension of MCW services, all of which were near-impossible for the RUDC to meet given its financial position.[87] Communist critics found it a relatively simple task to point out Labour's shortcomings in such situations, and to promise that were they elected, conditions and services would improve. Repeatedly the expectation that a Labour Council should do things for its people rather than sympathize with their plight was stressed.[88] Possibly these accusations alone would not have sufficed to turn the electoral tide against Labour on the RUDC in the mid-1930s but, when they were supplemented by scandals and public outrage concerning the issues of corruption and nepotism in Labour's administration, then the combined brew was potent indeed.

The temptations of office

I verily believe there was an element of corruption that came in, in the Depression period . . . I remember saying there at one stormy meeting, if we found out that there was a germ of truth in all these stories that everybody's got on their lips about corruption, we would have no hesitation in throwing them out of the Party. And one councillor, who was supposed to be the treasurer of the little group who were taking it, he said 'Why are you talking this load of rubbish when you can't prove anything.' We never could of course, because the man who gave the bribe was as bad, if not worse, than the poor fellow who received it. The Labour Party was deeply anxious about all these stories which were rife through the community; I'm quite satisfied there was truth in it. But I remember once arriving at the home of Owen Buckley and he was in a state of agitation: a teacher had been canvassing, to get a job as a Head Teacher, and he said 'George, what am I to do?' Well, when he'd gone, 'Look' he said, and he had three pound notes, now remember a miner's wage was two pounds ten, a week, three pound notes which were left behind on his seat, the seat of his chair. And I said, thinking the MP was God Almighty, before I became one, I said, 'I should go to Will John, and report it to him'. And you know, I thought that was severe, better than a High Court Judge. 'Tell him about it', I said, 'and send the money back to him, tell him that he won't get your vote.' So at any rate, he went to Will John who got furious, and said 'Why, why do you come and tell me about it, now you're making me an accessory after the act. I'm not supposed to know anything, don't tell me these things!' And he sent him away with a flea in his ear! There was a story about a Head Teacher who died, and he hadn't completed the year. And the bribe for a headship was supposed to be the difference between the salary of a class teacher and a Head Teacher, for the first year. That was the payment and could be made over the period. And the story was rife in Tonypandy, that his widow had been told he hadn't finished paying, so they wanted her to pay. You can imagine, remember it was a very difficult period. I heard Mark Harcombe in the Empire Cinema, Tonypandy, a Sunday afternoon meeting and I was in the chair, it was always packed, all men of course, it was different from nowadays, all men would come there, pack the meeting, the Cinema absolutely packed, and Mark was addressing them and he said 'I know the story that's going round, that you've only got to go to the Destructor at Porth and shout Harcombe, and every window will open.' And there was a roar of laughter because everybody had heard the story, and he said, 'What', he was a father mind of about eighteen or nineteen children, he said 'What sort of a father would I be if I didn't look after my own? And if I can't look after my own, do you think I'm fit to look after you?' And he had a storm of applause! I think they all put themselves in his shoes.

George Thomas, 1987[89]

Stories about the corruption and nepotism associated with the Labour Party in the south Wales coalfield abound. Their popularity, and their status as folk legend, make the subject as fascinating as it is awkward for the historian. Historical analysis consists of evaluating oral evidence and hearsay, and of attempting to draw conclusions from the few 'facts' that exist. However, whilst allegations of corruption may not be proven beyond reasonable doubt, and beyond the fear of unjust accusations, one can demonstrate that, at certain times in the inter-war years, such allegations were sufficiently widely held to have had electoral impact.[90]

Corruption is an all-inclusive term. In Rhondda, it can be broken down into four categories, two major and two minor. The major categories were those of nepotism in the making of appointments under the RUDC, and of the taking of bribes (for non-relatives) in the making of such appointments. The minor categories were of the misdemeanours and misfortunes of individual Councillors, and of the employment of individual Councillors by local government bodies. Overall the combined effect of these varieties of corruption was to damage seriously not only the reputation but also the political fortunes of the RBLP in the mid-1930s, and to turn voters away from Labour to Independents and, more significantly, to the Communists.

During the inter-war years three Urban District Councillors ended up being found guilty of embezzlement. In 1923 Gomer Jones, left-wing Labour Councillor and Naval colliery miner, was imprisoned for three years for having embezzled £2,000 from the Naval colliery Workmen's fund. Jones, an ILPer, had been elected to the RUDC in 1919 for the Penygraig Ward, but his wife Jane had died tragically at the age of thirty-one in August 1920, and Jones had begun gambling, drinking heavily, and making generous loans to his friends.[91] Liberal Councillor Emrys Harcombe (brother of Mark) was bound over for twelve months in 1929, having taken money from both the British Legion and the local Union Jack Club. Harcombe had served in the First World War (in Mesopotamia, Palestine and Egypt), having been mentioned in dispatches and promoted to sergeant. He had been secretary of both the Ynyshir branch of the British Legion, and of the Legion's Rhondda and Pontypridd District Committee. The embezzlement had been a desperate attempt to save the fortunes of his small business, under serious threat from the slump in the area's fortunes.[92] Finally, Labour Councillor Fred Quick, stalwart of Treherbert Trades and Labour Council and ILP, ended up in prison in 1932 having been found guilty of forgery, falsification and larceny in respect of £1,000 taken from customers of the Ton Industrial

Co-operative Society, which employed him as a clerk.[93] None of these men can be said to have directly used their positions as Councillors to make unlawful gains, but they can have done the image of Rhondda's public representatives no good whatsoever.

The second minor form of corruption was that of representatives obtaining employment under local authorities, sometimes under the very authorities upon which they sat. Most of these cases post-date the 1926 dispute, and can largely be explained as an individual reaction to unemployment and poverty. Labour County Councillor George Dolling became a rate collector for the RUDC in 1929, having lost his post as checkweigher at the Standard colliery; and a fellow County Councillor, Enoch Treharne, was appointed caretaker at the Carnegie Welfare Centre in Trealaw by the same authority when he stepped down from another checkweigher's post, this time at the Llwynypia colliery.[94] What might be considered a more blatant abuse of position occurred in 1932, when unemployed miner and sitting Labour Urban District Councillor Tom Rees was appointed to the post of slot collector by the very RUDC upon which he sat![95] He was followed in this path two years later by Llewellyn Jones (an ex-Tylorstown checkweigher and another Labour Councillor), and the following year Councillor Tom Thomas took a job working with the local Public Assistance Committee (PAC) under the new means-test regulations.[96] It is impossible to prove that such appointments were prejudiced in favour of these candidates, but suspicion that political service counted for more than merit was easy to arouse, and protests followed.[97]

Some within the Labour Party had been aware of the pitfalls of power from an early stage, the *Rhondda Socialist* in August 1912 commenting upon the amount of canvassing that went on in the appointment of teachers, and arguing that the principles of seniority and merit ought to be observed.[98] This was a problem which to some degree stemmed from the fact that the RUDC controlled its own educational provision, unlike other District Councils in Glamorgan. With the RUDC having the power to appoint teachers and headteachers, candidates for such posts could contemplate canvassing perhaps a majority of involved Councillors, given their geographical concentration. The whole business seems to have become quite organized: as George Thomas related above, a small number of Labour Councillors set the rules for hopeful candidates, who would have been well advised to know which Councillors to bribe and which not! It was commonly alleged that to obtain a simple teaching post, the bribe was fixed at one month's salary; to obtain a headteacher's post, the bribe was the difference for one year between the previous salary and the new.[99]

Protests at the acceptance of canvassing, whether it involved financial inducements or not, were long-standing. In 1919, during the teachers' dispute, both the Rhondda Certified Class Teachers' Association and some Labour Councillors appealed unsuccessfully for the introduction of a seniority scheme for promotions to headteacher.[100] In 1925 there were further protests from some within the Labour Group at the significance of canvassing and, in 1927, the RUDC passed a resolution that made canvassing for any appointments under the authority a disqualification, only to rescind it in 1929.[101] Subsequently, some Councillors became increasingly complacent and open about their behaviour and motivation. At a meeting of the Education Committee in July 1932 held to consider the procedure for appointing five headteachers it was noted that there was a short list of eighteen candidates, all of them local men. It was debated whether these should be interviewed, but, as James James remarked, interviewing was pointless given that the majority of committee members had already decided for whom to vote.[102]

Pressure mounted again in 1933 and 1934 for the adoption of seniority in appointing to headships, and at last the Education Committee agreed to evolve a new method of promotion. But when this scheme was brought forward in 1935 it was rejected by the Rhondda NUT as being 'a smoke screen to conceal the abuses complained of in the promotion of teachers'.[103] Overall, the record of the RUDC on this issue was not impressive, and was not enhanced by the public slating it received in 1933 at the hands of its recently retired director of education, R. R. Williams. In an article in *Y Ddraig Goch*, subsequently translated in the *Western Mail* and the *Glamorgan County Times*, Williams was forthright, claiming that 'some members of our education committee are unworthy of their responsibility', being open to bribery on every issue.[104] The problem with accusations of this kind was in being able to prove that corruption existed. Without proof, corrupt Councillors could ignore the rumours and the mud-slinging, and those who served alongside them could do little but feel uneasy. It was rare for individual cases of corruption to be brought to public notice; and when this happened, it was not without risk to the accusing party, as Communist Councillor George Maslin found out in the 'turkey case'.

In September 1927, Maslin made public allegations that some District Councillors were receiving bribes in return for votes. When pressed by the RUDC upon this matter he revealed that a colliery worker from the Gelli colliery, Daniel Jones, had approached him to ask him help secure a job for his daughter as a teacher of domestic science. Jones had told Maslin that if he co-operated he would be able to secure the unemployed Communist Councillor a job as storeman in the Gelli colliery (Maslin had previously been chairman of the Tylorstown Lodge). Maslin was subsequently given two £1 notes by Jones, which he handed over to the Ferndale and Tylorstown Joint Prisoners' Fund. The RUDC insisted that all this information be passed to the attorney-general, who responded by arranging for the prosecution of Jones, and, although reprimanding Maslin for having retained the money, found no grounds for his prosecution, much to the annoyance of some of his fellow Councillors.[105]

Business that had more serious consequences for the campaigning Maslin began in July 1929 with the appointment of an assistant solicitor to the RUDC, the successful applicant being J. E. Arnold James of Treherbert.[106] Maslin had voted for James, but alleged that he was surprised when, on Christmas Eve 1929, a turkey arrived at his home accompanied by a card carrying the message 'With the compliments of Arnold James'. Unemployed, with a family to feed, Maslin understandably, if naïvely, accepted the gift. Then, on 30 December 1929, Maslin was visited by Iorrie Thomas, who discussed the need to replace the clerk of the Finance Committee, who was a Liberal, with Arnold James. Thomas asked Maslin if he was not above accepting a gratuity. Maslin said that he did not know what Thomas meant. Subsequently, at a meeting of the Finance Committee held to discuss the appointment of a new clerk, Arnold James approached Maslin, thanked him and gave him two £1 notes 'for his support'. Maslin waited a few days and then revealed details of this episode, also stating that he would not be voting for Arnold James. James's response was to state that Maslin had concocted the whole story, and he instituted legal proceedings against him, whilst Iorrie Thomas denied that he knew what Maslin was talking about. The Council decided to send a statement of facts to the Ministry of Health, informing them that civil proceedings were pending.[107]

In November 1930 the case came for trial at the Glamorgan Assizes at Swansea, James taking slander action against Maslin, who conducted his own defence. The notes Maslin produced in court, claiming that they were from James, were found not to have been in circulation until July or August 1930, despite Maslin's contention that he had received them in January, and that they were the same ones he had produced before the RUDC in February. Maslin claimed he must have mixed the notes up. James won a judgement for £500, plus damages and costs, a decision which Maslin attacked as that of a 'class court'. Maslin was bankrupted as a result, and forced to resign his Council seat.[108] Whatever the truth of this episode, it indicated the personal dangers involved in the issue of corruption.

The cumulative effect of these instances and allegations of corruption was undoubtedly damaging to the reputation and standing of the RUDC and of the RBLP. But it was the issue of nepotism that was to prove to be the most direct electoral liability. The issue had first been raised at the 1925 RUDC elections when the Independent David Jenkins (a colliery clerk) challenged the Labour Councillor James James in Ward Four. Jenkins's election address stated that James had three sons and other relatives in Council employment, and the question was asked 'Why not give these jobs to ex-servicemen and disabled miners who are now unemployed?' The address finished by calling upon the electors to 'VOTE FOR David Jenkins, The Candidate who has no family to find jobs for.'[109] In October 1928 the RUDC received a formal protest from the NUR, Ystrad branch, at the 'preferential consideration in matters of employment' received by the children of Councillors, a protest sparked off by the appointment of James James's fourth son as a motor driver under the RUDC. The Council decided to prepare a list of employed relatives (excluding teachers) of Councillors for submission to the next meeting. Upon publication of the list (which revealed that the RUDC employed James James's brother and nephew as well as his sons, and employed two sons of Rhys Morgan Rees, two sons, a brother and two sons-in-law of Mark Harcombe and a total of nine other Councillors' relatives), Iorrie Thomas said that it seemed as though Councillors had exploited the fact that they had public confidence and had given preference to relatives when vacancies arose. Mark Harcombe defended himself by saying that he had found employment for dozens of men when his four boys were all unemployed, whilst James James claimed that his boys had entered Council employment at a time when better pay had been available in the pits. George Maslin proposed that all relatives of Councillors be dismissed. This went unseconded, and no action was taken.[110]

The issue revived in late 1932, protests arising in the Treorchy and Pentre areas that 'the local Councillors were determined to keep all the Council jobs for their relatives, and that no fair competition ever took place', or that jobs were actually created for Councillors' relatives. As a letter to the press remarked, 'We can plainly see that the Labour Party are not only out for themselves, but for their whole family and not for you.'[111] Boiling-point was eventually reached in September 1934 when an appointment was made to the post of porter and general assistant at the Isolation Hospital, Ystrad Rhondda. The Communist Councillors attempted to have the appointment deferred when they saw the short list, but failed, and the successful candidate was a certain John James, of Penrhys Road, Ystrad, who just happened to be the fifth son of James James. The appointment was immediately controversial: a public meeting was held in Ward Four, the populace of which were reputed to be 'seething with discontent', and a petition of over two thousand local government electors was collected from the ward, regarding the appointment of John James as 'distinctly unfair and biased', particularly as four of James James's sons were already employed by the Council! Demands were made for the dismissal of John James, on the grounds that he was not qualified for the post. Faced with this outcry the RUDC established a sub-committee to investigate the qualifications of John James for the post, and the more general allegations made by a deputation from Ward Four, concerning the recruitment of twenty Council employees believed to have received preferential treatment. However, it was found that John James was qualified for the position and therefore could not be dismissed, nor could any other of the investigated employees, whilst 'the allegation of the Deputation that Mr James James's membership of the Council contributed towards the appointment of Mr John James, is not supported by the evidence submitted'. The report was accepted by the Council amidst scenes of uproar and threatened violence.[112]

This episode, and the public revulsion it provoked, served to strengthen the growing Communist challenge to Labour's domination of the RUDC. The 1935 RUDC election results, which led to the defeat by Communists of two veteran Labour Councillors and to the return of two Communists, Jimmy Morton (Ward Ten) and Jesse Sweet (Ward Eleven), against Labour opposition, were seen as not so much a vote for Communism as a vote of no confidence in Labour, especially over the corruption issue. This may be too simplistic, especially when one considers the radicalizing impact of the means-test campaigns of early 1935, but Labour's 'unenviable repute' as W. H. Mainwaring termed it, could not be anything but an electoral liability.[113]

Labour's reputation was damaged by the storms of the mid-1930s, and although this did not lead to an irreversible decline in the party's fortunes, nevertheless it helps to account for the success of the Communist challenge at that time. To some voters it seemed as if the behaviour of a small number of Labour Councillors, and the readiness of some (though not all) others to whitewash what had happened, was nothing less than a betrayal of the working class, which could only be combated by lending support to the CPGB.

Little Moscows? A Communist culture

The existence of 'Little Moscow' was . . . an attempt, often deliberately, to create a counter-community within an existing one but based on its past traditions, frequently imitative of existing social formations, never excluding them whilst constantly offering what was thought of as a better alternative because more political, more proletarian, more conscious of its purpose.

Hywel Francis and David Smith[114]

Francis and Smith refer specifically to the historical experience of the community of Mardy at the upper end of Rhondda Fach, a settlement whose history perhaps best exemplifies the distinctive 'cultural' appeal of the CPGB during the 1920s and 1930s, and whose history has demanded such attention largely because of the political and industrial radicalism that earned it the tag 'Little Moscow'. The Mardy Lodge had a tradition of employing particularly left-wing checkweighers, from T. I. Mardy Jones through Noah Ablett to Ted Williams and Arthur Horner. It had had the first ILP branch in the 1890s and, with Ferndale, had been responsible for returning some of the first Labour representatives to Rhondda's local government bodies. After the First World War it had been the centre of a strong CP branch, which contributed strongly to the rejectionist challenge then working within the Rhondda Labour Party, and then, after disaffiliation, the radical Mardy Lodge and the Communist Party, led by Arthur Horner, had dominated the community's political and industrial life. Mardy remained militant when much of the rest of Rhondda was in retreat, and, as Francis and Smith suggest, it had a sense of its future in advance of that evident elsewhere. Ultimately that militancy was to be defeated, as part of both a fierce struggle within the SWMF and an assault from the external coercive agencies of the state. The Communist leadership of the community was imprisoned, driven out, or forced to acknowledge the political and economic reality of that community, one that left little scope for creative protest. But, for perhaps a decade, from the early 1920s to the early 1930s, Mardy represented the sharpest proletarian consciousness available in Rhondda and in south Wales.

Mardy's Communist history is unique: no other Rhondda settlement had that concentrated intensity of experience. It stemmed partly from the extreme conditions of unemployment that the settlement had to endure after 1926, from geographical location and relative isolation, and from the way in which the imaginative and broad-based leadership of the local Communists was able to draw in community support as part of a (still contested) Mardy identity. But although Mardy was unique, nevertheless the culture of Communist consciousness so manifest there was also displayed, albeit as part of a more varied local pattern, within the neighbouring settlements of Ferndale and Tylorstown, and to a lesser extent again in Mid-Rhondda, Porth, and in the lower Rhondda Fach settlements of Ynyshir, Stanleytown, Wattstown and Pontygwaith. Thus if one was a CPGB member then one might send one's children to the local Young Comrades League or Young Communist League that held weekly meetings and rallies. A sense of identity could be strong, and was developed by the wearing of Communist badges and favours, the donning of the 'uniform' of a khaki shirt and a red tie, and by taking part in symbolic acts, such as refusing to sing the national anthem, or expressing opposition to Empire Day. On a grander scale, May Day demonstrations and rallies, along with more combative and active protests forged corporate identification, whilst leading Communists took an active role in the NUWM, in coaching people for attendance at referees' courts, in organizing resistance to demands for the payment of loans or rates, and in generally serving as an extended advice bureau.[115] One might be able to play in or watch a Communist football team, and be buried at a Communist funeral.[116] One might read or deliver the Communist press, which frequently carried Rhondda news, and which at one time included the local party's own *Rhondda Vanguard*.[117] One could, up to a point, live and die in a world whose boundaries were defined by the Communist Party. This might have been particularly attractive in the Depression years, but should not be mistaken for escapism – to adopt a Communist perspective was to reiterate the purpose of one's life by placing it within the context of wider, international struggles, but it was also to accept that those struggles had to be fought, that oppression had to be faced, and that solace could not be found in anything but combative activity.[118]

One cannot be certain how many lives this culture touched: local branches of the CPGB did not have a very secure existence. Precise membership figures are unobtainable, but such evidence as there is suggests that it fluctuated considerably.[119] Perhaps this was less important than the fact that Communist Party influence was much greater than membership alone: activism was very high, and the same names can be found speaking, organizing and standing for election. The CP aimed not for mass membership but for a small, tightly-knit cadre of activists who could be capable of concerted decision-making and swift action, and could therefore begin to match the larger but more unwieldy Labour Party machine.[120] A particularly appealing feature of Rhondda Communism, and one that further assisted its progress, was its leadership by a number of talented and even charismatic figures. The best-known of these were Arthur Horner, Will Paynter and Lewis Jones, but they were complemented by less prominent activists such as George Maslin.[121] Much has already been written about Maslin's municipal struggles, and his indomitable spirit and commitment to the struggle are indicated by his recovery from bankruptcy in 1931 to take a seat again on the RUDC in 1934. He was born in Pontygwaith in 1892, the eldest of seven children, to parents who were staunch Conservatives. His father was a founder of the Tylorstown Conservative Club, and its long-serving chairman, whilst his mother was prominent in the Conservative Women's Guild. George started his working life as a pit boy (supplementing his earnings by boxing against and alongside Jimmy Wilde in the fairground booths) before a spell at sea with the merchant navy. When he married he returned to the mines, but contracted nystagmus and found work instead as a stoker working on the surface. Initially an Anglican, Maslin became a Christadelphian before attending local Central Labour College classes (run by, amongst others, Will Mainwaring) that converted him to Marxism. Thereafter well-read in both Dietzgen and the Bible (Maslin thought Christ the first Communist, and frequently used biblical imagery in his speeches, a trait that proved unpopular with some of his Communist colleagues), he was a conscientious objector during the First World War, a founding member of the CPGB in the Rhondda, a Co-operator, Tylorstown Lodge chairman, a leader of the local NUWM and a Hunger Marcher. Imprisoned during the 1926 dispute for obstructing the movement of coal, he was subsequently victimized by the colliery company and endured lengthy unemployment. Eventually he obtained work with the Mid-Rhondda Co-operative Society as a baker's roundsman, but after the Second World War went back to working in the mines. Frequently before the courts, Maslin was another of the Rhondda CP's 'Renaissance men', 'a genuine revolutionary', winning respect and admiration beyond party-political boundaries. When he died at the age of fifty-nine in 1951, his burial alongside other Communists at Penrhys cemetery was accompanied by a funeral ovation from Harry Pollitt.[122]

Although Communist affiliation or sympathy was a minority creed, the Party projected an energetic and vigorous image, with an inclusive culture, which compared favourably with the seeming apathy and complacency that had overcome the Labour Party since the mid-1920s. The latter's 'cultural dimension', evident from the end of the First World War through to the early 1920s, had been lost, and local party membership was consistently low and disappointing. The Labour Party appeared to have become less a living movement and more a self-perpetuating institution, to which success came by routine. In such circumstances the Communist Party could make its appeal as something fresh, new, challenging and unbowed by convention. A vote for the CP could appear to be a vote not only of protest but also a vote of hope.[123]

The appeal of Communist strategy

> The problem is, what is to be done? Our Party has the task to-day of solving this, and the first need is unity . . . whatever we do must be done together. We have called some of our leaders many things in the past and they are now full of bitterness, but this must be buried in the face of this new attack so that we can go forward with them against those responsible for the cuts. I believe we can get the Labour councillors to come with us in this.
>
> Mary Roberts, in Lewis Jones's *We Live*

Analysis of the political and electoral rise of Rhondda Communism in the 1930s has covered the problems and failings of Labour's administration of the RUDC, as well as the superior vitality of the Communist Party set against a rather tired Labour Party complacent in the seeming ease of its electoral domination. A yet more active contribution to its own success must be assigned to the CPGB's political strategy which, from 1933–4 onwards, to a large extent took the initiative away from Labour and enhanced the CP's popular reputation.

The so-called 'Third Period' or 'Class Against Class' strategy adopted by the Communist International and thus by Communist parties world-wide was a disaster, and the record of Communist fortunes in Rhondda supports the view that the 'New Line' was a mistake. Communist representation at local level was not advanced, whilst the relative progress of Arthur Horner as parliamentary candidate in the Rhondda East constituency between 1929 and 1931 can be taken as further confirmation of the consensus verdict. Horner, after all, had been one of the most prominent opponents of the New Line within the CPGB, and for his pains had been censured by Moscow as advocating a renegade, 'Hornerist' strategy.[124] The experience of the Mardy Lodge, which was expelled from the SWMF in February 1930 for refusing to withdraw its support from the RBLP (Disaffiliated) and the NUWM, is another solemn reminder of the futility of divisive and antagonistic action. Mardy's Communist militants cannot be blamed for the lodge's predicament in its totality, as they were treated unsympathetically by the Labour Party and its supporters within the SWMF leadership. But although heroic and legendary, the road they went down after expulsion was a cul-de-sac.[125]

Relief began to come in 1933, as the international Communist movement took note of the rise of Nazism and the threat it posed to peace and socialism. The Class Against Class strategy was shed, replaced by the traditional policy of working for a 'United Front': the unity of working-class organizations. In practical terms this meant that the CPGB should no longer try to struggle directly against the Labour Party, treating the latter as its enemy, but instead work with it against the common enemies of the working class.

The adoption of this strategy heralded a period, from 1933 until 1939, of unparalleled success for the CPGB at national level. But success there could only be built upon success at the grass roots, and what the Rhondda experience demonstrates is that, contrary to the opinions of some anti-Communist historians, local Parties could originate creative political strategies without necessarily awaiting directions from on high.[126] Furthermore, these strategies could cross the boundaries of national formulae such as the United Front and anticipate later innovations such as the Popular Front in their breadth and their imagination.[127]

It was the vision and the high work-rate of the Rhondda CPGB that did so much to assist its political advance in the 1930s. Communist campaigns were not revolutionary, but were essentially defensive, in that they concerned themselves with stopping the advance of Fascism, and with both protesting at the level of unemployment and mitigating its worst effects. Nevertheless, they attempted to challenge apathy and pessimism, and to speak for a community wider than that of their own party.

Much has been written about the extra-parliamentary struggles, demonstrations, hunger marches and direct-action protests led by Communists or those sympathetic to the CPGB during the 1930s, and it is not proposed to compete with existing histories for narrative detail.[128] Rhondda Communists were involved, often prominently, in each of the hunger marches that left south Wales; they were at the heart of the anti-BUF (British Union of Fascists), anti-Mosley demonstrations that culminated in violent disturbances in Tonypandy in 1936; and they also took a share in the running of anti-war demonstrations in 1935.[129] On a more prosaic level the CPGB also attempted to provide a lead in the sphere of local government policy. Progress here was slow, given the minority position the Communists faced, but individual candidates and Councillors paid great attention to the needs of their wards, and on the whole seem to have served their constituents as well as, if not better than, representatives of any other political colour.[130] In January 1935, before the RUDC elections, the *Daily Worker* proudly listed concessions supposedly won by the Communist group, ranging from the erection of MCW clinics and the provision of free milk, to the improvement of nurses' working conditions and the reduction of the cost of municipal electricity.[131] Such claims were not uncontested, and it is impossible given the formal presentation of Council minutes to ascribe individual reforms to Communist pressure; but it is significant that what might be considered fairly trivial matters were held as indicative of Communist advance. Lewis Jones expressed this belief in *We Live,* where (District Councillor) Mary Roberts defends herself in a CP meeting against criticism of over-stressing the importance of Council work:

I agree we mustn't concentrate the Party on one phase of the struggle, but neither must we neglect any phase. And all I've been trying to do is to get you comrades to see the importance of council issues to the people. It's these little things, such as parish, housing, child welfare, and so on, that affect the lives of our people in the quickest and most living way, and it's because of this the council can be made a mobilizer for bigger things and actions.[132]

Lewis Jones was living proof of this attitude. Having been elected to the GCC in 1936, he served on the local PAC, where his activities were such as to come to the notice of government officials, who remarked upon the fact that the Rhondda relief sub-committees were tending to grant the maximum levels of relief to claimants:

This tendency was accounted for in part by Communistic activity in the area and particularly by the activity of Mr Lewis Jones . . . Mr Jones has set himself out to educate his constituents as to their rights to Public Assistance. This he does in various ways. He has for example a motor van with a loud speaker by means of which he broadcasts to all in doubt as to their rights and invites all with a grievance to report their cases to local communist agents whose names and addresses are given; the agents pass on the particulars to Mr. Jones who then gives advice. He also holds crowded meetings every Sunday night in the Judge's Hall, Tonypandy at which he makes such statements as that there are hundreds of people in the Area not receiving the assistance to which they are entitled and advises them how this may be rectified. Particulars of the [Glamorgan] Scale are also published in a communist organ the *Rhondda Vanguard* which circulates in the Area . . . he is concerned with the operation of the guiding scale rather than with the relief of destitution, and . . . he suggests that the scale of relief should be granted more and more to the fullest amount permissible under the scale rather than to the extent demanded by the needs of applicants . . . I was informed that a very large number of people are now applying for out relief who, were it not for this propoganda [*sic*], would have refrained from asking for help . . . [133]

Jones spoke for himself in the *Rhondda Vanguard* of June 1936, where he set out his views on local government at length, arguing that the Labour Party had failed to see that the attacks made by the Government upon democratic institutions such as local governing bodies were actually attacks upon the conditions of the people:

This has resulted in a failure on the part of those leaders to see that their own strength and the safety of the institutions they occupy rests, not in themselves or the institutions, but in the working class and the organizations whom they represent. The working class and the democratic minded people can be lifted into mass action against all governmental attacks. To fail in this vital matter means that the local and county authorities and the representatives of the people within them become instruments to operate anti-working class legislation passed by the National Government instead of weapons in the hands of the working class to improve the living conditions. It is out of such an approach to the problem arises the false idea that it is better for Labour representatives to administer anti-working class regulations than a representative of the capitalist class. District and County Councils are thus forced to a policy that can only end in the bankruptcy of both. This is the problem now facing every authority in South Wales. It can only be solved by the closest united co-ordination between the existing working class majorities on these bodies linked up with a closer connection between these and the mass working class organizations. As it is now there is a complete separation between the representatives of the workers in the Trade Unions and those in the councils, although very often positions in both are filled by the same person.[134]

This is a complicated and slightly ambiguous passage, in that at one point Lewis Jones echoes the rejectionist rhetoric of the early 1920s. Yet this is outweighed by an awareness that local representative institutions cannot challenge the state alone, but that although they should not become the lackeys of anti-working-class action (a transition the Communists blamed Labour for permitting) they do need a great deal of assistance if they are to defend their people. The assistance that Jones envisages – 'united co-ordination' between 'existing working class majorities' and with 'mass working class organizations' – is also stressed by Mary Roberts as she speaks to her Communist branch in *We Live*:

'Take the question of unity between ourselves and Labour. Where are the leaders of the Labour Party?' she asked; then answered: 'In the Federation and the councils, isn't it? They are united with us in the Fed. against the non-pols. and the company, but they are miles away from us in the council. And that's just our problem. We've got to break down their opposition to us politically in one way or another, and I think the council is one way of doing it. If we can get Labour and Communist councillors marching together, on behalf of the unemployed for instance, I'm sure the mass of people would follow.'[135]

What Lewis Jones desired, in fiction and in fact, was a Rhondda version of the United Front, and indeed one that could become a Popular Front. This became an impressive reality in 1935, in the agitation against the means test.

The 1935 demonstrations against the implementation of Part II of the Unemployment Insurance Act of 1934 have been hailed as the most significant and effective direct-action protest of the inter-war years. It has been claimed that as a result of the volume of protest, the government froze and retreated. And the protests of the people of the south Wales coalfield were in the van of the struggle: Hywel Francis and David Smith see it as 'the greatest volcano of socio-political protest ever experienced in the region.'[136] Other historians have questioned this interpretation, claiming that the protests have to be seen alongside shifting alignments at the level of 'high' politics.[137] But whatever the retrospective assessments and moderations, contemporaries were struck by the size and the passionate nature of the 1935 protests. To a contemporary political journalist it was 'one of the greatest victories in the history of the British working-class movement'; to Rhondda East's MP W. H. Mainwaring it was 'a rising of mass indignation against the system'.[138]

Even when investigation of the means-test protest is confined to strictly political matters the event takes on considerable significance for its display of unity on the left and indeed into the centre. Although the Labour Party's national leadership and that of the TUC largely steered clear of active involvement in the movement, at the local level unity was extensive.

The Rhondda demonstrations in January 1935 were massive in the numbers they attracted and broad in their political support, organized at a coalfield level by the SWMF. The CPGB strategy was to work through local 'Fed' organizations such as the Combine Committees, rather than itself call directly for a United Front, a call that had not had much success during 1933 and 1934. This time mass meetings, *ad hoc* United Front committees, and deputations included SWMF speakers, representatives and delegates, who might be Labour or Communist, plus delegates drawn from both the Labour Party and the Communist Party themselves, all of whom worked together. These were supplemented by representatives of the Chamber of Trade, of the churches and chapels, of the unemployed clubs and even the Conservative Clubs and the local branch of Plaid Cymru![139]

The successes of early 1935 boosted the prestige and the confidence of Rhondda Communists. Subsequently, the ideal of United Front action from below reappeared for individual demonstrations and for hunger marches, such as the Rhondda League of Nations 'United Action for Peace' Day in September 1935.[140] In 1936, the spirit and some of the organizations of the United Front reappeared, focusing upon the Hunger Marchers of that year. An *ad hoc* body known as the Council of Action appeared, drawing representatives from religious organizations, trade unions, clubs and political parties, plus Councillors. A July demonstration against the means test saw prominent Labourites and Communists share the platform, a pattern repeated on occasions in subsequent years.[141] Although national Labour Party policy tended to be opposed to the United Front and the Popular Front, local opinion was often sympathetic, as was that of the SWMF leadership and membership.[142]

The problem for the Rhondda Labour Party was that although the causes undoubtedly appeared just, and although it was right to become involved in the demonstrations and committees, invariably it was the Communists who seemed to capitalize most on these joint efforts. As the CPGB was always calling for United Front action on any conceivable issue, inevitably it held the initiative when joint action took place. It had the personalities, the experience, and the flair, and however worthy and numerous Labour might appear, it was the CP that captured the limelight.[143]

This is clearly exemplified by the support for Republican Spain from 1936 until 1939. Again, whilst it is unnecessary to attempt to compete with the research of Hywel Francis on the attitudes taken by the south Wales miners towards the Spanish Civil War, certain general observations can be made.[144] Spain was not simply another international issue to Rhondda – reaction to it was urgent, inspired and sustained. Rhondda supplied the International Brigade with thirty-two volunteers, the largest valley contingent from within the ranks of the Welsh miners, and a larger contingent than all those volunteering from English coalfields.[145] Volunteering was only the tip of the iceberg: Aid for Spain Committees, meetings, rallies, demonstrations and fund-raising carried on apace at local level. Francis is probably right to claim that the RBLP 'seemed to be as active as the Communist Party' in these matters.[146] But, as his work implies, the depth of support for Republican Spain is inexplicable outside the context of a strong and dedicated Rhondda Communism, integral to which was an internationalist outlook. He is also correct

to note that Rhondda Communism lost many of its activists to Spain
– whether in the shape of volunteers or, as in the case of Lewis Jones,
those who worked themselves literally to death for the cause.[147] But
Spain also represented the capstone of Rhondda Communism's
achievements, and was a moment of heroism and endeavour, and
ultimately of humanity amidst the economic desolation of the
decade. Communist support in the Rhondda valleys derived from
dissatisfaction and disillusionment with the Labour Party, and took
sustenance from the cultural vibrancy of Communist Party life. But
ultimately the greatest explanatory burden for the CPGB's rise has to
be placed upon the courageous and original strategies that it, for a
time, articulated on behalf of Rhondda society as a whole.

The limits of Communism

> Communists can give both vigour and vision to all local authorities. In
> the case of those Councils which are Labour-controlled, a few
> Communist Councillors – or even one – can strengthen Labour's hands
> and infuse greater determination and drive into its efforts to improve the
> people's lot.
>
> Welsh Committee of the Communist Party, *Fighters for the People;*
> *A Record of the Activities of Communist Councillors in Wales*

The CPGB was able to pose a substantial challenge to Labour Party
domination in Rhondda, particularly in the 1930s. Such a challenge
was a rarity in inter-war Britain, and marks Rhondda out as being a
notable hotbed of political militancy. But having established the
strength of Rhondda Communism, it remains to be considered why it
did not have greater success, and remained unable to displace the
Labour Party at any level of political representation. The obstacles to
Communism's expansion, the limits of its success, can be located
largely within the decade of the 1930s, when Communism posed
Labour its greatest problems, and can be understood as a mirror
image of the sources of Communist strength. Thus consideration has
to be given to Labour's municipal successes as well as its failures, to
Labour's own internal struggles against corruption, and to the failure
of Communist achievement to match up to the levels of rhetoric and
criticism. The vibrancy of Communist Party culture provoked a
reaction in Labour Party circles, within which greater efforts were
made to build a sense of unity and purpose, whilst notions of
'respectability', sometimes allied with religious belief, were further

obstacles to Communist support. Finally, the CP's advance was impeded by the continuing reluctance of the Labour Party to enter into any permanent alliances with it, even at local level.

The burdens of office II

The Labour Group of the County Council has been subjected to caustic and ill-considered criticism by a certain section of the working-class movement, merely because it has not defied all Government Departments, and flouted the wishes of 'Whitehall' on every occasion. Had this mad policy been adopted, the probability is that democratic Local Government in Glamorgan would now be a matter of history. The powers possessed by the County Council are purely administrative, and let it be known definitely that every step taken by the Labour Group has been a step taken in the interests of the common people – their own fellow working men. Every member of the Group retains his belief in Socialism and is prepared to play his or her part in propagating the idea of social ownership and control, but not one pretends that he can establish and practise Socialism in County administration when the whole country is so obviously unripe for such a change. All the Labour County Council can do is to introduce as much humaneness into its administration as is possible, and thereby make the lives of the people a little bit easier during these terrible hard and difficult times.

Alderman Jack Evans, *Rhondda Clarion*, September 1935

The Labour Party's approach to local government administration, be it upon the GCC or RUDC, was financially and politically cautious, and thus open to attack from the CPGB. But it was not without its successes, one of which was the provision of milk to children of low-income families, and the sporadic provision of free coal and allotment produce. Medical experts visiting Rhondda acknowledged that were it not for the free distribution of milk widespread child malnutrition would follow, and observed that the RUDC was generous in its provision in comparison with other south Walian councils.[148] Allen Hutt, in his 1933 book *The Condition of the Working Class in Britain*, acknowledged the Glamorgan Labour Party's 'humane administration' of the means test.[149]

Paradoxically, the CP's own municipal advance was another obstacle to its progress. Taking office, sharing in administration, seeing its problems from the inside, all made impossibilist sloganizing and 'gesture politics' no longer quite so viable. Elizabeth Andrews for Labour called on voters to 'know the difference between a big noise and steady work, between walking out and creating scenes in the Council Chambers and facing facts and difficulties of administration and obtaining the maximum out of every Act of Parliament for the common good'.[150] In practice, differences between the two groups of Councillors became blurred, as both sought to work the system as well as to achieve party-political advantage. By the end of the 1930s there was increasing recognition that the problems and enemies faced by the RUDC were common to both Labour and Communist representatives.[151] Differences of style remained, and there was the occasional rancorous outburst but, with both parties adopting an essentially pragmatic, rather than rejectionist, outlook on local government, the potential for Communist vote-winning in this area became limited.

The temptations of office II

In each municipal election they [the Communists] have concentrated on the bias and prejudice against individuals in the Labour Movement, and have secured a small measure of success. But this tactic is now playing itself out, and the Communist Party will be judged by its performance in administrative positions.

Idris Williams, *Rhondda Clarion*, March 1936

Public revulsion at instances of Labour Party corruption had resulted in greater support being given to non-Labour Party candidates at local elections in the mid-1930s, and particularly in greater support for the CPGB. It would be wrong, however, to assume that involvement in, or even tolerance of corrupt practices was characteristic of the majority of Labour activists, and it is fair to say that the RBLP was eventually prompted by internal disquiet as well as external rebuffs into putting its own house into some sort of order, a measure that limited the damage the issue was able to do to the party's electoral fortunes, and thus restricted the opportunities for advance open to the CP.

By the early 1930s sections of the Labour Party were agitated by corruption. In January 1933, Ward Three RBLP urged the Rhondda West DLP to draw attention to the problem of Councillors' obtaining jobs for themselves and their relatives. In April 1933, the RBLP passed a resolution that Labour public representatives should, when making appointments, give preference to unemployed applicants when their qualifications were equivalent to those of employed applicants for the same post, but rejected another resolution that would force

Councillors wishing to take jobs under local authorities to resign their seats before applying for such jobs.[152] Following setbacks in the local elections of 1934 stronger action began to be taken, under stimulus from the local party and trade unions. The RBLP resolved that a Councillor must retire six months before a near relative could apply for a position under the authority of which that Councillor had been a member. The RBLP executive was also established as a Committee of Enquiry investigating corruption, and W. H. Mainwaring drafted its terms of reference:

1. Have Councillors used their positions for personal ends?
2. Have Councillors used their positions for their children and other relatives?
3. Is there any truth in the allegation of corruption?
4. Have there been obvious decisions on appointments difficult to justify?
5. Have the Councillors violated Party decisions?
6. Are Council employees prejudiced in their chances for promotion by other men appointed to positions?

All affiliated organizations were asked for their views and for any evidence, and in November 1934 the Committee of Enquiry reported its findings:

1. There is some ground for complaint . . . but given the Local Government Act 1933 . . . the Committee finds it unnecessary to make any additional recommendations. The Law stipulates that a Councillor must have left the Council for twelve months before he is eligible for any post.
2. The Committee finds that probably there is a great deal of exaggeration in the Public Mind, but, nevertheless, it was necessary to deal with the situation, and therefore recommend that Councillors should not do so, and that any Councillor canvassing for an appointment on behalf of a relative, be expelled from the Party. If a Councillor's son/daughter/brother/sister receive an appointment (excluding scholastic appointment) he/she shall not again be a party candidate, in the future.
3. It was felt that the question of promotion to Headships in the Teaching Profession underlies the whole of this, and therefore, it is recommended that present appointment method be abolished and a joint committee be set up to work out a new basis. If rumours become current, then councillors will be asked to clear their names.

4. Appointments have been made, that, undoubtedly, are difficult to justify for one reason or another, and in the interest of the Party, procedure should be tightened up and placed above suspicion.
5. Undoubtedly, Party resolutions have not been observed during the last two years, and Executive should deal with future cases, withholding endorsement of any delinquent thereafter, to stand as Party candidate.
6. Situation unsatisfactory, and joint committee to be set up and to bring forward a report before conference.[153]

The next month James James resigned from the Labour Party, and was followed in March 1935 by Eliza Williams.[154] Although these actions did not come in time to prevent substantial electoral damage to Labour in the 1935 elections, thereafter the urgency of the corruption issue waned. Indeed the Labour Party had the effrontery to begin to turn the criticism back on its Communist opponents. Communist Councillor George Maslin temporarily split from the CPGB in 1938 as a result of his failure to perform to pre-existing standards of Labour administration. Allegations were made that he had attempted to use his representative position to try to get a job for his son. Maslin denied this, and the fact that his son remained unemployed perhaps sums up the difference between the Labour Party and the Communist Party![155]

Only some Labour Councillors were involved in corruption in the 1930s, and it would be wrong to tar the whole of the Labour Group or the RBLP with the same brush. Some Labour activists deliberately went into Council work to try and right the prevailing image of Councillors as corrupt, whilst many others deserved no such image at all.[156] The political reaction of Rhondda electors, which was so important in the mid-1930s, was against the blatant misuse of power by certain individuals, but once action had been seen to have been taken there was no popular desire to remove all or even most Labour representatives. This is not to say that corruption did not continue: as far as it is possible to tell it did. But it was not quite so stark, it was therefore rather more tolerated, and perhaps, considering the virtues and achievements of the Labour Party at local and at national level into the 1940s and 1950s, it was not seen any longer as particularly important.

Labour's cultural and organizational renaissance

Although the Communist Party failed to win a parliamentary seat in Wales in the 1930s . . . their electoral success in Rhondda East provided

an important stimulus to the Labour Party to establish a cohesive
political organization in South Wales.

Ian McAllister[157]

The success of the Communist Party in the early to mid-1930s awoke
Labour from its docility and torpor. As Labour had come to dominate
parliamentary and local representation it had been barely impelled to
maintain an efficient party organization: success seemed to come
without too much effort, and there was little need to encourage high
levels of either membership or activity by party organizations. The
social vitality, evident up to the early 1920s, disappeared, and Labour
began to appear complacent and listless. For some years after
disaffiliation this continued to be true, and it was not until the shocks
of the 1933 by-election and the 1934 and 1935 local elections that
Labour began to pay greater attention to its internal organization and
its cultural dimension. Then the party decided upon a series of
reforms: organizational, cultural and strategic.[158]

Organizationally the internal structure of the Labour Party was
rationalized. Local public representatives were urged to report with
greater frequency to their Ward Parties and to the Borough Party.[159]
The official Labour Group on the RUDC was restructured to include
not only all Councillors, but also three representatives from each of
the Divisional Parties. A Liaison Group was established between the
Labour Group and the RBLP for better co-ordination of policy. Policy,
whether discussed by these groups, the RBLP, the Divisional Parties,
or the Ward Parties, often dealt with local matters such as bus routes,
the supervision of rents, public library facilities, the state of the
allotments or of the sewers, the price of milk, and the provision of
medical services. Ward committees would raise matters, and then
either approach their local public representatives directly, or pass on
the matter to the RBLP or perhaps the Divisional Party. In this way
the TLC functions that the Rhondda Labour Party should have taken
over with the reorganization of 1923 now came to receive greater
attention, and the RBLP set up its own Industrial Committee to
discuss particularly industrial or trade union issues, whilst restyling
itself the Rhondda Borough Labour Party and Trades Council.[160]
There was greater discussion of national policy issues, Labour Party
Conference resolutions were discussed, and encouragement was given
to public representatives to hold more public meetings in their wards
to explain local government policy.[161] Party finances were reorganized,

and there was greater emphasis placed on fund-raising and upon membership drives, although overall Rhondda's membership levels compared with other Labour Parties in Wales remained low.[162]

One innovation was the publication of the Rhondda Labour Party's newspaper, the *Rhondda Clarion* as a response to the CP's *Rhondda Vanguard*. The monthly *Clarion*, subtitled 'The Official Organ of the Rhondda Borough Labour Party', was established in September 1935, and ran for fourteen issues at a price of one penny until December 1936. W. H. Mainwaring was the motive force behind the *Clarion*, which ran articles on matters local and international. It included a Welsh-language column, a letters and notices section, book reviews and obituaries; but the overall impression was rather stilted and unexciting, and circulation was never sufficiently high to allow expansion or great confidence in the paper's long-term survival. The *Clarion*'s most important contribution was probably its provision of advice and information on unemployment regulations, another echo of the rival *Vanguard*, and the 1936 *Clarion* issue on the Unemployment Assistance Board (UAB) regulations was a sell-out.

More difficult to measure, but at least as important, was the Labour Party's renewed vigour in arranging social and cultural events from the mid-1930s onwards. Social evenings, victory celebrations, and public debates had never completely faded from the local scene but, with the rise of the CP threat, a greater number and a wider variety of such events were held.[163] There were plays, whist drives, flower shows, concerts, lectures, children's sports days, outings and May Day rallies.[164] A mock parliament reappeared, this time run at the Methodist Central Hall in Tonypandy, but very much Labour in tone.[165] Evidence that survives from the Labour Party Women's Sections also suggests that there was greater social and cultural activity, perhaps to the exclusion of more 'political' work. Such organizations placed great weight upon the sharing of personal and familial burdens, with the Sections electing 'sick visitors' to care for invalid members.[166]

Finally, the Labour Party also attempted to establish a youth organization, possibly in response to the CPGB's success with its Young Comrades League. A Labour Party League of Youth was formed in 1934, although its membership was very patchy across the wards, and there was some feeling that such success as it had was due to the interest of young people not in politics but 'in football teams, dances etc.'. The League continued to be active throughout the 1930s, and was revived after the war to try and bring more young people into the party.[167] Overall, although one must still concede that it was the CPGB that had the greatest cohesion and vibrancy, the Labour Party did make some efforts at self-improvement, and these may have played some part in restricting further Communist advance.

Religion and respectability

It has been brought to my knowledge that some members of the Christian Church have not only been regularly attending Communist meetings, but have even joined the Communist Party. It is impossible for anyone who is honourable to be a member of the Communist Party and of the Christian Church at one and the same time.

Reg Barker, 17 March 1935

A more substantial barrier to the spread of Rhondda Communism was organized religion: its attitude towards Communism and the more specific intermeshing of the Labour Party with Nonconformist culture. This, combined with a certain social prejudice against Communism as non-'respectable' meant that for a proportion of the population, Communist voting was unthinkable. There were CP activists who were religious, such as Congregationalists David Phillips of Ferndale and Samuel Davies of Mardy (Davies being a deacon as well as secretary of Mardy Lodge), and elements of Communist Party culture have been seen as operating along essentially religious lines.[168] Furthermore, sometimes the CP and religious organizations worked together for social reform, as in Mardy with the local Salvation Army.[169] But in general Communism and Christianity were seen as being in conflict. This was certainly the position adopted by the Methodist minister and Labour County Councillor at Central Hall, Tonypandy, Reg Barker, and by his successor Cyril Gwyther. Barker was unafraid to attack Communism as 'atheistic and irreconcilable with Christianity'.[170] Apocalyptically, Barker suggested that under Communism 'all the social and educational work of the churches would come to an end' and that 'even Sunday school trips to Barry would be forbidden'. Barker was a radical in his theology, refusing to believe in the Virgin Birth, and took an essentially Christian socialist position. His political involvement upset some chapel-goers.[171] Nevertheless, the 'cloak of religion' worked to Labour's benefit. Increasingly throughout the 1920s and into the 1930s Labour MPs and Councillors were found taking positions of responsibility in local churches and chapels, and being called upon to deliver sermons or lectures to church groups. Will John, Owen Buckley, and Tom Smith were all well-known Labour Nonconformists, and even someone such as W. H. Mainwaring, expelled from his chapel for refusing to believe that Lot's wife could have been turned into a pillar of salt, thought it prudent to put in the odd chapel appearance, albeit not in the pulpit! Mainwaring favoured a talk entitled 'Social Changes of the Bible'.[172] Whatever the claims of Communists that their beliefs were closer in spirit to the ideas of Christ, the challenge of the CPGB impelled the Nonconformist establishment further to embrace the Labour Party as a defence against the former's supposed atheism.

Labour's strategic closure

> There are those who see in this situation [the United Front] an opportunity for creating and spreading a mentality suitable to their own peculiar and irresponsible gospel. Every opportunity has and is being utilized by the Communist Party . . . Every fact and action is being distorted to the detriment of other people. There is absolutely no regard for the truth and no pretence at commonsense and reason. Every effort is concentrated in an attempt to inflame the passions of those who suffer and nullify all who counsel saner and more reasonable methods.
>
> Rhondda Borough Labour Party circular, 22 February 1936

The inspirational strategies pursued by the Rhondda CP in the mid-to-late 1930s have been rightly given much credit for the electoral successes of individual Communists in local and parliamentary contests. Undoubtedly it was the CP, not the Labour Party, that left its mark most distinctly upon these years. But there were also strategic reasons, which demand examination, for the CP's failure to make even greater progress. Within the context of the United Front, and later the Popular Front policies, it was the refusal of the Rhondda Labour Party to enter into a permanent rather than a temporary alliance with the CPGB, that limited the latter's opportunities, and closed down much of its potential for growth.

First, the CPGB was unable to extend temporary alliances over the means test, fascism or Spain into a permanent municipal electoral pact. A common Communist strategem was to suggest, before any local elections, that the Labour Party and the CPGB, plus all other working-class organizations, meet to select joint candidates, rather than go to the polls divided.[173] The standard RBLP executive committee's reply to such invitations was that no such arrangements were possible.[174] Indeed, the Labour Party usually preferred to risk defeat by splitting the left-wing vote rather than co-operate with the CPGB. Although the CP occasionally withdrew candidates as a friendly gesture, this was never formally reciprocated by the RBLP.[175]

The Communists had greater success with their United Front policy, particularly with agitation against the means test in 1935, as previously explained. But although a very impressive degree of unity was attained during the major demonstrations of that year, two of the CP's more ambitious objectives were not reached.

There is considerable evidence that Rhondda Communists, supported nationally by the *Daily Worker*, wished the means-test demonstrations to be only the beginning of a major campaign of extra-parliamentary action that would move from rectifying the specific injustices contained in the new legislation to challenging the system of poor relief.[176] Part of the political debate centred upon the issue of whether local government bodies should themselves refuse to operate the new regulations. At the RUDC, a motion calling upon the authority to invite the miners to 'down tools' in protest at the scales was moved by Labour's Jack 'Bolshie' Williams, but this was defeated in favour of the RUDC's calling upon the government to abolish the regulations. A resolution proposed by the Communist Jimmy Morton to ask the GCC to make up the benefit of any of the unemployed adversely affected by the new scales was defeated on the casting vote of the chairman of the Council, with the Labour Group split on this issue.[177] More dramatic was the CP's call of early February 1935, voiced in particular by Lewis Jones through the Cambrian Combine Committee, for a one-day stoppage throughout the area, to be combined with demonstrations at Unemployment Assistance Board offices and the establishment of United Front Committees throughout the coalfield. The strike was planned for 25 February, but in the event failed to materialize. Although Mid-Rhondda Chamber of Trade and the employees of Penygraig and Mid-Rhondda Co-operatives agreed to shut up shop for the day, miners' lodges outside the Cambrian Combine refused to support the move, following instructions from the SWMF executive and a conference of SWMF delegates. The Rhondda branch of the NUT voted five hundred to six not to strike. The Chamber of Trade and the Co-op then reversed their decision, and the various lodges of the Cambrian Combine followed suit.[178] The strike was 'postponed' for a month, and instead there was a mass demonstration of 20,000 marred by the shouting down of Labour speakers by the Communists.[179] Party-political unity was brief in January and February in 1935: it could reappear occasionally, but the Labour Party was consistent in its refusal to contemplate a permanent United Front with the CP.

This refusal was due to Labour's interpretation of the United Front as partly responsible for the Communist local and parliamentary advance. After the Labour Party's disastrous performance in the 1935 local elections, a special conference was held to discuss the operation of the United Front throughout the two valleys. Reports came in from each Ward Party, and in only one Ward, Treorchy, were the Communists not felt to be more trouble than they were worth. Repeatedly wards reported that they felt it was 'time to break away', that the Communists were using the United Front platforms purely for their own partisan purposes, that the committees had either turned into 'bear gardens', or that the Communists had already left the committees.[180] Party officials felt very much the same way at a meeting in May: that the United Front, such as it existed, represented a drain on the strength of the Labour Party.[181] These ideas were well received by the RBLP, and at the beginning of June 1935 the United Front was dissolved.[182]

Subsequently, the official RBLP view of the United Front was that it was a trick 'to further the power of the Communist Party machine', and the CPGB was regularly attacked in the pages of the *Rhondda Clarion*. How, it was asked, could one unite with a party that only wished to score points off the Labour Party?[183] More general attacks were made upon the insurrectionary intentions of the CPGB, and by 1936 there was no possibility of again organizing a United Front on a Rhondda-wide scale for any substantial period, and there was a similar fate for the Popular Front.[184]

The CP also found vital sources of sustenance cut off as the RBLP tightened its control of the political actions of affiliated organizations, in particular the miners' lodges. When the Ferndale Lodge was readmitted to the RBLP in 1936 it was on condition that it complied with Party rules and did not run candidates on its own account, or allow Communists to be delegates to Labour Party meetings.[185]

Capping Labour's determination to close off opportunities from the CP was the establishment of the South Wales Regional Council of Labour (SWRCL) in 1937, a deliberately anti-Communist body that aimed to co-ordinate the Labour movement in south Wales, and which barred CP members from being delegates.[186] Overall, once the CP began to present a serious threat to Labour in Rhondda in the mid-1930s, then Labour acted to close down the CP's avenues of advance, and did so effectively.

Epilogue: The return to one-party politics

The true test of Christian and Religious endeavour is to be found in the deed and not in mere belief. Apply this test to the Labour Government. During the past three years it has done more to build a New Jerusalem than any other Government in History. It is translating the Sermon on the Mount into our daily life. Labour is abolishing tyranny and oppression . . . It spreads the light of knowledge and truth. Labour is the only force in politics that works for the salvation of the human race.

RBLP Address to Electors, 1948 RUDC Elections

The outbreak of the Second World War made it easier for Labour to justify a separatist position, given the CPGB's confusion and neutralism until 1941. Labour experienced few doubts about the 'just' nature of the war, as is evidenced by John Thomas Davies's inaugural words upon accepting the chairmanship of the RUDC in 1940: 'The Rhondda has a great and important part to play in the prosecution of the world war now in progress to defeat Fascism and Nazism. I think that this war is a fight between evil and good, and I am fully convinced that eventually the powers of good will triumphantly prevail.'[187]

Upon the outbreak of war Labour immediately took the lead in organizing the community for its new challenges. The RBLP determined that each Ward Labour Party should establish committees to deal with food control, rents and the cost of living; with state assistance in the form of unemployment and social insurance; and with soldiers and sailors' military allowances and pensions.[188] Later, Labour also sank its efforts into the Rhondda Spitfire Fund, War Weapons Week and the establishment of a War Effort Committee to deal with information, propaganda, and morale.[189] In these circumstances the CP's efforts to perpetuate Popular Front activity through the medium of the People's Vigilance Movement had little success, with the highly suspicious Labour Party threatening any affiliated organizations that took an interest in the movement with expulsion.[190] A local variant also attempted by the CP was the Rhondda All-In Conference, meeting in the early months of 1940, which called for a broad campaign to increase allowances, public assistance, compensation payments, unemployment benefit and pensions. Although this was backed initially by some miners' lodges and Labour Party members, the SWRCL clamped down on support for this campaign as well, and the two Labour MPs also spoke out against it, Mainwaring stating baldly that 'I have not the slightest intention of co-operating with reactionary pro-fascist elements.'[191]

The German invasion of the Soviet Union in 1941 resulted in a wave of popular support for Russia that had beneficial side-effects for the CPGB. With the 1945 general election following hard on the heels of the Allied victory in Europe Harry Pollitt capitalized on the situation with a record vote and near-victory in Rhondda East. But without any local elections in that year the CP's success was brief, and as the Cold War began to descend upon the world the Party's momentum was frozen.

Labour's strongest card during the late 1940s was the Attlee Government. It was logical enough for voters who had backed a radical start to the peacetime compact in a general election to wish to extend that support to the level of local government.[192] The line taken against the CP was crude: 'at the most perilous moment in the history of this country, when we stood alone against the nazi hordes . . . they were willing to cringe and creep on their bellies to Hitler for a negotiated peace.' There was only one choice before the voters: 'Forge the Link between the Central Government and the Local Government. Make them PARTNERS IN ACTION.' The Labour Party had no truck with CP calls for joint candidacies and an electoral pact, and although the CP vote did not collapse in 1946, it was considered that they had reached 'the zenith of their power' in Rhondda.[193]

Over the following years Labour merely needed to repeat this message of first, the value of a Labour vote for the overall cohesion of Labour government throughout Britain, and second, the need to remember the Depression years and the importance in this context of loyalty to a long tradition of Labour support (true in most wards, if not all). The CP vote fell away, and by 1948 the local press was hailing 'the rout of the reds'.[194] On the whole Labour could now ignore the CP.[195] If required it could point to the Party's achievements locally with health care, education, public baths and parks, and to the house-building activity of the Labour government, its nationalization of the coal industry, its pensions and unemployment schemes. Communist calls to the electorate to 'Vote for Schools not Tanks, Health Centres not Bombs, Clinics not Atom Bombs' fell overwhelmingly on deaf ears, as did swipes at the advanced age of a number of Labour Councillors.[196] Indeed, as veteran Communists passed away, retired or were defeated, it was the CPGB that was most plagued by the problem of an ageing cadre of activists. Those that remained found it increasingly difficult to compete with Labour's new-found resonance. George Maslin, enjoying himself as chairman of the RUDC from 1945 until 1946, was praised for his work, particularly in the field of housing and the opening of new factories. Maslin, it was felt 'has a good deal of the temperament of a Horner or a Cook . . . but he is content to allow his divine discontent to find expression along quite respectable and constitutional lines, and he works in harness with his fellow councillors with scarcely a kick over the traces'.[197] Maslin himself considered his greatest achievement to be the establishment of a rheumatic clinic at Trealaw.[198] Communism was either becoming domesticated or out of step with the Cold War mood: either way it was irrelevant.[199] Labour had captured the political agenda and, on the subject of Rhondda's industrial reconstruction, all the fresh ideas were its own.[200] Come 1949 and the CP no longer had any representatives left on the RUDC. With their campaigns in decline, 'enshrouded in an air of unreality', lacking their 'old-time zest and determination', Labour found them less and less troubling. By 1954 the once-impressive CP challenge in Rhondda had faded to be of little more than 'nuisance value', on the margins of Rhondda politics alongside the Independents and Plaid Cymru. The Rhondda Labour Party, no longer preoccupied with external opposition, now began to generate its own internal controversies, as Bevanites sprang up on one side, and the Moral Rearmament movement appeared on the other. The Communist challenge had run out of steam, and a new, monochrome pattern of political activity had taken its place.

Conclusion: A Labour people

LOSS TO PORTH: DEATH OF ACTIVE PUBLIC WORKER
The death of County Councillor John James Garwood, 14 Lewis
Terrace, Llwyncelyn, Porth, has removed one of Porth's most esteemed
residents.

A native of Llandaff he came to Trehafod when a boy of four, and
started to work in the mines at the age of twelve. At a comparatively
early age the splendid qualities and initiative, for which he was to be
noted all his life, became evident, and he first won prominence as an
active member of the Lewis Merthyr Lodge of the Miners' Federation
and as secretary of the Checkweighers' Fund. He also became
workmen's representative on the Board of Management of the Cardiff
Infirmary, a position he held for thirty-five years, until the miners ceased
to contribute towards it. Another office he held was that of a trustee of
the Lewis Merthyr Workmen's Institute and Library. He served on
dispute committees, and was also a mines examiner, representing the
men at Lewis Merthyr. During the miners' strikes in 1921 and 1926 he
played a leading part.

In the depression following the 1926 strike he did outstanding work in
connection with the Lord Mayor's Fund, for which he received a letter of
thanks from HRH the Prince of Wales.

When twenty years of age Mr Garwood joined the St John's
Ambulance Corps, and soon became a foremost member in the local
division. The knowledge he gained was put to good use in the mines for
many years. After twenty-five years he ceased to be a member of the
Ambulance Corps but always kept its interest at heart. On the Saturday
before he passed away he performed his last duty to the organization,
through the medium of his devoted wife, by arranging a tea to follow
the National Coal Board ambulance competition at Llwyncelyn School.

Mr Garwood was thirty-two when he went to reside in Llwyncelyn,
where after two years he became a warden at St Luke's Church. He was
the main founder of the new St Luke's Church, and for twenty-eight
years rendered invaluable and faithful service.

In 1934 he was elected to the Glamorgan County Council. His chief
interests were child welfare and the care of the aged. He obtained for the

pensioners the use of the old Grand Cinema, where they could spend a
few hours of recreation every day. He always said: 'Look after the
children and the old folk; the others will manage pretty well.' He was
president of the Old Age Pensioners' Association.

During the war of 1939–45 he placed his services at the disposal of
the civil defence movement and became an ambulance driver at
Llwyncelyn First Aid Depot. He assisted in almost every organization
that was formed during the war, being Chairman of the Red Cross and
St John Fund, convener of the Repatriated Prisoners of War Fund, and a
member of the Prisoner of War Fund and War Savings Committees.

During 1941 he gave up his employment as a contractor at the Bertie
Pit, after being certified by the silicosis board. He suffered ill-health
until his death; he passed away in his sleep on May 7th. He is survived
by his widow, two sons and two daughters. Loved and respected by all,
his passing is a great loss to the community of Porth and district.

Rhondda Leader and Gazette, 22 May, 1948[1]

Johnny Garwood was a Labour Councillor. His obituary did not
mention his politics, but then, in listing his record of service to his
community, perhaps it did not need to do so. His life, and his life's
work, symbolized the overwhelmingly positive contribution made by
the Labour movement to Rhondda society from the end of the
nineteenth century onwards. It would be a mistake to suggest that
Johnny Garwood was in all ways typical of working-class public
representatives. His Anglicanism, for instance, was very much the
exception amongst such activists. He served on the County Council,
rather than upon the Urban District Council or Board of Guardians,
where for so long the larger levers of Rhondda power might be
manipulated. He refused a magistracy when it was offered. Yet he was
never tempted by the Communist Party, even after the 1926 dispute
(during which time he appeared as a jazz-band drummer) when he
was victimized and lost his job. He remained in the Labour Party and,
as his obituary indicates, placed himself at the disposal of his people.

There are many examples of such men and women to be found in
Rhondda's political annals and, during the researching of this work,
meetings took place with the families of a few of them.[2] Of the life
histories they recalled, perhaps the most common element was that of
the unrelenting dedication and hard work of their parents in a
number of different industrial, political, but ultimately social roles.
'Councillors', said George Thomas, 'were what I call ambidextrous.
They were all-purpose.'[3] In existing historical literature, much has

been made of the social centrality of Federation leaders within south Wales mining communities: in Will Paynter's words they were 'the guides, philosophers and friends', 'the village elders', 'the acknowledged social leaders'.[4] The same sort of role can be claimed for Labour (and indeed for Communist) public representatives, who were often Federation leaders wearing a different cap. They were the advice bureaux of their localities, a role for which they were occasionally named: Will 'Knowledge' Hughes, Dafydd Hughes 'Income Tax'. They made great personal sacrifices to perform effectively in such roles: according to their children they were always busy, they would be spending every evening in their front room (their 'surgery') or at a meeting, to which they might have to travel considerable distances on foot or by public transport. When they were at home they could expect to be called upon by friends, acquaintances and supplicants alike.

Being a public representative was not a passport to a comfortable existence. No doubt the office could confer some dignity, some pleasing recognition within the wider society. For a few it put temptation in their path, which they were not always able to resist.[5] But Rhondda society could forgive even those, if their service was seen as more important than their transgressions, most of which were on a minor scale. Mark Harcombe, the man at the centre of the Rhondda Labour Party's power and influence for decades, could joke about his reputation in public, because he knew what his contribution to Rhondda amounted to, and could feel secure in the knowledge that the majority of his constituents recognized it as well. Eleven times he put himself before his local electorate, and not once was he defeated, whilst for nearly fifty years he served his trade union in a variety of capacities. Harcombe, and others like him, could not delude his constituents into returning him to office. To understand his success one has to comprehend that the Rhondda Labour Party had an interactive relationship with its community that provided it with an integrity capable of defying any individual malfeasance. This relationship cannot properly be understood as 'machine politics' – with party leaders manipulating an electorate whose political senses were dulled by habitual tradition – currently a theme of emblematic significance in what is a shallow understanding of Labour domination.[6] Rather, it was a product of a class-conscious society that elevated its own representatives in a process of community redefinition that rested upon deep collective and personal loyalties, and upon a rich associational culture. Furthermore, much of the hard-earned success of the Rhondda Communist Party was built on an echo of this relationship. The chains of attachment between politicians and their society were of multiple form: whilst some public representatives were ingenuous reflections of the hopes of their people, others acted as prisms to refract those hopes on to a higher plane. Both types were serious engagements with present concerns and future desires.

Is it appropriate to view this society, from the mid-1920s onwards, as an 'alternative culture' in the valleys of the south Wales coalfield?[7] The characteristic elements of this culture have been defined as including a 'hostility to capitalism', 'a cultural shift . . . labelled "prolet-cult" by those who were most disturbed by it', and the increasing rejection of 'social, political and cultural norms'. All of these have been considered to have created a 'new behavioural pattern', evident in the 1925 anthracite strike but spread by the crisis of 1926, which 'precipitated a polarizing of class and community forces'.[8] During the strike and lock-out this 'alternative culture' was 'diversified and deepened so that it was founded on class discipline, resourceful quasi-political illegality, direct action resulting often in guerrilla and open warfare, collectivist action of various forms, perverse humour and escapism'. By the end of the year 'what emerged was in the manner of an alternative culture with its own moral code and political tradition: it was a society within a society'.[9] Evaluating this concept it is clear that Rhondda politics was able to create room within which an 'oppositional' or 'rejectionist' strategy had grown, a strategy that nurtured the Communist Party in the 1920s and provided much of its distinctive motivation in the 1930s. But a great deal of evidence has been garnered of 'rejectionism' that not only overlaps Communist–Labour party boundaries, but is also evident years before the General Strike and the lock-out of 1926.[10] Furthermore, explicit manifestations of (generally Communist) 'proletarian internationalism' cannot be understood except in the context of a much more protean (and Labour-voting) society that rested upon some of the personal and communal bonds outlined above. Essentially it was the human relevance of someone like Lewis Jones or Arthur Horner that accounted for their place in Rhondda society and Rhondda memory, not their ability to sloganize or to demonstrate their Communist Party credentials. Ultimately their contribution was not sectarian, but aligned itself in a unity across the parties of the left, using local institutions of the state (sometimes with pragmatism to the fore) and standing together against unsympathetic non-resident Welsh cultural élites, against the colliery companies, and against a predominantly Conservative national state. As has been shown for the 1930s, in practice, if not in rhetoric, the differences between Communist and Labour representatives were blurred. No ideological division can be ruled through south Walian history to place syndicalists and Communists on one side and Labour on the other, whether that be to exclude Labour from the nebulous 'Welsh radical tradition' or to marginalize the revelatory instances of extra-parliamentary protest. This was a common history shared out amongst a multiplicity of strategies. Fascinating and vital though syndicalism and Communism were, it was the strength of the Labour polity that enabled them to flourish.

However, this revised understanding of Rhondda (and by implication south Wales) society should not be misinterpreted as a minimization of that society's essential socialism. Important though it is to correct an over-enthusiastic reading of the political history of the inter-war south Wales coalfield, it is arguably both a more difficult but also more critical task to rescue the enterprise and vision of that history from the condescension and neglect of its academic detractors, of whatever political standpoint.

Some Marxist evaluations of the Labour Party deny it any role in contributing to the arrival of socialism.[11] Socialism, it is argued, is precisely what the Labour Party has failed to provide. Instead, perhaps in accordance with the ideological preferences of the whole working class itself from the post-Chartist era onwards, the party has expressed 'Labourism', frequently seen as a mongrel concoction of weak reformist ideas, suffering in comparison with 'accurate' Marxist theory.[12] But if spiritually deficient, this subordinate, defensive ideological form has also been wheeled in to explain the Labour Party's temporal strength by non-Marxist historians, eager to minimize the importance of socialist attachments.[13] For them, 'Labourism', '*ouvrier*ism', even working-class consciousness has been responsible for the electoral power of the Labour Party, at the same time as it has blocked out any intrinsic socialism. In a specifically south Walian context some historians have argued that the amount and significance of coalfield militancy, defined as 'membership of or support for political organizations to the left of the Labour Party, primarily the CPGB' has been over-estimated, and that the overwhelming support for the Labour Party exhibited throughout and beyond the inter-war years is indicative not of militancy but of conformity and an acceptance of 'the established order'.[14] The conclusion of this study of Rhondda working-class politics is that both traditional Marxist and non-Marxist views are misjudged, in the context of the south Wales coalfield at the very least, and that continuing support for the Labour Party and for other left-wing movements over many decades indicate the presence of a common socialist culture.

Initially the theoretical and methodological underpinnings of both views may be questioned. The Marxist interpretation that derided British 'Labourism' did so from an untenable faith in the viability of 'true', 'revolutionary' or 'political' consciousness – the purist talisman of Leninist and Lukacsian readings of class, politics and history. Not only may Marxist theoreticians now wonder whether such readings were ever feasible, but historians of whatever persuasion may agree that working-class consciousness arrives in a form that is never 'pure', but instead requires careful and sympathetic interpretation. As for the non-Marxist orthodoxy, its assumption that the working class is necessarily limited in its desire for social change rests upon insecure methodological foundations, and is at times more reminiscent of a naïve social anthropology than it is of an empathetic social history. The working class is viewed, not from inside, but from the perspective of national leaderships, bureaucracies, policy-makers and intellectuals. The allied definition of political militancy is restricted and ahistorical, for the south Wales coalfield, and in particular the Rhondda valleys, provided the Labour Party with one of its regional heartlands, and if 'militancy' is to have any historical meaning it must take account of this fact.[15] Support for the Rhondda Labour Party was not seen as support for the established order, for conformity or for acceptance.

This study, this 'history from below', has sought not to prejudge the 'meanings' of the beliefs of the activist and the voter, but to comprehend them as best one can with the evidence available. For whatever fallibilities can be discovered in what might now appear unsophisticated or vague conceptions of change and future social order (appearances themselves influenced by the partial survival of evidence and the inability of historical figures to explain those conceptions), respect for past mentalities demands that those self-perceptions be recognized rather than disparaged.[16] Their languages, their values and priorities, have to be taken seriously and accorded their own integrity. Of course many ordinary voters, perhaps many political activists, articulated conceptions of socialist progress which to us may seem incoherent, flimsy or vague. Even Arthur Horner himself was derided as a 'boy scout Communist' for his supposedly shallow understanding of Marxist theory by his great political rival Will Mainwaring. But we need to be wary of passing too hasty a judgement on these conceptions, these 'socialisms'. It is an academic fiction to deny the possibility of the alignment of working-class consciousness with socialist belief, for in south Wales that alignment took place.[17]

In the geographically but not intellectually circumscribed confines of the Rhondda valleys this socialism may be seen as having operated at three overlapping levels.[18] First, there were the mundane but nevertheless vital local concerns that Councillors and other representatives addressed as a matter of routine: street lighting, the state of pavements and public toilets, the working hours of municipal employees, the allotments, drains and bus routes. Second, there were the broader, national objectives that many would agree upon: the nationalization of the mines, the principles of full employment and of equal access to the education system, the availability of leisure time and facilities for working people. Of course these existed in a variable and general manner as a set of widely-held notions and desires, and altered from year to year: a concern with high rents and food prices in 1917 would have been replaced by worries over the Poor Law in the 1920s, and over the means test in the 1930s. These were not simply parochial issues, but issues that bore upon an understanding of contemporary national and international politics. Finally, whatever the programmatic content of political discourse, that discourse was suffused with socialist expectations and anticipation: oriented towards a future that would involve change and progress. They might disagree over the means, even over the priorities to be accorded to the different ends; but by the inter-war years the majority of Labour Party public representatives saw themselves as socialists, and as engaged in a struggle for socialism.

A final claim must be that the history of the Rhondda valleys during the period studied here is of central significance to the social history of the south Wales coalfield. Throughout, Rhondda spoke for the wider society, defining it successively as the arena of Labour representation, as the cutting edge of proletarian revolution, and as a resilient human community weathering economic adversity.[19] The claim of this work has not been that Rhondda was typical, or in some quantitative way 'representative'. Such notions are of little historical value, for the presumption of typicality that would lead one to investigate a particular area must necessarily be made on the basis of very little knowledge. Equally it is not clear that the average or typical experience is any more meaningful than any other experience. On the contrary, atypicality can cast new light upon trends and developments that might otherwise remain concealed. Had Rhondda been typical or representative it would not have had the force and the energy that enabled it to lead south Wales for seventy years. Rhondda acted instead as a beacon to the rest of the coalfield, signalling its history. It could be believed that what Rhondda experienced today, other parts of south Wales and of Britain with similar, working-class 'definitions of community', would experience tomorrow, even if that 'experience' was to be confined to the realm of political thought and debate, to capturing the imagination of theoretical advance.[20] In an important sense that realm had greater vitality and relevance than anything achieved on the ground, because it contributed to a collectivist, universalist definition of working-class and, indeed, Welsh identity that defied the linguistically exclusive 'Welshness' of a privileged minority. If those self-blinded visionaries had looked, they would have seen Wales not in Penyberth but in Penygraig, where national identity was, if not irrelevant, then marginal compared to an intermeshing of class and community solidarities whose horizons were truly international.

Statistical Appendix

Notes on Tables

1. *Political classifications*

A. 'Unknowns'
For certain times, particularly in the earlier period, it has not been possible to identify the political affiliation of all local government representatives or indeed of all candidates for local government office. It is possible that the proportion of 'unknowns' to total representatives might reflect the degree of politicization surrounding elections to a particular body, but such a view is problematic. First, no representative can be considered 'non-political', and given the prevailing hegemony of Liberalism in the early period it is likely that most 'unknowns' shared basic Liberal assumptions. Had they been Conservatives or Labour representatives this would have been recorded. That it was not, suggests their conformity rather than anything else. Second, candidates for both the RUDC and the PBG during the 1890s tended to be listed in the newspapers solely in terms of occupation, unlike the GCC, where politics were specified. But this did not mean that RUDC and PBG candidates were non-political: the political preferences of many can be discovered elsewhere in the press – in the published election addresses and in the columns of comment and prediction. Given the problems in assessing 'unknowns' alternative tables for the relevant periods have been provided.

B. Independents and others
After 1919 the local press favoured the use of the label 'Independent' where previously those of 'Liberal' or 'Conservative' would have been applied. As one paper might label a candidate an 'Independent' and another label the candidate a 'Liberal', it has been necessary to make a judgement as to which was the more accurate. The rule of thumb employed has been to ascertain whether the particular candidate had,

at any stage, been labelled either 'Liberal' or 'Conservative', or whether they were, or had been, involved in either political party. If they had, then the appropriate party label was applied. With candidates appearing under the label of 'Independent Labour', again individual judgements have had to be made. On the whole these were individuals whose occupational and social backgrounds were located within the Labour movement, but who might have either stood under their own steam, stood against an official Labour Party candidate, or become estranged from the official Labour movement. Finally, although there were public representatives or candidates who were members of the Communist Party before 1927, and who might make their Communism known in their election addresses or in other ways, as they were operating within the Labour Party up until the disaffiliation crisis, it has been considered appropriate to keep them within the Labour category. After disaffiliation, not only were Communists in opposition to Labour, but there were also candidates who appeared under such labels as 'People's Candidate', 'Workers' Candidate' or 'Independent Working Class Candidate'. These were either members of the CPGB standing under a United Front or Left Wing Movement/disaffiliated party label, or CPGB sympathizers who could not use the label 'Communist'. Individual differences have been noticed but, for the tables dealing with the political complexion of elected representatives of local government bodies all have been placed within the CPGB category, as on the whole they operated as a cohesive group.

2. Occupational classification

Throughout this work a sixfold occupational classification has been employed to distinguish between the relative political influence and office-holding of socio-economic groups. Such a classification naturally imposes order where none may exist, and the exercise is one of approximation not precision. Nevertheless, in terms of elucidating general principles and patterns, occupational analysis has its uses, and the following table represents a breakdown of exactly which occupations are included under each of the broad headings. It should be noted that married women or widows not themselves in paid employment have been placed in the category appropriate to their (late) husband, where this could be ascertained. It should also be noted that retired or unemployed individuals have remained in those categories which were appropriate during their working lives.

CAPITAL: coalowner; colliery manager; colliery agent; colliery accountant; colliery official; mining engineer; company director; railway inspector; company manager; colliery cashier; colliery clerk; personnel manager.

TRADESMEN: publican; hotelier; builder; estate agent; grocer; boot merchant; draper; butcher; ironmonger; undertaker; auctioneer; merchant; chemist; baker; bookseller; contractor; land agent; insurance agent; Co-op manager; tailor; postmaster; flannel merchant.

PROFESSIONALS: teacher; schoolmaster; lawyer; doctor; architect; surveyor; solicitor; headteacher.

MINISTERS: Nonconformist minister; Anglican priest.

FARMERS: gentleman farmer; farmer; landowner.

WORKERS: miner; checkweigher; miners' agent; haulier; lodge secretary; miners' librarian; collier; railway guard; winding engineman; miners' district official; nurse; telephone operator; Co-op clerk; railway clerk; ambulance attendant; milkman; caretaker; timekeeper; railwayman; groundsman; trade union organizer; colliery smith; shop assistant.

Table 1. The political complexion of Rhondda local government, 1894/5–1952[1]

Number of seats:

	Labour	IndLab	CPGB	Liberal	Con	Ind	Unknown	Total
1894/5	5	-	-	33	4	-	11	53
1898	3	-	-	34	2	-	12	51
1901	5	-	-	43	2	-	16	66
1904	8	-	-	40	2	-	16	66
1907	10	-	-	39	2	1	14	66
1910	16	-	-	38	6	1	9	70
1913	23	-	-	35	7	-	8	73
1919	43	1	-	19	2	8	-	73
1922	44	1	-	15	4	10	1	75
1925	40	4	-	14	4	14	-	76
1928	45	1	6	9	2	12	1	76
1928[2]	31	1	4	8	1	5	-	52
1931	39	-	1	4	-	8	-	52
1934	41	-	3	1	-	6	-	52
1937	37	1	7	-	-	7	-	52
1946	40	1	6	-	-	4	-	51
1949	48	-	-	-	-	3	-	51
1952	49	-	-	-	-	2	-	51

Democratic Rhondda

Table 1 cont.

In percentages:

	Labour	IndLab	CPGB	Liberal	Con	Ind	Unknown
1894/5	9.43	-	-	62.26	7.55	-	20.75
1898	5.88	-	-	66.67	3.92	-	23.53
1901	7.58	-	-	65.15	3.03	-	24.24
1904	12.12	-	-	60.60	3.03	-	24.24
1907	15.15	-	-	59.09	3.03	1.52	21.21
1910	22.86	-	-	54.29	8.57	1.43	12.86
1913	31.51	-	-	47.95	9.59	-	10.96
1919	58.90	1.37	-	26.03	2.74	10.96	-
1922	58.67	1.33	-	20.00	5.33	13.33	1.33
1925	52.63	5.26	-	18.42	5.26	18.42	-
1928	59.21	1.32	7.90	11.84	2.63	15.79	1.32
1928[2]	59.62	1.92	7.69	15.39	1.92	9.62	-
1931	75.00	-	1.92	7.69	-	15.39	-
1934	78.85	-	5.77	1.92	-	11.54	-
1937	71.15	1.92	13.46	-	-	13.46	-
1946	78.43	1.96	11.76	-	-	7.84	-
1949	94.12	-	-	-	-	5.88	-
1952	96.08	-	-	-	-	3.92	-

[1] The figures for 1894/5 are arrived at by pooling the results of the 1894 YUDC and PBG elections with those of the 1895 GCC elections. Triennial figures are given, as elections for both the GCC and PBG took place on this basis. Any substantial alterations in the intervening years would therefore result from the annual RUDC elections, tabulated later in this Appendix.
[2] 1928 figures excluding representatives on the PBG.

Table 2. The political complexion of Rhondda local government, excluding 'unknowns', 1894/5–1910

Number of seats:

	Labour	Liberal	Con	Ind	Total Known
1894/5	5	33	4	-	42
1898	3	34	2	-	39
1901	5	43	2	-	50
1904	8	40	2	-	50
1907	10	39	2	1	52
1910	16	38	6	1	61

In percentages:

	Labour	Liberal	Con	Ind
1894/5	11.90	78.57	9.52	-
1898	7.69	87.18	5.13	-
1901	10.00	86.00	4.00	-
1904	16.00	80.00	4.00	-
1907	19.23	75.00	3.85	1.92
1910	26.67	63.33	9.84	1.67

Table 3. The occupational complexion of Rhondda local government,
1894/5–1952

Number of seats:

	Capital	Tradesmen	Clergy	Profs.	Farmers	Workers	Unknown
1894/5	8	25	2	9	3	5	1
1898	9	25	1	9	3	3	1
1901	9	39	-	9	4	5	-
1904	11	36	-	6	4	8	1
1907	11	32	1	8	2	10	2
1910	12	30	1	9	1	17	-
1913	12	26	3	8	1	23	-
1919	4	16	2	6	-	44	1
1922	4	16	1	8	-	44	2
1925	5	15	1	8	-	44	3
1928	2	12	2	7	-	50	3
1928[1]	1	10	2	5	-	34	-
1931	2	7	2	4	-	37	-
1934	2	5	1	5	-	38	1
1937	2	5	-	2	-	39	4
1946	1	5	-	1	-	38	6
1949	1	5	-	2	-	30	13
1952	1	3	-	1	-	28	18

In percentages:

	Capital	Tradesmen	Clergy	Profs.	Farmers	Workers	Unknown
1894/5	15.09	47.17	3.77	16.98	5.66	9.43	1.89
1898	17.65	49.02	1.96	17.65	5.88	5.88	1.96
1901	13.64	59.09	-	13.64	6.06	7.58	-
1904	16.67	54.54	-	9.09	6.06	12.12	1.51
1907	16.67	48.48	1.51	12.12	3.03	15.15	3.03
1910	17.14	42.86	1.43	12.86	1.43	24.29	-
1913	16.44	35.62	4.11	10.96	1.37	31.51	-
1919	5.48	21.92	2.74	8.22	-	60.27	1.37
1922	5.33	21.33	1.33	10.67	-	58.67	2.67
1925	6.58	19.74	1.32	10.53	-	57.90	3.95
1928	2.63	15.79	2.63	9.21	-	65.79	3.95
1928[1]	1.92	19.23	3.85	9.62	-	65.38	-
1931	3.85	13.46	3.85	7.69	-	71.15	-
1934	3.85	9.62	1.92	9.62	-	73.08	1.92
1937	3.85	9.62	-	3.85	-	75.00	7.69
1946	1.96	9.80	-	1.96	-	74.51	11.76
1949	1.96	9.80	-	3.92	-	58.82	25.49
1952	1.96	7.84	-	1.96	-	54.90	35.29

[1] 1928 figures excluding representatives on the PBG.

Table 4. The political complexion of Rhondda representatives on the Glamorgan County Council, 1889–1952

	Labour	CPGB	Liberal	Con	Ind	Total
			Number of seats:			
1889	1	-	13	1	-	15
1892	3	-	13	-	-	16
1895	3	-	13	-	-	16
1898	2	-	13	-	-	15
1901	2	-	13	-	-	15
1904	2	-	13	-	-	15
1907	2	-	12	-	1	15
1910	2	-	14	-	1	17
1913	4	-	13	-	-	17
1919	11	-	6	-	-	17
1922	10	-	7	-	-	17
1925	10	-	7	-	-	17
1928	10	-	5	-	2	17
1931	15	-	1	-	1	17
1934	16	-	1	-	-	17
1937	15	1	-	-	1	17
1946	15	-	-	-	1	16
1949	15	-	-	-	1	16
1952	15	-	-	-	1	16

	Labour	CPGB	Liberal	Con	Ind
			In percentages:		
1889	6.67	-	86.67	6.67	-
1892	18.75	-	81.25	-	-
1895	18.75	-	81.25	-	-
1898	13.33	-	86.67	-	-
1901	13.33	-	86.67	-	-
1904	13.33	-	86.67	-	-
1907	13.33	-	80.00	-	6.67
1910	11.77	-	82.35	-	5.88
1913	23.53	-	76.47	-	-
1919	64.71	-	35.29	-	-
1922	58.82	-	41.18	-	-
1925	58.82	-	41.18	-	-
1928	58.82	-	29.41	-	11.77
1931	88.24	-	5.88	-	5.88
1934	94.12	-	5.88	-	-
1937	88.24	5.88	-	-	5.88
1946	93.75	-	-	-	6.25
1949	93.75	-	-	-	6.25
1952	93.75	-	-	-	6.25

Table 5. The political complexion of the Rhondda Urban District Council, 1894–1954

Number of seats:

	Labour	IndLab	CPGB	Liberal	Con	Ind	Unknown	Total
1894	2	-	-	10	2	-	1	15
1896	1	-	-	11	2	-	1	15
1897	1	-	-	12	1	-	1	15
1898	1	-	-	12	-	-	2	15
1899	2	-	-	21	1	-	6	30
1900	2	-	-	22	1	-	5	30
1901	3	-	-	22	-	-	5	30
1902	3	-	-	22	-	-	5	30
1903	4	-	-	21	-	-	5	30
1904	5	-	-	20	-	-	5	30
1905	5	-	-	21	-	-	4	30
1906	5	-	-	21	-	-	4	30
1907	6	-	-	21	1	-	2	30
1908	8	-	-	20	2	-	-	30
1909	8	-	-	20	2	-	-	30
1910	9	-	-	18	3	-	-	30
1911	11	-	-	17	2	-	-	30
1912	14	-	-	14	2	-	-	30
1913	13	-	-	16	4	-	-	33
1914	14	-	-	15	4	-	-	33
1915	15	-	-	14	4	-	-	33
1919	20	-	-	10	2	1	-	33
1920	22	-	-	8	2	1	-	33
1921	22	-	-	6	3	4	-	35
1922	20	-	-	6	4	5	-	35
1923	19	1	-	6	4	5	-	35
1924	17	3	-	6	4	5	-	35
1925	17	4	-	6	3	5	-	35
1926	21	3	-	4	2	5	-	35
1927	19	2	3	4	1	6	-	35
1928	21	1	4	4	1	4	-	35
1929	21	1	2	4	1	6	-	35
1930	22	-	2	4	1	6	-	35
1931	24	-	1	3	-	7	-	35
1932	27	-	-	3	-	5	-	35
1933	26	-	1	2	-	6	-	35
1934	25	-	3	1	-	6	-	35
1935	22	1	7	-	-	5	-	35
1936	21	1	7	-	-	6	-	35
1937	22	1	6	-	-	6	-	35

Table 5 cont.

	Labour	IndLab	CPGB	Liberal	Con	Ind	Unknown	Total
1938	24	1	5	-	-	5	-	35
1939	25	1	5	-	-	4	-	35
1946	25	1	6	-	-	3	-	35
1947	27	-	5	-	-	3	-	35
1948	30	-	2	-	-	3	-	35
1949	33	-	-	-	-	2	-	35
1950	33	-	-	-	-	2	-	35
1951	34	-	-	-	-	1	-	35
1952	34	-	-	-	-	1	-	35
1953	34	-	-	-	-	1	-	35
1954	33	-	-	-	-	1	-	34

In percentages:

	Labour	IndLab	CPGB	Liberal	Con	Ind	Unknown
1894	13.33	-	-	66.67	13.33	-	6.67
1896	6.67	-	-	73.33	13.33	-	6.67
1897	6.67	-	-	80.00	6.67	-	6.67
1898	6.67	-	-	80.00	-	-	13.33
1899	6.67	-	-	70.00	3.33	-	20.00
1900	6.67	-	-	73.33	3.33	-	16.67
1901	10.00	-	-	73.33	-	-	16.67
1902	10.00	-	-	73.33	-	-	16.67
1903	13.33	-	-	70.00	-	-	16.67
1904	16.67	-	-	66.67	-	-	16.67
1905	16.67	-	-	70.00	-	-	13.33
1906	16.67	-	-	70.00	-	-	13.33
1907	20.00	-	-	70.00	3.33	-	6.67
1908	26.67	-	-	66.67	6.67	-	-
1909	26.67	-	-	66.67	6.67	-	-
1910	30.00	-	-	60.00	10.00	-	-
1911	36.67	-	-	56.67	6.67	-	-
1912	46.67	-	-	46.67	6.67	-	-
1913	39.39	-	-	48.48	12.12	-	-
1914	42.42	-	-	45.45	12.12	-	-
1915	45.45	-	-	42.42	12.12	-	-
1919	60.60	-	-	30.30	6.06	3.03	-
1920	66.67	-	-	24.24	6.06	3.03	-
1921	62.86	-	-	17.14	8.57	11.43	-
1922	57.14	-	-	17.14	11.43	14.29	-
1923	54.29	2.86	-	17.14	11.43	14.29	-
1924	48.57	8.57	-	17.14	11.43	14.29	-
1925	48.57	11.43	-	17.14	8.57	14.29	-

Table 5 cont.

	Labour	IndLab	CPGB	Liberal	Con	Ind	Unknown
1926	60.00	8.57	-	11.43	5.71	14.29	-
1927	54.29	5.71	8.57	11.43	2.86	17.14	-
1928	60.00	2.86	11.43	11.43	2.86	11.43	-
1929	60.00	2.86	5.71	11.43	2.86	17.14	-
1930	62.86	-	5.71	11.43	2.86	17.14	-
1931	68.57	-	2.86	8.57	-	20.00	-
1932	77.14	-	-	8.57	-	14.29	-
1933	74.29	-	2.86	5.71	-	17.14	-
1934	71.43	-	8.57	2.86	-	17.14	-
1935	62.86	2.86	20.00	-	-	14.29	-
1936	60.00	2.86	20.00	-	-	17.14	-
1937	62.86	2.86	17.14	-	-	17.14	-
1938	68.57	2.86	14.29	-	-	14.29	-
1939	71.43	2.86	14.29	-	-	11.43	-
1946	71.43	2.86	17.14	-	-	8.57	-
1947	77.14	-	14.29	-	-	8.57	-
1948	85.71	-	5.71	-	-	8.57	-
1949	94.29	-	-	-	-	5.71	-
1950	94.29	-	-	-	-	5.71	-
1951	97.14	-	-	-	-	2.86	-
1952	97.14	-	-	-	-	2.86	-
1953	97.14	-	-	-	-	2.86	-
1954	97.06	-	-	-	-	2.94	-

Table 6. The political complexion of the Rhondda Urban District Council,
1894–1910, excluding 'unknowns'

Number of seats:

	Labour	Liberal	Con	Total Known
1894	2	10	2	14
1896	1	11	2	14
1897	1	12	1	14
1898	1	12	-	13
1899	2	21	1	24
1900	2	22	1	25
1901	3	22	-	25
1902	3	22	-	25
1903	4	21	-	25
1904	5	20	-	25
1905	5	21	-	26
1906	5	21	-	26
1907	6	21	1	28

Table 6 cont.

	Labour	Liberal	Con	Total Known
1908	8	20	2	30
1909	8	20	2	30
1910	9	18	3	30

In percentages:			
	Labour	Liberal	Con
1894	14.29	71.43	14.29
1896	7.14	78.57	14.29
1897	7.14	85.71	7.14
1898	7.69	92.31	-
1899	8.33	87.50	4.17
1900	8.00	88.00	4.00
1901	12.00	88.00	-
1902	12.00	88.00	-
1903	16.00	84.00	-
1904	20.00	80.00	-
1905	19.23	80.77	-
1906	19.23	80.77	-
1907	21.43	75.00	3.57
1908	26.67	66.67	6.67
1909	26.67	66.67	6.67
1910	30.00	60.00	10.00

Table 7. The political complexion of Rhondda representatives on the
Pontypridd Poor Law Board of Guardians, 1894–1928

	Labour	IndLab	CPGB	Liberal	Con	Ind	Unknown	Total
1894	-	-	-	10	2	-	10	22
1898	-	-	-	9	2	-	10	21
1901	-	-	-	8	2	-	11	21
1904	1	-	-	7	2	-	11	21
1907	2	-	-	6	1	-	12	21
1910	5	-	-	6	3	-	9	23
1913	6	-	-	6	3	-	8	23
1919	12	1	-	3	-	7	-	23
1922	14	1	-	2	-	5	1	23
1925	13	-	-	1	1	9	-	24
1928	14	-	2	-	1	6	1	24

Table 7 cont.

<table>
<tr><th colspan="8">In percentages:</th></tr>
<tr><th></th><th>Labour</th><th>IndLab</th><th>CPGB</th><th>Liberal</th><th>Con</th><th>Ind</th><th>Unknown</th></tr>
<tr><td>1894</td><td>-</td><td>-</td><td>-</td><td>45.45</td><td>9.09</td><td>-</td><td>45.45</td></tr>
<tr><td>1898</td><td>-</td><td>-</td><td>-</td><td>42.80</td><td>9.52</td><td>-</td><td>47.62</td></tr>
<tr><td>1901</td><td>-</td><td>-</td><td>-</td><td>38.10</td><td>9.52</td><td>-</td><td>52.38</td></tr>
<tr><td>1904</td><td>4.76</td><td>-</td><td>-</td><td>33.33</td><td>9.52</td><td>-</td><td>52.38</td></tr>
<tr><td>1907</td><td>9.52</td><td>-</td><td>-</td><td>28.57</td><td>4.76</td><td>-</td><td>57.14</td></tr>
<tr><td>1910</td><td>21.74</td><td>-</td><td>-</td><td>26.09</td><td>13.04</td><td>-</td><td>39.13</td></tr>
<tr><td>1913</td><td>26.09</td><td>-</td><td>-</td><td>26.09</td><td>13.04</td><td>-</td><td>34.78</td></tr>
<tr><td>1919</td><td>52.17</td><td>4.35</td><td>-</td><td>13.04</td><td>-</td><td>30.44</td><td>-</td></tr>
<tr><td>1922</td><td>60.87</td><td>4.35</td><td>-</td><td>8.70</td><td>-</td><td>21.74</td><td>4.35</td></tr>
<tr><td>1925</td><td>54.17</td><td>-</td><td>-</td><td>4.17</td><td>4.17</td><td>37.50</td><td>-</td></tr>
<tr><td>1928</td><td>58.33</td><td>-</td><td>8.33</td><td>-</td><td>4.17</td><td>25.00</td><td>4.17</td></tr>
</table>

Table 8. The political complexion of Rhondda representatives on the Pontypridd Poor Law Board of Guardians, 1894–1910, excluding 'unknowns'

	Labour	Liberal	Conservative	Total Known
1894	-	10	2	12
1898	-	9	2	11
1901	-	8	2	10
1904	1	7	2	10
1907	2	6	1	9
1910	5	6	3	14

		In percentages:	
	Labour	Liberal	Conservative
1894	-	83.33	16.67
1898	-	81.81	18.18
1901	-	80.00	20.00
1904	10.00	70.00	20.00
1907	22.22	66.67	11.11
1910	35.71	42.86	21.43

Table 9. The occupational complexion of Rhondda representatives on the Glamorgan County Council, 1889–1952

	Capital	Tradesmen	Clergy	Profs.	Farmers	Workers	Unknown
1889	5	3	1	4	1	1	-
1892	3	4	1	3	2	3	-
1898	2	6	-	4	1	3	-
1901	2	6	1	3	1	2	-
1904	2	8	-	2	1	2	-
1907	2	9	-	1	1	2	-
1910	2	8	-	2	1	2	-
1913	2	9	-	3	1	2	-
1919	-	4	-	2	-	11	-
1922	-	5	-	2	-	10	-
1925	-	5	-	2	-	10	-
1928	-	5	1	2	-	9	-
1931	-	5	-	-	-	12	-
1934	-	5	-	1	-	11	-
1937	-	4	-	-	-	12	1
1946	-	2	-	-	-	12	2
1949	-	2	-	-	-	10	4
1952	-	1	-	-	-	9	6

In percentages:

	Capital	Tradesmen	Clergy	Profs.	Farmers	Workers	Unknown
1889	33.00	20.00	6.67	26.67	6.67	6.67	-
1892	18.75	25.00	6.25	18.75	12.50	18.75	-
1898	12.50	37.50	-	25.00	6.25	18.75	-
1901	13.33	40.00	6.67	20.00	6.67	13.33	-
1904	13.33	53.33	-	13.33	6.67	13.33	-
1907	13.33	60.00	-	6.67	6.67	13.33	-
1910	13.33	53.33	-	13.33	6.67	13.33	-
1913	11.76	52.94	-	17.65	5.88	11.76	-
1919	-	23.53	-	11.76	-	64.71	-
1922	-	29.41	-	11.76	-	58.82	-
1925	-	29.41	-	11.76	-	58.82	-
1928	-	29.41	5.88	11.76	-	52.94	-
1931	-	29.41	-	-	-	70.59	-
1934	-	29.41	-	5.88	-	64.71	-
1937	-	23.53	-	-	-	70.59	5.88
1946	-	12.50	-	-	-	75.00	12.50
1949	-	12.50	-	-	-	62.50	25.00
1952	-	6.25	-	-	-	56.25	37.50

Table 10. The occupational complexion of the Rhondda Urban District
Council, 1894–1954

	Capital	Tradesmen	Clergy	Profs.	Farmers	Workers	Unknown
1894	5	4	1	2	1	2	-
1896	5	5	1	2	1	1	-
1897	6	5	-	2	1	1	-
1898	6	5	-	2	1	1	-
1899	8	14	-	4	2	2	-
1900	7	15	-	4	2	2	-
1901	6	14	-	5	2	3	-
1902	6	14	-	5	2	3	-
1903	7	12	-	5	2	4	-
1904	8	12	-	3	2	5	-
1905	8	11	1	3	2	5	-
1906	8	9	1	5	2	5	-
1907	8	10	1	4	1	6	-
1908	9	8	-	4	-	9	-
1909	9	9	-	4	-	8	-
1910	8	8	1	4	-	9	-
1911	7	7	2	4	-	10	-
1912	6	5	2	3	-	14	-
1913	7	7	2	4	-	13	-
1914	7	6	3	4	-	13	-
1915	6	7	3	3	-	13	-
1919	4	5	2	2	-	20	-
1920	4	2	2	3	-	22	-
1921	4	4	2	3	-	22	-
1922	4	6	1	4	-	20	-
1923	4	6	1	4	-	20	-
1924	4	6	1	4	-	20	-
1925	4	6	1	3	-	21	-
1926	3	5	1	3	-	23	-
1927	2	6	1	3	-	23	-
1928	1	5	1	3	-	25	-
1929	1	5	1	4	-	24	-
1930	2	3	1	5	-	24	-
1931	2	2	2	4	-	25	-
1932	-	2	2	5	-	26	-
1933	1	2	2	5	-	25	-
1934	2	-	1	4	-	27	1
1935	2	1	1	2	-	28	1
1936	2	1	1	2	-	28	1
1937	2	1	-	2	-	27	3

Table 10 cont.

	Capital	Tradesmen	Clergy	Profs.	Farmers	Workers	Unknown
1938	1	2	-	2	-	26	4
1939	-	2	-	2	-	27	4
1946	1	3	1	-	-	26	4
1947	1	2	-	1	-	24	7
1948	1	3	-	1	-	22	8
1949	1	3	-	2	-	20	9
1950	1	3	-	2	-	20	9
1951	1	3	1	-	-	20	10
1952	1	2	-	1	-	19	12
1953	1	2	-	1	-	18	13
1954	-	2	-	1	-	16	15

In percentages:

	Capital	Tradesmen	Clergy	Profs.	Farmers	Workers	Unknown
1894	33.33	26.67	6.67	13.33	6.67	13.33	-
1896	33.33	33.33	6.67	13.33	6.67	6.67	-
1897	40.00	33.33	-	13.33	6.67	6.67	-
1898	40.00	33.33	-	13.33	6.67	6.67	-
1899	26.67	46.67	-	13.33	6.67	6.67	-
1900	23.33	50.00	-	13.33	6.67	6.67	-
1901	20.00	46.67	-	16.67	6.67	10.00	-
1902	20.00	46.67	-	16.67	6.67	10.00	-
1903	23.33	40.00	-	16.67	6.67	13.33	-
1904	26.67	40.00	-	10.00	6.67	16.67	-
1905	26.67	36.67	3.33	10.00	6.67	16.67	-
1906	26.67	30.00	3.33	16.67	6.67	16.67	-
1907	26.67	33.33	3.33	13.33	3.33	20.00	-
1908	30.00	26.67	-	13.33	-	30.00	-
1909	30.00	30.00	-	13.33	-	26.67	-
1910	26.67	26.67	3.33	13.33	-	30.00	-
1911	23.33	23.33	6.67	13.33	-	33.33	-
1912	26.67	16.67	6.67	10.00	-	46.67	-
1913	21.21	21.21	6.06	12.12	-	39.39	-
1914	21.21	18.18	9.09	12.12	-	39.39	-
1915	18.18	21.21	9.09	9.09	-	39.39	-
1919	12.12	15.15	6.06	6.06	-	60.60	-
1920	12.12	6.06	6.06	9.09	-	66.67	-
1921	11.43	11.43	5.71	8.57	-	62.86	-
1922	11.43	17.14	2.86	11.43	-	57.14	-
1923	11.43	17.14	2.86	11.43	-	57.14	-
1924	11.43	17.14	2.86	11.43	-	57.14	-
1925	11.43	17.14	2.86	8.57	-	60.00	-

Table 10 cont.

	Capital	Tradesmen	Clergy	Profs.	Farmers	Workers	Unknown
1926	8.57	14.29	2.86	8.57	-	65.71	-
1927	5.71	17.14	2.86	8.57	-	65.71	-
1928	2.86	14.29	2.86	8.57	-	71.43	-
1929	2.86	14.29	2.86	11.43	-	68.57	-
1930	5.71	8.57	2.86	14.29	-	68.57	-
1931	5.71	5.71	5.71	11.43	-	71.43	-
1932	-	5.71	5.71	14.29	-	74.29	-
1933	2.86	5.71	5.71	14.29	-	71.43	-
1934	5.71	-	2.86	11.43	-	77.14	2.86
1935	5.71	2.86	2.86	5.71	-	80.00	2.86
1936	5.71	2.86	2.86	5.71	-	80.00	2.86
1937	5.71	2.86	-	2.86	-	77.14	8.57
1938	2.86	5.71	-	5.71	-	74.29	11.43
1939	-	5.71	-	5.71	-	77.14	11.43
1946	2.86	8.57	2.86	-	-	74.29	11.43
1947	2.86	5.71	-	2.86	-	68.57	20.00
1948	2.86	8.57	-	2.86	-	62.86	22.86
1949	2.86	8.57	-	5.71	-	57.14	25.71
1950	2.86	8.57	-	5.71	-	57.14	25.71
1951	2.86	8.57	2.86	-	-	57.14	28.57
1952	2.86	5.71	-	2.86	-	54.29	34.29
1953	2.86	5.71	-	2.86	-	51.43	37.14
1954	-	5.88	-	2.94	-	47.06	44.12

Table 11. The occupational complexion of Rhondda representatives on the Pontypridd Poor Law Board of Guardians, 1894–1928

	Capital	Tradesmen	Clergy	Profs.	Farmers	Workers	Unknown
1892	1	15	1	3	1	-	1
1898	1	14	-	4	1	-	1
1901	1	17	-	2	1	-	-
1904	1	15	-	2	1	1	1
1907	1	14	-	2	-	2	2
1910	2	13	-	2	-	6	-
1913	3	10	1	2	1	6	-
1919	-	7	-	2	-	13	1
1922	-	5	-	2	-	14	2
1925	1	4	-	3	-	13	2
1928	1	2	-	2	-	16	3

Table 11 cont.

In percentages:

	Capital	Tradesmen	Clergy	Profs.	Farmers	Workers	Unknown
1894	4.54	68.18	4.54	13.64	4.54	-	4.54
1898	4.76	66.67	-	19.04	4.76	-	4.76
1901	4.76	80.95	-	9.52	4.76	-	-
1904	4.76	71.45	-	9.52	4.76	4.76	4.76
1907	4.76	66.67	-	9.52	-	9.52	9.52
1910	8.70	56.52	-	8.70	-	26.09	-
1913	13.04	43.48	4.35	8.70	4.35	26.09	-
1919	-	30.44	-	8.70	-	56.52	4.35
1922	-	21.74	-	8.70	-	60.87	8.70
1925	4.17	16.67	-	12.50	-	54.17	12.50
1928	4.17	8.33	-	8.33	-	66.67	12.50

Table 12. The political complexion of competition for 'Rhondda seats' on the Glamorgan County Council, 1889–1954

A. 1889–1910

SINGLE SEAT

Type of contest	No. of contests
1 Liberal v. 1 Conservative	5
1 Liberal v. 1 Labour	7
1 Liberal v. 1 Independent	1
1 Liberal v. 2 Unknowns	1
2 Liberals	16
2 Liberals v. 1 Conservative	3
2 Liberals v. 1 Conservative v. 1 Labour	1
3 Liberals	1
1 Labour v. 1 Conservative	1
1 Labour v. 1 Unknown	1

DOUBLE SEAT

Type of contest	No. of contests
2 Liberals v. 1 Conservative	2
3 Liberals	1

TOTAL SEATS CONTESTED[1]	43
TOTAL CONTESTS	40
Total no. contests where no. Liberals > no. seats	22
Percentage contests where no. Liberals > no. seats	55

Table 12 cont.

B. 1910–1927

Type of Contest	No. of Contests
1 Labour v. 1 Liberal	8
1 Labour v. 1 Unknown	1
1 Labour v. 1 Liberal v. 1 Independent Labour	1
2 Liberals	1
TOTAL CONTESTS	11
Total no. contests where no. Labour > no. seats	0
Total no. contests where no. left-wing > no. seats[2]	1

C. 1927–1954

Type of Contest	No. of Contests
1 Labour v. 1 Liberal	6
1 Labour v. 1 Independent	13
1 Labour v. 1 Independent Labour	3
1 Labour v. 1 Unofficial Socialist	1
1 Labour v. 1 Communist	18
1 Labour v. 1 Liberal v. 1 Communist	1
1 Labour v. 1 Independent v. 1 Unofficial Socialist	1
1 Labour v. 1 Independent v. 1 Communist	11
1 Labour v. 1 Independent Labour v. 1 Communist	1
1 Labour v. 1 Communist v. 1 Plaid Cymru	1
1 Liberal v. 1 Communist	1
TOTAL CONTESTS	57
Total no. contests where no. Labour > no. seats	0
Total no. contests where no. left-wing > no. seats	37

[1] 'Total contests' refers to the actual number of elections, 'Total seats contested' to the total number of vacancies filled in those elections. Thus a two-member ward counts as two seats contested but only one contest.

[2] The category 'left-wing' is held to include Labour and Independent Labour candidates in the tables dealing with 1910–1927, and also to include Communist, Independent Socialist, Independent Communist, Unofficial Socialist and 'People's' candidates in the tables dealing with 1927–1954.

Table 13. The political complexion of competition for the Rhondda Urban District Council, 1894–1954

A. 1894–1910[1]

SINGLE SEAT

Type of contest	No. of contests
1 Liberal v. 1 Conservative	3
1 Liberal v. 1 Labour	13
1 Liberal v. 1 Labour v. 2 Unknown	1
1 Liberal v. 1 Unknown	5
1 Liberal v. 2 Unknown	1
1 Liberal v. 1 Conservative v. 1 Labour	1
2 Liberals	6
2 Liberals v. 1 Labour	1
2 Liberals v. 1 Labour v. 1 Unknown	1
2 Liberals v. 1 Unknown	1
2 Liberals v. 3 Unknown	1
3 Liberals	1
1 Labour v. 1 Conservative	4
1 Labour v. 1 Unknown	4
2 Unknowns	1

TRIPLE SEAT

Type of contest	No. of contests
1 Liberal v. 3 Unknown	1
2 Liberals v. 1 Labour v. 1 Conservative v. 5 Unknown	1
3 Liberals v. 1 Unknown	2
3 Liberals v. 2 Unknown	1
3 Liberals v. 3 Unknown	1
4 Liberals v. 1 Unknown	1
4 Liberals v. 1 Labour	1
4 Liberals v. 3 Unknown	1
4 Liberals v. 2 Unknown v. 1 Conservative v. 1 Labour	1
6 Liberals v. 2 Unknown v. 1 Conservative	1

TOTAL SEATS CONTESTED	77
TOTAL CONTESTS	55
Total no. contests where no. Liberals > no. seats	16
Percentage contests where no. Liberals > no. seats	29

Table 13 cont.

B. 1910–1927

SINGLE SEAT

Type of contest	No. of contests
2 Labour	2
1 Labour v. 1 Liberal	26
1 Labour v. 2 Liberal	1
1 Labour v. 1 Independent	6
1 Labour v. 1 Conservative	8
1 Labour v. 1 Unknown	5
1 Labour v. 1 Independent Labour	5
1 Labour v. 1 Liberal v. 1 Independent	1
2 Labour v. 1 Liberal	2
1 Labour v. 1 Liberal v. 1 Conservative	2
1 Labour v. 1 Unknown v. 1 Liberal	1
1 Labour v. 2 Liberal v. 1 Conservative	1
2 Labour v. 1 Unknown	1
1 Liberal v. 1 Conservative	1
1 Conservative v. 1 Nationalist	1
3 Indep. Labour v. 1 Unknown	1

DOUBLE SEAT

Type of contest	No. of contests
2 Labour v. 1 Independent	2
2 Labour v. 2 Independent	1
2 Labour v. 1 Conservative	1
2 Labour v. 1 Liberal v. 1 Conservative	1
1 Labour v. 3 Indep. Labour v. 1 Unknown	1
1 Labour v. 1 Conservative v. 2 Unknown	1
2 Labour v. 1 Liberal	1
1 Labour v. 2 Liberal	1
2 Labour v. 1 Liberal v. 1 Independent	1

TOTAL SEATS CONTESTED	84
TOTAL CONTESTS	74
Total no. contests where no. Labour > no. seats	5
Total no. contests where no. left-wing > no. seats	12

Table 13 cont.

C. 1927–1954

SINGLE SEAT	
Type of contest	No. of contests
1 Labour v. 1 Liberal	5
1 Labour v. 1 Independent	24
1 Labour v. 1 Conservative	3
1 Labour v. 1 Unknown	10
1 Labour v. 1 Independent Labour	2
1 Labour v. 1 Independent Socialist	1
1 Labour v. 1 People's Candidate	1
1 Labour v. 1 Communist	58
1 Labour v. 2 Communist	1
1 Labour v. 1 Liberal v. 1 Independent	1
1 Labour v. 1 Liberal v. 1 Communist	3
1 Labour v. 2 Liberal v. 1 Communist	1
1 Labour v. 1 Independent v. 1 Communist	20
1 Labour v. 2 Independent v. 1 Communist	1
1 Labour v. 1 Independent v. 1 OAP	1
1 Labour v. 1 Unknown v. 1 Communist	2
1 Labour v. 1 Independent Labour v. 1 Communist	3
1 Labour v. 1 Communist v. 1 Plaid Cymru	3
1 Labour v. 1 Independent v. 1 Independent Lab. v. 1 Communist	2
2 Labour v. 1 Conservative v. 1 Communist	1
2 Labour v. 2 Communist	1
1 Liberal v. 1 Communist	2
1 Independent v. 1 Communist	2
1 Independent v. 1 Communist v. 1 Unknown	1
1 Communist v. 1 Independent Communist	1

DOUBLE SEAT	
Type of contest	No. of contests
2 Labour v. 1 Communist	2
2 Labour v. 2 Communist	3
2 Labour v. 1 Independent	2
2 Labour v. 2 Independent	1
2 Labour v. 1 Independent v. 1 Communist	3
2 Labour v. 2 Independent v. 1 Communist	1
2 Labour v. 1 Independent Labour v. 1 Communist	1
1 Labour v. 1 Independent v. 2 Communist	2
2 Labour v. 1 Communist v. 1 Unknown	1
2 Independent v. 1 Communist	1

Table 13 cont.

TOTAL SEATS CONTESTED	186
TOTAL CONTESTS	168
Total no. contests where no. Labour > no. seats	2
Total no. contests where no. Left-Wing > no. seats	115

[1] Assessment of both this and Table 14 dealing with the PBG is complicated by the number of candidates whose political identities are unknown. On the RUDC in the period 1894–1910, 45% of contests included such a candidate, whereas on the PBG the figure was 83%. This undermines the usefulness of these tables for this period, but it is suggested that the figures for inter-Liberal competition on both bodies are almost certainly artificially low owing to this factor. If all the 'unknowns' were assumed to be Liberal then the three bodies would exhibit much more similar statistics for inter-Liberal competition (58% for the GCC, 55% for the RUDC, and 75% for the PBG) during the period.

Table 14. The political complexion of competition for Rhondda seats on the Pontypridd Board of Guardians, 1894–1927

A. 1894–1910	
SINGLE SEAT	
Type of contest	No. of contests
2 Liberals	1
DOUBLE SEAT	
Type of contest	No. of contests
1 Liberal v. 1 Conservative v. 1 Unknown	1
1 Liberal v. 2 Labour v. 2 Unknown	1
2 Liberals v. 1 Labour	2
2 Liberals v. 1 Unknown	2
3 Liberals	1
1 Labour v. 1 Conservative v. 1 Unknown	2
1 Labour v. 3 Unknowns	2
1 Conservative v. 3 Unknowns	1
1 Conservative v. 1 Independent v. 1 Unknown	1
3 Unknowns	2
4 Unknowns	1
TRIPLE SEAT	
Type of contest	No. of contests
3 Liberals v. 1 Unknown	1

Table 14 cont.

QUADRUPLE SEAT

Type of contest	No. of contests
2 Liberals v. 3 Unknowns	1
3 Liberals v. 2 Unknowns	1
5 Liberals v. 1 Labour v. 1 Conservative v. 1 Unknown	1

QUINTUPLE SEAT

Type of contest	No. of contests
1 Liberal v. 1 Conservative v. 5 Unknowns	1
3 Liberals v. 3 Unknowns	1
5 Liberals v. 1 Unknown	1

TOTAL SEATS CONTESTED	63
TOTAL CONTESTS	24
Total no. contests where no. Liberals > no. seats	3
Percentage contests where no. Liberals > no. seats	13

B. 1910–1927

SINGLE SEAT

Type of contest	No. of contests
1 Labour v. 1 Independent	2
1 Labour v. 1 Liberal v. 1 Conservative	1
1 Labour v. 1 Independent Labour	1

DOUBLE SEAT

Type of contest	No. of contests
2 Labour v. 1 Liberal	2
2 Labour v. 2 Liberal	1
2 Labour v. 1 Independent	5
2 Labour v. 2 Independent	2
2 Labour v. 1 Unknown	1
2 Liberal v. 1 Unknown	1
2 Labour v. 1 Independent v. 1 Liberal	1
2 Labour v. 2 Independent v. 1 Independent Labour	1
1 Labour v. 2 Unknown	1
1 Labour v. 1 Conservative v. 2 Unknown	1

Table 14 cont.

TRIPLE SEAT

Type of contest	No. of contests
2 Labour v. 1 Independent Labour v. 1 Unknown	1
3 Labour v. 1 Independent	1
3 Labour v. 2 Independent	1
3 Labour v. 2 Conservative	1
TOTAL SEATS CONTESTED	48
TOTAL CONTESTS	24
Total no. contests where no. Labour > no. seats	0
Total no. contests where no. left-wing > no. seats	2

Notes

Notes to Introduction

1 Writing in the *Barry Herald*. Cited in Ian Michael, *Gwyn Thomas* (1977), 35.
2 Rhondda West Divisional Labour Party (RWDLP) Minutes, 3 Nov. 1947.
3 E. P. Thompson, 'Homage to Tom Maguire', in *Essays in Labour History*, ed. Asa Briggs and John Saville (1960), 276–316; David Howell, *British Workers and the Independent Labour Party 1888–1906* (1983); Michael Savage, *The Dynamics of Working-Class Politics: The Labour Movement in Preston, 1880–1940* (1987); Duncan Tanner, *Political Change and the Labour Party 1900–1918* (1990).
4 Raphael Samuel and Gareth Stedman Jones, 'The Labour Party and Social Democracy', in *Culture, Ideology and Politics: Essays for Eric Hobsbawm*, ed. Samuel and Stedman Jones (1982), 320–9. 'Revisionist' historians have also called for more local studies of Labour. See Eugenio F. Biagini and Alastair J. Reid, 'Currents of Radicalism, 1850–1914', in *Currents of Radicalism: Popular Radicalism, Organised Labour and Party Politics in Britain, 1850–1914*, ed. Biagini and Reid (1991), 1–19, especially 15–16.
5 Christopher Howard, 'Expectations Born to Death: the Local Labour Party Expansion in the 1920s', in *The Working Class in Modern British History: Essays in Honour of Henry Pelling*, ed. Jay M. Winter (1983), 65–81; Joan Smith, 'Labour Tradition in Glasgow and Liverpool', *History Workshop Journal* 17 (1984), 32–56; John Marriott, *The Culture of Labourism: The East End Between the Wars* (1991); Stuart Macintyre, *Little Moscows* (1980); idem, *A Proletarian Science: Marxism in Britain, 1917–1933* (1986 edition).
6 The methodological rigour of Savage, *The Dynamics of Working-Class Politics*, is the best example. See also the new understanding of the Independent Labour Party (ILP) that has emerged not only from the work of Howell, *British Workers and the ILP*, but also from the study of the Party on the Clyde: A. McKinlay and R. J. Morris (eds.), *The ILP on Clydeside 1893–1932: From Foundation to Disintegration* (1991).

7 Howell, op. cit., 281–2; John Urry, 'Localities, Regions and Social Class', *International Journal of Urban and Regional Research*, 5 No.4 (1981), 454–73; Mike Savage, 'Understanding Political Alignments in Contemporary Britain: Do Localities Matter?', *Political Geography Quarterly* (1987), 53–76.

8 Patrick Joyce, *Visions of the People: Industrial England and the Question of Class, 1848–1914* (1990), 138–9.

9 Chris Williams, 'Britain', in *The Force of Labour: The Western European Labour Movement and the Working Class in the Twentieth Century*, ed. S. Berger and D. Broughton (1995), 107–35.

10 For this in a south Wales context see Gwyn A. Williams, 'Dic Penderyn, The Making of a Welsh Working-Class Martyr', *Llafur* 2 No.3 (1978), 110–20; Chris Evans, *'The Labyrinth of Flames': Work and Social Conflict in Early Industrial Merthyr Tydfil* (1993), 3–6; Chris Williams, 'History, Heritage and Commemoration: Newport 1839–1989', *Llafur* 6 No.1 (1992), 5–16.

11 Whether the study still bears an emphasis upon 'heroic periods of struggle' is another matter!

12 Philip Cooke, 'Class Relations and Uneven Development in Wales', in *Diversity and Decomposition in the Labour Market*, ed. Graham Day (1982), 147–75.

13 For an explanation of the early terminology of 'Labour' see Chapter 2, Note 1.

14 E. D. Lewis, *The Rhondda Valleys* (1984 edition); David Smith (ed.), *A People and A Proletariat: Essays in the History of Wales, 1780–1980* (1980); Hywel Francis and David Smith, *The Fed: A History of the South Wales Miners in the Twentieth Century* (1980); Dai Smith, *Wales! Wales?* (1984); Hywel Francis, *Miners Against Fascism: Wales and the Spanish Civil War* (1984). For a sympathetic critique of the existing trade union historiography, see Chris Williams, 'The South Wales Miners' Federation', *Llafur* 5 No.3 (1990), 45–56.

15 Andrew James Chandler, 'The Re-making of a Working Class: Migration from the South Wales Coalfield to the New Industry Areas of the Midlands c.1920–1940', Ph.D. thesis, University of Wales (Cardiff), 1988; D. K. Davies, 'The Influence of Syndicalism and Industrial Unionism on the South Wales Coalfield 1898–1921: A Study in Ideology and Practice', Ph.D. thesis, University of Wales (Cardiff), 1991; David Gilbert, *Class, Community and Collective Action: Social Change in Two British Coalfields, 1850–1926* (1992); Richard Lewis, *Leaders and Teachers: Adult Education and the Challenge of Labour in South Wales, 1906–1940* (1993); Dai Smith, *Aneurin Bevan and the World of South Wales* (1993). The journal of the Welsh Labour History Society, *Llafur*, serves as a barometer of the state of current research, see *Llafur* (1972–).

16 For a sample of Rhondda writing see Meic Stephens (ed.), *A Rhondda Anthology* (1993).

[17] Chris Evans, 'The Labyrinth of Flames', 2.

[18] Ioan Bowen Rees, *The Welsh Political Tradition* (1960); Emyr Humphreys, *The Taliesin Tradition: A Quest for the Welsh Identity* (1983).

[19] Kenneth O. Morgan, 'The Welsh in English Politics, 1868–1982', in *Welsh Society and Nationhood: Historical Essays Presented to Glanmor Williams*, ed. R. R. Davies, Ralph A. Griffiths, Ieuan Gwynedd Jones and Kenneth O. Morgan (1984), 232–50: 249–50.

[20] Peter Stead, 'Working-Class Leadership in South Wales, 1900–1920', *WHR* 6 No.3 (1973), 329–53; idem, 'The Language of Edwardian Politics', in *A People and a Proletariat: Essays in the History of Wales, 1780–1980*, ed. David Smith (1980), 148–65; idem, 'Establishing a Heartland: The Labour Party in Wales', in *The First Labour Party 1906–1914*, ed. K. D. Brown (1985), 64–88; J. Graham Jones, 'Wales and the "New Socialism", 1926–1929', *WHR* 11 No.2 (1982), 173–99. The best local studies are Deian Hopkin, 'The Rise of Labour: Llanelli, 1890–1922', in *Politics and Society in Wales, 1840–1922*, ed. Geraint H. Jenkins and J. Beverley Smith (1980), 161–82; Neil Evans, 'Cardiff's Labour Traditions', *Llafur* 4 No.2 (1985), 77–90; Susan E. Demont, 'Tredegar and Aneurin Bevan: A Society and its Political Articulation, 1890–1929', Ph.D. thesis, University of Wales (Cardiff), 1990; Martin Barclay, 'Aberdare, 1880–1914: Class and Community', MA thesis, University of Wales (Cardiff), 1985; Thomas John McCarry, 'Labour and Society in Swansea, 1887–1918', Ph.D. thesis University of Wales (Swansea), 1986; Jon Parry, 'Labour Leaders and Local Politics, 1888–1902: The Example of Aberdare', *WHR* 14 No.3 (1989), 399–416.

[21] Dai Smith, *Aneurin Bevan*, 4.

[22] E. P. Thompson, *The Poverty of Theory* (1978), 110. This position is considered at length by Christopher Lloyd, *Explanation in Social History* (1987), and by Ellen Meiksins Wood, 'Falling Through the Cracks: E. P. Thompson and the Debate on Base and Superstructure', in *E. P. Thompson: Critical Perspectives*, ed. Harvey J. Kaye and Keith McClelland (1990), 125–52.

[23] For the contribution of Antonio Gramsci to this theoretical standpoint see Joseph Femia, *Gramsci's Political Thought: Hegemony, Consciousness and the Revolutionary Process* (1987 edition).

[24] Geoff Eley and Keith Nield, 'Why Does Social History Ignore Politics?', *Social History* 5 No.2 (1980), 249–71.

[25] Tanner, *Political Change*, 11.

[26] This is the danger with some 'revisionist' work which, for all its intelligence, overvalues its originality and overstates its case. See Biagini and Reid, 'Currents of Radicalism'.

[27] Particularly Savage, *The Dynamics of Working-Class Politics*.

[28] Ibid., 193.

[29] Ibid., 3.

[30] Marriott, *Culture of Labourism*, 10–11. Savage's haste to exclude

consciousness and thus 'ideology' is in part responsible for his misleading presentation and subsequent denial of 'the autonomy of the political' as being necessarily centred upon the state (Savage, op. cit., 9). See also idem, 'Urban History and Social Class: Two Paradigms, *Urban History* 20 Pt.1 (1993), 61–77, especially 65–6.

31 Joyce, *Visions of the People*, 1. Joyce, for instance, operates with a crude and reductionist notion of 'class' to which few Marxists would subscribe, and often restates in different words what Marxist historians have already suggested.

32 Neville Kirk, 'History, Language, Ideas and Post-modernism: A Materialist View', *Social History* 19 No.2 (1994), 221–40: 239. As Kirk points out, an intellectual and ideological inspiration derived from (amongst others) Edward Thompson is quite compatible with anti-reductionism.

32 Gareth Stedman Jones, *Languages of Class: Studies in English Working Class History 1832–1982* (1983).

33 Chris Williams, 'Britain'.

34 For example, James Gillespie, 'Poplarism and Proletarianism: Unemployment and Labour Politics in London, 1918–34', in *Metropolis London: Histories and representations since 1800*, ed. David Feldman and Gareth Stedman Jones (1989), 163–88.

36 Savage, 'Urban History and Social Class', 72–7. See also Gillespie, op. cit., 164.

37 Much of this work relies upon a detailed understanding of the history of local government elections in the Rhondda valleys, a subject treated comprehensively in Christopher Mark Williams, 'Democratic Rhondda: Politics and Society, 1885–1951', Ph.D. thesis, University of Wales (Cardiff), 1991.

38 It is this articulation of working-class interests, separate from the programme of any political party, that is defined as 'Labourism'.

Notes to Chapter 1

1 *Western Mail (WM)* 1 Jan. 1901, cited in David Smith, 'Introduction', in *A People and a Proletariat: Essays in the History of Wales 1780–1980*, ed. David Smith (1980), 7–15: 10.

2 Joseph Conrad, *Lord Jim* (1986 edition), 220.

3 HTV Wales, 'Wings of Significance: A Portrait of Gwyn Thomas, 1913–1981', 1988.

4 Hywel Francis and David Smith, *The Fed: A History of the South Wales Miners' in the Twentieth Century* (1980), between 232 and 233; Dai (David) Smith, *Rhondda Lives* (1988), 13.

5 Rhondda's economic development is the subject of E. D. Lewis's *The Rhondda Valleys* (1958), a model of its kind and of its age.

6 Cited by E. D. Lewis, ibid., 14.

[7] Figure based upon tables in E. D. Lewis, ibid., 91–3, 103–4, 249, and information supplied by Dr W. D. Jones.

[8] Rhondda Urban District Council Minutes (hereafter RUDC), 28 Aug. 1896.

[9] *South Wales Coal Annual*, 1908.

[10] In south Wales the number of deaths caused by explosions and the frequency of major explosions were greater than in any other British coalfield region, with the central and eastern Glamorgan valleys (including Rhondda) notoriously susceptible. Trevor Boyns, 'Technical Change and Colliery Explosions in the South Wales Coalfield, *c.*1870–1914', *WHR* 13 No.2 (1986), 155–77.

[11] As E. D. Lewis, op. cit., 230, points out, this is an underestimate of total population growth in the Rhondda district, as parts of the lower Rhondda, where most of the early workings were concentrated, were included in the neighbouring parishes of Llantrisant (where population rose from 1,715 in 1801 to 4,181 in 1851) and Llanwynno (where population rose from 250 in 1,801 to 1,703 in 1851).

[12] The RUDC area may be taken to cover what is commonly known as the Rhondda valleys. Whilst in 1871 the population of Ystradyfodwg parish stood at 16,914, that of Rhondda district was 23,950.

[13] Rhondda's population is estimated at peaking in 1924 with 167,900 inhabitants. In 1921 Carmarthenshire had a population of 175,073.

[14] Ministry of Health, *Report of the South Wales Regional Survey Committee* (1921), 13.

[15] Philip N. Jones, *Mines, Migrants and Residence in the South Wales Steamcoal Valleys: The Ogmore and Garw Valleys in 1881* (1987). As Jones concludes (p. 89), 'All groups shared more or less equally the hazards of coalmining, and were bound up within the harsh class-based society which was being constructed.'

[16] 'South-West England' includes the counties of Cornwall, Devon, Somerset, Wiltshire, Gloucestershire and Herefordshire. See Philip N. Jones, 'Population Migration into Glamorgan 1861–1911: A Reassessment', in *Glamorgan County History VI: Glamorgan Society 1780–1980*, ed. Prys Morgan (1988), 173–202.

[17] Dot Jones, 'Serfdom and Slavery: Women's Work in Wales, 1890–1930', in *Class, Community and the Labour Movement: Wales and Canada, 1850–1930*, ed. Deian R. Hopkin and Gregory S. Kealey, (1989), 86–100; Rosemary Crook, '"Tidy Women": Women in the Rhondda Between the Wars', *Oral History Journal* 10 (1982), 40–6.

[18] Elizabeth Andrews, *A Woman's Work Is Never Done* (1948).

[19] For the 'Matron' column see *Rhondda Socialist* (*RS*) Jan., Feb., 11 May, 14 Sep., 26 Oct., 9 Nov., 21 Dec. 1912.

[20] RUDC, 12 July 1912.

[21] Industrial Unrest, Commission of Inquiry (Reports) No.7 Division, 1917–18, Cd.8668 xv.83, 14.

[22] Ibid., 12.

23 Ministry of Health, op. cit., 58.
24 C. R. Williams, 'The Welsh Religious Revival, 1904–5' *British Journal of Sociology* 3 (1952), 242–59.
25 *Rhondda Leader (RL)* 3 Dec. 1904, 7 Jan. 1905.
26 See forthcoming University of Wales (Cardiff) Ph.D. thesis of Andrew Croll, 'Popular Culture in Merthyr Tydfil, 1880–1914'.
27 H. S. Jevons, *The British Coal Trade* (1969 edition), 124–5.
28 Royal Commission on the Church of England and other Religious Bodies in Wales and Monmouthshire, 1910, Cd.5432 Vol.1 Pt.1, 57.
29 The comments of E. D. Lewis, *The Rhondda Valleys*, 218–23 upon this subject are characteristic of the all too prevalent 'chapel-worship' in the historiography of modern Wales. The notion that Nonconformist preachers became 'the natural leaders of Rhondda society' is plausible only for a brief period in the late nineteenth century, and even then ignores the insurmountable problems of denominational division, agnosticism and the competition of economic imperatives.
30 According to J. C. McVail, Rhondda housing was unattractive and 'the inmates have no pleasant surroundings. The alternative consolations to which they resort are said to be mainly two, of very different nature – religion, and drink. Many are very religious, and others are very intemperate.' Royal Commission on the Poor Laws and Relief of Distress, 1909, Cd.4573, Vol.XLII, 335, Appendix Vol.XIV, Appendix Vol.XV, 282.
31 Colin Hughes, *Lime, Lemon and Sarsaparilla: The Italian Community in South Wales 1881–1945* (1991), 70.
32 David Smith and Gareth Williams, *Fields of Praise: The Official History of the Welsh Rugby Union 1881–1981* (1980), 92, 104–8.
33 Brian Lile and David Farmer, 'The Early Development of Association Football in South Wales, 1890–1906, *Transactions of the Honourable Society of Cymmrodorion* (1984), 193–215.
34 Andrew Hignell, *A 'Favourit' Game: Cricket in South Wales before 1914* (1992); Gareth Williams, *1905 And All That: Essays on Rugby Football, Sport and Welsh Society* (1991), 122.
35 Gareth Williams, ibid., 125; Dai Smith, *Aneurin Bevan and the World of South Wales* (1993), 318–37.
36 All were Liberal in politics apart from the Conservative *Glamorgan County Times*.
37 Ceri W. Lewis, 'The Welsh Language: Its Origin and Later History in the Rhondda', in *Rhondda Past and Future*, ed. K. S. Hopkins (1975), 179–234. By 1921 Welsh was a minority language, spoken by 45 per cent of the population.
38 W. T. R. Pryce, 'Language Areas and Changes c.1750–1981', in *Glamorgan County History VI: Glamorgan Society 1780–1980*, ed. Prys Morgan (1988), 265–313; T. I. Williams, 'Language, Identity and Education in a Liberal State: The Anglicisation of Pontypridd, 1818–1920', Ph.D. thesis, University of Wales (Cardiff), 1989.

[39] E. John Davies, 'The Origin and Development of Secondary Education in the Rhondda Valleys (1878–1923), MA thesis, University of Wales (Cardiff), 1965; Gareth Elwyn Jones, *Controls and Conflicts in Welsh Secondary Education, 1889–1944* (1982).

[40] H. V. Morton, *In Search of Wales* (1932), 247; The Pilgrim Trust, *Men Without Work* (1938), 276; Richard Lewis, *Leaders and Teachers: Adult Education and the Challenge of Labour in South Wales, 1906–1940* (1993).

[41] *Rhondda Clarion* (RC) Nov. 1936.

[42] *WM* 12, 16 Apr. 1926.

[43] In contrast with the work of Anthony Mor O'Brien, 'Patriotism on Trial: The Strike of the South Wales Miners, July 1915', *WHR* 12 No.1 (1984), 76–104; idem, 'The Merthyr Boroughs Election, November 1915', *WHR* 12 No.4 (1985), 53–66.

[44] William Rosser Jones, Mardy, interviewed by Hywel Francis, 4 July 1973, South Wales Miners' Library (SWML).

[45] W. F. Hay, in *War! And the Welsh Miner* (1915) was quite explicit in his pragmatism concerning the conflict and his determination to use the opportunity to extract maximum advantage for the miners. See also the articles of Central Labour College (CLC) student Jack 'Bolshie' Williams in *Glamorgan Free Press* (*GFP*), Apr.–Dec. 1915, *passim*.

[46] W. Watkin Davies, an Edgbaston Congregational minister, in his *A Wayfarer in Wales* (1930), 199, justified his lack of interest in the coalfield at the time of its greatest depression by arguing that 'I am not going to concern myself with things which in no true sense belong to Wales, but are rather the hideous price which men are paying all the world over for an insane lust for gold and power.'

[47] E. D. Lewis, *The Rhondda Valleys*, 250.

[48] Ibid., 254. The 1931 census indicated that mining still accounted for two-thirds of the employed male labour force. Waged work amongst women had declined to covering only one-tenth of women of fourteen and above.

[49] L. J. Williams (ed.), *Digest of Welsh Historical Statistics*, 2 vols (1985), 1, 336.

[50] Work on this subject is in its infancy, but see my 'The South Wales Miners' Federation', *Llafur* 5 No. 3 (1990), 45–56; Trevor Boyns, 'Of Machines and Men in the 1920s', *Llafur* 5 No.2 (1989), 30–9; idem, 'Powell Duffryn: The Use of Machinery and Production Planning Techniques in the South Wales Coalfield', in *Towards a Social History of Mining*, ed. K. Tenfelde, (1992), 370–86; and idem, 'Jigging and Shaking: Technical Choice in the South Wales Coal Industry Between the Wars', *WHR* 17 No.2 (1994), 230–51.

[51] Andrew James Chandler, 'The Re-making of a Working Class: Migration from the South Wales Coalfield to the New Industry Areas of the Midlands, *c.* 1920–1940', Ph.D. thesis, University of Wales (Cardiff) 1988, 15.

[52] Ibid., 320–55; R. C. Whiting, *The View From Cowley, The Impact of Industrialization upon Oxford, 1918–1939* (1983).

[53] The Labour Party, *The Distress In South Wales*, (1928), 14.

54 Gareth Williams, op. cit., 179–80, 184.
55 Dai Smith, *Aneurin Bevan*, 321–3.
56 Chandler, op. cit., 10–14.
57 The phrase was used by Iorrie Thomas MP, in his maiden speech in the House of Commons on 4 April 1950.
58 Peter Stead, 'The Voluntary Response to Mass Unemployment in South Wales', in *Reactions to Social and Economic Change 1750–1939*, ed. Walter Minchinton (1979), 97–117.
59 Chandler, op. cit., 147–50; Sam Davies, 'The Membership of the National Unemployed Workers' Movement', *Labour History Journal* 57 Part No.1 (1992), 29–36.
60 Peter Stead, *Coleg Harlech, The First Fifty Years* (1977), 57–8, 73–4.
61 Wages had risen to eleven shillings per shift on average by October 1938.
62 Stuart R. Broomfield, 'South Wales During the Second World War: The Coal Industry and its Community', Ph.D. thesis, University of Wales (Swansea), 1979.
63 D. A. Thomas, 'War and the Economy: The South Wales Experience', in *Modern South Wales: Essays in Economic History*, ed. Colin Baber and L. J. Williams (1986), 251–77.
64 Rhondda miners, *Rebirth of the Rhondda: Nationalisation Souvenir Programme* (1947). Unemployment had fallen below 5 per cent of the insured labour force by the mid-1950s, although many older men continued to experience difficulty in finding regular work.

Notes to Chapter 2

1 W. H. Mainwaring Papers, National Library of Wales (NLW). The use of the term 'Labour' in the years prior to the emergence of the Labour Party either nationally or at Rhondda level is a matter of some complexity. Labour could mean manual labour in the most basic sense of the type of work undertaken. Or it could mean the 'interests' of manual labour, its rights and its collective dignity. Such a conceptualization was often political, and was even more so when the term also referred to an actual body of organized workers, such as the trade unions or the coalminers. But this need not have had anything whatsoever to do with the Labour Representation Committee or the Labour Party, although often any group of Lib-Labs. were referred to as a 'Labour party'. My understanding of Mainwaring's comment, therefore, is that he felt that the miners, through their appeal to organizational and class loyalties, were 'training people' to vote for candidates identified as representatives of 'Labour' (the 'interests of manual workers/trade unionists) before there was a formal Labour Party organization in existence in the locality.
2 For an example of this 'orthodoxy' see the work of Kenneth O. Morgan, especially *Wales in British Politics, 1868–1922* (1980 edition).

[3] Kenneth Owen Fox, 'The Emergence of the Political Labour Movement in the Eastern Section of the South Wales Coalfield, 1894–1910', MA thesis, University of Wales (Aberystwyth), 1965.

[4] *RL* 15 Feb. 1908.

[5] *Cardiff Times (CT)* 21 July 1883.

[6] *Pontypridd Chronicle (PC)* 7, 21 July 1883.

[7] E. W. Evans, *Mabon* (1959). Upon formation in 1877 known as the Cambrian Miners' Association (CMA), it subsequently divided into the RSCMA, and the Rhondda House Coal Miners' Association (RHCMA), Mabon remaining secretary to the former. The RSCMA, in 1885, was estimated to have had a membership of between twelve and fourteen thousand. It was very much a non-aggressive trade union, collecting its contributions via the colliery office. It was thus dependent on the goodwill of the employers for its continued existence. The dues were used to pay the salary of the agent, and the agent's role was to settle disputes via arbitration. Idem, *Miners of South Wales* (1961), 136–7.

[8] *PC* 19, 21 Jan., 5 July 1884, 3, 10 Jan. 1885; *CT* 26 July 1884.

[9] *PC* 23 Jan. 1885.

[10] Ieuan Gwynedd Jones, 'The Merthyr of Henry Richard', in *Merthyr Politics: The Making of a Working-Class Tradition*, ed. Glanmor Williams (1966), 28–57.

[11] *WM* 21 Jan. 1885; *PC* 16, 23 Jan. The first object of the Rhondda Liberal Association was 'to secure and maintain the Liberal representation of this Division in Local and Parliamentary Elections'.

[12] The Vice-Presidents included a landowner, two colliery managers, a Nonconformist minister, and the Ferndale collieries' doctor. John Jones Griffiths, a retired headmaster from Penygraig, was elected general secretary of the association, and the office of treasurer went to D. W. Davies, draper of Tonypandy.

[13] *PC* 6, 13 Mar., 17, 24 Apr., 15 May 1885; *WM* 17, 20 Apr. 1885; *South Wales Daily News (SWDN)* 12 May 1885.

[14] *PC* 10 Apr. 1885.

[15] Ibid. 24 Apr. 1885; *CT* 25 Apr. 1885.

[16] *CT* 15 Nov. 1884; *WM* 23 Apr. 1885.

[17] *SWDN* 15 May 1885; *WM* 20, 22 May, 15 June 1885.

[18] *SWDN* 5 May 1885.

[19] Ibid. 12 May 1885.

[20] Ibid. 14 May 1885.

[21] *PC* 15, 22, 29 May 1885; *WM* 18, 22, 25 May 1885.

[22] *WM* 20 May 1885.

[23] *SWDN* 16 May 1885.

[24] *WM* 30 May 1885.

[25] Ibid. 13 June 1885; *PC* 19 June 1885.

[26] *WM* 20 June 1885; *PC* 26 June 1885.

[27] *PC* 5, 26 June, 3, 17 July 1885; *WM* 29 June 1885.

28 There was never any serious possibility of a Conservative candidature. As the Liberal *South Wales Daily News* (26 Oct. 1885) put it with only mild exaggeration: 'The number of Tory votes is small enough to be absolutely inappreciable. The strides which the population have made have been so rapid, and the character of the people so exclusively industrial, that Toryism is an exotic plant totally unsuited to the vigorous Radical air which pervades everything.'

29 *SWDN* 3, 9 Oct. 1885; *WM* 3 Oct. 1885.

30 *SWDN* 23 July, 26 Nov. 1885; David Young, *A Noble Life: Incidents in the Career of Lewis Davis of Ferndale* (1888), 141–2.

31 *SWDN* 13, 16 July, 28 Oct., 9 Nov. 1885.

32 *PC* 24 July 1885; *SWDN* 1 Aug., 14 Nov. 1885.

33 *SWDN* 24 July, 9 Nov. 1885; *WM* 18 Nov. 1885.

34 *PC* 24 July, 30 Oct. 1885; *SWDN* 29 Oct., 13 Nov. 1885; *WM* 12, 18, 19, 21 Nov. 1885.

35 *WM* 8 Oct. 1885.

36 *SWDN* 6 Nov. 1885.

37 Ibid. 29 Oct. 1885; *WM* 29 Oct. 1885; *PC* 30 Oct. 1885.

38 *CT* 17 Oct. 1885.

39 *WM* 3 Dec. 1885.

40 Ibid. 4 Dec. 1885.

41 Ibid. 5 Dec. 1885; *PC* 18 Dec. 1885.

42 *PC* 25 Dec. 1885, 1 Jan., 19 Feb. 1886.

43 *SWDN* 4 Dec. 1885, 12 Feb. 1886; *WM* 23 June, 3 July 1886.

44 *SWDN* 18 Jan. 1889.

45 Ibid. 23 June 1892.

46 Ibid. 18 May 1892.

47 Ibid. 16, 27, 29, 30 June, 4, 7 July 1892. Morris described himself variously as an 'advanced Radical', a 'Republican', an 'Independent Labour candidate' and as 'Labour and Independent Liberal', but seemed prepared to distance himself from Mabon only on the details, not the principle, of Gladstone's Irish Home Rule Bill. The subtlety of such a policy eluded most of the electorate.

48 Ibid. 8, 9, 18, 23, 28 June, 1, 7 July 1892; F. J. Harries, *A History of Conservatism in the Rhondda* (1912), 34–6. Harries alleges that the explorer H. M. Stanley was asked by the RCA to stand as parliamentary candidate, but refused. No doubt Stanley felt that discovering a Conservative majority in Rhondda was likely to be a more difficult task than finding Livingstone in Africa!

49 *SWDN* 10, 18, 23, 24 June 1892; *PC* 10 June 1892; *Glamorgan Free Press (GFP)* 2 July 1892.

50 *SWDN* 21 June 1892. A similar point was made by Morris in a letter to Keir Hardie dated 25 Aug. 1893 (Francis Johnson Papers, British Library of Political and Economic Science 1893/88): 'Personally I feel that it is a pity that the men have lost confidence in him [Mabon] for I believe he is much more

honest than the men look upon him, but I cannot conceal the fact that the parties who most strenuously opposed him in 1885, are now his most ardent supporters, viz. Coal Owners, Royalty Owners, and Colliery Officials.'

51 *SWDN* 7, 9 July 1892. Morris subsequently claimed that on the day he had gone to Cardiff, intending to return to Pontypridd in time to enter his nomination, but that in Cardiff he had been drugged (by persons unknown) and subsequently missed his opportunity!

52 *GFP* 28 Jan. 1893, 14, 28 Apr., 22 Oct. 1894; *WM* July 1895 *passim*; *SWDN* 25 June, 5 July 1895; Harries, op. cit., 36.

53 *RL* May 1900 *passim*; *WM* 18, 20, 21, 25 Sept., 1 Oct. 1900; *SWDN* 1 Oct. 1900; Harries, op. cit., 37–44.

54 *GFP* 26 May 1900; *SWDN* 2 Oct. 1900; *WM* 2, 30 Oct. 1900.

55 *WM* 1, 3, 4, 8 Oct. 1900; *RL* 6 Oct. 1900.

56 *WM* 26 Sept. 1900; *RL* 29 Sept., 6 Oct. 1900.

57 *WM* 9 Oct. 1900; *SWDN* 10 Oct. 1900.

58 *WM* 1, 17 Jan. 1906; *SWDN* 2, 5, 10 Jan. 1906, 8 May, 25 Dec. 1909; *RL* 6 Jan. 1906; Harries, op. cit., 57–60.

59 *WM* 27 Nov. and Dec. 1909 *passim*; *SWDN* 15 Dec. 1909.

60 Rhondda No.1 District Minutes (RD) 11 Dec. 1909; *WM* 13, 16 Dec. 1909; *SWDN* 13 Dec. 1909; *RL* 25 Dec. 1909.

61 *WM* 16 Dec. 1909; *SWDN* 16 Dec. 1909; *RL* 25 Dec. 1909. Mabon had been heavily involved in supporting Lloyd George's budget during the year, and appeared on RLLA platforms.

62 *WM* 16 Dec. 1909.

63 *SWDN* 7 Jan. 1910.

64 *RL* Jan. 1910 *passim*.

65 Ibid. 8 Jan. 1910; *SWDN* 6 Jan. 1910.

66 *RL* 15, 22 Jan. 1910. To be sung to the tune of 'Men of Harlech'.

67 *SWDN* 21 Jan. 1910.

68 At a meeting in Ynyshir, Mabon was called upon to reply to the criticism that he was surrounded by too many socialists. His response was to assert that they were all socialists, even W. J. Thomas who was chairing the meeting. Lloyd George, Mabon said, was a 'practical socialist', whilst he himself was a 'revolutionary socialist'. It must remain doubtful whether other 'revolutionary socialists' were impressed by this new recruit to their ranks, who in 1907 had argued that he failed to see the difference between Liberalism and socialism – 'The Labour party are in favour of evolutionary Socialism, and not revolution. Dress it as you will [and Mabon certainly did!] that has always been the aim of Liberalism' (*GFP* 13 Dec. 1907; *SWDN* 17 Jan. 1910).

69 *Porth Gazette* (PG) 19 Feb. 1910.

70 *WM* 21 Nov. 1910.

71 *RL* 19 Nov. 1910.

72 Ibid. 3 Dec. 1910; *WM* 3 Dec. 1910; *SWDN* 1, 2 Dec. 1910; *The Clarion* 18 Nov. 1910.

73 *RL* 10 Dec. 1910; *WM* 6, 7 Dec. 1910.
74 *RL* 10, 17 Dec. 1910. Despite the non-appearance of a socialist candidate, Mabon continued to encounter difficulties, being taunted at meetings with his own phrase 'My friend, D. A. Thomas', and even 'Hen Wlad Fy Nhadau' found itself booed.
75 *SWDN* 6 Dec. 1910; *WM* 8, 15, 16 Dec. 1910.
76 For the classic example of which see the presentation of nearly £2,000 as a testimonial to Mabon 'in the evening of his life for his public services as a negotiator and arbitrator' in 1903, following his successful negotiation of an agreement with the coal-owners to introduce a conciliation board in place of the Sliding Scale (*SWDN* 13 Apr., 2 May 1903; NLW MSS. 12520 (Mabon's Testimonial Minute Book)).
77 Mabon operated in Parliament largely as an orthodox Liberal MP, but as a representative of Labour he did make important contributions as a member of three Royal Commissions. See the entry by Eric Wyn Evans and John Saville in the *Dictionary of Labour Biography (DLB)* (Volume I, 2–4); and Hywel John Davies, 'Mabon at Westminster: The Parliamentary Career of William Abraham M.P. 1885–1920', MA dissertation, University of Wales (Cardiff), 1990.
78 *WM* 3 Oct. 1885.
79 *PC* 3 Jan. 1885.
80 Ibid. 21 July 1883.
81 *SWDN* 16 July 1885.
82 *CT* 21 July 1883.
83 Both L. J. Williams, 'The First Welsh Labour MP', *Morgannwg* 6 (1962), 78–94 and Kenneth O. Morgan, 'The New Liberalism and the Challenge of Labour: The Welsh Experience, 1885–1929', *WHR* 6 No. 3 (1973), 288–312, are eager to see 1885 in the light of the subsequent 'alliance' between Labour and Liberalism in Rhondda. Mabon, after all, was not so 'firmly dedicated to the old Liberal premise of class collaboration' (Morgan, p. 292) that he was prepared to back down in 1885.
84 For accounts of Cymru Fydd see Morgan, *Wales in British Politics* and Emyr Wynn Williams, 'The Politics of Welsh Home Rule 1886–1929; A Sociological Analysis', Ph.D. thesis, University of Wales (Aberystwyth), 1986.
85 *SWDN* 10 Oct. 1888.
86 *SWDN* 15 June 1894.
87 Morgan, *Wales in British Politics*, 161–5; Emyr Williams, op. cit., 111–15, 121–4. Williams views the conflict as being between Lloyd George's 'popular democratic reformers' and D. A. Thomas's 'undemocratic and unscrupulous conservatives'. He argues that within 'proletarian South Wales in particular, Liberal Constituency Associations, where they existed, appear to have been notoriously undemocratic and unrepresentative'. This may have been the case, but little evidence is marshalled either in support of such characterizations, or to show that

north Walian Liberalism was any more 'democratic'. To divide the two wings of Welsh Liberalism between 'reformist' and 'conservative' axes is simplistic: Mabon was wary of the followers of Cymru Fydd precisely because of their lack, in his eyes, of 'democratic' or 'reformist' credentials (*SWDN* 13, 20 May, Nov. 1895 *passim; WM* 12 Nov. 1895; Kenneth O. Morgan (ed.), *Lloyd George: Family Letters, 1885–1936* (1973), 91–2.

[88] Eric Wyn Evans, 'Mabon and Trade Unionism in the South Wales Coalfield', in *Men of No Property: Historical Studies of Welsh Trade Unions*, ed. Goronwy Alun Hughes (1971), 51–8.

[89] Kenneth O. Morgan, *Rebirth of a Nation: Wales 1880–1980* (1981), 49.

[90] The YUSA tended to be known as the 'Local Board'. As for the YSB, a study of Rhondda does not bear out the suggestion of Jon Parry, 'Labour Leaders and Local Politics, 1888–1902: The Example of Aberdare', *WHR* 14 No.3 (1989), 399–416: 405, that School Boards were of primary importance.

[91] Absentee landlordism was characteristic of the Rhondda by the mid-nineteenth century (E. D. Lewis, *The Rhondda Valleys* (1984 edition) 16–17).

[92] *PC* 19 Feb. 1886. Such as Tom John, who joined the RLLA whilst remaining prepared to state his opinion that in 1885 'the intellect of the Rhondda had been with Mr. Davis'.

[93] Ibid. 3 June, 1 July 1892. Mabon discussed the parliamentary fund at a meeting of the CMA: 'the Miners had Liberal friends, and because they sent annually subscriptions to the Parliamentary Fund of the Rhondda Division – with all due respect to them, bear in mind; he didn't complain, though he felt pained sometimes – they thought they had a claim upon him and upon his services. It would not do for him . . . They thought they had a claim upon his services because they had contributed to the fund. For the sake of being free, he and the miners to be free, let them take that matter in hand . . .'

[94] This supports the view that the RLLA met annually to report progress and little else: Kenneth O. Morgan, 'Democratic Politics in Glamorgan', *Morgannwg* 4 (1960), 5–27; *SWDN* 15 Nov. 1895; and *RL* 3 Aug. 1907.

[95] There were occasional RLLA meetings on matters of importance: the Education Bill (1902); 'Welsh National Issues' (1906); the Licensing Bill (1908); the Budget (1909) (*GFP* 4 Oct. 1902, 5 Jan. 1906, 17 Sept., 8 Oct. 1909; *RL* 28 Mar., 7 Nov. 1908, 4, 11 Sept., 20 Nov. 1909). But banquets were often preferred, or there was the regular Rhondda Miners' Annual Demonstration, attracting important national politicians.

[96] In 1907, for example, the RLLA was estimated to have obtained the vote for four times as many lodgers as did the RCA (*RL* 12 Oct. 1907).

[97] Morgan, *Wales in British Politics*, 167–71, 243–5.

[98] *PC* 13 Sept. 1884; Harries, op. cit., 16.

[99] *PC* 24 May 1895; *GFP* 18 Dec. 1908; Harries, op. cit., 66–115.

[100] *WM* 4 July 1895. Rhondda saw no significant Primrose League activity in

this, the League's heyday. Ystrad Mynach, Dowlais, Aberdare, Pontypridd, Mountain Ash and Caerphilly all sported a measure of such populist Toryism: see Martin Pugh, *The Tories and the People* (1985), Appendix XVIII.

101 *SWDN* 10, 18, 19 Jan. 1889; *PC* 11, 25 Jan. 1889.

102 *SWDN* 3, 8 Jan. 1889.

103 Ibid. 4 Jan. 1889. Joseph Jones, miner, of Penygraig, chaired a RLLA meeting in support of John Jones Griffiths; John Williams, checkweigher, of Clydach Vale, chaired a meeting in support of Richard Lewis and W. G. Williams.

104 Ibid. 19 Jan. 1889.

105 Ibid. 23 Feb., 2 Mar. 1892; *PC* 26 Feb. 1892.

106 *SWDN* 25 Feb. 1892.

107 Ibid. 27 Feb., 1, 4 Mar. 1892.

108 *PC* 11 Mar. 1892.

109 *SWDN* 2, 4 Mar. 1892. An allegation that the Baptists had six candidates in the field was immediately countered by the observation that the Congregationalists had seven.

110 Interview with Brynna Jones, Gelli, 5 March 1986.

111 William Evans, born Fishguard 1864, is one of the best, and last, examples of a prominent local Liberal 'personality'. A Haverfordwest grocer, he came to Porth in 1885 and built a business reputation (through the 'Thomas and Evans' firm) far beyond the confines of Rhondda, whilst living in and serving the valley. Owen Vernon Jones, *William Evans 1864–1934* (1982), and BBC Wales TV, 'A View of the Rhondda: The "Prince of Porth"' (1984).

112 An anonymous letter-writer, in *GFP* 30 Aug. 1902.

113 The PLC, which called meetings of workmen in the locality and nominated the two candidates, was established shortly in advance of the 1892 GCC elections. The later Porth Trades and Labour Council (TLC) became active in the early years of the twentieth century.

114 *SWDN* 17, 24 Oct. 1896.

115 Ken John, 'Sam Mainwaring and the Autonomist Tradition', *Llafur* 4 No. 3 (1986), 55–66; *Merthyr Pioneer (MP)* 4 Mar. 1920; *Labour Leader* 16 June 1894.

116 Unlike Jon Parry, 'Trade Unionists and Early Socialism in South Wales, 1890–1908', *Llafur* 4 No. 3 (1986), 43–54.

117 *GFP* 20 June, 5, 11 July 1896, 20, 27 Mar. 1897; *ILP News* 1 No.1 (Apr. 1897); *PC* 26 Mar., 20 Aug. 1897; *Labour Leader* 4 June 1898.

118 *ILP News* 1 No.9 (Dec. 1897).

119 *Justice* 23 Oct. 1897.

120 *The Fed*, 1.

121 L. J. Williams, 'The Strike of 1898', *Morgannwg* 9 (1965), 61–79.

122 *Justice* 23 Apr., 7, 21 May 1898.

123 *ILP News* 2 No. 15 (June 1898); *Labour Leader* 28 May 1898.

[124] *ILP News* 2 Nos. 18–21 (Sept.–Dec. 1898); letter from Evan Vaughan (Mardy) to NAC, Oct. 1898; *Labour Leader 3* Dec. 1898.

[125] *ILP News* 2 Nos. 22–31 (Jan.–Oct. 1899).

[126] *ILP News* Nos. 34–7 (Jan.–Apr. 1900).

[127] *Labour Leader* 16 July 1898, 11 Feb. 1899. Willie Wright attacked the RLLA, observing that it received subscriptions from a number of coal-owners, not all of them Liberals, and that as such it could hardly claim to represent Rhondda miners.

[128] Hereafter references to 'the District' are to the No.1 District. This covered a far greater proportion of Rhondda miners than did the No.2 District.

[129] *RL* 22 Sept. 1900.

[130] *GFP* 12 Apr. 1902.

[131] Ibid. 13, 27 Jan. 1900; *RL* 13, 20 Jan. 1900.

[132] *RD* 13 May 1901.

[133] Ibid. 1 Apr. 1901; *PG* 16 Feb. 1901; *RL* 23 Feb. 1901. The Committee was composed of representatives of seven local lodges.

[134] *RL* 10 May 1902. This was a smokescreen for Liberal sympathies. In south Wales there was little likelihood of an appearance by a Conservative Labour man in Federation colours. By presenting the scheme as apolitical to the District, Watts Morgan could hope to circumvent any possible opposition from socialists, Conservatives, or those unenamoured of local Liberalism despite their possession of Liberal sympathies. This has been misunderstood by other historians. Morgan ('Democratic Politics in Glamorgan', 24–5); Michael J. Klarman, 'Osborne: A Judgment Gone Too Far?', *English Historical Review* 104 (1988), 21–39; idem, 'The Trade Union Political Levy, the Osborne Judgment (1909) and the South Wales Miners' Federation', *WHR* 15 No. 1 (1990), 34–57. The 'Pickard Scheme' was the brainchild of the Yorkshire miners' leader and president of the MFGB from 1889 until 1904, Ben Pickard. It was conceived as an attempt to secure parliamentary representation on an increased scale, whilst remaining within a general Lib-Lab context, rather than affiliating to the Labour Party. It was adopted by the MFGB 1902 annual conference, and consisted of a political fund which paid the salary and expenses of successful parliamentary candidates. Roy Gregory, *The Miners and British Politics 1906–1914* (1968), 19–24.

[135] *PG* 17 May 1902.

[136] *RD* 2 Feb. 1903; *RL* 7 Feb. 1903.

[137] *RD* 1 Feb. 1904.

[138] Ibid. 13 Mar. 1905; *RL* 21 July 1905.

[139] *RL* 5 Mar. 1904; *GFP* 12 Mar. 1904.

[140] *RD* 14 Mar. 1904.

[141] Ibid. 17 July 1905.

[142] *GFP* 27 Apr. 1901. The column discussed the relationship between socialism and Christianity, the housing problem, the land question, inequality, wealth and life expectancy.

[143] Frank Bealey and Henry Pelling, *Labour and Politics, 1900–1906: A History of the Labour Representation Committee* (1958), 51–2.

[144] *RL* Apr., May, June 1901 *passim*, 31 Aug. 1901.

[145] Bealey and Pelling, op. cit., 135; *The Democrat* 1, Nos.1–3 (June–Aug. 1902).

[146] NAC ILP 1–2 Dec. 1902; ILP Annual Conference Reports 1903–6; *RL* 12 Oct. 1901, 22 Nov. 1902, 10 Sept. 1904, 24 July 1905; *GFP* 29 Dec. 1905; *PG* Jan. 1906 *passim*.

[147] Gregory, op. cit., 28–31.

[148] *SWDN* 11 July 1906.

[149] E. W. Evans, *Mabon* (1959), 75–6; Gregory, op. cit., 125.

[150] *GFP* May–Aug. 1906 *passim*; Cambrian Lodge minutes (CL) 21 July 1906; *RL* 2 June 1906; *PG* 28 Apr., May 1906 *passim*.

[151] *RL* 4 Aug. 1906.

[152] RD 16 July 1906; *SWDN* 20 July 1906.

[153] *SWDN* 30 July 1906.

[154] Ibid. 17 July 1906; *GFP* 20, 27 July 1906; *RL* 4 Aug. 1906; *SWDN* 27 July, 1 Aug. 1906.

[155] *GFP* 3 Aug. 1906; Francis Johnson Papers 1906/272, letter from Mardy Jones to Keir Hardie, dated 19 July 1906, British Library of Political and Economic Science.

[156] *GFP* 17, 24 Aug., 2 Nov. 1906, 11, 28 Jan. 1907; *RL* 1 Dec. 1906; *PG* 21, 28 July, 15, 22 Sept., 10 Nov. 1906, 5 Jan., 2 Feb., 9 Mar., 11 May 1907.

[157] *GFP* 4 Jan. 1907.

[158] *RL* 18 May 1907.

[159] *GFP* 28 June 1907. For the campaign see ibid. May 1907 *passim*, 21 June, 12 July, 2, 16 Aug. 1907; *RL* 18 May, 24 Aug., 14, 21 Sept. 1907; *PG* 20, 27 July, 3 Aug. 1907.

[160] *RL* 26 Oct., 30 Nov., 7 Dec. 1907; *GFP* 13 Dec. 1907.

[161] *The Worker* 1 Aug. 1908. For the campaign see *GFP* 20 May, 10, 24 July, 14 Aug., 15 Sept., 2 Oct., 13 Nov., 4 Dec., 1908; *RL* Aug–Oct. 1908 *passim*, 28 Nov., Dec. 1908 *passim*; *PG* 17 Oct. 1908.

[162] *GFP* 22 Jan. 1909. The membership of the Porth Branch was reported as stationary, but the return of Noah Ablett from Ruskin College was expected to 'revive enthusiasm'.

[163] *RL* 23 Jan., 13, 27 Feb., 6 Mar., 3 Apr., 1 May, 13 June, 24 July, 11 Sept., Oct.–Nov.–Dec. 1909 *passim*; *GFP* 22 Jan., Feb. 1909 *passim*, 5 Mar., 21, 28 May, 11 June, July 1909 *passim*, 17, 24 Sept., 22 Oct., 19 Nov. 1909.

[164] *RL* 22 Jan. 1910; Report of the 18th Annual Conference (1910).

[165] *GFP* 1 June 1901.

[166] *GFP* 16, 23 Mar. 1906; *PG* 3, 10 Feb., 3 Mar. 1906.

[167] *GFP* 10 Feb. 1900.

[168] Ibid. 23 Mar. 1901.

[169] Ibid. 30 Mar. 1901.

[170] *PG* 28 Mar. 1903.

[171] *RL* 21 Feb. 1903.

[172] *PG* 4 Apr. 1903; *GFP* 4 Apr. 1903.

[173] *RL* 21 Mar. 1903.

[174] Traditional rivalry existed between the two largest lodges in the area, and Lewis Merthyr felt that as Cymmer Lodge was situated outside Ward Eight, it should concentrate on gaining representation in Ward Nine rather than capitalizing on the more favourable Ward Eight position.

[175] *RL* 26 Mar. 1904.

[176] Ibid. 20 Jan. 1906; *GFP* 23 Mar. 1906.

[177] *RL* Mar. 1907 *passim*; *GFP* 22 Mar. 1907. Morgan had already been returned unopposed to the GCC.

[178] *GFP* 8 Mar. 1907; *CL* 2 Feb. 1907; Labour Representation Committee (LRC) Correspondence Files 22/303: letter from Mid-Rhondda TLC (MRTLC) 23 Dec. 1907.

[179] Alan Clinton, *The Trade Union Rank and File: Trades Councils in Britain, 1900–40* (1977), 197.

[180] *RL* 13 Apr. 1901.

[181] Cornelius Gronow Collection University College, Swansea (UCS), Rules of No.9 Ward TLC (n.d.). The LRC No.9 Ward was established as a local committee, part of the first Rhondda No.1 District local government scheme. RD 13 Mar., 3 Apr. 1905. No other 'Labour committees', beyond an adapted PLC, were established, and LRC No.9 Ward rapidly assumed an autonomy from the District similar to that of a regular TLC, whilst all other areas that had been earmarked for a 'Labour committee' continued to refer their candidates for approval to the district. After the adoption of the second local government scheme, LRC No.9 Ward seems not to have had a role any different from that of the now-incorporated TLCs and the lodges.

[182] *RL* 15 June 1907; *PG* 16 Feb., 12 Oct. 1907.

[183] LRC No.9 Ward Minutes (LRC9) 12 July 1904; *GFP* 14 Feb. 1908.

[184] *PG* 11 Dec. 1909; *GFP* 9 Apr., 16 July 1909; *RL* 23 Mar. 1907, 29 Feb., 3 Apr., 11 Sept. 1909, 19 Feb., 8 Oct. 1910; MRTLC 1 Dec. 1909; MRTLC annual report 1910; RD 18 May 1908; *PG* 9 Oct. 1909.

[185] RUDC 22 May, 8 June, 14 Dec. 1906, 13 Mar. 1907, 11 June, 10 Sept. 1909.

[186] *RL* 1 May 1909.

[187] *RL* 3 Aug. 1907.

[188] Ibid. 29 Feb. 1908; RD 13 June 1908. The Rhondda scheme was therefore somewhat more elaborate than a scheme proposed by the SWMF EC, which allowed for 2*d*. to be set aside for local work. SWMF E1, report of sub-committee, Labour representation scheme (n.d.).

[189] *GFP* 10 Jan. 1908. The scheme was not welcomed by the Cambrian Lodge, which resented having to conduct its selection process through the Mid-Rhondda TLC. Squabbles between lodges and TLCs were frequent over where sovereignty lay in these matters. CL 26 Oct., 29 Nov., 7, 21 Dec. 1907; RD 19 Mar. 1909.

[190] *RL* 29 Feb., 14 Mar. 1908.
[191] Burton's opponent was in fact a hotelier.
[192] *RL* 14 Mar. 1908. According to T. I. Mardy Jones (*RL* 4 Apr. 1908) 'This is a fight between Capital and Labour.'
[193] *RL* Mar. 1908 *passim*, 4 Apr. 1908; RD 25 Apr. 1908.
[194] *RL* 11 Apr. 1908; *GFP* 17 Apr. 1908.
[195] *RL* 4 Apr. 1908.
[196] Ibid. Mar.–Apr. 1908 *passim*; SWMF EC 30 Mar. 1908.
[197] *RL* 11 Apr. 1908.
[198] *RL* 12 Dec. 1908, 9 Jan., Feb–Mar. 1909 *passim*, 3 Apr. 1909; 12, 19 Feb. 1910; *PG* Mar. 1909 *passim*; RD 19 Mar. 1909.
[199] Harries, op. cit., 17–18 and 55–6; Klarman, 'Osborne: A Judgment Gone Too Far?', 32–7.
[200] *RL* 9 Apr. 1910; RD 4 Oct., 1, 29 Nov. 1909; MRTLC 23 Feb. 1910.
[201] *RL* 12 Mar. 1910.
[202] *RL* 11 June 1904.
[203] Ibid. 23 Mar. 1907.
[204] 'Democratic Politics in Glamorgan', 23.
[205] It is in this light that the 1908 miners' ballot concerning affiliation to the Labour Party must be understood. The result in south Wales was a clear majority in favour of affiliation (74,463 to 44,571) paralleled in Rhondda No.1 District (15,371 to 9,027). With the national (MFGB) result also in favour, the union affiliated to the Labour Party at the beginning of 1909. Superficially this was an important step: the last of the major unions had eventually come over to the Labour camp. And it did cause a problem for miners' MPs such as Mabon, whose hearts remained in the Liberal Party. But the 1906 ballot had already shown south Wales miners in favour of affiliation, and at local government level the miners were advancing their own candidatures, irrespective of their union's affiliation, before 1908. Only at the parliamentary level did the ballot signal real change.
[206] See the account of the election of the SWMF general secretary Thomas Richards to the seat of West Monmouthshire in 1904 in Susan E. Demont, 'Tredegar and Aneurin Bevan: A Society and its Political Articulation, 1890–1929', Ph.D. thesis, University of Wales (Cardiff), 1990, 52–75.

Notes to Chapter 3

[1] *History of the South Wales Miners' Federation* (1938), 49.
[2] 'Tonypandy 1910: Definitions of Community', *Past and Present* 87 (1980), 158–84: 160.
[3] Dai Smith, *Wales! Wales?* (1984), 55–97. Prior interpretations were largely based upon David Evans, *Labour Strife in the South Wales Coalfield, 1910–1911: A Historical and Critical Record of the Mid-Rhondda, Aberdare Valley and Other Strikes* (1911).
[4] *Rhondda Socialist (RS)* Feb. 1912.

5 *RS* Oct. 1911. Mabon rarely attended SWMF EC meetings during 1911 and 1912 (SWMF EC *passim*) and experienced a health breakdown in 1913 (RD 6 Jan., 4 Apr. 1913).

6 *Merthyr Pioneer (MP)* 4 Jan. 1913; *RS* 4 Jan. 1918; *Porth Gazette (PG)* 23 Nov., 7 Dec. 1918; Kenneth O. Morgan, *Wales in British Politics 1868–1922* (1980 edition), 277.

7 SWMF EC , 4 Jan., 2 Feb. 1918; *Western Mail (WM)* 5 Dec. 1918. Mabon seems to have been in virtual retirement as an MP from as early as 1908 onwards. In that year he had been appointed to a Standing Committee but had failed to attend one of its sessions; in 1911 he made his last speech in the House; in 1915 he asked his last question (Parliamentary Debates, 1908–20 *passim*).

8 *Glamorgan Free Press (GFP)* 29 Nov. 1917, 10, 17 Jan. 1918; *Rhondda Leader (RL)* 12 Jan., 23 Feb. 1918; *PG* 19 Jan. 1918; *WM* 4 Dec. 1918.

9 *PG* 30 Nov. 1918; *GFP* 14, 21 Feb., 11 Apr. 1918; *RL* 13 Apr. 1918.

10 *South Wales News (SWN)* 5 Dec. 1918.

11 *WM* 4 Dec. 1918. See also ibid. 21, 26 Nov., 2, 3 Dec. 1918; *Glamorgan County Times (GCT)* 30 Nov., 7 Dec. 1918.

12 He joined on 4 Aug. 1914. *RL* 7 Nov. 1914; *GFP* 11 Mar. 1915; *Mid-Rhondda Gazette (MRG)* 4 Sept. 1915.

13 *GFP* 27 Jan. 1916, 9 Aug. 1917; *RL* 12 Jan. 1918; *WM* 24 Feb. 1933.

14 *RL* 21 Dec. 1918.

15 Rhondda No.1 District (RD) 16 Jan., 15 Mar., 12 Apr. 1920; Ferndale Lodge (FL) 10 Feb., 14 Mar. 1920; SWMF EC 27 Feb., 16 Mar. 1920; *RL* 6 Mar. 1920.

16 National Executive Committee (NEC) Labour Party 31 Aug. 1920; *WM* 22 Nov. 1920.

17 *GFP* 22 Apr. 1920; *RL* 5 Aug. 1920.

18 *WM* Dec. 1920 *passim*, and *GCT* 18 Dec. 1920.

19 The National Liberal Federation refused to endorse either candidate.

20 *RL* 16 Dec. 1920.

21 Ibid. 18 Nov. 1920.

22 *SWN* 15 Dec. 1920.

23 *SWN* 10, 14, 18, 20 Dec. 1920.

24 *RL* 2 Dec. 1920.

25 Ibid. 18 Nov. 1920; RD 4, 18 Oct., 15 Nov. 1920.

26 *RL.* 9, 16 Dec. 1920.

27 *GFP* 31 Dec. 1920; *RL* 6 Jan. 1921.

28 *RL* 26 Aug. 1920 and Dec. 1920 *passim*.

29 *SWN* 21 Dec. 1920.

30 *RL* 16 Dec. 1920.

31 Ibid. 30 Dec. 1920; *WM* 23 Dec. 1920.

32 NEC Labour Party 15 Feb. 1921; SWMF EC Political Committee, 8 Jan. 1921.

33 Sonia Evans (Porth) Collection, UCS.

34 For the 1922 campaign see *WM, SWN*, and *Glamorgan Free Press and
Rhondda Leader (GFPRL)* Oct.–Nov. 1922 *passim*. For the selection
procedures see *PG* 17 Sept. 1921, 25 Feb, 18 Nov. 1922; *Rhondda Fach
Gazette (RFG)* 28 Jan., 4 Feb. 1922.
35 For the 1923 campaign see *WM, SWN* and *GFPRL* Nov.–Dec. 1923
passim.
36 Will John's parliamentary gaffe of November 1921, when, attacking
royalty owners at Ton Pentre, he had characterized some MPs as 'three
parts drunk' in the Commons, and had been forced to apologize, was
thought to have offered Rowlands a better chance of success (*RL* 10 Nov.
1921, *WM* 7, 8, 9 Nov. 1921, *GFPRL* 3 Nov. 1922).
37 *WM* Oct. 1924 *passim*; *SWN* Oct. 1924 *passim*.
38 *WM* 1 Dec. 1923.
39 *GFP* 28 Jan. 1921, *RL* 3 Feb. 1921.
40 Mid-Rhondda TLC (MRTLC) 12 Oct. 1910; *RL* 5, 12 Nov. 1910; *WM* 5
Nov. 1910; *South Wales Daily News (SWDN)* 5 Nov. 1910.
41 *GFP* 27 Jan., 17 Feb. 1911; *RL* 28 Jan., 4 Mar. 1911.
42 *RL* 5 Nov. 1910. Also ibid. 12 Nov. 1910.
43 *PG* 12 Apr. 1913. The *Rhondda Socialist* (29 Mar. 1913) judged him 'a
Labourite and Socialist of the first rank'.
44 *RS* 30 Mar. 1912. However, in her first election she was the unofficial
Labour candidate, the victor being the official candidate David Thomas,
and some Labour movement suspicion may have been aroused by the fact
of her marriage to veteran Liberal County Councillor and Guardian Elias
Thomas Davies.
45 *RS* 25 Nov. 1911.
46 MRTLC 18 Jan. 1911, 30 Jan., 13 Feb., 3 Apr. 1912, 29 Jan. 1914; CL 27
Jan. 1911.
47 *RL* 11 Mar. 1911; Lewis Merthyr Lodge Minutes (LM) 28 Feb., 14 Dec.
1911, 23 Jan., 8 Feb. 1912, 9 May 1913. Also on Porth see *RS* 15 Mar. 1913;
PG 22 Feb., Mar. 1913 *passim*, 26 Apr. 1913; LM 10 Apr., 14 Nov. 1913.
48 *RL* 14 Jan., 28 Jan., 25 Feb., 4 Mar., 23 Sept., 9 Dec. 1911, 20 Jan., Feb.
1912 *passim*, 2 Mar. 1912, 15 Mar. 1913, 14 Mar. 1914; Labour
Representation Committee No. 9 Ward (LRC9) 6, 20 Feb. 1911, 3, 7 Mar.
1913; *PG* Jan. 1912 *passim*, 17 Feb. 1912, 8, 15 Feb. 1913, 21 Mar. 1914;
GFP 12 Jan. 1912; *RS* 1 Mar. 1913; Tylorstown Lodge Minutes (TL) 10
Mar. 1915.
49 *PG* 27 Feb. 1915. On Porth's squabbles see ibid. 3 Feb. 1912, 20 Feb. 1915,
Apr. 1915 *passim*; *RS* 1 Mar. 1913; LM 24 Feb. 1915; *MRG* 17 Mar. 1915.
50 RUDC 11 Feb., 13 Oct. 1916.
51 The GCC was accorded a lower priority by the Labour movement because
it was more expensive and time-consuming to send Councillors there,
whilst the RUDC's control of education gave it added importance.
52 Treherbert TLC(TTLC) 3 Feb. 1919; LRC9 5 Feb. 1919.
53 Electoral ephemera, Sonia Evans (Porth) Collection, UCS.

54 Electoral ephemera. Not only does this give a strong indication of how Labour's opponents were trying to counter the working-class 'definition of community' now in place, but it reinforces the point made earlier about the waning of organized Liberalism (and Conservatism), and its blending with Independents in a general anti-Labour morass. Such sentiment was behind the establishment of the Rhondda Property Owners and Ratepayers' Association (approx. 1921), which was seen as an inclusive anti-Labour body and one that backed the (politically Conservative) publican George Newman at the RUDC Treorchy elections of 1921 (*RL* 3 Feb. 1921; *Rhondda Gazette* (*RG*) 2 Mar. 1921).

55 Electoral ephemera.

56 In 1922 on the RUDC, for instance, Labour fielded nine out of a possible eleven candidates. For 1922, Park and Dare Lodge Minutes (PD) 22 Feb. 1922; *PG* Apr. 1922 *passim*; RD annual report, 1922. For 1923, *GFPRL* 23 Mar. 1923; LM 20 Mar. 1923.

57 LRC9 30 June 1919, Feb.–Mar. 1920 *passim*, 5 May 1920, 2 June 1920, 6 Oct. 1920.

58 *GFP* 20 Mar. 1919; *PG* 29 Mar. 1919, 31 Mar. 1923, 22 Mar. 1924, 2, 30 May, 6, 13 June 1925; LM 21 Feb. 1921; Sonia Evans (Porth) Collection, UCS.

59 TTLC 24 Feb., 10 Mar. 1919; *GFPRL* 14 Mar. 1924; Treherbert Ward Committee Labour Party, Feb.–May 1925 *passim*.

60 LRC9 26 Feb. 1920; *PG* 1 Mar., 29 Nov. 1924, 19 Dec. 1925.

61 *RL* 27 Feb, 6 Mar., 27 Nov. 1909.

62 Cambrian Lodge (CL) 5 May 1910; *RL* 11 June 1910; MRTLC 20 Dec. 1910.

63 SWMF EC 15 Nov. 1909.

64 *RL* 17 Dec. 1910.

65 LRC9 19 Dec. 1910.

66 *RS* Sept., Oct. 1911.

67 *RS* Oct. 1911.

68 Ibid. Oct., Dec. 1911; MRTLC 31 May, 28 June, 26 July, 30 Aug. 1911; *GFP* 7 July 1911; *RL* 8 July, 5 Aug. 1911; RD 14 Aug., 27 Nov. 1911; Labour Party correspondence files LP/AFF/6/337/2: copy of the rules and constitution of the Rhondda Labour Party, dated Dec. 1911.

69 *GFP* 4 Aug. 1911; MRTLC 27 Sept., 25 Oct. 1911.

70 *The Monthly Democrat* Mar. 1912.

71 *RS* Sept., Dec. 1911, Mar. 1912; Abergorky Lodge Minutes (AL) 12 Mar. 1913; *South Wales Worker* (*SWW*) 30 May 1914.

72 *MP* 4 Jan. 1913; *RS* 4 Jan. 1913.

73 *RL* 13 Dec. 1913.

74 Ibid. 22 Feb. 1913; *GFP* 17 July 1913.

75 *GFP* 15 June, 31 Aug., 23 Nov. 1916, 8 Mar., 27 Sept. 1917; MRTLC 31 Aug., 28 Sept. 1916.

76 *MP* 14 Oct. 1916; MRTLC 22 Feb., 29 Mar. 1917.

77 *MP* 7 July 1917; *GFP* 27 Sept. 1917; MRTLC 28 Mar. 1918.

78 *RL* 20 Apr. 1918.

79 TTLC 30 Sept. 1918.

80 *SWN* 15 Dec. 1920; SWMF EC Political Committee 5 Oct. 1922.

81 FL 2 Feb., 4 May, 1 Nov. 1922, 11 Jan., 1, 7 June 1923; Ton Co-operative Society Records 2 May 1922; TTLC 19 June 1922, 22 Jan., 12 Feb., 16 Apr. 1923. TTLC stopped terming itself a TLC and started terming itself a Ward Committee in Oct. 1923 – TTLC 30 Aug. 1923; Treherbert Ward Committee 15 Oct. 1923; MRTLC 11 May, 31 Nov. 1922; Labour Party NEC 2 May, 3 Oct. 1922 – Reports on the work of the District Organizers; RBLP Constitution adopted at a Delegate Conference of the Party held at Porth, 26 May 1923, approved by the NEC 18 June 1923, Labour Party Library 329 (LAB) A8; RD 6 Feb. 1922, 28 May, 12 June 1923.

82 RD annual reports, 1911–19, RD 16 July 1917, 28 May, 12 June 1923; LM 22 Feb. 1911. In 1914 the district supported twenty-five public representatives: by 1919 this had risen to forty-seven.

83 RD 27 Nov. 1911, 13 Sept. 1915, 31 Jan., 14 Feb., 23 Oct., 20 Nov. 1916; *RS* Dec. 1911.

84 Labour Party NEC 11 Nov. 1919.

85 *MP* 4 Jan. 1913; *RS* 4 Jan. 1913.

86 *GFP* 26 Aug. 1910; Labour Party NEC 24 Oct. 1911, 13 Feb. 1912.

87 RD 26 Jan., 25 May, 6 July 1914, 10 Sept., 30 Oct., 19 Nov. 1917; TL 3 July 1914.

88 CL Dec. 1923–Mar. 1926 *passim*.

89 Alan Clinton, *The Trade Union Rank and File: Trades Councils in Britain, 1900–40* (1977), 197; TTLC 22 Apr. 1918.

90 FL 27 Jan., 21 July, 4 Aug., 24 Nov., 8, 20 Dec. 1921; Mardy Lodge Minutes (ML) 29 Apr., 7 Aug. 1921; Robin Page Arnot collection, UCS, interview with Dai Lloyd Davies 20 July 1962.

91 *RL* 7, 28 Jan., 11 Mar., 5 Aug. 1911; MRTLC 5 Apr., 31 May 1911, 24 Apr. 1912, 7 May 1914, 13 May, 16 Dec. 1915, 22 Jan. 1920; *GFP* 7 Jan. 1915; *RFG* 16 Mar. 1918; TTLC 30 Sept. 1918, 4 Mar. 1919, 13 Apr. 1920.

92 Paul O'Leary, '"Syndicalist Teachers" in the Rhondda, 1913–19: A Comment', *Llafur* 4 No.3 (1986), 80–4: 83. For meetings, see *PG* 14 Jan., 18 Mar. 1911; *RL* 27 Apr., 17 June 1911, 16 Apr. 1912; MRTLC 13 Feb. 1912, 20 Dec. 1916, 1 Feb. 1917, 20 Nov. 1919, 10 June 1920, 25 May, 25 June 1922, MRTLC Relief Sub-Committee meeting 18 Oct. 1922; *SWW* 7 June, 19 July 1913; LRC9 14 Apr., 9 June 1915, 9 July 1919; *GFP* 15 June 1916.

93 MRTLC 10 Sept. 1914; RUDC 21 Mar., 9 June 1916; RD 19 June 1916; TTLC 30 June 1919.

94 *GFP* 23 Nov. 1916; RUDC 13 Aug. 1917; *MP* 10 Nov., 15 Dec. 1917; TTLC 17 Dec. 1917, 8 Apr., 27 May 1918, TTLC Food Vigilance Committee 18 Apr., 26 May 1918; LRC9 19 Dec. 1917, 10 Jan., 3 Dec. 1918, correspondence book Jan. 1919; *RL* 26 Jan., 16 Mar., 18 May 1918; RD 15 Dec. 1919.

95 MP Sept.-Nov. 1915 *passim*; MRTLC 29 Oct. 1915, 7 Mar., 4 Oct. 1918, 29 July 1920, 28 Sept. 1922; MRG 20 Nov. 1915; TTLC Food Vigilance committee June–Sept. 1918 *passim*, TTLC 23 June 1919, Oct.–Nov. 1920 *passim*, 14 Feb. 1921; LRC9 31 July, 15 Oct. 1918, correspondence book Aug. 1918 *passim*; RL 14 Sept. 1918; TL Oct. and Nov. 1918.

96 TTLC 6 Jan., Feb. and Mar. 1919 *passim*, 26 May, 25 Aug., 22 Sept. 1919, 22 Mar., 10 May, 7 June, 7 July, 5 Dec. 1920, 27 Nov., 17 Dec. 1922, 12 Feb. 1923, correspondence book 1920 *passim*; MRTLC 27 Sept., 27 Oct. 1921.

97 RL 28 Jan., 11 Mar., 8 Apr. 1911; SWW 7 June 1913; MRTLC 1 July 1915, 2 Nov. 1916, 31 Oct. 1918, 8, 23 May 1919, 22 Jan. 1920.

98 TTLC correspondence book 24 Oct. 1923; RBLP No.1 Ward 17 Dec. 1923.

99 RL 11 Mar. 1911, 14 Mar. 1914; MRTLC 31 May 1911, 30 Jan., 5, 20 June, 6, 20 Nov. 1912, 12 Feb., 12 Mar. 1913, 8 Jan. 1914; RD 2 Feb., 2 Mar. 1914, 11 Oct. 1915; SWW 7 Feb. 1914; PG 6, 13 Mar. 1915.

100 TTLC 22 July, 25 Aug. 1918, 19 Oct., 17 Nov. 1919, Feb. 1920 *passim*, Jan. 1921 *passim*, Nov. 1921 *passim*, 16 Jan., 13 Mar., 24 Apr., 2 May, 11 Sept. 1922; TTLC Sub-Committee on Payment of Local Representatives, 7 Oct., 11 Nov. 1919; TTLC correspondence book 16 Dec. 1920, 25 Apr. 1921, 20 Mar. 1922; MRTLC 22 Jan. 1920, 20 Jan. 1921, 24 Feb., 14 Mar., 31 Aug. 1922.

101 MP 24 Feb. 1917.

102 The existence of the National Democracy League and the SDF branch at Blaenclydach, and the Marxian Club there should be noted. There seems to have been no significant friction between SDF and ILP locally, rather unity and joint meetings.

103 GFPRL Sept.–Nov. 1910 *passim*; RL 18 Feb., 19 Apr., 20 May, June 1911 *passim*, 22 July, 5 Aug., Sept.–Oct. 1911 *passim*, 16 Mar., 25 May 1912; GFP 28 July, 8 Sept. 1911, 30 May, 18 July 1912; RS 19 Aug., Sept.–Oct. 1911, 15 Mar. 1913; SWW 16 Aug., 25 Oct. 1913.

104 Labour Party NEC 3 June 1919, and Report of the National Administrative Council presented to the ILP Conference of 1921 on 'Policy and Relations with the Labour Party', especially 60–1. ILP meetings were still held in the Rhondda, despite contraction of the organization. In 1920 there were 7 ILP branches within the 'Rhondda Federation'. See MP 22 Mar. 1919; GFPRL 18 Feb. 1928; ILP 1920 Conference Report, 1932 Conference Report (Mid-Rhondda ILP).

105 Co-operative Women's Guilds were formed at Porth, Ton, Ferndale and Blaenllechau, according to Council meeting 12 Sept. 1919. Mrs Andrews had formed Guilds for both men and women at Ton Pentre in 1914 (RL 7 Nov. 1914). Treherbert Women's Section was formed in 1918 (TTLC 6 May 1918, 24 June 1918); Ferndale, Blaenllechau, and Tylorstown sections were formed in 1919 (RFG 7 June 1919; NEC Report, 'The Work of Women in the Labour Party, 1918–1919', 3 June 1919). The year 1920 saw more established at Porth, Ystrad, Ton, Gelli, Tonypandy, Mardy, Clydach Vale, Cwmparc and Treorchy (RL 26 Aug., 9 Dec. 1920; *Workers' Bomb*

No.1). Some sections were short-lived – NEC June 1922: Notes on Women Organizers, NEC Report on Women's Organizations, 22 Sept. 1923, 22 Mar. 1924, 21 Jan. 1925; *RL* 20 Nov. 1948. For the efforts of Mrs Andrews, see NEC Oct. 1919, 20 Oct. 1923, NEC Report on Work of Women Organizers, 20 Jan. 1926; *RL* 9 Dec. 1920; NEC Report on Women's Organizations for 10 May 1924, which mentions that the Stanleytown Women's Section, established earlier that year, had caused some problems for Mrs Andrews in that its president and some of its members had actually campaigned for a Conservative candidate at the local elections! *Workers' Bomb* No.2; *GFPRL* 20 June 1924; *Free Press and Rhondda Leader (FPRL)* 17 Mar. 1934; Elizabeth Andrews, *A Woman's Work is Never Done* (1948).

[106] Constitution of the Rhondda Borough Labour Party adopted at a conference on 26 May 1923, approved by the NEC, 18 June 1923.

[107] This decision was confirmed with the adoption of the 1933 constitution, adopted in July and approved by the NEC in September (see RBLP 27 Apr., 27 July 1933; copy in Labour Party Library 329 (LAB) A8).

[108] This had the valuable side-effect of requiring the formal opening of the selection process to organizations other than the SWMF. As for Labour Groups, there is no record of any formal constitution of such groups, although occasionally the identities of the Groups' secretaries were revealed. The first recorded suggestion that a Labour Group on the RUDC be formed came in Dec. 1910, and one was also noted as working on the PBG by 1912. By 1915, Transport House was informed that there was a 'strong Labour group' on the RUDC. War Emergency Workers' National Committee (WNC 26 Feb. 1916 – letter dated 9 Jan. 1915); MRTLC 20 Dec. 1910, 20 June 1912, 1 Sept. 1914.

[109] Under the 1933 constitution the EC drew more heavily from the trade unions, and the bimonthly 'conferences' of the RBLP were replaced by General Committee meetings every six weeks. Alongside the RBLP EC was established an Industrial Committee to deal explicitly with 'trade council' matters, and the RBLP became known as the Rhondda Borough Labour Party and Trades Council (RBLP 1932–5 *passim*; RWDLP 4 Nov. 1946; RBLP 9 June–July 1936 *passim*, Sept.–Oct. 1949 *passim*, July 1951 *passim*; *FPRL* 11 Feb. 1939).

[110] *MP* 8 May 1920.

[111] *RS* 1911 *passim*.

[112] Kenneth O. Morgan, 'Socialism and Syndicalism: The Welsh Miners' Debate, 1912', in Society for the Study of Labour History, *Bulletin* 30 (1975), 22–37; *GFP* 16 June 1912; *RFG* 10 Nov. 1917.

[113] *MP* 26 May 1917, 27 Apr., 11 May 1918; *GFP* 26 July 1917.

[114] *RL* 27 Apr. 1918.

[115] *MP* 24 Jan., 19 June 1920; TTLC 24 Apr., 2 May 1922. Women's organizations also began to provide a range of social activities, such as whist drives, outings, Christmas parties, dances and more generalized

'socials' or teas. These were to become more important in the 1930s (*GFPRL* 29 Aug. 1924).

116 Richard Lewis, *Leaders and Teachers: Adult Education and the Challenge of Labour in South Wales, 1906–1940* (1993).

117 Ibid. 53–6; *RL* 26 Sept. 1908. The RUDC discontinued its sponsorhip once it realized that Mardy Jones was converting his students to be 'Socialists and infidels'!

118 Richard Lewis, op. cit., 1–47 *passim*; *GFP* 6 Nov. 1908; *RL* 13 Mar. 1909; *PG* 1 May 1909.

119 Richard Lewis, op. cit., 59–79; *GFP* 9 Apr. 1909; *Plebs* Feb., Apr., June 1909; Michael Woodhouse, 'Rank and File Movements Among the Miners of South Wales, 1910–1926', D.Phil. thesis, University of Oxford, 1969, 43.

120 W. W. Craik, *The Central Labour College, 1909–1929: A Chapter in the History of Adult Working-Class Education* (1964); Industrial Unrest, Commission of Inquiry (Reports) No.7 Division, 1917–18, 17/99–18/100; *Plebs* Sept. 1911, Feb., Sept., Nov. 1912, Mar., Apr. 1913, Oct. 1916, Jan., Dec. 1917.

121 Conservative Clubs seemed to have less of a role post-war than pre-war: see *GFPRL* Apr. 1923 *passim*; *PG* 10 May 1925, for how Liberals and Conservatives had 'abandoned the citadel to the enemy'.

122 *RL* 12 Nov. 1910, 28 Jan. 1911, 3 Jan., 22 Aug. 1914; *MRTLC* 13 Feb., 8 Mar. 1911; *RS* Sept. 1911, 16 Mar., 11 Apr. 1912, 12 Apr., 10 May 1913; *SWW* 10 Jan., 7, 21 Feb., 21 Mar., 4 Apr., 30 May, 27 June 1914; *GFP* 30 July 1914; *MP* 24 Jan. 1920; *RG* 9 Feb. 1924; George Phippen, *The Origin of the Ystrad Rhondda Labour Club* (n.d.).

123 *MP* 28 Feb., 8 May, 26 June 1920; *ML* 10 Jan. 1925.

124 *GFPRL* Feb.–Apr. 1924 *passim*, Sept.–Nov. 1924 *passim*, Jan.–Apr. 1925 *passim*, 9 Oct. 1925, 3 Nov. 1928; testimony of John Hughes (Tonypandy), son of Will 'Knowledge' Hughes. Later there was a similar institution run at Tonypandy (*GFPRL* 11 Apr. 1924).

125 Some felt the Party needed to put much more effort into this area – see the comments of Councillor William Harris of Pontllanfraith in *The Colliery Workers' Magazine* (*CWM*) 1 No.1 (Jan. 1923), 9–10. Demont, 'Tredegar and Aneurin Bevan', especially 352–4, finds much more activity of this sort than in the Rhondda, although one wonders whether this was sustained after the mid-1920s.

126 Christopher Turner, 'Conflicts of Faith? Religion and Labour in Wales, 1890–1914', in *Class, Community and the Labour Movement: Wales and Canada, 1850–1930*, ed. Deian R. Hopkin and Gregory S. Kealey, (1989), 67–85; W. R. Lambert, 'Working Class Attitudes Towards Organised Religion in Nineteenth Century Wales', *Llafur* 2 No.1 (1976), 4–17; C. E. Gwyther, 'Methodism and Syndicalism in the Rhondda Valley – 1906 to 1926', Ph.D. thesis, University of Sheffield, 1967; idem, 'Sidelights on Religion and Politics in the Rhondda Valley, 1906–1926', *Llafur* 3 No.1 (1980), 30–43. Assessment of Gwyther's work is complicated by the

author's first-hand experience of Rhondda life in the late 1930s, but one wonders whether or not the project ('to examine the interaction of Methodism and Syndicalism' – p.1) was not flawed from the beginning. The conclusions reached seem to owe more to the author's recollections of his Tonypandy ministry than they do to any convincing historical argument. The most valuable parts of the research are those in which Gwyther cites from correspondence with various Rhondda Labour leaders.

127 *GFP* 11 May 1901; *PG* 23 Mar. 1907; *RL* 13 Apr. 1912.

128 *RS* 11 Apr. 1912.

129 RD 23 March 1908; Mr and Mrs D. J. Davies, Ystrad Rhondda, interviewed by Hywel Francis 14 Oct. 1974, South Wales Miners' Library (SWML); letter from Charlie Gibbons to Cyril Gwyther (n.d.).

130 *RS* 20 July 1912. An angry reaction followed in *GFP* 13 June 1912. A similar critique of Nonconformity was made in *MP* 21 Oct. 1916 by W. H. Mainwaring, and in *RS* 12 Apr. 1913. The general point was made that organized religion's hostility to the Labour movement was turning people against the Church and chapels.

131 *RL* 7, 14 Dec. 1907.

132 RUDC 11 June 1909, 14 Oct., 20 Dec. 1910.

133 RUDC 13 Jan. 1911. See also ibid. 10 Feb., 13, 21 Oct. 1911; *RL* Jan. 1911 *passim*, 18 Feb. 1911; MRTLC 14 Jan. 1911; RD 27 Feb. 1911; *RS* 19 Aug., Sept. 1911.

134 Later (31 Aug. 1912) the *Bomb* accused Thomas of hypocrisy and of playing to the gallery. See also ibid. Feb. 1912; *GFP* 18 Dec. 1913.

135 RUDC 10 Dec. 1915, 10 Mar., 14 Apr., 14 July, 10 Nov. 1916, 12 Nov. 1919; *GFP* 13 Apr. 1916; *RL* 22 Apr. 1916, 16 Mar. 1918, 22 Nov. 1919; RD 22 May 1916, 5 June 1916.

136 *GFP* 1 Nov. 1907; *RL* 28 Mar., 25 Apr., 12 Dec. 1908; Turner, 'Conflicts of Faith?', 81; Gwyther, 'Methodism and Syndicalism', 294.

137 *GFP* 11 May 1901, 10 July 1908; *RL* 12 Sept. 1908, 9 July 1910, 18 May, 17 Oct. 1918; *GFPRL* 24 Apr., 15 May 1925.

138 *RS* Sept. 1911; *GFP* 2 Apr. 1914.

139 *RL* 30 Mar. 1912. There may have been something in Phillips's allegations, albeit rather less sinister and more pragmatic. The atheist and ILPer William Phippen was apparently dropped from the position of Labour's first-choice candidate in Ward Four and replaced by James James, who was felt to be more acceptable as he was a chapel-goer at Bodringallt (Mr and Mrs D. J. Davies (Ystrad Rhondda), interviewed by Hywel Francis 14 Oct. 1974).

140 *RL* 17 Dec. 1904, 22 Aug., 5 Sept. 1908, 6 Feb. 1909, 15 Oct. 1910, 30 Mar. 1912; *MP* 4 May 1912; *GFPRL* 15 Feb. 1924. Penygraig ILP's proposal to establish a Labour Church found opposition from the RUDC: see RUDC meeting 15 Dec. 1911.

141 David Smith, 'Tonypandy 1910', 184.

Notes to Chapter 4

1   *Western Mail* (*WM*) 27 Nov. 1909.
2   *Rhondda Leader* (*RL*) 5, 12 Nov. 1910; *WM* 5 Nov. 1910; *South Wales Daily News* (*SWDN*) 5 Nov. 1910.
3   *Glamorgan Free Press* (*GFP*) 1 Mar. 1912.
4   *Rhondda Socialist* (*RS*) 19 Aug. 1911.
5   David Evans, Trealaw, in *RL* 10 Jan. 1914.
6   *RS* 28 Sept. 1912.
7   Another author of *The Miners' Next Step*, W. H. Mainwaring, was responsible for setting in motion the events that led to the formation of the Rhondda Labour Party.
8   *The Miners' Next Step*, 24 and 25, reprinted in *Democracy in the Mines*, ed. Ken Coates (1974), 16–30.
9   *RS* 19 Aug. 1911. In ibid. Oct. 1911 an article was published arguing that to be considered a socialist one had to agree with the following objectives:
    1. Nationalization of land, mines, railways, factories and workshops.
    2. Equal opportunity.
    3. Full employment.
    4. Leisure to cultivate higher faculties.
    5. A co-operative, not a competitive society.
    6. Public bodies to work for the improvement of the workers.
    The idea of publishing a Labour newspaper had been announced in June 1911. Production of *The Rhondda Socialist Newspaper, being the BOMB of the Rhondda Workers* shifted from monthly to fortnightly and the paper was expanded from a four-page folded sheet to six and then eight pages. The paper began to have financial problems by the end of 1912. In an effort to expand its circulation it changed its title in May 1913 to *The South Wales Worker* (*SWW*)and reached out to the rest of Glamorgan. It survived until 1915.
10 *RS* 15 Mar. 1913.
11 *Merthyr Pioneer* (*MP*) 2 Sept. 1916.
12 Letter from Clement Edwards to Winston Churchill, 17 Feb. 1911, HO45/10638/204636: Appointment of JPs in Glamorgan in connection with Glamorgan coalfield.
13 *Porth Gazette* (*PG*) 6 Mar. 1909; *RL* 4 July 1914; *SWW* 11 July 1914.
14 *GFP* Sept.–Oct. 1914 *passim*.
15 *RL* 6 Nov. 1915; Council 12 Nov. 1915, 11 Feb. 1916. The Pentre Labour and Progressive Club expelled conscientious objectors.
16 *GFP* 6 Nov. 1915, 6 Jan. 1916, 4 Jan., 18 Oct., 22 Nov. 1917; *MP* 23 Oct., 6 Nov. 1915, 8 Aug. 1917; Mid-Rhondda TLC (*MRTLC*) 16 Dec. 1915; *Workers' Dreadnought* (*WD*) 6 Oct. 1917; *RL* 11 Dec. 1915, 8 Dec. 1917, 16 Mar., 20 Apr. 1918; Treherbert TLC (*TTLC*) 24 Jun. 1918, 3 Feb. 1919; *PG* 30 Nov. 1918.
17 David Egan, 'The Swansea Conference of the British Council of Soldiers' and Workers' Delegates, July 1917: Reactions to the Russian Revolution of February 1917, and the Anti-War Movement in South Wales', *Llafur* 1

No.4 (1975) (1983 facsimile edition), 162–87; *RL* 7 July 1917; *GFP* July–Sept. 1917 *passim*; *MP* 16 June, 28 July, 4 Aug. 1917.

18 *Rhondda Fach Gazette (RFG)* 16 Apr. 1918.

19 *MP* 9 Mar. 1918.

20 *GFP* 17 Jan. 1918. Presumably the 'Holy Temple of Mum' is the Council Chamber, and the 'Great Presence' refers to Walter Nicholas, the clerk of the Council.

21 *MP* 9 Feb. 1918; *RL* 5 July 1919.

22 For a full account see Christopher Mark Williams, 'Democratic Rhondda: Politics and Society, 1885–1951', Ph.D. thesis, University of Wales (Cardiff), 1991; Martin Lawn, 'Syndicalist Teachers: The Rhondda Strike of 1919', *Llafur* 4 No.1 (1984), 91–8; and Paul O'Leary, ' "Syndicalist Teachers" in the Rhondda, 1913–19: A Comment', *Llafur* 4 No.3 (1986), 80–4.

23 This was at the time the largest teachers' strike in British history.

24 For instance, Labour had eight out of fourteen representatives on the Salaries Sub-Committee which handled the teachers' claim.

25 *RL* Oct.–Dec. 1917 *passim*; *GFP* 18 Oct. 1917; *PG* 27 Oct. 1917.

26 *GFP* 15 Nov. 1917, 6, 27 Mar. 1919; TTLC 3 Dec. 1917; LRC9 2 Oct. 1918; *RL* 12 Oct. 1918, 8, 29 Mar. 1919; Labour Representation Committee No.9 Ward (LRC9) 5 Feb., 30 June 1919; MRTLC 2 Oct. 1919. W. H. Mainwaring and T. I. Mardy Jones backed the RCTA.

27 *RL* 8, 22, 29 Mar. 1919.

28 RUDC, Reports of the Medical Officer of Health and the School Medical Officer, 1914-1927.

29 Parliamentary Debates 1919, vol.114, Fifth Series, 7 Apr. 1919, Col.1706.

30 *RL* 21 Feb. 1920; *PG* 14 Feb. 1920.

31 Ferndale Lodge (FL) 1, 16 Mar. 1920; RUDC 14 Apr. 1920.

32 FL 2 May 1920.

33 *PG* 15 May 1920.

34 FL 6, 9 May 1920; *WD* 29 May 1920.

35 FL 30 June 1920.

36 RUDC 7, 14, 27 July, 8 Sept. 1920, 9 Mar. 1921; Housing Committee 23 Dec. 1920, 22 Mar., 26 Apr., 21 June 1921.

37 RUDC: Reports of the Medical Officer of Health and the School Medical Officer, 1922–1932.

38 FL 8 Jan. 1921.

39 Ibid. 29 May 1920; Council 12 May 1920; *RL* 20 Oct. 1917, 17, 24 June 1920; *GFP* 18 Oct. 1917; TTLC 14 June 1920.

40 TTLC 14 Sept. 1920, Correspondence Book 14 Sept. 1920.

41 TTLC 27 Sept., 11, 18 Oct. 1920. TTLC 25 Oct. 1920, Correspondence Book 17 Nov. 1920; Labour Party Correspondence Files CA/GEN/936, letter to J. S. Middleton from Tom Llewellyn, 12 Dec. 1920; MRTLC : Report of the Council of Action 21 Oct. 1920.

42 TTLC 18 Oct. 1920.

43 *Workers' Bomb* No.2 Dec. 1920; Central Canteen Committee (CCC) 11 May, 1 June, 12 Dec. 1921, 19 Sept. 1924; RUDC 1 July 1921; Education Committee (EdC) 20 July 1921, 4 Jan. 1922.
44 Finance Committee (FC) 30 May 1921; RUDC 1, 13 July 1921.
45 RUDC 9 Mar. 1921; Roads Committee (RoC) 26, 31 Oct. 1921.
46 RUDC 9 Nov. 1921: report of the Conference of Necessitous Areas, London, 26 Oct. 1921.
47 RUDC 29 Nov. 1921; RoC 29 Dec. 1921.
48 RUDC 10 May 1922; RoC 26 July 1922; RUDC 29 July 1924.
49 RUDC 14 June, 12 July, 13 Sept., 11 Oct. 1922, 9 Sept. 1925; Special Staffing Committee (SSC) 4, 14 July, 5, 12 Sept., 10 Oct. 1922, 4 Feb. 1924.
50 SSC 14 July 1922.
51 SSC 16 Oct., 5 Dec. 1922, 8, 22 Jan., 5 June 1923; SSC Sub-Committee 20, 27 Nov. 1922; RUDC 8 Nov. 1922, 10 Jan. 1923, 14 Oct. 1925.
52 FC 4 Sept. 1923; *WM* 24 Feb., 12 Mar. 1925; Council 14 Oct. 1925.
53 School Management Committee (SMC) 16 Sept. 1925; RD 7 Dec. 1925; RUDC 9 Dec. 1925; *GFPRL* 18 Dec. 1925; *RFG* 19 Dec. 1925.
54 Report on the administration of outrelief in the Bridgend and Cowbridge, Pontypridd, Bedwellty, and Merthyr Tydfil areas by the Local Government Board Inspector H. R. Williams, on 12 July 1910, cited in (Ministry of Health File) MH 57/106: Poor Law Relief and Unemployment: Distressed Areas, South Wales, Inspector's Report (James Evans) 30 Apr. 1919.
55 See the report of 26 Oct. 1916, made to the Local Government Board by M. D. Propert, the district auditor (106,340/16.A). Cited in MH 57/106: Poor Law Relief and Unemployment: Distressed Areas, South Wales, Inspector's Report 30 Apr. 1919.
56 Williams's report, MH 57/106, 12 July 1910; Evans's report, MH 57/106, 30 Apr. 1919.
57 Meeting of Committee appointed to consider preparation of a Scale of Outdoor Relief for the Pontypridd Union, 11 June 1919.
58 Relief Advisory Committee (RAC) 4 Apr. 1921. Letter from the clerk to the Guardians, William Spickett, 1 Apr. 1921.
59 MH 79/297 Public Assistance: General Strike and Coal Strike 1921–1926, H. W. S. Francis 19 July 1921.
60 Recommendations of the Relief Advisory Committee (RAC) upon Applications for Poor Law Relief due to Unemployment, 4 Apr. 1921.
61 RAC 25 Apr., 2 May 1921. Up to this juncture the PBG was relieving single able-bodied men, a category which, under the Ministry of Health's interpretation of the Merthyr Tydfil judgement of 1900, should have been denied outrelief. See MH 57/94: The Effect of the Poor Law System of the General Strike and Coal Dispute 1926, II. The Merthyr Tydfil Judgement 1900, pp.2–7. The judgement was evaded by treating the 1921 dispute as a lock-out rather than as a strike. Afterwards the Ministry conceded that 'the practical difficulties raised by the judgement were so serious as to make it almost unworkable . . . The system of granting relief on loan and

of tacitly relieving the striker by inflating the relief afforded to his family rendered it difficult for the Auditor to strike at the root of the illegality.'

62 PBG 2, 11 May, 15 June, 13 July 1921; RAC 4, 18 May 1921; *Rhondda Gazette (RG)* 21 May 1921, 27 Oct., 10 Nov. 1923, 2 Feb. 1924; *PG* 8 Aug. 1925.

63 PBG 13 July 1921; RAC 27 July, 5 Oct., 2 Nov. 1921; *RFG* 24 Sept. 1921, 15 Sept. 1923; MH 57/107: Poor Law Relief and Unemployment, Distressed Areas, South Wales: Memo: The New 'Subsistence Level' Wage in South Wales, Effect on Out-Door Relief, by James Evans, 9 Dec. 1921; and H. W. S. Francis's letter to W. P. Elias, General Inspector of the Ministry of Health, 14 Dec. 1921.

64 *RG* 27 Oct., 10 Nov. 1923, 2 Feb. 1924; PBG 20 Dec. 1922, 31 Jan. 1923; RAC Sub-Committee Sept. 1923–May 1924 *passim*; *WM* 30 Dec. 1926.

65 FL 8 Apr. 1925.

66 RAC 11 Nov. 1921; *WM* 13 Feb. 1922.

67 *RFG* 4 Mar. 1922.

68 FL 15 Feb. 1925; Mardy Lodge (ML) 9, 11, 18, 20 Feb., 18 Mar. 1925; *Glamorgan Free Press and Rhondda Leader (GFPRL)* 27 Feb. 1925.

69 CCC 11 May 1921; RAC 6 Oct. 1924, 7 Sept. 1925; *RFG* 17 Sept. 1921, 19 Dec. 1925; SMC 16 Sept. 1925; PBG 28 Oct. 1925; RD 7 Dec. 1925; RUDC 9 Dec. 1925; *GFPRL* 18 Dec. 1925; *Workers' Weekly (WW)* 26 Feb. 1926; FL 8, 15 Dec. 1925.

70 PBG 19 Apr. 1922; *Glamorgan County Times (GCT)* 3 Mar. 1923.

71 Gibbons opposed the 'fetish of political action', characterizing County Council and District Council work as 'futile'. He argued that, as the organization was short of money, what it had should be spent in the industrial field: 'The Miners' Organization had failed to give us a bread and cheese basis of life, and if we failed to force the Government, what hopes had local Authorities to do so?' FL 21 Feb. 1922. See also ibid. 13 Feb. 1922.

72 FL 16, 27 Feb., 4, 29 Oct. 1922, 11, 23 Jan., 19, 25 Apr., 8 June 1923, 14 Jan. 1924; *WW* 24 July 1925.

73 RUDC 10 Jan. 1923; Lewis Merthyr Lodge (LM) 1 Feb., 6 Oct. 1924, 17 Feb. 1925; FL 11 Feb. 1924.

74 Labour Party Conference Agenda, 1924; FL 19 June, 3, 10 July 1924; Pontypridd Trades Council and Labour Party (PTCLP) 2 Feb. 1925.

75 *RG* 27 Oct., 10 Nov. 1923, 2 Feb. 1924.

76 *GCT* 26 Apr. 1924.

77 Tromans argued that: 'The real enemies of the working class, was those people who by their continuous agitation had opened the eyes of the County Court Judges who were stating that relief granted by Guardians was making for the prolongation of strikes.' The motion of censure was lost. FL 15 Feb., 2 Nov. 1925. The Ferndale Lodge refused to accept the Oct. decision. Horner's strategy was responsible for alienating the services of the Co-operative movement. When they were approached by the Rhondda No.1 District at the beginning of 1926 to see if they would be

prepared to supply food on credit during any forthcoming industrial dispute, the Co-op pointed out that they had yet to be repaid for what they had supplied in 1921, and that they had to look after the interests of their own members first of all (FL 2 Feb., 28 Apr. 1926).

78 FL 28 July, 11, 22 Aug., 13 Oct. 1925.

79 SWMF E2 – Investigation and Report of the FL Dispute, 18 Aug. 1925. SWMF EC 29 June, 19 Sept., 19 Oct. 1925. FL 3 Mar., 8, 21 Apr., 10 June, 6 Oct. 1925.

80 FL 27 Feb., 17 Nov. 1924, 15 Feb., 23 Sept., 13 Oct. 1925; GFPRL 17 Oct. 1924.

81 FL 25 Nov., 1 Dec. 1925.

82 PBG 13 May, 2 Sept. 1925, 21 Apr., 23 June 1926; RFG 23 May 1925; PG 8 Aug. 1925; SMC 16 Sept. 1925; GCT 20 Mar., 26 June 1926.

83 For the operation of the Poor Law during the industrial crisis see Patricia Ryan, 'The Poor Law in 1926', in *The General Strike*, ed. Margaret Morris (1976), 358–78. For south Wales, see Hywel Francis, 'South Wales', in *The General Strike, 1926*, ed. Jeffrey Skelley (1976), 232–60, and Paul Jeremy, 'Life on Circular 703: The Crisis of Destitution in the South Wales Coalfield during the Lockout of 1926', *Llafur* 2 No.2 (1977), 65–75.

84 MH 57/94: The Effect Upon the Poor Law System of the General Strike and Coal Dispute 1926, 1.

85 Ibid., 2–7.

86 Ibid. and WM 31 May 1926.

87 WM 10 Apr. 1926; PTCLP 12 Apr. 1926.

88 WM 12 Apr. 1926; PBG 14 Apr. 1926; WW 16, 23 Apr. 1926; RAC 3 May 1926.

89 PBG AGM 21 Apr. 1926.

90 Circular 703, issued 5 May 1926; RAC 10 May 1926.

91 RAC 10 May 1926; CCC 11 May 1926.

92 RAC 21 May 1926; WM 31 May, 2 June 1926.

93 CCC 5, 11 May 1926; RAC 10 May 1926; Maternity and Child Welfare Committee (MCW) 11 May 1926.

94 Evans's report (see note 84); CCC 11 May 1926; RUDC 12 May 1926; PTCLP 17 May 1926; Secondary EdC 18 May 1926.

95 RAC 21 May 1926; WM 31 May 1926, 2 June 1926.

96 CCC 26 May 1926; EdC 28 May, 2 June 1926; PTCLP 31 May, 7 June 1926.

97 Joint Meeting of the RAC and the representatives of EdCs and MCWs, 7 June 1926; CCC 8 June 1926; RUDC 9 June 1926; SMC 16 June 1926; RG 19 June 1926.

98 CCC 11 May 1926; MH57/116: Coal Dispute 1926: Relief of Miners and Dependants / Daily Lists 25 May 1926, 1 June 1926; RAC 4 June 1926; PTCLP 7 June 1926.

99 PBG 8 June 1926; WM 9 June 1926; GCT 11 June 1926.

100 RFG 5 June 1926; MH57/116, 14 June 1926; 15 June 1926; PBG 14 June 1926; WM 15 June 1926; GFPRL 18 June 1926; WW 18 June 1926.

101 MH79/297, memo 14 Dec. 1926, unsigned and untitled.

[102] CCC 28 June, 12 July 1926; FC 29 June 1926; EdC 7 July 1926; *GFPRL* 10 July, 11 Dec. 1926; RUDC 14 July, 8 Dec. 1926; FC 29 Nov. 1926, 3 Jan. 1927; *WM* 9 Dec. 1926.

[103] PTCLP 7 June, 5 July, 20 Sept., 4 Oct. 1926; *WM* 7, 8 July 1926; *GFPRL* 10 July 1926; RAC 12 July 1926; *RFG* 17 July 1926; *WW* 30 July 1926.

[104] RUDC, Report of Medical Officer of Health and School Medical Officer, 38; CCC 11 May 1926; MCW 11 May 1926; *GFPRL* 4, 11 Sept. 1926, 15 Jan. 1927. The Ministry had shown its awareness of this problem of evasion in Circular 703: 'It will be realized of course that the powers conferred upon Local Education Authorities by the Education Act, 1921, in regard to the provision of meals are not intended to be so used as to throw the burden of the relief of destitution upon the Education rate.'

[105] MH57/117 3 Nov. 1926; MCW 10, 30 Aug. 1926; RUDC 1, 8 Sept., 13 Oct. 1926; PBG 1 Sept. 1926; *GFPRL* 4, 25 Sept., 2 Oct. 1926; RAC 6, 20 Sept., 1, 15 Nov. 1926; MCW 8, 21 Sept., 23 Nov. 1926; *WM* 20 Sept. 1926.

[106] MH57/94; MH57/117 2, 23 Oct. 1926; *WM* 20 Sept. 1926.

[107] CCC 3, 14, 21 Dec. 1926; RUDC 8, 28 Dec. 1926; *WM* 9 Dec. 1926; *GFPRL* 11 Dec. 1926; EdC 28 Dec. 1926.

[108] EdC 5, 11 Jan. 1927; RAC 10 Jan. 1927; RUDC 11 Jan. 1927; *GFPRL* 15, 22 Jan. 1927; PBG 19 Jan. 1927; SMC 19 Jan. 1927.

[109] The vote was 10,266 to 1,936. CCC 24 Jan., 14 Feb. 1927; ML 28 Jan. 1927; LM 8 Feb. 1927; PBG 16 Feb. 1927; *GFPRL* 19 Feb. 1927; FL 30 Jan., 22 Feb. 1927; *The Times* 3 Mar. 1927; *SWN* 3 Mar. 1927; *WM* 3, 14 Mar. 1927; *Workers' Life* (*WL*) 18 Mar. 1927.

[110] EdC 2 Mar. 1927; CCC 7 Mar. 1927; RUDC 9 Mar. 1927; *WL* 18 Mar. 1927; *WM* 10 Mar. 1927.

[111] Cited in John Stevenson and Chris Cook, *The Slump* (1979 edition), 70. West Ham Board of Guardians had been superseded in 1926.

[112] Sian Rhiannon Williams, 'The Bedwellty Board of Guardians and the Default Act of 1927', *Llafur* 2 No.4 (1979), 65–77.

[113] Ibid., 73–4.

Notes to Chapter 5

[1] L. J. MacFarlane, *The British Communist Party* (1966), 94–9, 142–51, 189–92, 210–15; Henry Pelling, *The British Communist Party: A Historical Profile* (1958), 39–41; James Klugmann, *History of the Communist Party of Great Britain, Vol. I*, (1969), 166–81; Noreen Branson, *History of the Communist Party of Great Britain, 1927–1941* (1985), 1–16; NEC 25 July, 31 Oct. 1923, 2 Sept., 9 Dec. 1924, 28 Jan., 7 Feb., 24 June, 2, 28 Oct. 1925, 9 Aug. 1926.

[2] NEC 2 Feb., 21, 23 June, 28 July, 7 Sept., 27 Oct. 1926, 6–7 Feb. 1927.

[3] MacFarlane, op. cit., 44–72; Klugmann, op. cit., 13–72; Pelling, op. cit., 1–14; and M. A. S. Shipway, 'Anti-Parliamentary Communism in Britain 1917–1945', D.Phil. thesis, University of Manchester, 1985, 45–6, 204.

4   *Rhondda Fach Gazette (RFG)* 1 Sept. 1917; *Workers' Dreadnought (WD)* 6
    Oct. 1917, 16 Mar. 1918, 28 June 1919; *Rhondda Leader (RL)* 19 Jan.
    1918, 8 Feb. 1919; Sylvia Pankhurst, *The Home Front* (1932), especially
    221–4 and 413.
5   *WD* 10 Apr. 1920.
6   *WD* 28 Feb., 27 Mar., 5, 19 June, 11, 18 Sept. 1920; *The Communist* 30
    Sept., 1 Oct. 1920; Michael Woodhouse, 'Rank and File Movements
    Among the Miners of South Wales, 1910–1926', D.Phil. thesis, University
    of Oxford, 1969, 187.
7   Interview with George A. Maslin (Ferndale), 7 May 1990; Billy Griffiths
    interviewed by Hywel Francis, Nov. 1969; Archie James interviewed by
    Hywel Francis and David Smith, 14 Nov. 1973; Ben Davies interviewed by
    Hywel Francis, 11 June 1973; *Workers' Weekly (WW)* 1 Sept. 1923, 25 July,
    8 Aug., 7 Nov. 1924, 23 Jan., 24 July, 15, 28 Aug. 1925, 21 May 1926.
8   NEC 25 Apr. 1923.
9   *WW* 21 Sept. 1923, 10 Oct. 1924; Ferndale Lodge (FL) 17 Nov., 2 Dec.
    1924.
10 *WW* 27 Feb. 1925. These votes were repeated in 1926: *WW* 30 Apr. 1926;
    FL 20 Apr. 1926.
11 NEC 20 Jan. 1926.
12 *Western Mail (WM)* 3, 12, 14 Mar. 1927; *South Wales News (SWN)* 3
    Mar. 1927.
13 *Colliery Workers' Magazine (CWM)* Dec. 1924.
14 Cambrian Lodge (CL) 9 Mar. 1927; *WM* 14 Mar. 1927; *SWN* 14 Mar.
    1927; FL 15 Mar. 1927; *Workers' Life (WL)* 18 Mar. 1927; Mardy Lodge
    (ML) 18 Mar. 1927; *Glamorgan Free Press and Rhondda Leader (GFPRL)*
    19 Mar. 1927; *Porth Gazette (PG)* 19 Mar. 1927.
15 *SWN* 19 Mar. 1927; *GFPRL* 26 Mar. 1927. The reaffiliation of the RBLP
    was approved by the NEC on 23 March 1927.
16 Lewis Merthyr Lodge (LM) 2 Dec. 1926; *WM* 5, 23 Mar. 1927; ML 18, 25
    Mar., 7, 22 Apr., 13 Dec. 1927; *WL* 18, 25 Mar., 29 Apr., 29 May 1927;
    RFG 26 Mar. 1927; FL 6, 26 Apr., 5, 12 July, 9 Aug. 1927.
17 FL 27 July, 1 Nov. 1927, 14 Feb. 1928; CL 19 Oct. 1927; ML 13 Jan. 1928;
    Rhondda No.1 District (RD) 21 May 1928.
18 *GFPRL* 2 July, 15, 29 Oct., 24 Dec. 1927, 7 July 1928, 12, 19 Jan., 6 Apr.,
    11, 18 May, 1 June 1929; *SWN* 18 Mar. 1927; *WM* Apr.–May 1929 *passim*.
19 Labour Party Correspondence Files LP/MIN/28/25, Circular 17 Feb. 1928;
    PG 18 Feb., 14 July 1928, 8 June 1929; *WL* 8 June, 19 Oct. 1928, 25 Jan.,
    Apr.–May 1929 *passim*.
20 *GFPRL* 19 Oct. 1928 and letter from Ramsay MacDonald to Mrs Watts
    Morgan, 27 Mar. 1929, in PRO 30/69, 1439/3/2227.
21 *WM* Apr.–May 1929 *passim*, 1, 3 June 1929; *RFG* 6 Apr., 25 May 1929; *PG*
    13 Apr. 1929.
22 *WM* Oct. 1931 *passim*; *Glamorgan Free Press (GFP)* Oct. 1931 *passim*.
23 *PG* 31 Oct. 1931.

[24] NEC 22 Mar. 1933; *WM* 23 Feb.–20 Mar. 1933 *passim*; *The Times* 2 Mar. 1933; SWMF EC C.1 3 Mar. 1933; *GFP* 4 Mar. 1933; *Glamorgan County Times (GCT)* 8 Apr. 1933; *PG* 11 Mar. 1933.

[25] *GFP* 25 Mar. 1933; *WM* 21, 23, 25 Mar. 1933; RBLP EC Propaganda Sub-Committee 15, 23 Aug., 5 Sept. 1933; Mainwaring Election Special, Arthur Horner Collection, UCS; John Mahon, *Harry Pollitt: A Biography* (1976), 180.

[26] Horner Election Special, Addresses and Handbills, Return of election expenses, Arthur Horner Collection, UCS; Arthur Horner, *Incorrigible Rebel* (1960), 128–9.

[27] Mainwaring Election Special. For the campaign, see *Daily Worker (DW)* 7 Mar. 1933; *The Times* 16, 17 Mar. 1933; *WM* 16, 24, 27 Mar. 1933; *PG* 18 Mar. 1933; *RFG* 25 Mar. 1933; Mahon, op. cit., 179–80.

[28] *WM* 30 Mar. 1933; *The Times* 28 Mar. 1933; *DW* 29 Mar. 1933; *PG* 1 Apr. 1933; *Free Press and Rhondda Leader (FPRL)* 8 Apr. 1933; SWMF EC C.1 27 May, 23 June 1933.

[29] *WM* 28, 31 Oct., 1 Nov. 1935; *FPRL* 2 Nov. 1935.

[30] *WM* 29 Oct., 8 Nov. 1935.

[31] Ibid. 2, 13 Nov. 1935.

[32] *DW* 5, 7, 13, 14 Nov. 1935.

[33] Ibid. 25 Oct. 1935; *WM* 1 Nov. 1935; 1935 Rhondda East Special, Arthur Horner Collection, UCS.

[34] *DW* 17, 23 Oct., 2 Nov. 1935; *The Miners' Monthly* Nov. 1935; *Rhondda Vanguard (RV)* Aug.–Sept. 1935.

[35] *PG* 28 Sept. 1935; *WM* 13 Nov. 1935; *DW* 18, 28 Nov. 1935.

[36] *PG* 12 Oct., 9 Nov. 1935.

[37] *PG* 23 Nov. 1935.

[38] Richard Sibley, 'The Swing to Labour During the Second World War: When and Why?', *Labour History Review* 55 No.1 (1990), 23–34.

[39] John Attfield and Stephen Williams (eds), *1939: The Communist Party and the War* (1984).

[40] *FPRL* 8, 22 Feb., 29 Mar., 3 May 1941; *GCT* 8 Feb. 1941; 21st Report of the Annual Congress, South Wales District, Communist Party, Feb. 1941. There was a seven-month-long debate in the *FPRL* from Jan. 1941 onwards.

[41] Interview with Idris and Dora Cox, 21 June 1987.

[42] *FPRL* 20 Sept., 18, 25 Oct., 1 Nov., 6 Dec. 1941, 3 Jan. 1942; *GCT* 25 Oct., 1, 8 Nov. 1941; Park and Dare Lodge (PD) 29 Oct., 5 Nov., 21 Dec. 1941, 14 Jan., 12, 19 Aug. 1942, 14 Feb., 21 July, 11 Aug., 1 Dec. 1943, 29 Mar., 17 May 1944; SWMF Conference Reports 9–11 Apr. 1942, 29 Apr.–1 May 1943; Tylorstown Lodge (TL) 15 Oct. 1942; *PG* 26 Feb. 1944.

[43] *PG* 27 Sept., 18 Oct. 1941, 25 July, 22 Aug. 1942; *FPRL* 27 Dec. 1941, 17 Jan. 1942.

[44] *PG* 6 May, 10 June, 19 Aug., 2 Sept. 1944; *Rhondda Fach Leader (RFL)* 24 Feb., 14 Apr. 1945; Mahon, *Harry Pollitt*, 305.

45 Mahon, ibid., 308; *RFL* 16 June 1945; *WM* 18 June 1945; *RL* 4 Aug. 1945; Idris Cox, 'Story of a Welsh Rebel', Idris Cox Collection, UCS, 76; NUM (South Wales Area) EC, Special EC Meeting with Miners' MPs; FL 11 Jan. 1945.

46 Interview with Cyril Gwyther, 28 July 1987. See also *RFG* 28 Apr. 1945; *WM* 26 June 1945; *RL* 7 July 1945.

47 *WM* 27 July 1945; Reg Fine, interviewed by Hywel Francis, 2 July 1973; interview with Idris and Dora Cox; Mr and Mrs D. J. Davies, Ystrad Rhondda, interviewed by Hywel Francis, 14 Oct. 1974; Mahon, op. cit., 308; interview with Iorwerth and Hilda Price, 17 Aug. 1987; interview with Cliff Prothero, 19 Aug. 1987; interview with Cyril Gwyther; E. George Thomas, Treherbert, interviewed 5 Nov. 1973 by Hywel Francis; South Wales Regional Council of Labour 14 May 1946.

48 *RL* 4 Aug. 1945. For more on the campaign see *RL* 14 Apr. 1945, 30 June, 14 July 1945; *RFL* 28 Apr. 1945.

49 Cox, op. cit., estimates that Welsh membership, which stood at 3,000 in 1945, had fallen to 1,450 by 1950.

50 *RL* 28 Jan., 18 Feb. 1950; *WM* 18 Feb. 1950; Mahon, op. cit., 334–40.

51 *RL* 4 Mar. 1950; *WM* 25 Feb. 1950.

52 *RL* 18 Nov. 1950, 20 Oct., 3 Nov. 1951; Mahon, op. cit., 334–40; Oliver Stutchbury, *Too Much Government? A Political Aeneid* (1977), 16.

53 *RL* 4 Feb., 4 Mar. 1950. Electoral ephemera (broadsheet 1950).

54 RWDLP 24 Mar., 11 Sept. 1950, 9 Feb., 20 Apr., 15 June, 17 Aug., 7 Sept. 1951.

55 Electoral address; electoral ephemera.

56 Cited in D. Hywel Davies, *The Welsh Nationalist Party, 1925–1945* (1983), 234.

57 *RFG* 29 Jan. 1927, 29 Sept. 1928, 1 Feb., Mar. 1930 *passim*; *PG* 5 Apr. 1930, 2, 9 Nov. 1940.

58 *GFPRL* 18 Dec. 1926, 17 Mar. 1928; *RFG* 5 Apr., 31 May 1930.

59 Interview with Elwyn Wales (nephew) Pentre, 2 June, 1990; conversation with D. J. Davies, 29 Aug. 1986.

60 Interview with Mrs Elias (widow), Pentre, 2 June 1990.

61 *RL* 14, 28 Apr., 30 June, 14 July 1945; *RFL* 28 Apr. 1945.

62 *GFPRL* 10 Nov. 1928; *FPRL* 23 Jan. 1932; *Y Ddraig Goch* 1931–2 *passim*; *Welsh Nation* 1932–44 *passim*; *PG* 13 Feb. 1932; *WM* 27 Mar. 1933; *GCT* 15 Jan. 1938; Jesse Clark (Tonypandy) collection: letter from A. B. Oldfield-Davies, 15 June 1945; UCS; D. Hywel Davies, op. cit., 202–3.

63 Davies, op. cit., 203, 217.

64 Ibid., 204.

65 Ibid., 146; *Welsh Nation* 15 Apr. 1933, May 1934; *Mid-Rhondda Outlook* (*MRO*) Nov. 1934.

66 *Rhondda Clarion* (*RC*) Nov. 1936.

67 *PG* 26 June 1943; *Welsh Nation* 1944–51 *passim*.

68 Davies was Hon. Sec. to the Deputation to the Prime Minister from

Representatives of Churches in Wales and Members of Parliament for Welsh Constituencies on the Subject of the Distressed Areas in Wales. Cited in Premier's Papers, PREM 1/182, 10.

69 Cyril Gwyther, *The Valley Shall Be Exalted: Light Shines in the Rhondda* (1949), 70–1; H. W. J. Edwards, *The Good Patch* (1938), 80–2; interview with H. W. J. Edwards, Trealaw, 7 May 1990.

70 Hywel Francis and David Smith, *The Fed: A History of the South Wales Miners in the Twentieth Century* (1980), 248.

71 Parliamentary Debates Vol.215, Cols 878–9, 26 March 1928.

72 RUDC 21 Aug., 27 Nov., 11 Dec. 1929.

73 PBG 9, 27 Apr. 1927; RAC 2 May, 12 Dec. 1927, 9 Jan. 1928; Sub-Committee Collectors' Committee 16 May 1927; *GFPRL* 18 Dec. 1926, 5, 26 Nov. 1927.

74 Goschen Committee 10 Dec. 1926, 23 Feb. 1927; Special Estimates Committee 8 Apr. 1927.

75 RUDC 30 Mar., 13 Apr. 1927; Goschen Committee 19 Mar. 1928.

76 Special Estimates Committee 8, 13 Apr. 1927; RUDC 13 Apr. 1927.

77 RUDC 27 Apr. 1927, 8 Feb. 1928; Education Committee (EdC) 7 Sept. 1927; RD 30 Jan., 27 Feb. 1928.

78 Central Canteen Committee (CCC) 6 May, 19 Oct., 1 Nov. 1927; RUDC 11 May, 13 July, 19 Oct., 1 Nov. 1927; EdC 6 July, 19 Oct., 1 Nov. 1927; *GFPRL* 16 July 1927; *RFG* 23 July 1927.

79 RUDC 13 Apr. 1927; EdC 6 July, 7 Sept., 1 Nov. 1927; *GFPRL* 17 Sept. 1927; *RFG* 17 Sept. 1927.

80 EdC 7 Sept., 19 Oct., 1 Nov. 1927, 4 Jan. 1928; CCC 19 Sept., 19 Oct., 1 Nov. 1927; RUDC 19 Oct., 1 Nov. 1927; RAC 12 Dec. 1927, 9 Jan. 1928.

81 CCC 18 Jan., 15 Feb. 1928; The Labour Party, *The Distress in South Wales* (1928), 8; MH55/691 Children – Physical Condition in Welsh Mining Areas Board of Education Report, 5; and Charles Webster, 'Health, Welfare and Unemployment during the Depression', *Past and Present* 109 (1985), 204–30, especially 215–16.

82 Goschen Committee 10 Dec. 1926, 19 Mar. 1928; RUDC Rating Committee 31 Aug. 1927; *GFPRL* 11 Feb. 1928; RUDC 13 Apr., 11 July, 12 Sept. 1928, 13 Feb. 1929; Finance Committee (FC) 30 July 1928.

83 RUDC 11 Jan. 1928; Sub-Committee re: Arrears of Housing Rentals 13 Jan. 1928; *GFPRL* 14 Jan. 1928.

84 RUDC 13 Feb. 1929.

85 *WL* 21, 28 June 1929; FC 1 July 1929.

86 RUDC 12 Oct. 1927; *FPRL* 16 Jan., 12 Mar., 2 July 1932; *GCT* 16 Jan., 12, 27 Mar. 1932; *RFG* 24 Dec. 1932; Horner, *Incorrigible Rebel*, 113–19.

87 RUDC 8 Feb. 1928, 21 Aug., 25 Sept., 9 Oct. 1929, 2 July 1930; Roads Committee (RoC) 20 Feb. 1928; RD 30 Jan., 27 Feb. 1928; *GFPRL* 21 May 1927, 21 Sept. 1929, 22 Sept. 1934, 15 Feb. 1936; *RFG* 11, 18 Oct., 8, 22 Nov. 1930.

88 *FPRL* 22 Nov. 1930, 22 Sept. 1934; *RFG* 22 Nov. 1930; Gwen Ray Evans's

election address, RUDC Ward Nine 1929, W. H. Mainwaring Papers, NLW; E. George Thomas's election address, RUDC Ward Three 1935, E. George Thomas Collection, UCS; *DW* 21 Jan. 1935; TL 22 Nov. 1934.

[89] Interview with George Thomas, 17 Aug. 1987. George Thomas's assertion that Harcombe had 'eighteen or nineteen children' is an exaggeration: he had seven sons and three daughters. Corroborative testimony by Will Whitehead, interviewed 12 June 1990.

[90] All of this material has been provided for the author via either oral or written testimony, via the records of the RUDC or through the pages of the local press. No allegations are made that have not already been made in one form or another. The originality of this section lies rather in the bringing together of such evidence as exists, and the insertion of such evidence into an overarching political and electoral interpretation.

[91] *GFPRL* 23 Nov. 1923.

[92] *GFPRL* 11 Sept., 4 Dec. 1926, 22 Jan. 1927, 23 Nov. 1929.

[93] *FPRL* 21 Mar. 1931.

[94] RBLP 24 Oct., 25 Nov. 1933, 12 Jan. 1934; *FPRL* 18 Apr. 1936.

[95] *PG* 5 Nov. 1932; *RFG* 5, 19 Nov. 1932.

[96] *PG* 14 Apr. 1934, 23 Mar. 1935; *FPRL* 12 Nov. 1935.

[97] *GFPRL* 19 May 1928; *FPRL* 16 June 1934; RUDC 9 Nov. 1932, 9 May 1934; RBLP 3 Dec. 1932.

[98] *RS* 3 Aug. 1912.

[99] Interviews with Elwyn Wales; Will Whitehead.

[100] EdC 6 June 1919; School Management Committee (SMC) 20 June 1919; RUDC 11 July 1919.

[101] RUDC 14 Jan. 1925, 9, 13 Nov. 1929; *RFG* 19 Nov. 1927.

[102] *GFPRL* 15 Sept. 1928; *FPRL* 9 July 1932.

[103] *FPRL* 10 Nov. 1934, 6 Apr., 8 June, 7 Sept. 1935; RBLP 30 June 1933, 22 Feb. 1934; *PG* 22 July 1933.

[104] *Y Ddraig Goch* June 1933, reprinted in *GCT* 17 June 1933.

[105] *GFPRL* 11, 24 Sept., 15 Oct. 1927; RUDC 21 Sept. 1927; *RFG* 27 Oct., 12 Nov. 1927.

[106] RUDC 30 July 1929.

[107] RUDC 12 Feb., 12 Mar. 1930; *FPRL* 15 Feb., 17 May 1930; *DW* 14 Feb. 1930.

[108] *FPRL* 22 Nov., 6 Dec. 1930; RUDC 27 Nov. 1930; *PG* 29 Nov., 6 Dec. 1930; *RFG* 25 Apr. 1931; *GCT* 25 Apr. 1931; Maslin bankruptcy documents in the possession of Mr George A. Maslin (son); interview with Mr George A. Maslin.

[109] David Jenkins's Election Address Ward Four RUDC 1925, electoral ephemera; *GFPRL* 17 Apr. 1925.

[110] RUDC 10 Oct. 1928; *GFPRL* 19 Oct., 24 Nov. 1928.

[111] *FPRL* 17, 24 Dec. 1932; *PG* 17 Dec. 1932.

[112] RUDC 12 Sept., 10 Oct. 1934, 13 Mar. 1935; Sub-Committee re: Allocation of Appointments in No.4 Ward, 22, 31 Oct., 15, 23, 30 Nov., 14

Dec. 1934, 10, 17, 30 Jan., 5 Feb. 1935; *FPRL* 22 Sept., 13, 20 Oct. 1934, 16 Mar. 1935; TL 13 Sept., 29 Nov. 1934, 20 Feb. 1935; *GCT* 13 Oct. 1934.
113 *Mid-Rhondda Outlook (MRO)* Jan., May 1935.
114 Francis and Smith, *The Fed*, 161.
115 Reg Fine, interviewed by Hywel Francis; Mrs Jo Evans, Mardy, interviewed by Hywel Francis, 11 June 1973; Mardy, Ferndale and Tylorstown CP local leaflet 17 Apr. 1932, W. H. Mainwaring Papers, NLW.
116 *WW* 24 Apr. 1925; *GFPRL* 21 May 1927; *FPRL* 26 Dec. 1931; interview with George A. Maslin.
117 *DW* Jan.–Apr. 1935, *passim*.
118 Hywel Francis, *Miners Against Fascism: Wales and the Spanish Civil War* (1984), Chapter Nine, *passim*.
119 E. George Thomas, interviewed by Hywel Francis; Archie James, interviewed by Hywel Francis and Dai Smith; Will Picton, Mardy, interviewed by Hywel Francis and Dai Smith, 9 May 1973.
120 Interview with Idris and Dora Cox; interview with Iorwerth and Hilda Price; *WL* 25 Jan. 1929; interview with Cyril Gwyther.
121 Will Paynter, *My Generation* (1972), and also Hywel Francis, 'Tribute to Will Paynter (1903–1984)', *Llafur* 4 No.2 (1985), 4–9. For Lewis Jones see the introductions to his novels by David Smith; idem, *Lewis Jones* (1982); idem, *Wales! Wales?*, 138–40. Horner, apart from starring in *The Fed*, provides us with his own *Incorrigible Rebel*.
122 Interview with George A. Maslin; Billy Griffiths interviewed by Hywel Francis.
123 Low levels of Labour Party membership were noted by Party Organizer George Morris in Dec. 1932 as 'depressing' (RBLP 30 Dec. 1932, 7 Jan. 1933, 6 Dec. 1935). Rhondda's average membership figures in the 1930s, for effectively two Constituency Parties, were less than many Welsh Parties based on only one constituency (*Labour Party Conference Reports*).
124 Francis, *Miners Against Fascism*, 47–8; and Horner himself in *Incorrigible Rebel*, 109–12.
125 Stuart Macintyre, *Little Moscow*, 37–41, 45, 124; Horner, op. cit., 109; Francis and Smith, *The Fed*, 164–70.
126 Pelling, op. cit., 183, 186–9.
127 Francis and Smith, *The Fed*, 270.
128 In particular, see Francis and Smith, op. cit., and Francis, *Miners Against Fascism*. Also Peter Kingsford, *The Hunger Marchers In Britain, 1920–1940* (1982), 40–1, 82–6, 133; Wal Hannington, *Unemployed Struggles 1919–1936: My Life and Struggles Amongst the Unemployed* (1977 edition), 156–68, 219–20; Richard Croucher, *We Refuse to Starve in Silence: A History of the National Unemployed Workers' Movement, 1920–1946* (1987), 87–9.
129 *WL* 1 Feb. 1929; *WM* 3, 12 Oct. 1931; *MRO* Nov. 1934; *SWM* 23 Oct. 1934; *DW* 27 Sept., 8 Oct. 1935; *FPRL* 11 Aug. 1934, 5, 12 Oct. 1935, 8 Feb., 2, 30 May, 13, 20 June 1936; *GCT* 5 Oct. 1935, 11 July 1936; *RC* Oct. 1935; *RV* Aug.–Sept. 1935.

130 For Communist proposals for local government, see the election addresses of Gwen Ray Evans (RUDC Ward Nine 1929), W. H. Mainwaring Papers, NLW, and E. George Thomas (RUDC Ward Three 1935), E. George Thomas Collection, UCS. Thomas juxtaposed a call for a playground for children in his ward (point five of his programme) with a call for the abolition of war and fascism (point six)!

131 *DW* 21 Jan. 1935.

132 *We Live* (1978 edition), 225–26

133 Cited in Webster, 'Health, Welfare and Unemployment', Appendix. For full details, see MH79/312 Public Assistance Out Relief – Rhondda Administration 1936. D. J. Roberts, Report on 'Rhondda Out Relief', 19 July 1936.

134 *RV* No.10, June 1936.

135 Lewis Jones, *We Live*, 226.

136 Francis and Smith, *The Fed*, 253.

137 John Stevenson and Chris Cook, *The Slump* (1979 edition), 183–4, 193–4; John Stevenson, 'The Politics of Violence', in *The Politics of Reappraisal 1918–1939*, ed. Gillian Peele and Chris Cook (1975), 146–65, especially 162; idem, 'The Making of Unemployment Policy, 1931–1935', in *High and Low Politics in Modern Britain: Ten Studies*, ed. Michael Bentley and John Stevenson (1983), 182–213, especially 203–9.

138 Parliamentary Debates Vol.297, 28 Jan. 1935.

139 *DW* Jan. 1935 *passim*; *WM* 21, 22 Jan. 1935; *FPRL* 25 Jan. 1935; *PG* 26 Jan. 1935; *MRO* Jan., Feb. 1935.

140 *DW* 28 Feb. 1935; *FPRL* 2 Mar. 1935.

141 *FPRL* 25 July, 1 Aug., Sept. 1936 *passim*, 3 Oct. 1936, Feb.–Mar. 1938 *passim*; *PG* 1 Aug. 1936, 5 Mar., 14 May 1938; *RC* Sept. 1936; *FL* 23 Jan., 16 July 1936, 27 May, 9, 27 June 1938; Cambrian Combine Special Committee 19 Mar. 1936, All-Organizations Conference 7 May 1936; CL Correspondence Book 10 Aug. 1936, 15 Sept., 25 Oct. 1938; Francis and Smith, op. cit., 270–1; Cambrian Combine Committee 18 Sept., 1 Dec. 1938.

142 *Miners' Monthly* Oct. 1936.

143 R. J. Barker, *Christ in the Valley of Unemployment* (1936), 31.

144 Francis, *Miners Against Fascism*, and idem, 'Rhondda and the Spanish Civil War: A Study in International Working-Class Solidarity', in *Rhondda Past and Future*, ed. K. S. Hopkins (1975), 66–83.

145 Francis, 'Rhondda and the Spanish Civil War', 73.

146 Ibid., 80.

147 Ibid., 81.

148 For the milk scheme see MH79/312 Public Assistance Out Relief, – Rhondda Administration 1936, Minute from J. Owain Evans to Mr Ure, 19 June 1936; MH55/691 Report on Rhondda Milk Scheme by D. Llewelyn Williams and Howell E. James, to Sir George Newman, 8 Feb. 1928; report by Dr Dilys Jones, 8 Feb. 1928; note from A. B. McLachlan (Minister of

Health) to Sir George Newman, 13 Feb. 1928; MH55/629, Maternal Mortality in the Special Areas J. G. Howell, A. T. Jones 9 Oct. 1936, Appendix IV, Expenditure on Milk under the MCW scheme; and also Inquiry Into the present conditions as regards the effects of continued unemployment on health in certain areas of South Wales and Monmouth, 23 Oct. 1936.

[149] Allen Hutt, *The Condition of the Working Class in Britain* (1933), 49.

[150] RC Oct. 1935.

[151] See the corroborative testimony of Mavis Llewellyn, Nantymoel, interviewed by Hywel Francis 20 May 1974.

[152] FPRL 14 Jan. 1933; RBLP 10 Feb., 22 Apr., 3 Aug. 1933.

[153] RBLP Committee of Enquiry: Summary of Recommendations. Issued 25 Nov. 1934. RBLP 25 May, 23 June, 6 July, 3 Nov. 1934, 13 Apr. 1935; Special Committee of Enquiry, 20 July, 3 Aug., 25 Nov. 1934.

[154] RBLP 14, 29 Dec. 1934, 9 Mar., 13 Apr., 18 May 1935.

[155] Billy Griffiths interviewed by Hywel Francis; interview with George A. Maslin; FPRL 6 Mar. 1938.

[156] Interview with Brynna Jones, 5 Mar. 1986.

[157] Ian McAllister, 'The Labour Party in Wales: The Dynamics of One-Partyism', *Llafur* 3 No.2 (1981), 79–89: 80.

[158] Interview with Cliff Prothero, 19 Aug. 1987; RBLP 13 Apr. 1935.

[159] RBLP 17 June, 23 July, 1 Oct. 1932; 28 Jan., 24 Oct. 1933.

[160] RBLP 23 July, 3 Sept., 1, 5 Oct., 3 Dec. 1932, 9 Sept., 2 Oct., 25 Nov. 1933; 26, 28 Apr., 16 Aug. 1934. RBLP No.9 Ward (RBLP9) 4 June, 14 July 1936; FPRL 11 Feb. 1939; conversation with D. J. Davies.

[161] RBLP 7 Jan., 2 June, 24 Oct., 14 Nov., 9, 12 Dec. 1933, 12, 13 Jan., 10 May, 26 July 1934, 12 July, 17 Oct. 1935; EC Joint May Day Sub-Committee, 26 Jan. 1933.

[162] RWDLP Account books, 1925–55; PG 12 Mar. 1932; LM 8 Nov. 1932; conversation with D. J. Davies; Labour Party Annual Conference Reports, 1928–50.

[163] For a flurry of events in the late 1920s see GFPRL 5 Feb., 16 Apr., 10 Sept., 10 Dec. 1927, 7 Jan., 12 May, 16 June, 1 Sept., 19 Oct., 10 Nov. 1928, 7 Sept., 19 Oct. 1929; FPRL 28 Dec. 1929, 15 Nov. 1930.

[164] FPRL 9 May 1931, 5, 12 Mar., 22 Oct. 1932, 8 July 1933, 12 May, 16 June 1934, 20 Dec. 1935, 29 Aug., 12, 19 Sept. 1936, 18 Jan. 1941; MRO Jan. 1937, Feb., Dec. 1938; PG 19 Oct. 1935, 21 Mar. 1936; RFG 28 Jan. 1933.

[165] MRO Feb. 1938; interview with Cyril Gwyther.

[166] Tonypandy Women's Section Labour Party Minute Book (in the possession of George Thomas, Cardiff), 1942–6; interview with Cyril Gwyther; Treorchy Ward Labour Women's Section Treasurer's Book, 1935–54.

[167] Interview with Cliff Prothero; RBLP 23 July, 3 Sept. 1932; League of Youth Conference, 14 June 1935; League of Youth Meeting, 23 June 1935; RWDLP 14 Sept., 5 Oct. 1948, 1 Feb., 7 Mar. 1949; RBLP9 25 July 1938, 7

Feb. 1949; *FPRL* 20 Jan. 1934, 20 Nov. 1937; *MRO* Mar., Aug., Sept. 1935; *RFL* 15 Sept. 1945; *RL* 10 May 1947.

[168] Francis, *Miners Against Fascism*, 49.

[169] Trevor Davies interviewed by Hywel Francis, 3 July 1973.

[170] *The Tribune* Mar. 1935.

[171] *WM* 22 Mar., 1, 6, 10 Apr. 1935; interview with Cyril Gwyther; Gwyther, *The Valley Shall Be Exalted*, 70–2; Barker, op. cit., 60–1.

[172] *GFPRL* 10 Nov. 1928; *FPRL* 28 Dec. 1929, 18 Jan., 13 Sept., 1 Nov. 1930, 20 Feb. 1932, 22 Feb. 1936.

[173] *RV* Feb. 1936.

[174] *RBLP* 9 Mar. 1935; *RV* Aug.–Sept. 1935; *TL* 13 Nov., 12 Dec. 1935.

[175] The CP withdrew two candidates before the 1935 RUDC elections ostensibly to prevent any split in the 'United Front vote', according to the *DW* 31 May 1935.

[176] *DW* 2, 4, 13, 14, 16 Feb. 1935.

[177] *RUDC* 9 Jan., 13 Feb. 1935; *FPRL* 9 Feb. 1935; Francis and Smith, *The Fed*, 256–7.

[178] *DW* 1, 9, 20, 21, 23, 25 Feb. 1935; *CL* 17, 24 Feb. 1935; *TL* Jan.–Feb. 1935 *passim*; *WM* 25 Feb. 1935; *FPRL* 2 Mar. 1935.

[179] *DW* 28 Feb. 1935.

[180] *RBLP* 26 Apr. 1935.

[181] *RBLP* 10 May 1935.

[182] *RBLP* 18 May, 6 June 1935; *DW* 31 May, 10 June 1935.

[183] *RC* Oct. 1935, Jan., Mar.–May 1936 *passim*.

[184] *RBLP* 22 Mar. 1935; *PG* 23 Mar., 4 Apr. 1935. Francis, in *Miners Against Fascism*, 92, drawing from the *DW* 8 July 1936, notes that the RBLP in 1936 'instructed its ward committees to form, with the Communist Party, a "common front against Fascism".' All evidence indicates that this was a temporary unity forged in the struggle against the local appearance of the British Union of Fascists.

[185] *FL* 13 Nov. 1935, 30 Apr., 11 June, 16 July 1936, 24 Mar., 12, 27 May, 9 June 1938.

[186] The South Wales Regional Council of Labour: Labour Party (Wales) Archives, Vol.I, 1937–8.

[187] *GCT* 11 May 1940.

[188] Circular from Ben Harcombe, 25 Sept. 1939, CL Correspondence Book; CL 8 Oct. 1939; CL Files, C20 circular from No.6 Ward Labour Party Committee 5 Aug. 1940; *GCT* 14 Oct. 1939; *FPRL* 23 Sept., 14 Oct. 1939.

[189] *FPRL* 5, 12 Oct. 1940, 29 Mar. 1941; *MRO* Sept., Nov. 1940; *PD* 20 May 1942.

[190] Stuart R. Broomfield, 'South Wales during the Second World War: The Coal Industry and its Community', Ph.D. thesis, University of Wales (Swansea), 1979, 587–94; South Wales Regional Council of Labour 8 Oct., 3, 10 Dec. 1940, 14 Jan., 18 Feb., 11 Mar. 1941; SWMF EC 17 Sept. 1940, 4 Jan. 1941; *PD* 23 Feb., 25 Mar. 1941; CL Correspondence Book, circular

from the RBLP 20 Apr. 1940; CL Correspondence Book, 20, 28 Sept., 9 Oct. 1940, 2 Jan. 1941.

[191] Central Committee All-In Conference, Feb.–Mar. 1940 *passim*; letter from Will John to E. George Thomas, Secretary of the Conference, 13 Mar. 1940; letter from W. H. Mainwaring to E. George Thomas, 11 Mar. 1940, E. George Thomas Collection, UCS.

[192] *Labour's Call to Rhondda* (RUDC and GCC), electoral ephemera, RBLP Ward One Address.

[193] CP handbill, South Wales District CP Records; Will Picton Collection, UCS – Communist Message to the People of the Rhondda; George Thomas's electoral address, E. George Thomas collection, UCS; *RL* 19 Jan., 9 Feb., 16 Mar., 6 Apr. 1946.

[194] RWDLP 14 Apr. 1947; RBLP9 14 Apr., 15 Dec. 1947; *RL* 16 Mar. 1946, 10 May 1947, 29 Mar. 1947, 5 Apr. 1947, 1 Nov. 1947, Feb.–Apr. 1948 *passim*; RBLP9 22 Mar. 1948.

[195] Labour Party Message to the electorate in Wards Four, Six, Seven, Nine, Ten, 1947.

[196] George Baker's handbill, Ward Four GCC 1949; CP Handbill for local elections, 1946; *RL* 17, 24 Nov., 8 Dec. 1945, 10 May 1947, 17 Apr., 8 May, 17 July, 10 Dec. 1949.

[197] *RL* 16 Feb. 1946.

[198] Interview with George A. Maslin.

[199] *RL* 27 July, 23 Nov. 1946, Feb.–Mar. 1947 *passim*, 24 May, 7 June 1947.

[200] Ibid. 2 Nov. 1946, 25 Jan. 1947.

Notes to Conclusion

[1] I am grateful for this reference, and for other information concerning Mr Garwood, to Mr Victor Garwood (son) and his wife. Conversation with them at Llwyncelyn, Porth, 16 May 1990.

[2] In particular, and in addition to the family of Johnny Garwood, much was gained from the families of Arthur Davies, Glyn Elias, Len Elston, Samuel Hedditch, David Hughes, Will 'Knowledge' Hughes, Reg Travess, and Albert Trotman. Some first-hand insights into the ethos of Labour Party public representatives were gained from a meeting with Brynna Jones, whilst slightly different angles were provided by the families of a Conservative Party activist, Annie Tamplin, and of the Independent Councillor, Glyn Wales. Conversation with Mrs Megan Lewis (daughter of Arthur Davies), Litchard, Bridgend, 26 May 1990; conversation with Mrs J. G. Elias; conversation with son, daughter and daughter-in-law of Len Elston, Tonypandy, 11 September 1990; conversation with Mrs A. G. Hedditch (daughter-in-law), Ton Pentre, 16 May 1990; conversation with Mr D. E. Hughes (son), Barry, 19 May 1990; communication with Ms Freda Travess (daughter), Treherbert, 9 June 1990; conversation with Mr Alun Trotman (son) and his wife Shirley, Llwynypia, 17 June 1987;

conversation with Mr Elwyn Wales; interview with Brynna Jones; conversation with Alfred Tamplin (son), and his wife Edith, Wattstown, 24 June 1987.
3 Interview with George Thomas.
4 Will Paynter cited in Chris Williams, 'The South Wales Miners' Federation', *Llafur* 5 No. 3 (1990), 45–56: 47.
5 In no sense is this meant to imply that any of the above-named individuals were involved in such corruption as existed in the Rhondda Labour Party during the inter-war years.
6 For an appropriate 'defence' of Labour's reputation elsewhere, see Kenneth O. Morgan, 'The Challenges of Democracy', in *The City of Swansea: Challenges and Change*, ed. Ralph A.Griffiths (1990), 51–66, especially 62, where Morgan observes that 'Labour dominated Swansea's local government not because it was corrupt but because it was committed . . . Democratic machine-run politics in Swansea may have had their price at times, but they also had genuine social rewards and achievements.'
7 Hywel Francis and David Smith, *The Fed: A History of the South Wales Miners in the Twentieth Century* (1980), 54–6.
8 Hywel Francis, 'The Anthracite Strike and Disturbances of 1925', *Llafur* 1 No.2 (1973), 53–66 (facsimile edition).
9 Francis and Smith, op. cit., 66.
10 Francis and Smith, op. cit., 52, seem to contradict themselves with regards to the chronology of 'alternative culture': 'The period from the outbreak of the Great War to the commencement of the General Strike and miners' lock-out was one which saw a deepening of the radicalization of the South Wales miners which had been apparent in certain parts of the coalfield during the tumultuous years of 1910–11.'
More succinctly, see Dai Smith, *Wales! Wales?* (1984), 96–7: 'The working class of mid-Rhondda in 1910, in their anticipation of the more generalized struggles of the 1920s and 1930s, stand for the working class of South Wales.'
For other works stressing the significance of 1910–11 see idem, 'Tonypandy 1910. Definitions of Community', *Past and Present* 87 (1980), 158–84; idem, 'Wales Through the Looking-Glass' in *A People and a Proletariat: Essays in the History of Wales, 1780–1980*, ed. David Smith (1980), 215–39: 218–24; idem, 'The Valleys: Landscape and Mindscape', in *Glamorgan County History VI: Glamorgan Society 1780–1980*, ed. Prys Morgan (1988), 129–49: 144–5.
11 Ralph Miliband, *Parliamentary Socialism: A Study in the Politics of Labour* (1972 edition).
12 John Saville, 'The Ideology of Labourism', in *Knowledge, Belief and Politics*, ed. Robert Benewick, R. N. Berki, and Bhikhu Parekh (1973), 213–26; 215: 'Labourism . . . was a theory and practice which accepted the possibility of social change within the existing framework of society; which rejected the revolutionary violence and action implicit in Chartist

ideas of physical force; and which increasingly recognized the working of political democracy of the parliamentary variety as the practicable means of achieving its own aims and objectives. Labourism was the theory and practice of class collaboration . . . '

[13] Ross McKibbin, *The Evolution of the Labour Party, 1910–1924* (1974). The position is exemplified by the comment (xiv–xv) that 'the class consciousness which produced the Labour Party at the same time deprived it of any ideological exactness and excluded it from many areas of working-class life.' A more sophisticated version of this position is offered in idem, *The Ideologies of Class: Social Relations in Britain 1880–1950* (1990), 294–5, in revision of comments by Jay M. Winter, 'Trade Unions and the Labour Party in Britain', in *The Development of Trade Unionism in Great Britain and Germany, 1880–1914*, ed. Wolfgang J. Mommsen and Hans-Gerhard Husung (1985), 359–70. McKibbin argues latterly that the British industrial working class was contained within a 'ritualized' political and social system, and therefore was necessarily on the defensive for historical and practical rather than inherent reasons.

[14] Ina-Maria Zweiniger-Bargielowska, 'Industrial Relationships and Nationalization in the South Wales Coalmining Industry', Ph.D. thesis, University of Cambridge (1989), 103–11. See also David John Rossiter, 'The Miners' Sphere of Influence: An Attempt to Quantify Electoral Behaviour in Mining Areas Between the Wars', Ph.D. thesis, University of Sheffield (1980), 3–4.

[15] Furthermore, to note, as does Rossiter, op. cit., that only once, in parliamentary elections in Rhondda East, did Communist votes rise above one-third of the total electorate is not to say that Rhondda East did not exhibit strong Communist support. Such support has to be measured by relative (British) historical criteria, not absolute and abstract numerical ones. A contrasting view of the significance of Communist support is offered by James Griffiths, 'Welsh Politics in my Lifetime', in *James Griffiths and His Times*, ed. J. Beverley Smith (1977), 16–57: 32.

[16] Thus Michael Savage, *The Dynamics of Working-Class Politics: The Labour Movement in Preston, 1880–1940* (1987), 5: 'What ordinary people thought, and the way in which they expressed it, matters and ought to be taken seriously by historians; what the politically active among them demanded cannot be assessed in abstraction from their own needs, desires, and capacities.'

[17] A welcome recognition of this alignment is provided by R. Merfyn Jones, 'Beyond Identity? The Reconstruction of the Welsh', *Journal of British Studies* 31 (1992), 330–57: 340.

[18] This classification does not conform with what, in this instance, is Savage's inappropriate distinction between 'practical' and 'formal' politics.

[19] As Dai Smith, 'The Valleys: Landscape and Mindscape', 145, suggests, Rhondda might also have spoken in a very different way, had the visions of

another of its figures, D. A. Thomas, Lord Rhondda, been realized. Thomas represented the leading edge of capitalist advancement, his Liberalism, rooted as it was in 'American Wales', having shaken off the sentimental trappings of Cymru Fydd and the remainder of the ideological props of Welsh-speaking Liberal Wales. The future which Thomas represented was curtailed: by his own death in 1918, and by the collapse of the coalfield's economic fortunes between the wars. With this 'alternative' of an indigenous, present south Walian capitalist leadership wrenched out of history, and with the self-serving deceits of Welsh Liberal Nonconformity exposed by the blood and violence of 1910, there was no 'alternative' to the working-class leadership of coalfield communities, in defeat as much as in victory.

[20] And in this sense Rhondda was an 'alternative culture', a 'society within'.

Bibliography

A.   INTERVIEWS, CORRESPONDENCE AND PERSONAL
     COLLECTIONS
  I   Interviews
  II Correspondence
  III Transcripts of Interviews Undertaken by the South Wales
      Coalfield History Project
  IV Personal Collections

B.   OFFICIAL PAPERS AND RECORDS

C.   POLITICAL PARTY, TRADE UNION AND
     MISCELLANEOUS RECORDS
  I   Political Party Records
  II Trade Union Records
  III Miscellaneous Records

D.   NEWSPAPERS AND JOURNALS

E.   WORKS OF REFERENCE

F.   PUBLISHED WORKS

G.   THESES, DISSERTATIONS AND BROADCASTS
  I   Theses and Dissertations
  II Broadcasts

A. Interviews, Correspondence and Personal Collections

I. Interviews

Idris and Dora Cox (Talywaun). 21 June 1987.
Mr D. J. Davies (Preston). 29 August 1986.

Mr H. W. J. Edwards (Trealaw). 7 May 1990.
Mrs J. G. Elias (Pentre). 2 June 1990.
Mr L. Elston and family (Tonypandy). 11 September 1990.
Mr and Mrs Victor Garwood (Porth). 16 May 1990.
Ms M. Glanville (Llwynypia). 9 June 1990.
Cyril Gwyther (Pembroke Dock). 28 July 1987.
David Harcombe (Treherbert). 25 February 1986.
Mrs A. Hedditch (Pentre). 16 May 1990.
Mr D. E. Hughes (Barry). 19 May 1990.
John Hughes (Tonypandy). 22 April 1990.
Brynna Jones (Gelli). 5 March 1986.
Megan Lewis (Bridgend). 26 May 1990.
Mr Maltby (Sully). 16 June 1990.
George A. Maslin (Ferndale). 7 May 1990.
Iorwerth and Hilda Price (Barry). 17 August 1987.
Cliff Prothero (Penarth). 19 August 1987.
Alfred Tamplin (Wattstown). 24 June 1987.
George Thomas (Cardiff). 17 August 1987.
Albert Trotman (Llwynypia). 17 June 1987.
Elwyn Wales (Pentre). 2 June 1990.
Will Whitehead (Bristol). 12 June 1990.

II. Correspondence

Rita Ashman (Llwynypia). 1 July 1990.
Mrs M. Cadogan (Ystrad). 4 May 1990.
Mr T. H. Cann (Porth). 28 May 1990.
Gordon R. Coles (Treherbert). 4 June 1990.
D. Collingbourne (Pontygwaith). 12 June 1990.
Eira Davies (Ferndale). 25 June 1990.
Mr G. Davies (Tonypandy). 17 May 1990.
Mrs P. M. Evans (Ton Pentre). 3 June 1990.
Mr S. Hobbs (Treherbert). 16 May 1990.
Mr M. Lewis (Treherbert). 14 June 1990.
Mr M. Speed (Pentre). 14 June 1990.
Mr T. J. Street (Pontygwaith). 24 September 1990.
Freda Travess (Treherbert). 9 June 1990.
Will Whitehead (Bristol). 15 June 1990.
Mr H. C. Winter (Ystrad). 8 May 1990.
Mr E. G. Wynne (Ton Pentre). 10 June 1990.

III. Transcripts of Interviews Undertaken by the South Wales Coalfield History Project

George Baker
Alfred Beams and Richard Williams
Jake Brookes

Jesse Clark
Ben Davies
D. J. and B. Davies

Dai Lloyd Davies
Penry Davies
R. B. Davies
Mrs T. Davies
Trevor Davies
B. Edwards
Dai Dan Evans
Mrs J. Evans
John Evans
Reg Fine
Max Goldberg
Billy Griffiths
Bert Hutley
Archie James
Len Jefferies
Mr W. Knipe
Mr and Mrs William Rosser Jones
Mr and Mrs Bryn Lewis
Miss Mavis Llewellyn
Mrs Eddie Lloyd

A. J. Martin
D. J. Matthews
Abel Morgan
Arthur Morgan
Octavius Morgan
Mr and Mrs Fred Morris
Will Paynter
Will Picton
Anne Thomas
(E.) George Thomas
William Thomas
Will 'Box' Thomas
Jim Vale
Alun Menai Williams
Frank Williams
Gwilym Williams
Mrs Maria Williams
W. H. Mainwaring (interviewed by David Smith: notes in possession of interviewer).

IV. *Personal Collections*

NLW MSS 12520 (Mabon's Testimonial Minute Book)
Robin Page Arnot (UCS)
Edgar Chappell (NLW)
Jesse Clark (UCS)
Idris Cox (SWML). Includes unpublished autobiography 'Story of a Welsh Rebel'.
Beatrice Davies (UCS)
Sonia Evans (UCS)
Anita Gale (Cardiff)
Cornelius Gronow (UCS)
Cyril Gwyther (Pembroke Dock)
Arthur Horner (UCS)
Francis Johnson Papers (British Library of Political and Economic Science).
Lewis Jones (SWML)
W. H. Mainwaring Papers (NLW)
Austin Pearce (UCS)
Will Picton (UCS)
Gwilym Richards (UCS)
David Thomas MA (Wales) (NLW)
Emlyn Thomas (UCS)
(E.) George Thomas (Treherbert) (UCS)
Frank Williams (UCS)
Also: various materials in possession of individuals interviewed (see A.I above).

B. Official Papers and Records

Census Reports: 1871, 1881, 1891, 1901, 1911, 1921, 1931, 1951, 1961
Parliamentary Debates
Parliamentary Papers:
  Boundary Commission 1884–5 (Report) XIX, C.4287
  Redistribution of Seats Act 1885 (Constituencies), 1884–5, LXII (Commons), 1886, VIII
  Accidents in Mines, Final Report of Commissioners. 1886, XVI, C.4699
  Reports of the Inspectors of Mines, for 1885. 1886, XVI, C.4760
  Employers' Liability Act (1880) Amendment Bill. Report from Select Committee (Commons), 1886, LII.
  Local Government Boundaries Commission, Report. 1888, LI, C.360; (Commons), 1894, XXXV
  Royal Commission on the Poor Laws and Relief of Distress, 1909, Cd.4573
  Royal Commission on the Church of England and other Religious Bodies in Wales and Monmouthshire, HMSO, 1910, Cd.5432–9
  Industrial Unrest, Commission of Inquiry (Reports) No.7 Division, 1917–18, Cd.8668
  Boundary Commission Report and Appendices, 3 vols, 1917, Cd.8756–8
Returns of Election Expenses: (Commons) 1886, LII; (Commons) 1901, LIX; (Commons) 1906, XCVI; (Commons) 1910, LXXIII; (Commons)1911, LXII
Parliamentary Constituencies: (Commons) 1901, LIX; (Commons) 1902, LXXXII; (Commons) 1903, LIV; (Commons) 1904, LXXVIII; (Commons) 1905, LXII; (Commons) 1906, XCIV, Cd.2807; (Commons) 1907, LXVI; (Commons) 1908, LXXXVII; (Commons) 1909, LXX; (Commons) 1910, LXXIII, Cd.4975; (Commons) 1911, LXII; (Commons) 1912–13, LXVII; (Commons) 1914, LXV; (Commons) 1914–16, LII; (Commons) 1918, XIX; (Commons) 1919, XL
Home Office Files: 45/10638/204636; 45/263275/274, 315, 318; 144/A55059/B/58
Education Board File ED/108/52
Board of Trade File BT/31/18313/96196
Cabinet Papers CAB/24
Premier's Papers PREM 1/182
PRO 30/69 (Ramsay MacDonald files)
Ministry of Health Files: MH55/629, 691; MH57/94, 106–10, 116–19, 125–6; MH 79/297, 304, 312
Ystradyfodwg Urban Sanitary Authority Minutes
Ystradyfodwg School Board Minutes
Rhondda Urban District Council Minutes
Reports of the Medical Officer of Health and the School Medical Officer, Rhondda Urban District Council
Pontypridd Board of Guardians Minutes
Glamorgan County Council Diaries

C. Political Party, Trade Union and Miscellaneous Records

I. Political Party Records

ILP NAC Minutes; Annual Conference Reports
Fabian Society Reports
Labour Party NEC Minutes; Correspondence Files: LRC/CORR; LP/AFF; WEWNC/WNC; CA/GEN; LP/MIN; LP/CO; Library LAB Files (Constitutions); Annual Conference Reports and Agendas
South Wales Regional Council of Labour Minutes
Welsh Regional Council of Labour Minutes
Rhondda Borough Labour Party Minutes; Balance Sheets
Rhondda West Divisional Labour Party Minutes; Account Books
Rhondda Borough Labour Party No.9 Ward Minutes
LRC No.9 Ward: Minutes and Rules; Correspondence Books
Mid-Rhondda TLC Minutes and Rules
Treherbert TLC Minutes; Correspondence Book
Treherbert Labour Party Ward Committee Minutes
Tonypandy Women's Section Labour Party Minute Book
Treorchy Ward Labour Women's Section Treasurer's Book
Pontypridd Trades Council and Labour Party Minutes
Communist Party of Great Britain (South Wales District) Annual Report
Electoral Ephemera – Treorchy Public Library Local History Collection

II. Trade Union Records

South Wales Miners' Federation Minutes and Files
NUM (South Wales Area) Minutes and Files
MFGB/NUM Directories
Rhondda No.1 District Minutes
SWMF Area No.4 Records
Abergorky Lodge Records
Cambrian Lodge Records
Ferndale Lodge Records
Ferndale Lodge Workmen's Band Records
Lewis Merthyr Lodge Records
Mardy Lodge Records
Mardy Workmen's Hall and Institute Records
Park and Dare Lodge Records
Tylorstown Joint Lodges Records
Tylorstown Lodge Records
Cambrian Combine Minutes
Powell Duffryn Combine Minutes
Cory Combine Minutes

III. Miscellaneous Records

British Legion Records
Lily of the Valley Lodge of Oddfellows, Ystrad Rhondda, Records

Maes-yr-Haf Educational Settlement Records
Saint David's Unity of Ivorites, Ystrad Rhondda District, Records
Ton Co-operative Society Records

D. Newspapers and Journals

The Cardiff Times
The Clarion
The Colliery Workers' Magazine
The Communist
The Communist Daily
The Daily Herald
Daily Worker
The Democrat
Y Ddraig Goch
Forward
Free Press and Rhondda Leader
Glamorgan County Times
Glamorgan County Times and Free
  Press
Glamorgan Free Press
Glamorgan Free Press and Rhondda
  Leader
Glamorgan Free Press, Pontypridd
  and Rhondda Chronicle
The Glamorgan Times and Rhondda,
  Merthyr, Aberdare and Rhymney
  Valleys Reporter
I.L.P. News
Inprecorr
Justice
Labour
Labour Leader
Labour Magazine
Llais Llafur
Merthyr Pioneer
Mid-Rhondda Gazette
The Mid-Rhondda Outlook
Miners' Monthly
The Monthly Democrat
The [Pontypridd] Observer
Plebs
Pontypridd and Rhondda Valleys
  Chronicle
Pontypridd and Rhondda Weekly
  Post

Pontypridd Chronicle
The Pontypridd District Herald and
  Rhondda Valley, Llantrisant,
  Caerphilly and Mountain Ash
  News
Pontypridd Observer
The Porth Gazette
The Porth Gazette and Rhondda
  Leader
Red Dawn
The Rhondda Chronicle
The Rhondda Clarion
Rhondda Fach Gazette
Rhondda Fach Leader
Rhondda Fach Leader and Gazette
The Rhondda Gazette
The Rhondda Gazette and General
  Advertiser of the Rhondda Fach
  and Ogmore Valleys
The Rhondda Leader
The Rhondda Leader and Gazette
The Rhondda Leader, Maesteg,
  Garw and Ogmore Telegraph
The Rhondda Post
The Rhondda Socialist Newspaper
Rhondda Vanguard
Rhondda Workers' News Service
The Schoolmaster
The Schoolmaster and Women
  Teachers' Chronicle
The Socialist
South Wales Daily News
South Wales Democrat
South Wales Echo
South Wales Journal of Commerce
South Wales Miner
South Wales News
South Wales Voice
The South Wales Worker
Sunday Worker

The Times
The Tribune
Wales
The Welsh Labour Outlook
Welsh Nation
Welsh Nationalist
Welsh Outlook

Western Mail
The Wheatsheaf
The Worker
Workers' Bomb
The Workers' Dreadnought
Workers' Life
The Workers' Weekly

E. Works of Reference

Dictionary of Labour Biography
Dictionary of Welsh Biography
Kelly's Directory of South Wales and Monmouthshire
The Labour Annual
Labour Year Books
List of Mines
South Wales Coal Annual

F. Published Works

Andrews, Elizabeth, *A Woman's Work is Never Done* (Ystrad Rhondda, 1948).

Arnot, Robin Page, *South Wales Miners: I – 1898–1914* (London, 1967).

—— *South Wales Miners: II – 1914–1926* (Cardiff, 1975).

Attfield, John, and Williams, Stephen (eds), 1939: *The Communist Party and the War* (London, 1984).

Barker, R. J., *Christ in the Valley of Unemployment* (London, 1936).

Bealey, Frank, and Pelling, Henry., *Labour and Politics, 1900–1906: A History of the Labour Representation Committee* (London, 1958).

Biagini, Eugenio F., and Reid, Alastair J., 'Currents of Radicalism, 1850–1914'. In *Currents of Radicalism: Popular Radicalism, Oganised Labour and Party Politics in Britain, 1850–1914*, ed. Biagini and Reid (Cambridge, 1991), 1–19.

Board of Trade, *An Industrial Survey of South Wales* (London, 1932).

Boyns, Trevor, 'Technical Change and Colliery Explosions in the South Wales Coalfield, *c.*1870–1914', *WHR* 13 No.2 (1986), 155–77.

—— 'Of Machines and Men in the 1920s', *Llafur* 5 No.2 (1989), 30–9.

—— 'Powell Duffryn: The Use of Machinery and Production Planning Techniques in the South Wales Coalfield'. In *Towards a Social History of Mining*, ed. K. Tenfelde (Munich, 1992), 370–86.

—— 'Jigging and Shaking: Technical Choice in the South Wales Coal Industry Between the Wars', *WHR* 17 No.2 (1994), 230–51.

Branson, Noreen, *Poplarism 1919–1925: George Lansbury and the Councillors' Revolt* (London, 1979).

—— *History of the Communist Party of Great Britain, 1927–1941* (London, 1985).

Clinton, Alan, *The Trade Union Rank and File: Trades Councils in Britain, 1900–40* (Manchester, 1977).

Cooke, Philip, 'Class Relations and Uneven Development in Wales'. In *Diversity and Decomposition in the Labour Market*, ed. Graham Day (Aldershot, 1982), 147–75.

Craik, W. W., *The Central Labour College, 1909–29: A Chapter in the History of Adult Working-Class Education* (London, 1964).

Crook, Rosemary, '"Tidy Women": Women in the Rhondda Between the Wars', *Oral History Journal* 10 (1982), 40–6.

Croucher, Richard, *We Refuse to Starve in Silence: A History of the National Unemployed Workers' Movement, 1920–1946* (London, 1987).

David, Wayne. 'The Labour Party and the "Exclusion" of the Communists: The Case of the Ogmore Divisional Labour Party in the 1920s', *Llafur* 3 No.4 (1983), 5–15.

Davies, D. Hywel, *The Welsh Nationalist Party, 1925–1945* (Cardiff, 1983).

Davies, David James 'Guardians of the Needy Found Wanting: A Study in Social Division during the Industrial Crisis of 1926', *Carmarthenshire Historian* 19 (1982), 54–69.

Davies, Paul, *A. J. Cook* (Manchester, 1987).

Davies, Sam, 'The Membership of the National Unemployed Workers' Movement 1923–1938', *Labour History Review* 57 Part No.1 (1992), 29–36.

Davies, W. Watkin, *A Wayfarer in Wales* (London, 1930).

Deacon, Alan, 'Concession and Coercion: the Politics of Unemployment Insurance in the Twenties'. In *Essays in Labour History*, Vol. III, ed. Asa Briggs and John Saville (London, 1977), 9–35.

Edwards, H. W. J., *The Good Patch* (London, 1938).

Edwards, Ness, *History of the South Wales Miners' Federation* (London, 1938).

Egan, David, 'The Swansea Conference of the British Council of Soldiers' and Workers' Delegates, July 1917: Reactions to the Russian Revolution of February 1917, and the Anti-War Movement in South Wales', *Llafur* 1 No.4 (1975) (1983 facsimile edition), 162–87.

—— 'The Unofficial Reform Committee and The Miners' Next Step: Documents from the W. H. Mainwaring Papers, with an Introduction and Notes', *Llafur* 2 No.3 (1978), 64–80.

—— 'Noah Ablett, 1883–1935', *Llafur* 4 No.3 (1986), 19–30.

Eley, Geoff, and Nield, Keith, 'Why Does Social History Ignore Politics?', *Social History* 5 No.2 (1980), 249–71.

Evans, Chris, '*The Labyrinth of Flames': Work and Social Conflict in Early Industrial Merthyr Tydfil* (Cardiff, 1993).

Evans, David, *Labour Strife in the South Wales Coalfield, 1910–1911: A Historical and Critical Record of the Mid-Rhondda, Aberdare Valley and Other Strikes* (Cardiff, 1911).

Evans, E. W., *Mabon* (Cardiff, 1959).

—— *Miners of South Wales* (Cardiff, 1961).

Evans, Eric Wyn, 'Mabon and Trade Unionism in the South Wales Coalfield'. *In Men of No Property: Historical Studies of Welsh Trade Unions*, ed. Goronwy Alun Hughes. (Caerwys, 1971), 51–8.

Evans, Neil, 'Cardiff's Labour Traditions', *Llafur* 4 No.2 (1985), 77–90.

Femia, Joseph, *Gramsci's Political Thought: Hegemony, Consciousness and the Revolutionary Process* (London, 1987).

Francis, Hywel, 'The Anthracite Strike and Disturbances of 1925', *Llafur* 1 No.2 (1973), (1983 facsimile edition), 53–66.

—— 'Rhondda and the Spanish Civil War: A Study in International Working-Class Solidarity'. In *Rhondda Past and Future*, ed. K. S. Hopkins (Rhondda, 1975), 66–83.

—— 'South Wales'. In *The General Strike, 1926*, ed. Jeffrey Skelley (London, 1976), 232–60.

—— *Miners Against Fascism: Wales and the Spanish Civil War* (London, 1984).

—— 'Tribute to Will Paynter (1903–1984)', *Llafur* 4 No.2 (1985), 4–9.

Francis, Hywel, and Smith, David, *The Fed: A History of the South Wales Miners in the Twentieth Century* (London, 1980).

Gilbert, David, *Class, Community and Collective Action: Social Change in Two British Coalfields, 1850–1926* (Oxford, 1992).

Gillespie, James, 'Poplarism and Proletarianism: Unemployment and Labour Politics in London, 1918–34'. In *Metropolis London: Histories and Representations since 1800*, ed. David Feldman and Gareth Stedman Jones (London, 1989), 163–88.

Gregory, Roy, *The Miners and British Politics 1906–1914* (Oxford, 1968).

Griffiths, James, 'Welsh Politics in my Lifetime'. In *James Griffiths and His Times*, ed. J. Beverley Smith (Ferndale, 1977), 16–57.

Gwyther, Cyril, *The Valley Shall Be Exalted: Light Shines in the Rhondda* (London, 1949).

Gwyther, C. E., 'Sidelights on Religion and Politics in the Rhondda Valley, 1906–1926', *Llafur* 3 No.1 (1980), 30–43.

Hannington, Wal, *Unemployed Struggles 1919–1936: My Life and Struggles Amongst the Unemployed* (London, 1977 edition).

Harries, F. J., *A History of Conservatism in the Rhondda* (Pontypridd, 1912).

Hay, W. F., *War! And the Welsh Miner* (Tonypandy, 1915).

Hignell, Andrew, *A 'Favourit' Game: Cricket in South Wales before 1914* (Cardiff, 1992)

Hopkin, Deian, 'The Rise of Labour: Llanelli, 1890–1922'. In *Politics and Society in Wales, 1840–1922*, ed. Geraint H. Jenkins and J. Beverley Smith (Cardiff, 1988), 161–82.

Hopkins, K. S. (ed.), *Rhondda Past and Future* (Rhondda, 1975).

Horner, Arthur, *Incorrigible Rebel* (London, 1960).

Howard, Christopher, 'Expectations Born to Death: the Local Labour Party Expansion in the 1920s'. In *The Working Class in Modern British History: Essays in Honour of Henry Pelling*, ed. Jay M. Winter (Cambridge, 1983), 65–81.

Howell, David, *British Workers and the Independent Labour Party 1888–1906* (Manchester, 1983).

Hughes, Colin, *Lime, Lemon and Sarsaparilla: The Italian Community in South Wales 1881–1945* (Cardiff, 1991).

Humphreys, Emyr, *The Taliesin Tradition: A Quest for the Welsh Identity* (London, 1983).

Hutt, Allen, *The Condition of the Working Class in Britain* (London, 1933).

Jeremy, Paul, 'Life on Circular 703: The Crisis of Destitution in the South Wales Coalfield during the Lockout of 1926', *Llafur* 2 No.2 (1977), 65–75.

Jevons, H. S., *The British Coal Trade* (Newton Abbot, 1969 edition).

John, Ken, 'Sam Mainwaring and the Autonomist Tradition', *Llafur* 4 No.3 (1986), 55–66.

Jones, Dot, 'Serfdom and Slavery: Women's Work in Wales, 1890–1930'. In *Class, Community and the Labour Movement: Wales and Canada, 1850–1930*, ed. Deian R. Hopkin and Gregory S. Kealey (Aberystwyth, 1989), 86–100.

Jones, Gareth Elwyn, *Controls and Conflicts in Welsh Secondary Education, 1889–1944* (Cardiff, 1982).

Jones, Gareth Stedman, *Languages of Class: Studies in English Working-class History, 1832–1982* (Cambridge, 1983).

Jones, Ieuan Gwynedd, 'The Merthyr of Henry Richard'. In *Merthyr Politics: The Making of a Working-Class Tradition*, ed. Glanmor Williams (Cardiff, 1966), 28–57.

Jones, J. Graham, 'Wales and the "New Socialism", 1926–1929', *WHR* 11 No.2 (1982), 173–99.

Jones, Lewis, *From Exchange and Parish to the PAC: For Decency Instead of Destitution* (Tonypandy, 1934).

—— *South Wales Slave Act Special* (Tonypandy, 1935).

—— *Cwmardy* (London, 1978 edition).

—— *We Live* (London, 1978 edition).

Jones, Owen Vernon, *William Evans 1864–1934* (Porth, 1982).

Jones, Philip N., *Colliery Settlement in the South Wales Coalfield 1850–1926* (Hull, 1969).

—— *Mines, Migrants and Residence in the South Wales Steamcoal Valleys: The Ogmore and Garw Valleys in 1881* (Hull, 1987).

—— 'Population Migration into Glamorgan 1861–1911: A Reassessment'. In *Glamorgan County History VI: Glamorgan Society 1780–1980*, ed. Prys Morgan. (Cardiff, 1988), 173–202.

Jones, R. Merfyn, 'Beyond Identity? The Reconstruction of the Welsh', *Journal of British Studies* 31 (1992), 330–57.

Joyce, Patrick, *Visions of the People: Industrial England and the Question of Class, 1848–1914* (Cambridge, 1990).

Kingsford, Peter, *The Hunger Marchers in Britain, 1920–1940* (London, 1982).

Kirk, Neville, 'History, Language, Ideas and Post-modernism: A Materialist View', *Social History* 19 No.2 (1994), 221–40.

Klarman, Michael, 'Osborne: A Judgment Gone Too Far?', *English Historical Review* 104 (1988), 21–39.

—— 'Parliamentary Reversal of the Osborne Judgment', *Historical Journal* 32 (1989), 893–924.

—— 'The Trade Union Political Levy, The Osborne Judgment (1909), and the South Wales Miners' Federation', *WHR* 15 No.1 (1990), 34–57.

Klugmann, James, *History of the Communist Party of Great Britain*, Vol. I (London, 1969).

The Labour Party, *The Distress in South Wales* (1928).

Lambert, W. R., 'Working Class Attitudes Towards Organised Religion in Nineteenth Century Wales', *Llafur* 2 No.1 (1976), 4–17.

Lawn, Martin, 'Syndicalist Teachers: The Rhondda Strike of 1919', *Llafur* 4 No.1 (1984), 91–8.

Lewis, Ceri W., 'The Welsh Language: Its Origin and Later History in the Rhondda'. In *Rhondda Past and Future*, ed. K.S. Hopkins (Rhondda, 1975), 179–234.

Lewis, E. D., *The Rhondda Valleys* (Cardiff, 1984 edition. First published 1958.).

Lewis, Richard, *Leaders and Teachers: Adult Education and the Challenge of Labour in South Wales, 1906–1940* (Cardiff, 1993).

Lile, Brian, and Farmer, David, 'The Early Development of Association Football in South Wales, 1890–1906', *Transactions of the Honourable Society of Cymmrodorion* (1984), 193–215.

Lloyd, Christopher, *Explanation in Social History* (Oxford, 1987).

McAllister, Ian, 'The Labour Party in Wales: The Dynamics of One-Partyism', *Llafur* 3 No.2 (1981), 79–89.

MacFarlane, L. J., *The British Communist Party* (London, 1966).

Macintyre, Stuart, *Little Moscows* (London, 1980).

—— *A Proletarian Science: Marxism in Britain, 1917–1933* (London, 1986 edition).

McKibbin, Ross, *The Evolution of the Labour Party, 1910–1924* (Oxford, 1974).

—— *The Ideologies of Class: Social Relations in Britain 1880–1950* (Oxford, 1990).

McKinlay, A. and Morris, R. J. (eds.), *The ILP on Clydeside 1893–1932: From Foundation to Disintegration* (Manchester, 1991).

Mahon, John, *Harry Pollitt: A Biography* (London, 1976).

Marriott, John, *The Culture of Labourism: The East End Between the Wars* (Edinburgh, 1991).

Martin, Roderick, *Communism and British Trade Unions 1924–1933: A Study of the National Minority Movement* (Oxford, 1969).

Michael, Ian, *Gwyn Thomas* (Cardiff, 1977).

Miliband, Ralph, *Parliamentary Socialism: A Study in the Politics of Labour* (London, 1972 edition).

Ministry of Health, *Report of the South Wales Regional Survey Committee* (London, 1921).

Morgan, Kenneth O., 'Democratic Politics in Glamorgan', *Morgannwg* 4 (1960), 5–27.

—— 'The New Liberalism and the Challenge of Labour: The Welsh Experience, 1885–1929', *WHR* 6 No.3 (1973), 288–312.

—— 'Socialism and Syndicalism: The Welsh Miners' Debate, 1912', Society for the Study of Labour History, *Bulletin* 30 (1975), 22–37.

—— *Wales in British Politics, 1868–1922* (Cardiff, 1980 edition).

—— *Rebirth of a Nation: Wales 1880–1980* (Oxford, 1981).

—— 'The Welsh in English Politics, 1868–1982'. In *Welsh Society and Nationhood: Historical Essays Presented to Glanmor Williams*, ed. R. R. Davies, Ralph A. Griffiths, Ieuan Gwynedd Jones and Kenneth O. Morgan (Cardiff, 1984), 232–50.

—— 'The Challenges of Democracy'. In *The City of Swansea: Challenges and Change*, ed. Ralph A. Griffiths (Stroud, 1990), 51–66.

—— (ed.), *Lloyd George: Family Letters, 1885–1936* (Cardiff, 1973).

Mor O'Brien, Anthony, 'Patriotism on Trial: The Strike of the South Wales Miners, July 1915', *WHR* 12 No.1 (1984), 76–104.

—— 'The Merthyr Boroughs Election, November 1915', *WHR* 12 No.4 (1985), 538–66.

Morton, H. V., *In Search of Wales* (London, 1932).

Newton, Kenneth, *The Sociology of British Communism* (London, 1969).

O'Leary, Paul, ' "Syndicalist Teachers" in the Rhondda, 1913–19: A Comment', *Llafur* 4 No.3 (1986), 80–4.

Pankhurst, Sylvia, *The Home Front* (London, 1932).

Parry, Jon, 'Trade Unionists and Early Socialism in South Wales, 1890–1908', *Llafur* 4 No.3 (1986), 43–54.

—— 'Labour Leaders and Local Politics, 1888–1902: The Example of Aberdare', *WHR* 14 No.3 (1989), 399–416.

Paynter, Will, *My Generation* (London, 1972).

Pelling, Henry, *The British Communist Party: A Historical Profile* (London, 1958).

—— 'The Politics of the Osborne Judgment', *Historical Journal* 25 (1982), 889–909.

Phippen, George, *The Origin of the Ystrad Rhondda Labour Club* (n.d.).

The Pilgrim Trust, *Men Without Work* (Cambridge, 1938).

Pitt, Bob, 'Educator and Agitator: Charlie Gibbons, 1888–1967', *Llafur* 5 No.2 (1989), 72–83.

Pryce, W. T. R., 'Language Areas and Changes *c.*1750–1981'. In *Glamorgan County History VI: Glamorgan Society 1780–1980*, ed. Prys Morgan (Cardiff, 1988), 265–313.

Pugh, Martin, *The Tories and the People* (Oxford, 1985).

Rees, Ioan Bowen, *The Welsh Political Tradition* (Cardiff, 1960).

Rhondda Miners, *Rebirth of the Rhondda: Nationalisation Souvenir Programme* (1947).

Ryan, Patricia, 'The Poor Law in 1926'. In *The General Strike*, ed. Margaret Morris (Harmondsworth, 1976), 358–78.

Ryan, P. A., '"Poplarism" 1894–1930'. In *The Origins of British Social Policy*, ed. Pat Thane (London, 1978), 56–83.

Samuel, Raphael, and Jones, Gareth Stedman, 'The Labour Party and Social Democracy'. In *Culture, Ideology and Politics: Essays for Eric Hobsbawm* ed. Raphael Samuel and Gareth Stedman Jones (London, 1982), 320–9.

Savage, Michael, *The Dynamics of Working-Class Politics: The Labour Movement in Preston, 1880–1940* (Cambridge, 1987).

Savage, Mike, 'Understanding Political Alignments in Contemporary Britain: Do Localities Matter?', *Political Geography Quarterly* 6 No.1 (1987), 53–76.

—— 'Urban History and Social Class: Two Paradigms', *Urban History* 20 Pt.1 (1993), 61–77.

Saville, John, 'The Ideology of Labourism'. In *Knowledge, Belief and Politics*, ed. Robert Benewick, R. N. Berki and Bhikhu Parekh (London, 1973), 213–26.

Sibley, Richard, 'The Swing to Labour During the Second World War: When and Why?', *Labour History Review* 55 No.1 (1990), 23–34.

Smith, David (see also under Smith, Dai), 'The Struggle Against Company Unionism in the South Wales Coalfield, 1926–1939', *WHR* 6 No.3 (1973), 354–78.

—— 'The Future of Coalfield History', *Morgannwg* 19 (1975), 57–70.

—— 'Leaders and Led'. In *Rhondda Past and Future*, ed. K. S. Hopkins (Rhondda, 1975), 37–65.

—— 'Tonypandy 1910: Definitions of Community', *Past and Present* 87 (1980), 158–184.

—— 'Introduction'. In *A People and a Proletariat: Essays in the History of Wales, 1780–1980*, ed. David Smith (London, 1980), 7–15.

—— 'Wales Through The Looking Glass'. In *A People and a Proletariat: Essays in the History of Wales, 1780–1980*, ed. David Smith (London, 1980), 215–39.

—— *Lewis Jones* (Cardiff, 1982).

Smith, Dai, *Wales! Wales?* (London, 1984).

—— *Rhondda Lives* (Cardiff, 1988).

—— 'The Valleys: Landscape and Mindscape'. In *Glamorgan County History VI: Glamorgan Society 1780–1980*, ed. Prys Morgan (Cardiff, 1988), 129–49.

—— *Aneurin Bevan and the World of South Wales* (Cardiff, 1993).

Smith, David (ed.), *A People and a Proletariat: Essays in the History of Wales, 1780–1980* (London, 1980).

Smith, David, and Williams, Gareth, *Fields of Praise: The Official History of the Welsh Rugby Union 1881–1981* (Cardiff, 1980).

Smith, Joan, 'Labour Tradition in Glasgow and Liverpool', *History Workshop Journal* 17 (1984), 32–56.

South Wales Coalfield History Project, *Final Report* (Swansea, 1974).

Stead, Peter, 'Working-Class Leadership in South Wales, 1900–1920', *WHR* 6 No.3 (1973), 329–53.

—— *Coleg Harlech, The First Fifty Years* (Cardiff, 1977).

—— 'The Voluntary Response to Mass Unemployment in South Wales'. In *Reactions to Social and Economic Change 1750–1939*, ed. Walter Minchinton (Exeter, 1979), 97–117.

—— 'The Language of Edwardian Politics'. In *A People and a Proletariat: Essays in the History of Wales, 1780–1980*, ed. David Smith (London, 1980), 148–65.

—— 'Establishing a Heartland: The Labour Party in Wales'. In *The First Labour Party 1906–1914*, ed. K. D. Brown (Beckenham, 1985), 64–88.

Stephens, Meic (ed.), *A Rhondda Anthology* (Bridgend, 1993).

Stevenson, John, 'The Politics of Violence'. In *The Politics of Reappraisal 1918–1939*, ed. Gillian Peele and Chris Cook (London, 1975), 146–65.

—— 'The Making of Unemployment Policy, 1931–1935'. In *High and Low Politics in Modern Britain: Ten Studies*, ed. Michael Bentley and John Stevenson (Oxford, 1983), 182–213.

Stevenson, John, and Cook, Chris, *The Slump* (London, 1979 edition).

Stutchbury, Oliver, *Too Much Government? A Political Aeneid* (Ipswich, 1977).

Tanner, Duncan, *Political Change and the Labour Party 1900–1918* (Cambridge, 1990).

Thomas, D. A., 'War and the Economy: The South Wales Experience'. In *Modern South Wales: Essays in Economic History*, ed. Colin Baber and L. J. Williams (Cardiff, 1986), 251–77.

Thompson, E. P., 'Homage to Tom Maguire'. In *Essays in Labour History*, ed. Asa Briggs and John Saville (London, 1960), 276–316.

—— *The Making of the English Working Class* (Harmondsworth, 1968 edition).

—— *The Poverty of Theory* (London, 1978).

Turner, Christopher, 'Conflicts of Faith? Religion and Labour in Wales, 1890–1914'. In *Class, Community and the Labour Movement: Wales and Canada, 1850–1930*, ed. Deian R. Hopkin and Gregory S. Kealey (Aberystwyth, 1989), 67–85.

Unofficial Reform Committee, *The Miners' Next Step*. In *Democracy in the Mines*, ed. Ken Coates. (Nottingham, 1974), 16–30.

Urry, John, 'Localities, Regions and Social Class', *International Journal of Urban and Regional Research* 5 No.4 (1981), 454–73.

Webster, Charles, 'Health, Welfare and Unemployment during the Depression', *Past and Present* 109 (1985), 204–30.

Whiting, R. C., *The View from Cowley, The Impact of Industrialization upon Oxford, 1918–1939* (Oxford, 1983).

Williams, Chris, ' "An Able Administrator of Capitalism?" The Rhondda Labour Party, 1917–1921', *Llafur* 4 No.4 (1987), 20–33.

—— 'The South Wales Miners' Federation', *Llafur* 5 No.3 (1990), 45–56.

—— 'History, Heritage and Commemoration: Newport 1839–1989', *Llafur* 6 No.1 (1992), 5–16.

—— 'Britain'. In *The Force of Labour: The Western European Labour Movement and the Working Class in the Twentieth Century* ed. Stefan Berger and David Broughton (Oxford, 1995), 107–35.

—— ' "The Hope of the British Proletariat": The South Wales Miners, 1910–1947'. In *Miners, Unions and Politics: 1910–1947*, ed. Alan Campbell, Nina Fishman, and David Howell (Aldershot, 1996), 121–44.

Williams, C. R., 'The Welsh Religious Revival, 1904–5', *British Journal of Sociology* 3 (1952), 242–59.

Williams, Gareth, *1905 And All That: Essays on Rugby Football, Sport and Welsh Society* (Llandysul, 1991).

Williams, Gwyn A., 'Dic Penderyn: The Making of a Welsh Working-Class Martyr', *Llafur* 2 No.3 (1978), 110–20.

Williams, Huw, 'Merthyr Tydfil and the General Strike of 1926', *Merthyr Historian* 2 (1978), 122–34.

Williams, L. J., 'The First Welsh Labour MP', *Morgannwg* 6 (1962), 78–94.

—— 'The Strike of 1898', *Morgannwg* 9 (1965), 61–79.

—— (ed.), *Digest of Welsh Historical Statistics*, 2 vols (Cardiff, 1985).

Williams, Sian Rhiannon, 'The Bedwellty Board of Guardians and the Default Act of 1927', *Llafur* 2 No.4 (1979), 65–77.

Winter, Jay M., 'Trade Unions and the Labour Party in Britain'. In *The Development of Trade Unionism in Great Britain and Germany, 1880–1914*, ed. Wolfgang J. Mommsen and Hans-Gerhard Husung (London, 1985), 359–70.

Wood, Ellen Meiksins, 'Falling Through the Cracks: E. P. Thompson and the Debate on Base and Superstructure'. In *E. P. Thompson: Critical Perspectives*, ed. Harvey J. Kaye and Keith McClelland (Oxford, 1990), 125–52.

Young, David, *A Noble Life: Incidents in the Career of Lewis Davis of Ferndale* (London, 1888).

G. Theses, Dissertations, Papers and Broadcasts

I. Theses and Dissertations

Barclay, Martin, 'Aberdare, 1880–1914; Class and Community'. MA, University of Wales (Cardiff), 1985.

Broomfield, Stuart R., 'South Wales During the Second World War: The Coal Industry and its Community'. Ph.D., University of Wales (Swansea), 1979.

Chandler, Andrew James, 'The Re-making of a Working Class: Migration from the South Wales Coalfield to the New Industry Areas of the Midlands c.1920–1940'. Ph.D., University of Wales (Cardiff), 1988.

Davies, D. K., 'The Influence of Syndicalism and Industrial Unionism on the South Wales Coalfield 1898–1921: A Study in Ideology and Practice'. Ph.D., University of Wales (Cardiff), 1991.

Davies, E. John, 'The Origin and Development of Secondary Education in the Rhondda Valleys (1878–1923)'. MA, University of Wales (Cardiff), 1965.

Davies, Hywel John, 'Mabon at Westminster: The Parliamentary Career of William Abraham M.P. 1885–1920'. MA (Dissertation), University of Wales (Cardiff), 1990.

Demont, Susan E., 'Tredegar and Aneurin Bevan: A Society and its Political Articulation, 1890–1929'. Ph.D., University of Wales (Cardiff), 1990.

Fox, Kenneth Owen, 'The Emergence of the Political Labour Movement in the Eastern Section of the South Wales Coalfield, 1894–1910'. MA, University of Wales (Aberystwyth), 1965.

Gwyther, Cyril E., 'Methodism and Syndicalism in the Rhondda Valley – 1906 to 1926'. Ph.D., University of Sheffield, 1967.

Howells, Kim, 'A View From Below: Tradition, Experience and Nationalisation in the South Wales Coalfield, 1937–1957'. Ph.D., University of Warwick, 1979.

McCarry, Thomas John, 'Labour and Society in Swansea, 1887–1918'. Ph.D., University of Wales (Swansea), 1986.

Rossiter, David John, 'The Miners' Sphere of Influence: An Attempt to Quantify Electoral Behaviour in Mining Areas Between the Wars'. Ph.D., University of Sheffield, 1980.

Shipway, M. A. S., 'Anti-Parliamentary Communism in Britain 1917–1945'. D.Phil., University of Manchester, 1985.

Williams, Christopher Mark, 'Democratic Rhondda: Politics and Society, 1885–1951', Ph.D. University of Wales (Cardiff), 1991.

Williams, Emyr Wynn, 'The Politics of Welsh Home Rule 1886–1929: A Sociological Analysis'. Ph.D., University of Wales (Aberystwyth), 1986.

Williams, T. I., 'Language, Identity and Education in a Liberal State: The Anglicisation of Pontypridd, 1818–1920'. Ph.D., University of Wales (Cardiff), 1989.

Woodhouse, Michael, 'Rank and File Movements Among The Miners of South Wales, 1910–1926'. D.Phil., University of Oxford, 1969.

Zweiniger-Bargielowska, Ina-Maria, 'Industrial Relationships and Nationalization in the South Wales Coalmining Industry'. Ph.D., University of Cambridge, 1989.

II. Broadcasts

BBC Wales. 'A View of the Rhondda: The "Prince of Porth"'. 1984.

HTV Wales. 'Wings of Significance: A Portrait of Gwyn Thomas, 1913–1981'. 1988.

Index

Ablett, Noah 12, 23, 68, 110, 115, 122, 125, 181
Abraham, William (Mabon) 5, 29–45, 57–8, 93
  and Cymru Fydd 44–5
  and RLLA 40, 48
  announces intention to retire 85
  appointed as SWMF president 61
  as archetypal Lib-Lab 29–30, 31, 42–3, 45
  as RSCMA secretary 32
  as spokesman for the 'rights of Labour' 31, 43–5, 57–8
  attacked by Lewis Davis 34
  attacked in Ferndale 35
  campaign in 1885 35–7, 43–4
  campaign in January 1910 40–1
  career 31
  election victory (1900) 39
  electoral history 38
  fails to win RLA nomination (1885) 33, 54
  intervention in Rhondda West by-election (1920) 88
  intervention in teachers' strike (1919) 128
  involvement in local elections 49
  leadership in 1898 dispute 61
  nominated as Labour candidate (1885) 32
  opposed by Nonconformist ministers (1885) 114
  opposes affiliation to Labour Party (1906) 68, 70
  policies 35
  president of Rhondda Parliamentary Recruiting Committee 124
  reconciliation with Liberals 37–8
  retirement 86, 100
  returned unopposed (1886) 37
  returned unopposed (1895) 39
  returned unopposed (1906) 39
  returned unopposed (1918) 84–5
  socialist challenge to (December 1910) 42, 100
  support for in 1885 33, 36
  support for First World War 124
  takes Labour Whip 40
  unpopularity over Sliding Scale 38, 59
adult education 22
Ajax, Howell 36

'alternative culture', concept of 114, 208
Amalgamated Association of Mineworkers 32
Andrews, Elizabeth 16, 107, 192
Attlee government 203

Baker, James 64, 65, 75
Barker, George 23
Barker, Reg 198
Bedwellty Board of Guardians 149
Benjamin, Morgan 'Mog' 98
Boer War 39
Bowen, John 136, 139
Broadhurst, Henry 33
Brooks, Joseph 73–4
Buckley, Owen 117, 129, 174, 199
Burton, George 78–9

Cambrian Combine Committee 200
Cambrian Miners' Association Executive Committee 57
Chalke, Dr R. D. 157, 158
Clynes, J. R. 88
Co-operative Society 26
Co-operative Women's Guild 16, 106, 107
coal industry
  dangers of 240 n.10
  decontrol of (1921) 25, 131
  depression in 25–7
  development of in Rhondda Valleys 13–14, 17–18
  mechanization of 25–6
  nationalization of 5, 13, 25, 27–8; debate in Judge's Hall, Trealaw 23
  ownership of 24
  revival of 27
  working methods in 14
Coffin, Walter 12
Cold War 163, 203–4
colliery companies 24, 33, 37, 51
Colliery Worker's Magazine, The 154
Commission of Enquiry into Industrial Unrest (1917) 19, 111
Communist Party 141, 168, 206, 208–9
  affiliation to the Labour Party 151–6, 163
  and extra-parliamentary protest 186
  character of 153
  councillors 191
  decline of 203–4
  in Mardy 181–4

local government fortunes 166
membership of 183
policy towards the poor law 137
political culture of 182
recruitment of members (1935) 161
Rhondda branches 153
Second World War, policy on 162
support for 169
Third Period 155–6, 166, 185
United Front 168, 185, 189–90, 199–201
Young Communist League 182
Young Comrades League 182, 197
Communist Party (British Section Third International)/Communist Party of South Wales 153
community leadership 113, 207
company unionism 25
Condition of the Working Class in Britain, The 192
Conservative clubs 49, 111
Cook, Arthur James 5, 110, 128, 129, 153, 157, 204
corruption 170, 173–81, 193–5
Cory, Clifford J. 51
Cove, William G. 110
Cox, Dora 162
Cox, Idris 164, 165
Cule, Aneurin 36
Cymru Fydd 45

Daily Worker 200
Davies, Ben 73–4, 95
Davies, Dai Lloyd 137, 139–40, 148, 157
Davies, David 164
Davies, David A. 153
Davies, Elias Henry 50, 55
Davies, Elias Thomas 55
Davies, Elizabeth 95
Davies, Enoch 54
Davies, Evan 54
Davies, Evan Naunton 52, 74
Davies, Henry Naunton 52
Davies, Jack (John Leigh) 158, 159
Davies, James Kitchener 161, 164, 165, 166, 168
Davies, John Thomas 96–7, 202
Davies, Revd T. Alban 168
Davies, Samuel 198
Davies, T. Eric 116
Davies, Thomas 36
Davies, Thomas Rees 123, 148
Davies, W. Watkin 242 n.46
Davies, William Thomas 52, 55, 66
Davis, Frederick Lewis 33, 34, 35
    attacked 35, 43–4
    campaign in 1885 35–7

elected to Glamorgan County Council, (1889) 49
retirement from politics 51
selected as parliamentary candidate 34
support for 36, 114
Davis, Lewis 33–4
    appointed president of RLA 33
    attacks Mabon 34
    declines to stand as parliamentary candidate 33
    selected as parliamentary candidate 33
    views on Labour representatives 33
'definitions of community' 21–3, 59, 118
Demos 125–6
Dolling, George 41, 110, 153, 155, 176
Drew, Sammy 141
Driscoll, J. P. 164

Edwards, John Salisbury 36, 49
Edwards, Ness 83
elections (parliamentary)
    1885 4, 31–7, 44, 57
    1892 38–9
    1900 38–9
    January 1910 38, 39–41
    December 1910 42, 99, 100
    1918 84–6
    Rhondda West by-election (1920) 86–9, 102
    1922 23, 89–90
    1923 89–91
    1924 89, 91
    1929 157–8
    1931 3, 158–9
    Rhondda East by-election (1933) 159–60
    1935 160–1
    1945 161–3, 203
    1950 163–5
    1951 163–5
Elias, Glyn 167
Evans, Daniel 58
Evans, David (Bodringallt) 49
Evans, David (Clydach Vale) 100
Evans, David (Ynyshir) 128, 148–9
Evans, David Charles 95
Evans, Griffith 74
Evans, Jack 192
Evans, James 55
Evans, Sir Samuel T. 40
Evans, Thomas Owen 137
Evans, Tom 40, 74, 76, 111
Evans, William 'Corona' 55, 98
Evans, William (Mabon Bach) 57
Eveleigh, William 74
eviction disturbances, Mardy (1931) 173

Eynon, Daniel 50

Ferndale Free Church Council 40
First World War 24, 85, 105, 124–5
Francis, Hywel 12, 60, 181, 189, 190

Garwood, John James 205–6
George, David Lloyd 40, 45, 100
George, Tom 40, 93
Gibbons, Charlie 122, 130, 139, 153
Gill, Edward 23
Glamorgan Free Press 71, 73
Glamorgan Free Press and Rhondda Leader 113
Glamorganshire County Council
    1889 elections for 49
    1892 elections for 49–50
    administration of means test 192
    Labour weakness on (1910) 79
    Labour majority upon (1919) 92
    Rhondda representation upon 46
Grayson, Victor 42, 71
Griffiths, James 160
Griffiths, John Jones 49, 52, 55
Griffiths, Rhys Samuel 52
Griffiths, Thomas 95
Gronow, Cornelius 99
Gwyther, Cyril 162–3, 198

Halliday, Thomas 32
Harcombe, Emrys 175
Harcombe, Mark 93, 95, 117, 132, 148, 155–6, 174, 179, 207
Harries, Tom 78, 80, 93
Harris, Oliver 154
Hartshorn, Vernon 40, 69
Hay, William Ferris 122, 153, 242 n.45
Heale, Frederick William 89–91
Hedditch, Samuel 148
historical methodology 7–10
Hodges, Frank 23, 88
Hopla, John 87, 117
Horner, Arthur 5, 153, 156, 163, 181, 183, 204, 208, 211
    and eviction disturbances, Mardy (1931) 173
    and PBG 139–40, 143
    election campaign (1929) 157–8
    election campaign (1931) 158–9
    election campaign (1933) 159–60
    'Hornerism' 185
housing question 96, 99, 121, 127
    post-war crisis 129–30
Howell, David 1
Hughes, Dafydd 'Income Tax' 207
Hughes, Jack 110

Hughes, John 73–4, 98, 148
Hughes, R. Moelwyn 157, 158
Hughes, Robert 39
Hughes, Will 'Knowledge' 207
Hutt, Allen 192

Independent Labour Party 153
    branches 62, 95, 99, 110, 123; Cardiff 59; Clydach Vale 109; Ferndale 68, 70; Mardy 59, 62, 181; Mid-Rhondda 42; Pentre 70; Penygraig 68, 70; Porth 68, 70; Treherbert 78; Ystrad Rhondda 111
    1909 membership 71
    declines (1899–1901) 62
    growth of 30, 68, 70–71
    propaganda campaigns 71
    relationship with Labour Party 106, 107
    role in 1898 dispute 61
    significance of rise of 62, 103
    support for MFGB affiliation to Labour Party 68–70
Independent Labour candidates 98–9
industrial disputes
    1893 dispute 59
    1898 dispute 30, 60–2
    Pentre colliery dispute (1910) 79
    Cambrian Combine dispute (1910–11) 24, 41–2, 80, 83, 87
    'Great Unrest' (1910–14) 24, 30
    1912 dispute 24
    1915 dispute 24
    1921 dispute 25, 131, 132, 133, 139
    1926 dispute 23, 25, 142–9, 151, 169, 184, 206, 208
    stay-down stoppages (1935) 6
industrial unionism, *see* syndicalism
Isaac, T. Daronwy 50

Jacob, Abel 130, 141, 148
James, James 79, 97, 131, 148, 177, 179, 180, 195
Jenkins, David 64, 179
Jenkins, T. Pascoe 36, 50
Jenkins, William 37, 49, 51
Jevons, H. Stanley 20
John, Tom 36, 52, 93
John, William 90, 93, 102, 110, 117, 156, 157, 158, 159, 160, 170, 174, 199
    career 87
    election campaign (1920) 86, 88–9
    parliamentary gaffe (1921) 255 n.36
    retirement of 1
Jones, Daniel Richard 54–5, 74
Jones, Edward 80
Jones, Gareth Stedman 1, 9

Jones, Gomer 175
Jones, J. R. 90
Jones, John Talwrn 148
Jones, Lewis 5, 143, 183, 184, 186–9, 191, 200, 208
Jones, Llewellyn 97, 148, 176
Jones, Philip N. 15
Jones, Samuel 72
Jones, Thomas Isaac Mardy 23, 79, 181
    and First World War 124
    and Labour Party municipal strategy 121
    and organization of Labour Party 101–3
    and workers' education 110–11
    challenges for parliamentary nomination 125
    supports Mabon (1910) 40
    supports affiliation to Labour Party 68–70
Jones, Tom Ayton 98
Jones, William Thomas 54

Kirk, Neville 9

Labour and Progressive Club, Penygraig 112
Labour Clubs 111–12
Labourism 209–10, 243 n.1
Labour Party
    disaffiliation crisis 149, 151–6, 172
    discipline of 92
    domination of local government 91–2
    domination of politics of south Wales coalfield 3–4
    historiography of 1–2, 6, 9–10, 29–31
    Junior Labour League 112
    League of Youth 109, 197–8
    municipal policy 77, 96, 120–2, 124–7
    organization of 99–103, 106–9
    policy on necessitous feeding 148–9
    policy on poor law 138–41
    political culture of 109–14, 117
    reaction to United Front 201
    reorganization of in 1930s 196–7
    Rhondda Borough Labour Party Committee of Enquiry (1934) 194–5
    Rhondda Borough Labour Party (Disaffiliated) 155–6, 185
    Women's Sections 197
Lawrence, David 32, 36
Left Wing Movement 152, 153, 155–6
Lewis, Dr Ivor Ajax 52
Lewis, Dick 155
Lewis, Richard (boot merchant) 36
Lib-Labism 29–30, 45, 59, 68

historiography of 56–7, 81–2
Liberals, domination of local government 46
Lloyd, Gwilym 98
Lloyd, Harold 39, 41, 42, 43
Lloyd, Hugh 59
Local Government Act 1929 171
Loxton, Henry 74
LRC No.9 Ward 75, 78, 97, 98, 100

Mabon, *see* Abraham, William (Mabon)
McAllister, Ian 196
MacDonald, Ramsay 71
Maes-yr-Haf Educational Settlement (Trealaw) 27
magistrates, appointment of 99, 122, 124
Mainwaring, Sam 59
Mainwaring, William H. 29, 181, 189, 199, 203, 211
    and *Rhondda Clarion* 197
    and workers' education 110, 183
    calls for organization of Labour Party 99
    election campaign (1933) 159–60
    election campaign (1935) 160–1
    election campaign (1945) 161–3
    election campaigns (1950, 1951) 163–5
    investigation into corruption (1934) 194
Making of the English Working Class, The 1
Malkin, Benjamin Heath 13
Maltby, Henry Edward 95
Mann, Tom 42, 59, 159
Marriott, John 8
Marxian Club (Blaenclydach) 68
Maslin, George 183–4, 195, 204
    and 'turkey case' 177–9
Mathias, William Henry 51
means test 170, 211
    demonstrations against (1935) 189, 200
Merthyr Pioneer 122
Merthyr Tydfil judgement 143, 144
Methodist Central Hall, Tonypandy 197
Mid-Rhondda Free Church Council 40, 117
milk, supply of 132, 147
Miners' Next Step, The 6, 110, 122-3
Mineworkers' Federation of Great Britain 30
    affiliation to Labour Party 30, 56–7, 68, 99
Ministry of Health, 129, 132, 134–5, 142–50, 171–2
Minton, John 96, 117
Morgan, David Rees 96
Morgan, David Watts 72, 74, 75
    death 159

defeated in GCC election (1899) 64
early career 64
elected to GCC (1902) 65
election campaign (1922) 89–90
election campaign (1923) 89–90
election campaign (1929) 157–8
election campaign (1931) 159
favours Labour representation 64–7, 78, 80
involvement with RLLA 64
maiden speech 129
opposes affiliation to Labour Party 68, 70
opposition to 125
returned unopposed (1918) 84–5, 88
selected as parliamentary candidate 125
wartime record 86, 89, 124
Morgan, J. Vyrnwy 55
Morgan, John 36
Morgan, John 137
Morgan, Kenneth O. 46, 56, 81, 82
Morgan, Thomas Charles 52
Morgan, Walter H. 23, 36, 49
Morgan, William 49, 74
Morgan, William Herbert 78, 93
Morris, Morgan Charles 36
Morris, Morris 40, 53
Morris, Richard 38, 52
 1892 GCC elections 50
 challenge to Mabon (1892) 38–9
Morris, Thomas Charles 77, 84, 110, 127
Morris, William 36
Morris, William (Rhosynnog) 50
Morris, William Meredith 116
Morton, Jimmy 180, 200
Moses, Moses 57, 75

National Brotherhood Movement 116
National Democratic League 67–8
National Unemployed Workers' Movement 27, 137–8, 140–2, 154, 157, 182, 184–5
Naval and Military War Pensions Committee 105
nepotism, *see* corruption
New Theology 116
Newman, George 148
Nicholas, James 117
Nicholas, Sir Walter 22–3, 126
Nicholls, George 164
Nonconformity 19–20, 241 n.29
 and Communism 198–9
 and local politics 52
 attitudes towards Labour movement 114–15
 prohibition of Sunday meetings 115–16

O'Leary, Paul 105
Orchard, Alfred John 89–91, 97
Osborne Judgement 79, 250 n.134
Owen, Tom 148

Parliamentary Executive Committee 32
Paynter, Will 5, 183, 207
Phillips, David 198
Phillips, Horatio 40
Phillips, W. F. 117
Plaid Cymru 164, 166–8, 189
Plebs' League 111
political competition
 1889–1910 47
 1910–1927 92
 1927–1955 166
'politics of personality' 50–6, 58–9
Pollitt, Harry 156, 159, 184, 203
 election campaign (1935) 160–1
 election campaign (1945) 161–3
 election campaign (1950) 163–4
Pontypridd Board of Guardians 136–50
 and 1921 dispute 134–5
 and 1926 dispute 144–9
 criticism of administrative procedures 133–4
 demise of 171
 experimental boot-centre (1926) 147
 financial difficulties 133–5, 139, 143–6, 149
 Labour advance on (1910) 79
 Labour domination of (1919) 92
 Labour minority on (1926) 143–5, 149
 recovery of outrelief 134–5, 138–42
 Rhondda representation upon 46
Porth Cottage Hospital 73
Porth Labour Committee 57, 72, 73, 74, 75
pragmatism 119–20, 136, 209
Pritchard, Roman 113
Progressive Theology League 116
prohibition issue (1920) 87
proletarian internationalism, concept of 24, 208
Propaganda Committee of Labour and Socialist Clubs of the Rhondda 112
Powell, J. Francis 157, 158
Prichard, Wilfred A. 157, 158

Quick, Fred 175

railway accident, Hopkinstown (1911) 93
Ratepayers' Association 167
Red Dawn 141
Rees, Noah 79, 111, 122
Rees, Rhys Morgan 148, 179
Rees, Tom 95, 148, 176

Reform Act, Third (1884–5) 4, 14, 32
rejectionism 119–120, 123–4, 126, 129, 138, 188, 208
Religious Revival (1904–5) 19–20
Representation of the People Act (1918) 85
Representation of the People Act (1928) 157
Rhondda Borough Council 28
Rhondda Certificated Class Teachers Association 177
Rhondda Clarion 22, 192, 193, 197, 201
Rhondda Class Teachers Association 76
Rhondda Conservative Association 85, 86, 127, 128
  fails to put forward candidate (1895) 39
  fails to put forward candidate (1906) 39
  marginality of 47, 48–9
  preparations for 1900 General Election 39
  preparations for January 1910 General Election 39
  role in 1892 General Election 38
Rhondda Fach Gazette 125
Rhondda Food Control Committee 105
Rhondda's history
  interaction of local and national themes in 2–3
  centrality to history of south Wales coalfield 4–5, 12
Rhondda Labour and Liberal Association 38, 59, 88
  approaches Rhondda No.1 District for financial support (1900) 64
  backs Mabon (January 1910) 40
  backs Mabon (December 1910) 42
  backs Watts Morgan (1899) 64
  decides not to contest parliamentary seat (1918) 85–6
  disorganization 85
  domination by middle-class 59
  failure to contest Rhondda West by-election (1920) 86
  formation 37
  lack of control over local government candidates 49–50, 57
  organization 48–9
  social and political orientation 48
  threatened by ILP 62
Rhondda Leader 73, 80, 93
Rhondda Liberal Association 32–4, 35, 59
  absorbed into RLLA 37–8
  formation 32
  procedures for selection of candidate (1885) 32–5
Rhondda Parliamentary Recruiting Committee 124

Rhondda Socialist Newspaper 17, 100, 114, 119, 123, 176, 262 n.9
Rhondda Socialist Society 42, 106, 123, 152
Rhondda Socialistic Propaganda Organization 42
Rhondda Steam Coal Miners' Association 31–2, 35, 48, 57
  creation of Parliamentary EC (1885) 32
  conflict with RLA 32
  backs Mabon 34
Rhondda Urban District Council, 74, 127, 140, 144, 148, 166, 171
  1899 elections for 72
  administrative record of 121–2
  and 1926 dispute 144–9
  Central Canteen Committee 147–8
  closure of halls on Sundays 115–16
  control of secondary education provision 22
  Education Committee 147–8
  education policy 127–8
  financial difficulties 129–30, 132–3, 134–5, 146–9, 171–3
  Labour control upon (1919–) 91–2
  Labour Group on 151, 170
  Labour position on (1908) 79
  rise of Labour upon 47
  Special Estimates Committee 171–2
  Special Staffing Committee 132–3
Rhondda Valley Property Owners and Ratepayers Association 106
Rhondda valleys
  Anglicization of 21
  community identity in 18–19
  demographic growth 15
  health and welfare in 26–7
  housing conditions in 17–18
  leisure activities in 20–1
  migration from 26
  migration into 15
  newspaper press 21
  occupational structure of 15–16
  political culture of 4, 5, 16–17
  population density of 18
  reconstruction policy, impact of 27
  Second World War, impact of 27
  spectator sport in 20–1, 26
  structure of representative politics 46
  unemployment in 25
Rhondda Vanguard 156, 182, 187, 197
Rhondda Workers' Committee 153
Richards, Dan 141
Richards, Evan 36, 40
Richards, Thomas 135
riots, Tonypandy (1910) 5, 24, 42, 80, 83–4, 93, 124, 165

Roderick, Evan Joshua 93, 116, 121
Rowlands, Gwilym 86, 87, 88, 89, 90, 97
Royal Commission on Church in Wales (1910) 20
Ruskin College, Oxford 23, 79, 110–11
Russian Revolution 125, 126

Samuel, John 54
Samuel, Raphael 1
Savage, Michael 1, 8–10
schoolchildren, feeding of 121, 132–3, 138–40, 144, 147–9, 171–2
Second World War 202–3
Simons, Emrys 165
Smith, Dai 7, 12, 60, 83, 118, 181, 189
Smith, David (Ferndale) 53
Smith, Tom 93, 148, 199
Social Democratic Federation 42
    1898 meetings 61
    Blaenclydach branch 68
    establishment in Rhondda 59
Social-Democratic Party 100
socialism
    growth of interest in 67
    socialism and Christianity 116–17
South Wales Association of Labour Members 104
south Wales coalfield
    political history of 3–4, 6
    historiography of 5, 6
South Wales Daily News 33
South Wales Miners' Federation 83, 84, 88–9, 99
    affiliation to MFGB (1899) 61
    ballots on affiliation to Labour Party 30
    claims Rhondda East and Rhondda West as miners' seats 85
    establishment of (1898) 60–1
    organization 63–4
    political role 103–4
    rebuilding of 6, 169
    Rhondda No.1 District 12, 63, 68, 74, 78, 104
        1908 election circular 78
        and workers' education 110–11
        approached by RLLA for financial support (1900) 64
        drive for parliamentary representation 67
        involvement in election campaigns (1910) 39–40
        intervention in 1920 Rhondda West by-election 88
        Labour Representation Fund scheme 65–6, 75

Labour Representation Scheme 76–8, 103
lodges: Abergorky 63, 155; Cambrian 63, 99; Cymmer 65, 73; Ferndale 103, 104, 130–1, 136, 138–41, 157, 201; Fernhill 98; Hendrewen 98; Lewis Merthyr 74, 139, 205; Llwynypia 87, 110, 117; Maindy 96; Mardy 95, 103, 104, 137, 139, 156, 157, 181, 185, 198; National 65; Park 164; Tylorstown 157; Tylorstown United 97; Ynyshir 57; Ynyshir House Coal 63
    organization of 63–4
    policy on poor law 138–41, 145, 148
    relationship with Labour Party 102–4
    role in promoting Labour representation 63
    selection of parliamentary candidate (1918) 125
    support for teachers' strike (1919) 128
South Wales Miners' Industrial Union 25
South Wales Regional Council of Labour 201, 203
South Wales Socialist Society 152, 153
Soviet Union, reaction to invasion of 161–2, 203
Spanish Civil War 190
Spickett, William 140
Stacey, Enid 59
Stanton, Charles 68, 69
Starr, Mark 110
Stutchbury, Oliver 164, 165
Sweet, Jesse 180
syndicalism 119, 122–4, 126, 209

Tanner, Duncan 1, 8
teachers, appointment of 176–7
teachers' strike 127–30
Thomas, David Alfred (Lord Rhondda) 24, 45
Thomas, George (Viscount Tonypandy) 173–4, 176, 206
Thomas, Gwyn 5, 12
Thomas, Iorwerth 113, 164–5, 178–9
Thomas, Ivor 143
Thomas, Jimmy 88
Thomas, Thomas 94
Thomas, Tom 153, 176
Thomas, William David 159–60
Thomas, Dr William Evans 52, 97, 116, 148
Thomas, W. P. 51, 54
Thomas, William James 41, 51

Thompson, Edward 1, 7
Tillett, Ben 42, 68
Trades and Labour Councils 66, 99, 101–6, 129, 131
  composition 75–6
  Council of Action 107, 131
  electoral role 76
  financial problems 79
  form part of RBLP (1923) 106–7
  functions of 75–6
  Mid-Rhondda 75, 95, 98–9, 101, 104, 106, 115
  Pentre 75, 95–6, 131
  Porth 95, 105, 131
  propaganda campaigns 106
  role during the First World War 105–6
  role in promoting Labour representation 63
  Treherbert 75, 78, 95, 98, 105–7; electoral success (1907) 74; foundation of 74
  Treorchy 76, 95, 104
Ton Co-operative Society 78
Treharne, Enoch 176
Treharne, John 134
Treorchy Mock Parliament 112–13
Tromans, Noah 110, 130, 134, 136, 137, 138, 139, 140, 141, 143

unemployment 96, 131–2, 169
  public works programmes 132
Unemployment Grants Committee 132
Unemployment Insurance Act (1934) 189
Unofficial Reform Committee 123, 152–3

Wales, Glyn 167
We Live 186–7, 188
Wells, William 148
Welsh Political and Educational Leaders of the Victorian Era 55
'Welsh radical tradition' 6, 209
Western Mail 35, 121

White Fang 112
Whitehead, Edgar T. 153
Wight, William Dundas 79
Williams, David 36
Williams, Eliza 148, 155, 195
Williams, Frank 141
Williams, Henry 58
Williams, Idris 193
Williams, Jack 'Bolshie' 98, 110, 148, 155, 200, 242 n.45
Williams, John (Ferndale) 130
Williams, Morgan 57, 64, 75
Williams, Morris 167–8
Williams, R. R. 177
Williams Ted 110, 181
Williams, Tim 21
Williams, William Gwrtydd 50
Winstone, James 68, 69
women
  political activism 16–17, 71, 107
  waged work 16
Women's Co-operative Guild *see* Co-operative Women's Guild
Worker Looks At History, A 110
workers' education 110–11
Workers' Educational Association 111
Workers' Suffrage Federation 152
Workmen's Compensation Act (1897) 60
Workmen's Institutes
  Fernhill 78
  Lewis Merthyr Workmen's Institute and Library 205
Wright, Willie 61–2

Ynyshir Labour Committee 64
Young, Tom 135–6
Ystradyfodwg School Board 46
Ystradyfodwg Urban District Council 14, 46
Ystradyfodwg Urban Sanitary Authority 46
Ystrad Rhondda Labour Club 111–12